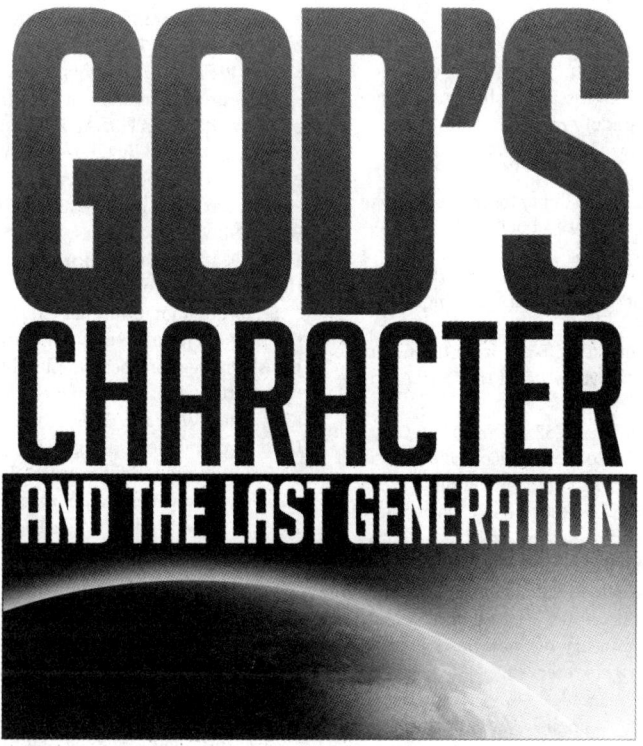

GOD'S CHARACTER
AND THE LAST GENERATION

MOSKALA · PECKHAM

Pacific Press®
Publishing Association

Nampa, Idaho | Oshawa, Ontario, Canada
www.pacificpress.com

Cover design by Gerald Lee Monks
Cover design resources from Dreamstime.com/Sebastian Kaulitzki
Inside design by Aaron Troia

The authors assume full responsibility for the accuracy of all facts and quotations as cited in this book.

Additional copies of this book may be purchased by calling toll-free 1-800-765-6955 or by visiting AdventistBookCenter.com.

ISBN 978-0-8163-6361-2

March 2018

Dedication

Dedicated to those who are diligently searching to understand the Word of God regarding God's character of love and the fulfillment of our God-given mission in these last days of human history.

Table of Contents

Contributors

Cortez, Félix H., PhD, associate professor of New Testament, Seventh-day Adventist Theological Seminary, Andrews University, Michigan

Davidson, Jo Ann, PhD, professor of Theology, Seventh-day Adventist Theological Seminary, Andrews University, Michigan

Davidson, Richard M., PhD, J. N. Andrews Professor of Old Testament Interpretation, Seventh-day Adventist Theological Seminary, Andrews University, Michigan

Fortin, Denis, PhD, professor of Historical Theology, Seventh-day Adventist Theological Seminary, Andrews University, Michigan

Hanna, Martin, PhD, associate professor of Systematic Theology, Seventh-day Adventist Theological Seminary, Andrews University, Michigan

Jankiewicz, Darius W., PhD, professor of Historical Theology, Seventh-day Adventist Theological Seminary, Andrews University, Michigan

Jerončić, Ante, PhD, associate professor of Ethics and Theology, Seventh-day Adventist Theological Seminary, Andrews University, Michigan

Moskala, Jiří, ThD, PhD, dean and professor of Old Testament Exegesis and Theology, Seventh-day Adventist Theological Seminary, Andrews University, Michigan

Peckham, John C., PhD, associate professor of Theology and Christian Philosophy, Seventh-day Adventist Theological Seminary, Andrews University, Michigan

Stefanovic, Ranko, PhD, professor of New Testament, Seventh-day Adventist Theological Seminary, Andrews University, Michigan

Swanson, H. Peter, PhD, professor of Pastoral Care, emeritus, Seventh-day Adventist Theological Seminary, Andrews University, Michigan

Whidden, Woodrow, PhD, professor of Religion, emeritus, College of Arts and Sciences, Andrews University, Michigan

Preface

In London's Trafalgar Square, a statue of the famous naval officer Horatio Nelson towers above visitors to the square and reminds them of the former power of the British Empire as ruler of the seas. Three of the four additional plinths in that same square honor kings and other military leaders; together they stand for all that is best in human power and abilities. For a while, however, one column was left out of this display of authority. This plinth was reserved instead for a variety of different sculptured figures and faces. In 1999, it housed a statue that seemed out of place in this celebration of human might. And the size—only six feet tall, the height of a regular man—was dwarfed by the huge statues that surrounded it. The statue, *Ecce Homo* (Behold the Man), caused considerable debate; some arguing it was inappropriately placed. Others were delighted to see Jesus Christ represented this way in this place. The humble among the proud; the One who could bring salvation through humility among those who needed that salvation but didn't know it. The Servant among the self-proclaimed powerful. The true Savior among the apparent saviors.

In the twenty-first century, the place of faith, of a life lived in the power of the gospel, has become too often denigrated as a life of weakness or irrelevance. Luke 18 asks us the question, "When the Son of Man comes, will he find faith on the earth?" (verse 8, NIV). A faith that is persistent in its longing for the second coming of Christ, a faith that has power not because of the person who exercises it, but the One whose sacrifice validates that faith.

This collection of essays focuses on that very intersection: the reality of Christ's coming back to earth, and the role He plays in the lives of those of us who live in this generation. Appropriately, the essays are written by theologians of the Seventh-day Adventist Church who are passionate about the gospel as expressed through the theology of the church. It is also appropriate, because these themes are so central to the theology and eschatology of the Seventh-day Adventist Church. We are uniquely positioned to speak of these things.

We are uniquely positioned, first because as a church we do believe unequivocally in the saving power of Christ's sacrifice through faith alone. The five-hundredth-year celebration of the Reformation, 2017, is an appropriate time to remember how our history aligns with those ideals. Our faith is not in human power but in the power of Christ, that is, the moral power of His love. Yet linked to this Adventist conviction of the centrality of the gospel and our justification through the blood of Christ is also our unique commitment to the imminence of the Second Coming that will change the alignment of authority and power forever. That is when we will finally understand unequivocally that true authority and power reside squarely in the character of God. So it is out of a commitment to the intersection of these two important beliefs (justification by faith and the reality of the Second Coming) that this book speaks to its readers, inviting a renewed commitment to faith through Christ alone and to an active belief in the second coming of Christ.

This intersection, of course, does not come without challenges and questions. Throughout the history of the Seventh-day Adventist Church, not unlike the wider Christian church, debates have emerged regarding exactly how our eschatology affects the balance between salvation through faith alone and the importance of how we live. How does Christ's role as mediator deepen our understanding of the Savior's role in salvation? Can we ever move beyond our life of sinfulness to live a pure life as Christ lived? Is that even a goal to seek?

As a church, we do have high standards for living a life of holiness. While justification by faith is the basis of salvation, that knowledge of salvation and a continually deepening relationship with our Savior should change the way we live. Yet that never leaves behind our reliance on the sacrifice of Christ and the reality that our holiness is His holiness. To do otherwise not only leads to an overemphasis on our right actions, with an ensuing discouragement at the reality of our humanness, it also leads us too easily into the path of judging others, whom we might perceive

as holding back the Second Coming due to not living more perfectly. Both are dangerous positions because they shift focus away from Christ and in effect repeat the danger of Trafalgar Square—reliance on the human rather than the divine.

As an educator, I have seen too often how a personal conviction of the need to live a pure life results in promises that are made with fervor but are not kept because of the human condition. As the reality of human frailty becomes clear, the joy of the gospel and the anticipation of the Second Coming are replaced with personal discouragement and a fear of the judgment. In the meantime, the beauty of the gospel is veiled. A commitment to the total efficacy of the Savior does not mean, as is so well expressed in Romans 6, that we can do whatever we want, just to experience God's grace. It does mean that we can face the darkness of the human condition in the confidence that God is in ultimate control.

I was asked the other day whether the events we see around us at this point in history lead me to any particular conviction about the second coming of Christ. My answer was that I continue to believe that Jesus will come in His time and that our responsibility is to continue to keep our eyes focused on Him, not on the power of this world, and to show His character to others as He shines through our lives. I see the future in the reality of God's moral power, not our human efforts, and that is where my confidence lies.

Are these issues important? Critically so. This book and its writers seek to remind us of the importance of keeping our focus on our faith and our mission at this important time of history. It reminds us of the dangers of overdetermining the future that is God's or of focusing too much on the human rather than the divine. In doing so, this book firmly places salvation at the cross and sees our actions as a reflection of the character of God, which we are reminded of daily. These theologians are also individuals of faith. They speak from a range of perspectives, but all focus on the same message—the one reiterated at the beginning of Hebrews 12, "And let us run with perseverance the race marked out for us, fixing our eyes on Jesus, the pioneer and perfecter of faith. For the joy set before him he endured the cross, scorning its shame, and sat down at the right hand of the throne of God. Consider him who endured such opposition from sinners, so that you will not grow weary and lose heart" (verses 1–3, NIV).

Andrea Luxton
President, Andrews University

A Word From the Editors

This book, *God's Character and the Last Generation*, deals with the theological understanding, lifestyle, and choices pertinent to those who, like us, believe that they live at the time of the end and face unprecedented conditions that demand a sound interpretive approach and careful scrutiny in light of biblical teachings. This book, then, is not meant as a polemic against last generation theology but aims to provide a positive, constructive approach to these issues that are important for all Adventists.

Some chapters of this publication are broader in scope, while some deal more specifically with certain crucial and pertinent issues raised by last generation theology. But all of the chapters aim at more clearly understanding and presenting the teachings of Scripture and the additional insight given by Ellen G. White on some of the most crucial issues facing Christians who live before the second coming of Christ.

We are now living in a so-called post-truth era where xenophobia is a prevalent feature of societal behavior. But as followers of Christ, we cannot allow fear to be a dominant factor in our lives or to lead our decisions. Our focus must always be on God's love and His grace manifested in Christ and experienced in the power of the Holy Spirit. The love of God casts away fear, as John declares, "Perfect love drives out fear" (1 John 4:18, NIV).

The prophet Daniel reveals that at the very end of time, God's faithful followers will live in a perilous age but will never be alone, because Christ will stand for His people: "At that time Michael, the great prince who protects your people, will arise. There will be a time of distress such as has not happened from the beginning of nations until then. But at that time your people—everyone whose name is found written in the book—will be delivered" (Daniel 12:1, NIV). We can thus face tomorrow with courage, trusting that our Lord will provide, in His loving care, whatever we need for abundant life (John 10:10).

The apostle Paul assures us that our God will never leave nor forsake those who believe in Him, because there is no power, thing, or person on earth or in the entire universe that can separate us from our loving and faithful Lord (Romans 8:38, 39). We can trust that the process of redemption and transformation that Christ started in us, He is able to culminate at His glorious second coming: "Being confident of this very thing, that He who has begun a good work in you will complete it until the day of Jesus Christ" (Philippians 1:6, NKJV).

It is our prayer and hope that you will find in this book solid and edifying material, which will encourage you in your walk with the Lord and will give you assurance of your salvation in Jesus Christ, faith in His leadership and providence, lasting inner joy, and satisfying answers to some of your perplexing questions. When our self-confidence and assumptions are challenged, we may be able to find more solid ground for our faith and understanding of the truth. Let's remember that even our best formulations and expressions of truth are rudimentary, because only God, who is our ultimate Judge, has the last word. May our gracious, caring, holy, and awesome Lord inspire each reader to follow the path of truth in this complicated world in which we live as we serve and await the glorious coming of our Lord and Savior Jesus Christ.

Nihil sine Deus. Soli Deo gloria!

Jiří Moskala & John C. Peckham
Editors

Great Controversy Issues

John C. Peckham

God is love. This recognition is central to theology as a whole and plays a crucial role in the great-controversy motif, which is itself a crucial component of Adventist theology.[1] Put broadly, the great controversy refers to a conflict between God and Satan regarding the character of God and God's moral government. Just how God's character is vindicated over and against the claims of the devil is an important matter in Adventist theology. How one approaches and understands this issue has far-reaching ramifications for many other areas of theology and practice. Therefore, to provide a better understanding of the questions and issues that will be addressed in the following chapters of this book, this chapter provides a brief introduction to the great controversy and the issues raised relative to God's character and the last generation within that context.[2]

The cosmic conflict over God's character

According to the Adventist understanding of the great controversy, the devil has charged and continues to charge that God is not wholly loving and good and that His government and law are not fair.[3] Therefore, this conflict is not one about sheer power or brute force. Since God is all powerful (omnipotent), no one could stand against Him were He to exercise His power to quell rebellion. Yet no show of force would effectively answer the charges raised against God's character and government. Since the cosmic conflict is a conflict about character, it cannot be settled by force, but only by a demonstration of character that refutes the charges raised against God's character.

This is due, in large part, to the nature of love. In this view, love by its very nature must be freely given; it cannot be compelled or determined.[4] Therefore, God has granted significant (but also limited) freedom of will to creatures, which He will not revoke because doing so would be against the principles of His character and government of love.[5] This cosmic conflict originated when the devil, created by God as a perfect angel, exercised his free will to rebel against God, slandering God's character in heaven as a means to usurp God's rule, leading some angels to rebel along with him (see Ezekiel 28:12–18; cf. Isaiah 14:12–14; Revelation 12:4, 7–9).[6] Satan then appeared as a serpent in the Garden of Eden, who questioned and slandered God's character (Genesis 3:1–5).[7] In doing so, he led Eve and Adam into distrusting and disobeying God and eating the forbidden fruit, introducing sin and evil into this world (verses 6–19). Ever since, all humans, as descendants of Adam and Eve, have struggled with sin and the devastating consequences of evil.

But even in the midst of the Fall, God revealed His plan of redemption—that Christ would finally defeat the serpent and redeem humanity (verse 15). Indeed, God "so loved the world" that He has made a way for "whoever believes" in Christ to be saved (John 3:16). Christ Himself, the Second Person of the Godhead, would become human, live a life untainted by sin, and willingly die on the cross as a perfect sacrifice in the place of sinners (John 10:18; Philippians 2:5–8), simultaneously upholding God's law and definitively demonstrating God's completely righteous character of love (Romans 3:25; 5:8).

Broadly speaking, this concept of a cosmic conflict between God and Satan is by no means unique to Adventist thinking, but it is uniquely essential to Adventist theology. It provides a great deal of the framework within which many doctrines of Adventist theology make sense, including, but not limited to, the doctrine of last things and the second coming of Christ (eschatology) and the nature of God's judgment and the sanctuary doctrine.

Differing understandings of the great controversy

Although the basic features of the great controversy outlined above are generally accepted among most Adventists, there are significant departures among some regarding just how the controversy over God's character is settled and the part that humans are to play in this cosmic drama of the great controversy, in which, as Paul puts it, "we have become a spectacle [or theater] to the world, both to angels and to men" (1 Corinthians 4:9).[8] This book aims to address these questions in order to help provide a clearer picture of God's character and the last generation for the benefit of the church.

On one hand, many Adventists affirm that God provides for Himself the means and grounds of victory in the great controversy, by definitively defeating Satan at the cross. Christ's work provided sufficient and effective grounds to refute the charges of the enemy and thus fully vindicate God's character before the onlooking universe. In this view, the role of humans is a missional role of proclamation and witnessing to the truth of God's unimpeachable character, spreading the good news, and reflecting God's character as a means to help people to recognize that God truly is wholly good and loving and thus cause them to give themselves unreservedly to Him. While this missional role has real and significant ramifications in helping people to recognize God's love and to choose to receive His free gift of salvation, the activity of humans does not provide any *grounds* for the vindication of God's character or God's victory in the great controversy. Humans merely proclaim and witness to the vindication of God's character, helping people to recognize God's perfect character without contributing in any way to actually making it true that God's character is perfect (cf. Romans 3:4). The essential point here is that God Himself wins the victory in the great controversy, and this victory is not contingent upon something added by mere creatures. Christ effectively refuted Satan's false charges against God's character, law, and moral government by His perfect life and death and has thus defeated the enemy (Revelation 12:10).[9]

On the other hand, some Adventists affirm what has come to be known as last generation theology (LGT). The following chapter will provide a historical and theological overview regarding just what LGT is. For now, we might minimally define it as the view that there must be a last generation of humans who become absolutely sinless and "perfect" in order to provide the grounds to vindicate God's character and win the great controversy. In this regard, generally speaking, LGT affirms that an additional phase of atonement is necessary, beyond the ministry of Christ, in order to finally defeat Satan. Specifically, there must be a final, entirely sinless generation of humans that, by completely overcoming sin, provides the grounds for the vindication of God's character, playing a crucial role in deciding the victor in the great controversy.[10] In this view, then, Satan was not defeated at the cross; some group of humans must become perfectly sinless in order for Satan to be defeated.

Issues and questions pertinent to LGT

This approach of LGT raises a number of issues that have far-reaching theological implications. For one thing, LGT makes God's victory in the great controversy dependent upon the fidelity of mere creatures, thus requiring the view that divine revelation and action are insufficient to win the great controversy but must be supplemented by human action.

Further, the idea that at least some group of humans must be sinlessly "perfect" prior to the Second Coming in order to provide the grounds for the vindication of God's

character requires one to believe that it must be possible for humans to become absolutely sinless prior to glorification—that is, prior to the transformation of the redeemed by Christ at the Second Coming (1 Corinthians 15:52–55). But this raises significant questions relative to the human condition, particularly to the doctrine of sin. If sin is thought of only as actions that are freely chosen, then one might become sinless by the force of one's will. If, on the other hand, sin is more than freely chosen actions, if it is also a bent disposition of the human condition with unchosen propensities toward evil, then it seems humans would not be able to *perfectly* overcome sin (in this broad sense) by the force of their will because the human will would itself be infected by sin.

Bound up with these issues relative to overcoming sin, many concerns and confusions arise regarding the conditions and process of salvation. In this regard, whereas many Adventists understand justification to be a forensic or legal declaration of righteousness, some advocates of LGT argue that justification is not merely forensic; it also includes the process by which the believer is made righteous (i.e., sanctification).

More disagreement and confusion arise when it comes to the nature of sanctification, which many Adventists view as the process of becoming more and more holy or growing in one's character to love more completely even as God does. In this view, whereas justification is a declaration of God made in a moment, sanctification is the work of a lifetime, yet both are by faith and depend upon the primary and prior (or "prevenient") action of God. In this view, Christians may achieve character "perfection," but this kind of perfection is not the same as the absolutist conception of perfection fostered by Greek philosophy.

On the other hand, last generation theology advocates perfection*ism*, which maintains that humans can become absolutely sinless. This tends to place the emphasis on human works and suggests that one might reach a point prior to glorification when one is perfectly "sanctified" and thus no longer in need of the imputed righteousness of Christ. In this view, one can follow in Christ's footsteps to become absolutely (morally) perfect.

Just how one views the conditions and process of salvation, particularly regarding the issue of "perfection," has abundant implications for what one considers to be holy living. Adventists generally agree that Christians should aim for Christlikeness and holiness, but there is considerable disagreement over what such holiness looks like and how it might be achieved.

Some emphasize external obedience and focus on abstaining from committing sins by the sheer, disciplined exercise of one's will. Others recognize the importance of obedience and of abstaining from committing sin but also emphasize that obedience and the overcoming of sinful *actions* can be accomplished only by a work of God in us that we embrace by faith, while our sinful inclinations will remain until glorification. In this latter view, abstaining from committing external sins is not enough; our sinful nature itself must be reckoned with, and when it comes to sins, there are not only sins of commission but also sins of omission. In this regard and many others, there are wide differences of belief regarding how Adventists should live in light of the soon coming of Jesus.

All this closely relates to one's perspective concerning the struggle with sin, which has significant ramifications for mental health. I have personally encountered and ministered to many Adventists who have tried—and failed—to be absolutely sinless and perfect (in the perfectionist sense described above). Because they believed they *could* achieve this absolutely sinless state if they simply made the right decisions and had to do so in order to have an assurance of salvation in the last days, their failure to achieve this state had devastating consequences for their faith and well-being.

Many had been taught that they *can* and *must* be just like Jesus in order to be worthy of salvation. Some came to believe that if they failed in doing so they were lost and that even doubting that they could and should become absolutely perfect in this sense amounted to doubting God's power and goodness and the effectiveness of Christ's ministry for and in them.

This relates closely to a common LGT argument: we can be absolutely sinless *even as* Jesus was absolutely sinless. In order for Christ to be our example, it is argued, He must have been *just like us*. Specifically, the claim goes, Christ must have inherited the same sinful condition and inclinations toward sinning that plague us; if He did not, then He was not fully human like us. If Christ was just like us, it is argued further, the fact that He never sinned (which is generally agreed upon by those in this discussion [see 1 John 3:5; cf. John 14:30]) demonstrates that humans may also overcome sin and achieve a state of perfect sinlessness.

Others, however, while agreeing that Christ was absolutely sinless, question whether Jesus was really *just like us* in accordance with the premises of LGT that (1) in order to be *fully* human one must inherit the sinful condition, and (2) Christ would need to be *just like us* in order to be our example. This relates closely to the aforementioned doctrine of sin. If sin is a condition that requires salvation from outside and Christ inherited this condition, then it seems that He would Himself be in need of a Savior. But this cannot be so.

In this regard, in at least some forms of LGT, the perfect example of Christ is considered to be insufficient to demonstrate that God's law is perfect and just. The argument, as some put it, is that a generation is needed who is in a *worse* situation than Christ, having inherited even further moral degeneration than LGT claims Christ did, in order to demonstrate that God's law can be kept perfectly by humans who possess a terribly deteriorated and sinful human nature.[11]

This raises many questions relative to just what Jesus accomplished on the cross and whether Christ's atonement was and is actually sufficient for us. In this respect, there are related disputes among Adventists regarding whether the atonement was complete at the cross, with some arguing (as noted earlier) that a further phase of human action is required for atonement and for God to win the great controversy, whereas others argue that atonement is complete through what Christ accomplished on the cross while atonement is not yet "completed" in reference to its application to humans.[12]

Once again, much of this discussion centers upon how and by whom the great controversy is finally resolved. This includes debates over the depiction of the state of the last generation in Revelation and elsewhere. If the last generation of believers is to be blameless and spotless (cf. 2 Peter 3:14), those who follow the Lamb wherever He goes (Revelation 14:4), does that mean that they are absolutely sinless? If they "must live in the sight of a holy God without an intercessor," does that mean that they must have fully overcome sin, in all respects, prior to glorification and in a way that they no longer need the work of Christ on their behalf?[13]

In these and other aspects, LGT argues, Christ's work alone is not sufficient to vindicate God's character from the slander of the enemy. In addition to Christ's work, there must be a group of humans who become perfectly sinless and thus provide the grounds for God's character to be vindicated by demonstrating that God's law can be perfectly kept by fallen humans.[14] In this view, Christ has not returned yet because He is waiting for this group to provide the sufficient grounds to close the great controversy.[15]

Addressing the issues:
The remainder of this book

Much more could be said about issues and implications that arise in relation to LGT, which will be taken up in more detail in the following chapters. To begin this discussion, in the next chapter, Woodrow Whidden provides a historical and theological overview that addresses the question, What is last generation theology?

Following this, in chapter 3, Martin Hanna takes up the question, What is sin? This is a crucial question because, as briefly explained above, some advocates of LGT tend to reduce sin to merely actions and choices whereas other Adventists emphasize that sin includes choices but is more than merely that which humans choose. This has massive implications regarding what it means to have victory over sin and how that is accomplished.

With this understanding of sin in the background, the discussion turns in the following chapters to just how to understand the salvation of sinners. Similar to the way in which sin is variously understood, the ideas concerning the nature and mechanics of how humans are saved vary depending on how one views sin, among a host of other factors. In chapter 4, Richard Davidson begins this discussion of salvation by addressing the nature of justification and how it functions, taking up questions such as: What does it mean to be justified? How can a sinner stand before the perfectly holy God?

Denis Fortin then moves to a discussion of the process of sanctification and issues related to "perfection" in chapter 5. As noted earlier, one's understanding of perfection and perfectionism is closely bound to one's understanding of the nature and process of sanctification. Here Fortin not only provides a discussion of what sanctification means and does not mean—emphasizing the proper ground of salvation in Christ and by faith alone—but he also takes up such crucial questions as, What does it

mean to be "perfect"? In what sense does God command humans to be perfect?

After this, in chapter 6, Ante Jerončić addresses the issue of holy living, particularly how we might inhabit the kingdom of God. In this chapter, Jerončić deals with the questions of what it means to be holy and how we should live in light of the soon coming of Jesus. In the next chapter, Peter Swanson contends with the psychology of perfection, discussing how we should understand our struggle with sin and how might it affect our mental health. In this chapter, he addresses the struggle in the mind of sinners as they attempt to overcome sin and, particularly, the danger of becoming so discouraged that they give up.

Chapter 8 turns to a discussion of the nature and work of Christ; the latter of which is expanded upon in the chapters that follow. In chapter 8, Darius Jankiewicz explains how Jesus, as both fully divine and fully human, can be our Savior as well as our example. In the discussion over LGT, much attention has been given to the humanity of Christ, and Jankiewicz takes up this issue, asking whether Jesus was really just like us and indeed whether He needed to be just like us in order to be our example.

In chapter 9, Félix Cortez explains the work of Christ at the cross, addressing the question: What did Jesus accomplish on the cross? Here Cortez explains how the cross provides the solution to the problems that arose from the Fall, how Jesus defeated the enemy at the cross, and how the cross provides the supreme manifestation of God's love and righteousness. Jiří Moskala follows up this discussion in chapter 10 by providing a treatment of the significance, meaning, and role of Christ's atonement. This chapter addresses the thorny issue of whether and when atonement was complete and the questions raised by LGT over the sufficiency of Christ's atoning work.

In chapter 11, Ranko Stefanovic takes up the question: What is the state of the last generation? Here Stefanovic provides an analysis of the biblical portrayal of the generation who will be alive at the Second Coming, addressing disputes—among other things—on whether this final generation is depicted as absolutely sinless. Jiří Moskala follows this in chapter 12 by introducing and addressing five myths in Adventism that have contributed to the misinterpretation of end-time issues and that have caused

some Adventists to have a shortage of confidence in the assurance of salvation.

Then in chapter 13, Jo Ann Davidson concludes the discussion of last things (eschatology) by addressing the issue of the "delay" of Christ's second coming, taking up such questions as: Why hasn't Jesus returned yet? Has Christ not yet returned because He is waiting for a final generation of absolutely sinless humans who will demonstrate to the universe that it is possible for fallen humans to be perfect, thus winning the great controversy? Finally, chapter 14 will conclude the discussion by briefly revisiting the issues and questions raised and addressed throughout the book, emphasizing the final triumph of God's love.

Endnotes

1. Seventh-day Adventist Fundamental Belief 8, on the great controversy, reads as follows: "All humanity is now involved in a great controversy between Christ and Satan regarding the character of God, His law, and His sovereignty over the universe. This conflict originated in heaven when a created being, endowed with freedom of choice, in self-exaltation became Satan, God's adversary, and led into rebellion a portion of the angels. He introduced the spirit of rebellion into this world when he led Adam and Eve into sin. This human sin resulted in the distortion of the image of God in humanity, the disordering of the created world, and its eventual devastation at the time of the global flood, as presented in the historical account of Genesis 1–11. Observed by the whole creation, this world became the arena of the universal conflict, out of which the God of love will ultimately be vindicated. To assist His people in this controversy, Christ sends the Holy Spirit and the loyal angels to guide, protect, and sustain them in the way of salvation. (Gen. 3; 6–8; Job 1:6–12; Isa. 14:12–14; Ezek. 28:12–18; Rom. 1:19–32; 3:4; 5:12–21; 8:19–22; 1 Cor. 4:9; Heb. 1:14; 1 Peter 5:8; 2 Peter 3:6; Rev. 12:4–9.)." Seventh-day Adventist Church, "The Great Controversy," https://www.adventist .org/en/beliefs/salvation/the-great-controversy/.

2. For more on the Adventist understanding of the great-controversy motif, see the collection of essays in Gerhard Pfandl, ed., *The Great Controversy and the End of Evil* (Silver Spring, MD: Biblical Research Institute, 2015). See also Frank B. Holbrook, "The Great Controversy," in *Handbook of Seventh-day Adventist Theology*, ed. Raoul Dederen (Hagerstown, MD: Review and Herald®, 2000), 969–1009; Richard M. Davidson, "Cosmic Metanarrative for the Coming Millennium," *Journal of the Adventist Theological Society* 11, nos. 1–2 (2000).

3. The first such recorded charge is found in Genesis 3, when the serpent insinuates that God is a liar and does not have Eve's best interests in mind (verses 1–5). Elsewhere, Satan challenges God's judgment regarding Job's character. In this and other ways, the devil (*diabolos*, which means "slanderer") antagonizes God and His people throughout Scripture, functioning as "the accuser of our brethren" who "accuses them before our God day and night" (Revelation 12:10). All Scripture quotations in this chapter are from the NASB unless otherwise noted.

4. One should be careful not to conflate "determined" and "compelled." Many who believe in de-

terminism also agree that God does not "compel" but believe that God does determine everything that happens, including the very will and choices of all creatures. On the nature of love, see John C. Peckham, *The Love of God: A Canonical Model* (Downers Grove, IL: IVP Academic, 2015).

5. As Ellen G. White puts it, "The exercise of force is contrary to the principles of God's government; He desires only the service of love; and love cannot be commanded; it cannot be won by force or authority. Only by love is love awakened. To know God is to love Him; His character must be manifested in contrast to the character of Satan. This work only one Being in all the universe could do. Only He who knew the height and depth of the love of God could make it known." Ellen G. White, *The Desire of Ages* (Mountain View, CA: Pacific Press®, 1940), 22. This is not to say, however, that human beings possess an unfettered free will. Although God never compels the will, due to the Fall all humans have a sinful nature or bent to sin, which will be discussed further in Martin Hanna's chapter.

6. See Richard M. Davidson, "Ezekiel 28:11-19 and the Rise of the Cosmic Conflict," in Pfandl, *The Great Controversy and the End of Evil*, 57–69. See also Richard M. Davidson, "And There Was Gossip in Heaven," *Adventist Review*, January 24, 2013, 22–24.

7. In this narrative, the serpent subtly raises a question about God's character (Genesis 3:1) and then explicitly asserts that God is a liar and has a nefarious motive for lying when he declares, contrary to what God had said, "You surely will not die! For God knows that in the day you eat from it your eyes will be opened, and you will be like God, knowing good and evil" (verses 4, 5).

8. By "we," Paul refers specifically to the apostles, but the idea that this world is a "theater" to both angels and men applies more broadly in the context of the great controversy.

9. "When Christ died on Calvary's cross, he exclaimed in his expiring agony, 'It is finished;' and Satan knew that he had been defeated in his purpose to overthrow the plan of salvation." Ellen G. White,

"The Unchangeable Character of the Law," *Signs of the Times*, September 23, 1889, 577. While Christ has won the victory at the cross, the enemy's rule continues for some time after the cross event until the final consummation and execution of judgment. In this regard, see Jo Ann Davidson's chapter on the "delay" of Christ's second coming.

10. As M. L. Andreasen puts it, "To complete Christ's work and make it efficacious for man, such a demonstration [of the perfection of the last generation saints] must be made. It must be shown that man can overcome as Christ overcame." M. L. Andreasen, *The Book of Hebrews* (Washington, DC: Review and Herald®, 1948), 59. In his view, "the last generation of men living on the earth . . . will [demonstrate] that it is possible to live without sin." Further, it is in "the last generation that God is vindicated and Satan defeated." M. L. Andreasen, *The Sanctuary Service* (Washington, DC: Review and Herald®, 1947), 302, 304.

11. See the discussion of this issue in Woodrow Whidden's chapter in reference to writings that appeared on Larry Kirkpatrick's website in 2007.

12. See the discussion of this issue in Jiří Moskala's chapter on the atonement.

13. Ellen G. White, *The Great Controversy Between Christ and Satan* (Mountain View, CA: Pacific Press®, 1950), 614.

14. This is attractive to some Adventists, particularly devout young Adventists, because it provides a concrete mission and goal to achieve for God and thus usher in the Second Coming.

15. As one advocate of LGT puts it: "God will wait for the maturing of Christian character in a significant number of people as the chief condition determining those events, such as the latter rain, loud cry, sealing, and Sunday law, which affect the time when probation for the world shall close and thus the time of the Second Coming." Larry Kirkpatrick, "LGT14: The 14 Points of Last Generation Theology," Last Generation Theology, http://www .LastGenerationTheology.org/lgt/ori/ori-lgt14.php (website discontinued).

2

What Is Last Generation Theology?
What Are the Historical Roots of Last Generation Theology?

Woodrow Whidden
With contributions from George R. Knight and Ángel Rodríguez

Introduction

When one speaks about last generation theology (LGT)[1] in the context of the history of Seventh-day Adventist theology, it immediately raises issues and questions regarding Christ's final intercessory and judging work in the Most Holy Place of the heavenly sanctuary. All who have entered into this discussion seem to agree on the following conviction: there is currently a special phase of the atoning work of Christ transpiring in the heavenly sanctuary that is vitally interconnected with His second coming. All are also agreed that this work includes a special spiritual work of character change among God's professed people that is, and will be, the fruit of Christ's forgiving and transforming grace.

And in a more special, focused sense, this work of Christ in the Most Holy Place of the heavenly sanctuary (which began in 1844) is called the "final atonement"[2] and is also closely associated with the pre-Advent "investigative judgment." Furthermore, all the participants in this discussion believe that one of the major reasons for this work of judgment is so that God can vindicate Himself in the face of charges that Satan has laid against His nature and character as He governs His created, but sin-warped, universe. Therefore, this judgment serves to vindicate God as He makes the final revelation as to who should receive eternal life or eternal death. But along with these numerous agreements, there has also been a long-simmering controversy regarding what is actually involved in the vindication of God's character as He reveals Himself to be the just and rightful moral governor of the universe.

What follows seems to be at the core of the controversy regarding this final atonement. The LGT that has been especially associated with well-known Ellen White–influenced and Bible-believing writers, such as E. J. Waggoner, M. L. Andreasen, Herbert Douglass, C. Mervyn Maxwell, Dennis Priebe, Kevin Paulson, and Larry Kirkpatrick (to name only the most prominent writers), lays down the following strong claim: This final atonement demands a level of sinless perfection from the last generation of God's professed believers that will allegedly vindicate God's demands for perfect obedience to His law. If God does not receive this vindication from this last generation of the perfectly sinless remnant, He loses out in the great controversy that has been going on between Christ and Satan!

In contrast to these earnest claims are the basic perspectives and claims that have been put forth by many writers who also profess to be Ellen White–affirming and Bible-believing Seventh-day Adventists. And the essence of the settled convictions of this latter group is the following: Although they will be faithfully responsive to Christ and will give evidence (in the records of their lives) that their faith was, and is, a genuine faith in Christ that has persistently produced the witness of the fruit of the Spirit in their lives of grace-empowered discipleship, God is *not* dependent on the last generation to prove anything. Furthermore, God has used in the past, and will continue to use in the present and into the future, the holy lives of the redeemed of all ages (not just the "last generation") as witnesses who will (at least in some sense) vindicate His decisions in the investigative judgment. Thus, they believe that, in Christ and His righteousness—both imputed (meritoriously) and imparted (evidentially)—all of the redeemed (including the remnant) will be the justified and sanctified beneficiaries of eternal salvation.

Furthermore, this latter group of thinkers has firmly held that it was the incarnate Christ's faith in God's imparted Holy Spirit power that has once and for all settled the question as to whether perfect obedience to the will of God (His holy law) through faith in God's imparted power is possible. (Christ did not need imputed grace—forgiveness of sins—since He had no sin.) And the key evidence they cite can be found in numerous Ellen G. White references that will be invoked later.

With these preliminary observations in hand, the major objective of this chapter is to lay out the historical background of this lengthy and often controversial debate. This historical overview will focus on the key ideas and figures that have provided the conceptual framework for LGT, especially the ideas and convictions of E. J. Waggoner and M. L. Andreasen, as well as a brief review of their more recent admirers, imitators, and adapters.

While there will be some brief assessments of LGT ideas, the major burden of this chapter will be to try to get at what have been the actual teachings of the key precursors and subsequent developers of this theology and their major polemical responders. Stated more succinctly, we are trying to objectively ascertain what LGT advocates and their critics have thought and taught on the issue of what has also been called the "truth" of the final atonement.

Who developed LGT?

In the known history of the major modern thinkers (since the late eighteenth century) who have set forth LGT issues, there appear to be four or five key persons who have greatly shaped the contours of this genre of theology. And it is to the thought of these major precursors of the contemporary LGT writers that we now turn our attention.

First of all is Edward Irving (1792–1834), who ministered in Reformed (Calvinistic) circles in Scotland and England during the early decades of the nineteenth century. He seems to be the forerunner of those who in the nineteenth and twentieth centuries emphasized the key ideas involved in the so-called post-Fall nature of Christ's humanity. Though more recent scholarship has not yet found definitive documentary connections, Irving does appear to be the major source of the theology of E. J. Waggoner and A. T. Jones regarding the post-Fall humanity of Christ.[3]

Notably, Irving stated, "If it be said, that our Lord's human nature differed in any of its properties from ours—that it was Adam's before it fell; or as ours shall be in the resurrection, immortal and incorruptible; or in any condition intermediate between these two, different from this fallen condition in which flesh ever hath found, from the first man down to the present generation of men—then that may be called a supposititious, or hypothetical, or imaginary humanity; but the humanity which I understand and know, it is not."[4]

What has also become quite evident is that Irving is the theological source for the so-called post-Fall Christology of the major twentieth-century non-Seventh-day Adventist theologians who have adopted this brand of Christological reflection. And these figures include such notables as Karl Barth and T. F. Torrance, along with some other thinkers of lesser scholastic stature, such as Harry Johnson of twentieth-century English Methodism.

Furthermore, it seems safe to conclude that for Seventh-day Adventist theology, the substantive fathers of the post-Fall (or "postlapsarian") views on Christ's humanity have been E. J. Waggoner and A. T. Jones. Therefore it should also come as no surprise that E. J. Waggoner was the effectual father of the Seventh-day Adventist version of the so-called last generation theology, which holds that God needs a last, or final, generation of tested believers to finally vindicate God's demand for perfect obedience to His holy law.

And finally, the very thorough research that Paul Evans has done on the history of these LGT ideas in Seventh-day Adventist history has vindicated this writer's earlier published research into Waggoner's thought regarding the historical sources for LGT. My original research was set forth in my biography of E. J. Waggoner: *E. J. Waggoner: From the Physician of Good News to Agent of Division* (Hagerstown, MD: Review and Herald®, 2008). Two years later, the above mentioned LGT research of Paul Evans emerged, ably exhibited in his 2010 dissertation titled "A Historical-Contextual Analysis of the Final-Generation Theology of M. L. Andreasen"

Evans, after presenting a carefully detailed body of evidence for the emergence of LGT, did directly affirm that Waggoner was the primary historical source for the development of LGT in Seventh-day Adventist theology during the nineteenth through the twenty-first centuries. (Further comment on Evans's conclusions will be given later when we engage in a more thorough discussion of Waggoner's and M. L. Andreasen's subsequent impact on LGT teaching.)

Therefore, a question arises: Could it be that E. J. Waggoner—especially during his eleven years of service in Britain and continental Europe from 1892 to 1903—was reading Irving on the post-Fall human nature of Christ? We will probably never be able to definitively answer this question because Waggoner never directly quotes Irving. Furthermore, we do not have access to Waggoner's personal library, since it has seemingly been lost.

But one of the key questions of this study

is this: Did Edward Irving promote the idea of an alleged last generation vindication of God that could have conceptually influenced Waggoner and later Seventh-day Adventist writers, including Uriah Smith, W. W. Prescott, and M. L. Andreasen? As of this writing, it seems that the most important idea that Irving may have contributed to the LGT later expressed by E. J. Waggoner and M. L. Andreasen was his view on Christ's humanity. This writer has not been able, at this juncture, to identify any concept in Irving's thought that God's vindication before the universe is dependent on the obedience of a last, or final, generation of perfected believers.

With these findings in hand, we can now turn to the thought of E. J. Waggoner, the most apparent, original developer of LGT in Adventist history.

The contribution of E. J. Waggoner

While the theme of last generation vindication or perfection received little, if any, expression during Waggoner's writing ministry before 1890, it would begin to receive increasing attention as the 1890s and the early years of the twentieth century unfolded. Thus, what follows provides a summary overview of the development of this theme in Waggoner's published writings from the early 1890s onward.[5]

Waggoner began his expositions with some very straightforward observations that clearly proclaimed that the major reason the Bible teaches that there will be a judgment according to works is that God's fairness in judging has been called into question. So "evidently," in the "judgment God's righteousness will be made

manifest," and it will "appear that he is indeed true, and that everything opposed to him is a lie. Thus God will be clear when he judges"—in other words, He will be vindicated. And thus "God condescends in all his ways to submit them to the judgment of the people, and thus he educates their sense of right and wrong," even including the "wicked" who "will thus acknowledge God's justice."[6]

Probably no informed Seventh-day Adventist who accepts the basic outlines of Ellen G. White's expositions of the great-controversy theme would take issue with Waggoner's sound teaching as to the reasons for a judgment of this nature—whether it includes the successive phases of pre-Advent, during the millennium, or at the end of the millennium! And while Waggoner would go on in a subsequent article to suggest how precious will be the witness of the changed lives of the believers when they are displayed in the great judgment,[7] he then went on to make some interesting comments to the effect that God does not really need any human witnesses to vindicate Himself against the devil's charges that obedience is impossible: "Men have nothing to do with giving Christ His kingdom. All they are called upon to do is to yield themselves to the Holy Spirit, that they may be fashioned into a fit subject for the kingdom which the Lord God will give unto them."[8]

But the next two pieces of commentary are even more explicit: "What if all the professed Christians in a province apostatised, and his work seemed to have been entirely in vain? 'Nevertheless the foundation of God standeth sure.' The truth is no more true because many men, and even great men, believe it; and it is no less true because many reject it. Jesus was just as much the Son of God when all forsook Him and fled, as He was when the multitude followed Him, shouting, 'Blessed be the King that cometh in the name of the Lord.' "[9]

> The Gospel does not derive its character from the character of men who profess it. It comes from God. Men may live ungodly lives, but that does not disprove the Bible. On the contrary, it makes the truth the more vivid by the contrast. Men may deny the faith; they may apostatise and say that it is all a sham; but that does not shake the Gospel any more than it would make the fortress of Gibraltar fall down if some of the men who are now stationed there should desert, and say that it is built on cardboard. It is solid rock, no matter what may be said of it.[10]

If these statements asserting God's sovereign ability to vindicate Himself, without the help of either friend or foe, are quite clear, the following is even more explicit regarding God's sovereign, independent ability to take care of the issues concerning His own vindication: "His [God's] honour is at stake. He has declared that the table shall be filled, and the inheritance fully occupied. He has pledged His very existence to that. Therefore, 'Some *must* enter therein.' So necessary is it, that if all the men on earth should refuse to come, God would raise the children to Abraham from the stones of the ground. Matt. iii. 9."[11]

Thus, according to Waggoner, God will have witnesses, but if need be, in the face of universal apostasy and rejection, He will produce these witnesses from the very "stones of the ground."[12]

Clearly, the thoughts expressed in this latter statement seem to bring an interesting wrinkle to the discussion. Even though Waggoner had earlier said that God does not need any witness from any person, he now says that the sovereign God will have witnesses, even if He has to unilaterally manufacture such witnesses from the ground—the "stones" of the earth. But this strong emphasis on divine sovereignty would be notably modified as Waggoner's "vindication" theology continued to unfold.

Such modifications would be forthrightly and openly manifested at Lincoln, Nebraska, during the 1897 Seventh-day Adventist General Conference Session. On March 6, 1897, Waggoner put forth the following path-breaking concept: "God has left the vindication of His character to His children. He has, as it were, risked His character with men."[13] With these notable and unmistakable lines, Waggoner declared God's sovereignty to be no longer dependent on His ability to transform the "stones of the ground" into vindicating witnesses; now God is viewed as almost totally dependent upon human beings to vindicate Himself—"He has, as it were, risked His character with men."

This unfolding case would be stated in even more unmistakable terms in December 1898. Referring to the work of the 144,000, pictured in Revelation 14, Waggoner made God totally dependent on their witness: "In them He [God] sees the work that He designed to do for men, and He is willing that these shall be known everywhere as the proofs of His saving power. He is willing to be judged by these results and He puts His own seal upon them. . . . His commandments are known to them as life everlasting, and Christ dwells in them, so that they have the faith of Jesus. They are His perfect representatives."[14]

But Waggoner was just warming up in these initial comments. He continued in the same issue of *The Present Truth*:

God has never left Himself without witness in what is termed the works of nature; but that witness is insufficient; man, the highest of God's creatures, must witness to Him as well as the lower things that God has made. . . . It is not merely single individuals, but a body of people "called out,"—the congregation, the church,—that constitutes God's house. Before the end comes, and at the time of the coming of Christ, there *must* be a people on earth, not necessarily large in proportion to the number of inhabitants of earth, but large enough to be known in all the earth, in whom "all the fullness of God" will be manifest even as it was in Jesus of Nazareth. God will demonstrate to the World that what He did with Jesus of Nazareth He can do with anyone who will yield to Him.[15]

But Waggoner could not leave this demonstration as a matter of some extra, bonus witness. In one of the most remarkable arguments ever entertained by his creative mind, he would go on to claim that without the witness of the end-time followers of Jesus, the very witness of the life of Jesus was not sufficient to vindicate the justice and mercy of God! Carefully weigh his sentiments:

Jesus Christ was the perfect temple of God; but if He were to be the only one in whom such fulness is revealed, then the too common idea that Jesus was a unique specimen, not made in all things like unto His brethren, and that it is impossible for anybody else to be in all things like Him, would be warranted; and Satan would not fail to charge God with incapacity and failure, saying that He is not able to make a man born in sin, and bring him to perfection. Day after day he is making this charge through men who, either despondently, or in self-justification, say that "Christ was different from us, for He was begotten by the Holy Ghost, and being born sinless had the advantage of us." The Lord wants all to understand that the new birth puts men in the same position that Christ occupied on this earth, and He will demonstrate this before all the world. The life of Jesus *is to be perfectly reproduced in His followers*, not for a day merely, but for all time and for eternity.[16]

What is truly remarkable about this claim (that God needs an end-time group to perfectly reproduce the life of Jesus in their character development) was that Waggoner would later, paradoxically, once more make it seem that everything was riding on the perfect obedience of Jesus. What follows is the most astounding statement that this writer has ever read on this issue:

> If Christ had failed or become discouraged because of the difficulties of His task, God's oath would have been broken; but if God's oath had been broken, God's own life would have been forfeited; and since He is the Creator and upholder of all things, everything would have ceased to be. Now we can see how well tried is this foundation upon which we are asked to build. God placed Himself and the weight of the entire universe upon it, and it stood the test. Therefore, we can rest upon it in confidence. It is a precious stone to those who believe.[17]

If God and His governance of the universe—even the very existence of the universe—was at stake and was settled by the faithfulness of Christ, what further need would there be for any other witness from His church? Here is a paradox, if not a contradiction, in Waggoner's thinking. Was God at risk? The better part of Waggoner's thought was to throw all the weight of this risk onto the faithfulness and obedience of the person of the incarnate Christ. The more questionable proposition—of God risking His vindication on the performance of His church—is one of the more uncertain moments in the doctrinal history of E. J. Waggoner.

Tensions would remain in Waggoner's thought for a time between the idea of the sovereign God risking the vindication of His character and the moral governance of His incarnate Son and the idea that God allegedly needed the witness of His church (His professed people) in order to vindicate His character. But it was the latter version—that of a human-centered, subjective, "victory over sin" exoneration of God—that ultimately triumphed in Waggoner's thinking. Carefully ponder the later developments in his "vindication" teachings: "Who is to clear the Infinite One of Satan's accusations? God created this world to be inhabited with a race of beings who would reflect His image, who would be loyal to Him. He has such confidence in man whom He has created, that He is willing to risk His character with him, and to this end He calls upon men to be His witnesses, witnesses of His lovingkindness, of His great mercy, of His willingness and power to forgive sin—witnesses who will tell the truth, the whole truth and nothing but the truth."[18]

In May 1901, Waggoner unequivocally laid out the idea of the vindication of God through the "mortal flesh" of His professed people:

> Before this corruptible body is made incorruptible, and the natural, sinful body is exchanged for the spiritual, sinless body, God will demonstrate what He can do in spite of corruption and mortality. He has condemned sin in the flesh, showing that even in sinful flesh He can live a sinless life. His perfect life will be manifested in mortal flesh, so that all will see it.
>
> . . . *This wonder must be worked out in sinful man, not simply in the person of Jesus Christ, but in Jesus Christ reproduced*

and multiplied in the thousands of His followers.[19]

While Waggoner's paradoxical thoughts finally landed on the side of the necessity of a demonstration of vindicating, faithful obedience by the professed last-day people of God, he did lay out a more positive, practical, and down-to-earth possibility for that witness:

> But before probation ends, there will be a people so complete in him [God] that in spite of their sinful flesh, they will live sinless lives. They will live sinless lives in mortal flesh, because he who has demonstrated that he has power over all flesh lives in them,— lives a sinless life in sinful flesh, and a healthful life in mortal flesh, and that will be a testimony that cannot be gainsaid,—a witness than which no greater can be given. Then the end will come. This will be the kingdom of God manifested to all nations for a witness to God's power. "The kingdom of God is within you."[20]

In these last two statements, a number of themes present themselves for a succinct summation.

First, the positive theme that God wants to use the end-time witness of His sanctified servants as a practical missionary witness to a doomed and hopeless world is most laudable. One could only wish that Waggoner would have stuck to this sort of motivation for living "sinless" lives in "sinful flesh." But to claim that such victorious living was a "must," a required

demonstration to get God off the hook of the great adversary's charges that obedience is impossible, not only places an enormously trying burden on the struggling people of God but also reveals very troubling theological presuppositions.

Yet there is one other matter that should be considered that has to do with Waggoner's constantly repeated, even predictably repetitive, theme of redemptive subjectivity: "They will live sinless lives in mortal flesh, because he who has demonstrated that he has power over all flesh lives in them" and such living of "sinless lives in mortal flesh" will be a "witness to God's power. 'The kingdom of God is within you.'"[21]

While there were a few positive aspects of this vindication thesis, the real point was that this theme provided Waggoner with one more occasion to further promote and elaborate the great, overriding theme of his salvation thought—especially during this last phase of his public ministry in the Seventh-day Adventist Church. And what was this theme?

It was that Christ literally dwells in His followers, His wonders to perform. That the immanent Christ is the very embodiment (in redeemed, sinful flesh) of "the kingdom of God within you." The subjective aspects of the presence of the immanent Christ were once more manifesting themselves as the all-consuming feature of Waggoner's salvation theology.

It thus seems abundantly evident that Waggoner's views of the indwelling Christ not only played a decisive role in his understanding of the atonement and personal salvation but also exercised a collective impact on his eschatology, especially with reference to the notable influence it exerted on his views regarding the vindication of God by the final generation in the great controversy.

The crucial role of
M. L. Andreasen and his LGT

There is little doubt that E. J. Waggoner had some degree of lasting influence on Andreasen. It is known that Andreasen studied at the newly founded Emmanuel Missionary College in Berrien Springs, Michigan, but there is no clear evidence that he was there during the 1903–1904 school year, which was the only year that Waggoner taught there. But whether or not Waggoner was a major, direct source of Andreasen's ideas on LGT, it is clear that the similarities between their positions are striking.[22]

It is impossible to overestimate the influence of M. L. Andreasen on later twentieth-century Adventist theology. Andreasen was Adventism's most influential theologian in the 1930s and 1940s, and his influence did carry over into the 1950s and 1960s and onward. Andreasen's special field of interest was the sanctuary and Christ's atonement. Quite clearly, his foremost contribution to Adventist theology has been his brand of LGT, which was fully developed by the time he published the first edition of his key book *The Sanctuary Service* in 1937. And it is at this juncture that we will look at his theology from the 1930s and 1940s; a theology that never essentially changed.

Before examining Andreasen's LGT, it might prove helpful to carefully ponder some of the theological concepts that undergirded his LGT thinking. First is his emphasis on a dual, or parallel, cleansing of the sanctuary on the antitypical day of atonement. According to this theology, aspects of which extend back to O. R. L. Crosier and Joseph Bates in the 1840s, God's people on earth must cleanse their soul temples while Christ is cleansing the sanctuary in heaven.[23]

A second concept is Ellen G. White's idea, presented in the books *The Great Controversy* and *Early Writings*, that the final generation will go through the time of trouble without a mediator. A third idea relates to the statement in *Christ's Object Lessons* that "Christ is waiting with longing desire for the manifestation of Himself in His church. When the character of Christ shall be perfectly reproduced in His people, then He will come to claim them as His own."[24]

A fourth concept underlying Andreasen's theology is the teaching of Jones, Waggoner, and Prescott that Jesus became incarnate in human flesh just like that of Adam *after the Fall*, with all of its sinful tendencies. Thus Jesus can, in every way, be our example in developing a perfect life.

A fifth idea at the foundation of Andreasen's LGT centers on the same line of thought that had led Waggoner to conclude that God's end-time people would be a demonstration to the universe—a people whose lives would proclaim, "Here are they that keep the commandments of God, and the faith of Jesus" (Revelation 14:12, KJV).

Thus M. L. Andreasen became the theological link between the post-1888 (not 1888) Jones, Waggoner, and Prescott theology and those Adventist groups that would arise in the 1960s and 1970s (and even until the present) in reaction to the book *Questions on Doctrine*.

A further concept crucial to a clear understanding of Andreasen's theology is his firm belief that Christ's atonement remained unfinished at the cross—an idea going back to Crosier's early treatment of the heavenly sanctuary and the Adventist understanding that the antitypical day of atonement began in October 1844. Andreasen set forth the atonement as having three phases. The first had to do with Christ living a perfect life. The second focused on events climaxing with the cross, where "the sins which [Christ] had met and conquered were placed upon Him, that He might bear them up to the cross and annul them."[25]

It is the third phase of his theology that became especially important to Andreasen's thought, because it contained what he saw as the special Adventist contribution to the topic. "In the third phase," he penned, "Christ demonstrates that man can do what He did, with the same help He had. This phase includes His session at the right hand of God, His high priestly ministry, and the final exhibition of His saints in their last struggle with Satan, and their glorious victory. . . . The third phase is now in progress in the sanctuary above and in the church below" as Christ is "eliminating and destroying sin in His saints on earth."[26]

The part of the third phase that deals with the perfecting of the saints on earth is central to the most influential chapter in Andreasen's book *The Sanctuary Service.* That chapter appears in the 1937 and 1947 editions. We will quote from the 1947 version at some length as we seek to grasp Andreasen's foremost contribution to Adventist theology.

"The final demonstration," he writes, "of what the gospel can do in and for humanity is still in the future. Christ showed the way" by taking a human body. "Men are to *follow His example and prove that what God did in Christ, He can do in every human being who submits to Him. The world is awaiting this demonstration. . . . When it has been accomplished, the end will come.*"[27]

Andreasen then went on to note that "the plan of salvation must of necessity include not only forgiveness of sin but complete restoration. Salvation *from* sin is more than forgiveness of sin."[28] Then he describes the process of sanctification as a point-by-point overcoming of behavioral and attitudinal sins. As the sinner has been "victorious over one besetment, so he is to become victorious over every sin." When an individual has accomplished this and clearly demonstrated that "he is ready for translation. . . . He stands without fault before the throne of God. Christ places His seal upon him. He is safe, and he is sound. God has finished His work in him. The demonstration of what God can do with humanity is complete. Thus it shall be with the *last generation* of men living on the earth. . . . *They will demonstrate that it is possible to live without sin. . . .* It will become evident to all that the gospel really can save to the uttermost. God is found true in His sayings."[29]

Next the seven last plagues fall, but nothing can make God's people sin.

They "keep the commandments of God, and the faith of Jesus." Rev. 14:12. . . .

It is in the last generation of men living on the earth that God's power unto sanctification will stand fully revealed. The demonstration of that power is God's vindication. It clears Him of any and all charges which Satan has placed against Him. *In the last generation God is vindicated and Satan defeated.*[30]

A little later on in this same chapter, Andreasen set forth the interesting thesis that even though Satan "failed in his conflict with Christ," that failure did not defeat him. The cross and the Resurrection were a setback to be sure, but the scene now shifts to the final generation. Satan goes out to " 'make war with the remnant of her seed, which keep the commandments of God and have the testimony of Jesus Christ.' Rev. 12:17. *If he could overcome them he might not be defeated.*"[31]

Thus, we can see the importance of the last generation for Andreasen. For him, the last (or final) generation holds the central spot in the great controversy between Christ and Satan, and it is no exaggeration to say that this final generation plays the most important part in the atonement. Satan had challenged God that people really couldn't keep the law. God needs a generation of people, the 144,000 of Revelation, to whom He can point and supply an answer to Satan:

"Here are they that keep the commandments of God, and the faith of Jesus." Rev. 14:12. . . .

. . . *God has reserved His greatest demonstration for the last generation.*[32]

In the last generation God will stand vindicated. In the remnant Satan will meet

defeat. The charge that the law cannot be kept will be met and fully refuted. God will produce not only one or two who keep His commandments, but a whole group, spoken of as the 144,000. They will reflect the image of God fully. They will have disproved Satan's accusation against the government of heaven.[33]

The supreme exhibition has been reserved until the final contest. . . .

[And thus to make the demonstration complete, God] . . . hides Himself. The sanctuary in heaven is closed. The saints cry to God day and night for deliverance, but He appears not to hear. God's chosen ones are passing through Gethsemane. . . . Seemingly they must fight their battles alone. They must live in the sight of a holy God without an intercessor.[34]

In the last generation God gives the final demonstration that men can keep the law of God and that they can live without sinning. . . . *Through the last generation of saints God stands fully vindicated. Through them He defeats Satan and wins His case.* . . . *The cleansing of the sanctuary in heaven is dependent upon the cleansing of God's people on earth.* How important, then, that God's people be holy and without blame! In them every sin must be burned out, so that they will be able to stand in the sight of a holy God and live with the devouring fire.[35]

Andreasen's powerful arguments put Adventism, as the people of the third angel of Revelation 14:12, at the very center of the atonement and the great controversy. That heady message took Adventism by storm. It became the denomination's dominant (but not exclusive) theology of the 1940s and 1950s. Andreasen had skillfully woven the insights of *pre*-1888 Adventism with those of the *post*-1888 Jones, Waggoner, and Prescott camp and had created an integrated eschatological theology that had great appeal to Adventists.[36]

Similarities between Waggoner's and Andreasen's LGT concepts

With Andreasen's LGT thought essentially in hand, we need to compare it with that of Waggoner. Can we justifiably conclude that the core of Waggoner's ideas was the direct seedbed for Andreasen's theology of the last generation?

First, as one reads through Virginia Steinweg's biography of Andreasen—*Without Fear or Favor: The Life of M. L. Andreasen* (Washington, DC: Review and Herald®, 1979)—there seems to be very little, if any, evidence of direct personal contact between Andreasen and Waggoner. During most of Andreasen's early years in ministry, Waggoner was ministering in Britain and continental Europe (1892–1903) and had essentially sidelined himself from the church after moving in 1904—against Ellen G. White's counsel—to Battle Creek from Emmanuel Missionary College, where he had taught for one year in Berrien Springs, and joining with John Harvey Kellogg in a steady slide into apostasy. But it could have been that Andreasen was reading articles and books written and published by Waggoner during these crucial years of

transition for both of these men.

Furthermore, it could also very well be that Andreasen was exposed to some of Waggoner's themes through his more direct association with the influential A. T. Jones, who was Andreasen's teacher at Battle Creek College in 1899 and his sometime conversation partner during social outings on Sundays at Lake Goguac near Battle Creek.[37]

What is also quite evident is that Jones and Waggoner shared a strikingly similar post-Fall view of Christ's human nature. The essential core of this theology regarding the humanity of Christ was reflected in Andreasen's theology. Furthermore, while Jones shared very similar views with both Waggoner and Andreasen on the end-time saints gaining the victory over sin, it does *not* appear that Jones was as emphatic in expressing the ideas of a last generation vindication of God that were so typical of E. J. Waggoner and Andreasen.[38] Despite this difference between Jones and the duet of Waggoner and Andreasen on the vindication of God, solid documentary evidence cogently points to the striking similarities between the LGT concepts regarding the vindication of God that were so evident in the commonly held thought of both Waggoner and Andreasen. And these ideas were essentially the same riveting concepts that were to become so influential on the later eschatology of twentieth- and twenty-first-century Seventh-day Adventism. Thus, it seems more than proper to conclude that Waggoner's theology had a manifest influence on that of Andreasen. We invite the reader to carefully ponder their following conceptual commonalities.

Waggoner clearly taught that God required a demonstration of perfect obedience by His last-day remnant that would take place "before the end, and at the time of the coming of Christ."[39] This demonstration (especially as it was clearly portrayed by Waggoner in his article "God's Witnesses," in the June 1, 1899, issue of *The Present Truth*) was very similar (including its location in time) to what was later described by Andreasen. And for Waggoner, the ones who would give this vindicating demonstration would be "a body of people . . . the church" who will "demonstrate to the world that what He [God] did with Jesus . . . He can do with anyone who will yield to Him."[40] Furthermore, Waggoner expressed the idea that the demonstration of Jesus' obedience was not sufficient to make the case, since "Jesus was a unique specimen"—a charge that Waggoner attributed to Satan.[41]

So while we cannot adduce any totally direct literary dependency of Andreasen on Waggoner, their conceptual similarities are so striking as to suggest that there was some sort of influential linkage between the teachings of the older E. J. Waggoner and the much younger Andreasen (and his later admirers).

The later advocates of Waggoner's and Andreasen's LGT ideas[42]

Even though Andreasen never considered the perfection of the last generation to be meritorious, his teaching contributed in the church to the presence of a strong element of unwitting legalism—the idea that good works performed in any subjective human experience of sanctification help to secure our meritorious acceptance with God. During the 1960s and 1970s, his ideas were variously modified, misused, or even rejected by many.

During the 1960s, Robert David Brinsmead, a layman from Australia, accepted and developed some of Andreasen's ideas. But Andreasen's most significant influence on Brinsmead was related to his teachings on the last generation. Like Andreasen, Brinsmead maintained that God's final answer to Satan's charges concerning the impossibility of keeping His law was to be given through the last generation.

But Brinsmead tended to radicalize Andreasen's views. He believed that the cleansing of the heavenly sanctuary was the cleansing of God's name, His vindication.[43] He even concluded that humans were created "to vindicate His [God's] name and exonerate His law, and to help bring to an end the work of Satan."[44] The eternal antidote for sin was not simply the cross, but the collective life of the last generation who will live without sinning and without a mediator. Thus God will demonstrate that there is no reason for the presence of sin in the universe. Brinsmead took Andreasen's ideas to an extreme, teaching that the perfection of the last generation will take place during the judgment, at which time "humanity will be united (married) to divinity" and the individual "will be as sinless in the flesh as Christ was sinless in the flesh."[45] Brinsmead's emphasis on perfectionism ultimately ended when he accepted what he deemed to be the Reformers' understanding of justification by faith. This was a theological move that then took him to an evangelical form of practical antinomianism (something many of the Reformers were most careful to eschew) and eventually resulted in Brinsmead's permanent separation from the Adventist Church.

Interestingly enough, the influence of Andreasen's views resurfaced in the 1970s. This time it was developed into a more sophisticated form by theologians in leading positions in the church. Two of the most influential were Herbert E. Douglass and C. Mervyn Maxwell. Herbert E. Douglass was a college religion teacher and president who later became one of the editors of the *Review and Herald*. It was especially in this latter position that his views became widely influential.[46] Using statements from Ellen G. White, Douglass established what he called "the harvest principle as an explanation for the delay of the Second Advent."[47] The condition of the church "determines when the landlord returns to his faithful servants."[48] Christ is waiting "until His church on earth had vindicated truth—His character—in their lives."[49] Christ is waiting "until the gospel seed has produced a sizable and significant group of mature Christians in the last generation."[50] According to Douglass, "Jesus proved that man in sinful flesh could live without sinning."[51]

In contrast with Andreasen, Douglass suggested that Christ's earthly ministry demonstrated that Satan was a liar, that the law was just, that God was love, and that justice and mercy can coexist. Christ vindicated God.[52] How, then, does the last generation contribute to God's vindication? Doubts may still linger, says Douglass, particularly among humans, who may doubt that we can overcome like Jesus did. So in order "to silence that last lingering

question . . . Jesus now waits for His church to reproduce what He achieved, thus proving again that man with fallen human nature can live without sinning. This demonstration will complete the vindication of God's character and government and will settle the question of His justice and mercy forever."[53] Like Andreasen, Douglass does not consider character development to be a contribution to our salvation but considers it a response of gratitude to the Lord for redeeming us. He also tried to distinguish his views from a sinless perfection that places the individual beyond temptation and the possibility of sinning.[54] Douglass's influence diminished a little during the latter years of his life, but in his final years he began to write again on the topic, and at the present time, his ideas have again become a topic of discussion among Adventists.[55]

C. Mervyn Maxwell, a professor at Andrews University Theological Seminary, also invoked the core of Andreasen's view, including a questionable view of the right relationship between faith and works. Faith is expressed in different ways, including "laborious and taxing" actions.[56] This is not legalism, he said, because legalism is about why we do things and not about what we do.[57] Grace is effective only for those who keep their eyes on Jesus and express faith through works.[58] Maxwell asked the rhetorical question, "Who will say that all this diligent effort of ours has nothing to do with our personal salvation?"[59] He connected that work of perfection with the cleansing of the heavenly sanctuary, arguing that the cleansing takes place first in the hearts of believers through the power of Christ.[60] Concerning the last generation,

Maxwell commented that "the saints who stand invincible in the sight of a holy God will not *commit* sin, in whatever manner the term is defined."[61] They are still sinners, but victorious sinners. He was willing to use the phrase "sinless perfection," but he defined it as "perfection that triumphs over every sinful prompting of human nature and dynamically emulates the virtues of Jesus Christ."[62]

Now quite likely a number of these positions could be understood as faith being the *root* and works of obedience being the *fruit* of the dynamics of genuine faith. But when Maxwell moves on to the issue of the vindication of God's character, through the last generation's state of perfection, things then begin to become a bit too anthropocentric (human centered). Thus, the last generation "adequately represents God's love and truth to the fallen in this world and the unfallen in worlds afar. By revealing the true glory of God in their daily lives, they can help God secure the eternal loyalty of the universe and the consent of sinners to be saved."[63] Once more, while there might be some legitimate vindicating truth in these statements, they do tend to imply that the sinless life and substitutionary sacrifice of Christ was not enough to vindicate God.[64]

The theology of the perfection of the last generation was more critically addressed and critiqued by two Adventist theologians, Edward Heppenstall and Hans K. LaRondelle.[65] They both approached the question of perfection from a more biblically informed perspective. Heppenstall defined sin as a *state of being* as well as *acts which are* contrary to God's will.[66]

Biblical perfection consists in establishing a personal relationship with God—a total commitment to Him.[67] Therefore, biblical perfection is not sinless perfection, but it is a "spiritual maturity and stability that is possible in this life."[68] Sin has been dethroned, but it still remains. Through the Spirit, God awakens and develops the desire for full freedom from sin, for freedom from sin in all its forms, but the full actualization of that desire will occur at the return of the Lord. He adds that in the Christian life "imperfection persists, not in the sense of committing willful sin, but in the sense of coming short of the ideal in Jesus Christ."[69] Consequently, we will always need to ask for forgiveness. Since we are spiritually disabled by sin, "we will always live by the grace of God."[70] For Heppenstall, a last generation that is morally and spiritually different from previous generations was not theologically defensible.

Hans K. LaRondelle argued that in the Old Testament the human awareness of sinfulness was addressed through divine forgiveness that broke the power of sin.[71] Therefore, there was not perfection independent of the cultic atonement symbolized in the Israelite sanctuary services. Christian perfection "is not striving after ethical ideals or even the endeavor to imitate or copy Christ's life independent of Him, but it is a wholehearted, undivided belonging to Him and living with Him by His saving and sanctifying power."[72] In a sense, perfection is a present gift; but at the same time, it is a promise that will be fulfilled at the Second Coming. When we are justified by faith, LaRondelle commented, we are transferred from the dominion of sin to the kingdom of grace and we are commanded not to allow sin to reign over us (Romans 6:12).[73] The Christian walk is a walk in constant "dependence on God's forgiving and keeping grace."[74] It is only on that basis that we can "attain victory over every sin and reach in this life the standard of Christian perfection of character."[75] Perfection is dependent not only on Christ's forgiving grace but also on constant growth in holiness.

With respect to the last generation, LaRondelle did not say much. Based on Revelation 14, he suggested that the last proclamation of the gospel will climax in a manifestation of primitive godliness through the reception of the Spirit. That means that "all Christians will practice the gift of saving and sanctifying grace as perfection in action, visible in all their social relationships so that God will be glorified and praised."[76]

The influence of Andreasen's theology did not end with the theological debate we have just summarized. Some of the independent and self-supporting ministries within the church have continued to promote perfection of character, based on Christ as a model who overcame sin in a fallen human nature. These groups have been influenced not only by Andreasen but also by theologians who have continued to promote some of his views. Colin Standish and his late brother Russell Standish have argued that victory over sin is not self-centeredness and that it has no merits for salvation. But they continued to maintain that good works serve "to vindicate the character of God against the false charge of Satan that God's law is unjust and impossible for fallen man to keep."[77] This "work

of character perfection and sin cleansing will be complete before the close of probation."[78] Donald K. Short observed that "the spiritual maturity, or character perfection of the final generation, is inseparably joined to Christ taking the human nature of Adam after the Fall."[79] The perfection of the last generation is, as in the case of Andreasen, connected to the day of atonement. The cleansing of the heavenly sanctuary, the blotting out of the record of our sins from the heavenly books, could not take place "unless first of all the sin itself is blotted out of the human heart."[80] The forgiving ministry of Christ should come to an end and a sealing should occur "from which there will never be a turning away. This is equivalent to the blotting out of sins, and is a preparation for the coming of Jesus."[81] Others will argue that the perfection of the last generation will make them "safe to save."[82]

As we complete this survey, one contemporary figure should be mentioned, though he is not alone. Adventist pastor Larry Kirkpatrick[83] has been one of a number of polemicists that has led out in challenging many of the opponents of LGT, including the treatment of M. L. Andreasen's theology found in George Knight's *A Search for Identity: The Development of Seventh-day Adventist Beliefs* (Hagerstown, MD: Review and Herald®, 2000).

What is especially striking about Kirkpatrick's response to Knight is his claim that the reason Jesus needs a final generation—the very last, in fact, before the Second Coming—to vindicate Him in His demand for perfect obedience is that Jesus' humanity was not sufficiently degenerate at the time of His incarnation for Him to truly be our effective exemplar as we battle with temptation in our time. This rationale is based on the assumption of most post-Fall Christology advocates that Jesus had to be just like fallen humanity in His fallen, sinful nature. If Jesus' human nature was not just like fallen sinners—"in the likeness of sinful flesh" (Romans 8:3)—then He cannot effectually succor sinners in their resistance to temptation. Thus, Kirkpatrick goes on to make the following case.

Agreeing with Ellen G. White that the moral degeneration of the human race has continued apace since the Fall, he draws the following conclusion: Since we are now many generations removed from the time of Christ's incarnation, Jesus was thus not degraded enough in His human nature to be our effectual exemplar. And then Kirkpatrick proceeds to conclude that Jesus will be somehow dependent on the very last generation of earth's saints to vindicate His requirements for perfect obedience. Thus, he makes the point that Jesus really cannot be an effective exemplar unless He can point to the last generation of saints as His example of being totally dependent on the Holy Spirit.

Clearly Kirkpatrick raises some very relevant questions in his efforts to vindicate last generation theologians' earnest efforts to justify their theology. But the answers to these questions, and others, will be more fully dealt with in later chapters. At this juncture, we need to briefly summarize the historical developers of LGT and then pose the key questions that need to be pondered in response to their earnest efforts to articulate their ideas regarding the vindication of God.

Conclusions and further challenges to ponder

There is little doubt that the key shapers of LGT have sincerely sought to clarify Adventism's great-controversy theme. And for them the key question has been the following: Who will be the key persons among God's last-day believers (the remnant) who will step forward to exonerate God and His grace as He seeks to vindicate Himself in the face of Satan's challenge that He has acted unfairly in His dealings with Lucifer's sin and challenge? Furthermore, at the heart of Satan's challenge to God's governance has been the claim that God was unfair in requiring perfect obedience to His holy law, and thus He should not destroy any sinner. And the major shapers of this LGT have been (in chronological order) E. J. Waggoner (late nineteenth and early twentieth centuries), M. L. Andreasen (early to mid-twentieth century), Herbert Douglass and C. Mervyn Maxwell (mid-twentieth to early twenty-first centuries), and key contemporary figures such as Dennis Priebe, Kevin Paulson, and Larry Kirkpatrick, to mention only three of the most able writers and advocates for LGT.

Furthermore, at the heart of all LGT teaching is the basic idea that God needs a significant group of the remnant, Christian believers who will perfectly obey the law of God. And when God finds such a perfected remnant group, it will effectively, by faith, refute Satan's challenge that perfect obedience to God's law is impossible. And it will be through this remnant that God will (must) be vindicated in His requirements of "perfect obedience" to His holy law.

But in pointed opposition to this line of

thought, there have been those writers and speakers who have taken the position that in the great controversy between Christ and Satan it has been Christ Himself, the unique God-man, who has effectively vindicated God's demand for perfect obedience by His incarnate life, atoning death, heavenly intercession, and the various phases of God's investigative and executionary judgments (pre-Advent, millennial, and at the end of the millennium). So the key question that remains to be answered in subsequent chapters of this volume is this: Who has the best evidence, from (a) the Bible, (b) the longer Christian tradition of theological reflection (especially its Protestant version), and (c) the writings of Ellen G. White, as to how God will be vindicated in all of His dealings with sin, sinners (both angelic and human), and their terrible rebellion that has caused such horrific losses in God's reeling universe? May the marvelous grace of God continue to be with us all!

Endnotes

1. Henceforth last generation theology will be referred to as LGT.

2. Ellen G. White, *Early Writings* (Washington, DC: Review and Herald®, 1945), 253.

3. See Remwil Tornalejo, "A Comparative Study of the Christology of Edward Irving, Ellet Joseph Waggoner, and Alonzo Trevier Jones" (MTh thesis, Adventist International Institute of Advanced Studies, 2009).

4. Cited from Edward Irving, *The Orthodox and Catholic Doctrine of Our Lord's Human Nature* (London: Ellerton and Henderson, 1830), as quoted in Tornalejo, "Comparative Study," 38, 39.

5. What follows over the next several pages is drawn from this writer's above mentioned biography of Waggoner, *E. J. Waggoner: From the Physician of Good News to Agent of Division* (Hagerstown, MD: Review and Herald®, 2008). Reprinted by permission.

6. E. J. Waggoner, "Romans 3:9-12. (Concluded)," *Signs of the Times*, August 25, 1890. A very similar line of thought came nine years later: "In order that rebellion shall be put down for ever, never more to have any possibility of arising, every creature in the universe must see and acknowledge the righteousness of God. . . . The great Judgment is not for the purpose of enabling God to judge of the character of men, but to cause all men to see the true character of God. . . . The time will come when every secret thing will be brought to light. Then all will see that God has always been true and good. Every knee will bow, and every tongue will confess." E. J. Waggoner, "The Gospel of Isaiah. The Great Case at Law," *Present Truth*, January 5, 1899, 4.

7. E. J. Waggoner, "Witnesses for God," *Present Truth*, December 14, 1893, 577, 578.

8. E. J. Waggoner, "The Authority of Christ," *Present Truth*, April 12, 1894.

9. E. J. Waggoner, "The Gospel Does Not Depend Upon Man," *Present Truth*, May 10, 1894.

10. E. J. Waggoner, "Not of Man," *Present Truth*, June 7, 1894.

11. E. J. Waggoner, "Front Page," *Present Truth*, August 30, 1894 (emphasis in original).

12. This very same point would be repeated some three years later: "So absolutely necessary is it that some must enter into the rest that God has prepared, and which can be entered into only by faith, that even if every man should be false and faithless, God would still remain true to His promise (Rom. iii. 3, 4), for He could take some of the ground and raise up children to Abraham. Matt. iii. 9." E. J. Waggoner, "Lessons From the Book of Hebrews. The Rest That Remains," *Present Truth*, November 11, 1897.

13. E. J. Waggoner, "Witnesses for God," *General Conference Bulletin* 2, no. 1 (1897): 55.

14. E. J. Waggoner, "Notes on the International Sunday-School Lessons. The Captivity of Judah. Jeremiah lii. 1-11," *Present Truth*, December 8, 1898, 770.

15. E. J. Waggoner, " 'The Sanctuary of God,' " *Present Truth*, December 8, 1898, 774 (emphasis added).

16. Ibid. (emphasis added). This compelling line of expression has been essentially and effectively "reproduced" by most of the twentieth- and twenty-first-century adapters of Waggoner's end-time vin-

dication theology. We will reinforce this point later. It must also be acknowledged that Ellen G. White uses similar language in the book *Christ's Object Lessons* (Washington, DC: Review and Herald®, 1941), 69. While this language is similar to that of Waggoner's, it is clearly given in a setting where Christ is seeking to urge this transformation of character as a means to the end, or goal, of the corporate spreading of the gospel to the world.

17. E. J. Waggoner, "The Gospel of Isaiah. The Sure Foundation," *Present Truth*, May 11, 1899, 293. A somewhat similar line of thought can be found in Ellen G. White's reflections on the great test brought by Satan to Christ in Gethsemane: "Everything was at stake with him [Satan]. If he failed here, his hope of mastery was lost; the kingdoms of the world would finally become Christ's; he himself would be overthrown and cast out. But if Christ could be overcome, the earth would become Satan's kingdom, and the human race would be forever in his power. With the issues of the conflict before Him [Christ], Christ's soul was filled with dread of separation from God." Ellen G. White, *The Desire of Ages* (Mountain View, CA: Pacific Press®, 1940), 687. Also referring to the terrible struggle of Christ in Gethsemane is the following: "The awful moment had arrived which was to decide the destiny of the world. The heavenly hosts waited the issue with intense interest. The fate of humanity trembled in the balance." Ellen G. White, *The Spirit of Prophecy*, vol. 3 (Battle Creek, MI: Steam Press of the Seventh-day Adventist Pub. Assn., 1878), 99. And finally, "For a period of time Christ was on probation. He took humanity on Himself, to stand the test and trial which the first Adam failed to endure. Had He failed in His test and trial, He would have been disobedient to the voice of God, and the world would have been lost." "Christ Glorified," *Signs of the Times*, May 10, 1899, 2, quoted in Ellen G. White Comments, in *The Seventh-day Adventist Bible Commentary*, ed. Francis D. Nichol, vol. 5 (Washington, DC: Review and Herald®, 1980), 1082, 1083. Ellen G. White seemed a bit less apocalyptic than Waggoner. For Waggoner, the cosmic universe would have imploded as a result of Christ's possible failure. For Ellen G. White, sinful humanity would have been entirely lost.

18. E. J. Waggoner, "God's Witnesses," *Present Truth*, June 1, 1899, 339.

19. E. J. Waggoner, "Back Page," *Present Truth*, May 9, 1901, 304 (emphasis added). A very similar expression was to come about six weeks later: "Now, however, are we sons; and God will demonstrate His mercy and His power, and vindicate His righteousness before all the universe, by demonstrating that He can work that which is good and well pleasing in His sight in a corruptible body as well as in an incorruptible one." "The Editor's Private Corner. The New Birth—a Spiritual Man," *Present Truth*, June 20, 1901, 391.

20. E. J. Waggoner, "Sermon," *General Conference Bulletin*, Thirty-Fourth Session, First Quarter, April 9, 1901, 147.

21. Ibid.

22. What follows in this section is adapted from George R. Knight's *A Search for Identity: The Development of Seventh-day Adventist Beliefs* (Hagerstown, MD: Review and Herald®, 2000), 144ff.

23. For confirmation of this point, see Frank B. Holbrook, ed., *Doctrine of the Sanctuary*, Daniel and Revelation Committee Series, vol. 5 (Silver Spring, MD: Biblical Research Institute, 1989), 134, 135, 144, 145; and Paul Evans, "A Historical-Contextual Analysis of the Final-Generation Theology of M. L. Andreasen" (PhD diss., Andrews University, 2010), 27, 29.

24. White, *Christ's Object Lessons*, 69.

25. M. L. Andreasen, *The Book of Hebrews* (Washington, DC: Review and Herald®, 1948), 59.

26. Ibid., 59, 60.

27. M. L. Andreasen, *The Sanctuary Service* (Washington, DC: Review and Herald®, 1947), 299 (emphasis added).

28. Ibid., 300 (emphasis added).

29. Ibid., 302 (emphasis added).

30. Ibid., 303, 304 (emphasis added).

31. Ibid., 310 (emphasis added).

32. Ibid., 310–312 (emphasis added).

33. Ibid., 315 (emphasis added).

34. Ibid., 316–318 (emphasis added).

35. Ibid., 319–321 (emphasis added).

36. This concludes this writer's adaptation of George Knight's material.

37. See Virginia Steinweg, *Without Fear or Favor: The Life of M. L. Andreasen* (Washington, DC: Review and Herald®, 1979), 50–52.

38. Paul Evans has carefully made this point: while A. T. Jones and other contemporaries shared very similar ideas on perfection and the last generation, it was Waggoner who was the main man in making the point that it would be the last generation that would finally settle the issue of whether perfect obedience

was possible or not—all done in that generation's final vindication of God. See Evans, "Historical-Contextual Analysis," 150–182, with special focus on page 158.

39. Waggoner, " 'The Sanctuary of God,' "774.

40. Ibid.

41. Ibid.

42. What follows is adapted from an enlarged and revised version of Ángel Rodríguez's paper entitled "Theology of the Last Generation: A Chapter in Adventist Theological Discussions," originally published in *Al Aire del Espíritu: Festschrift al Dr. Roberto Badenas*, ed. Ramon Gelabert and Víctor Armenteros (Libertador San Martin, Argentina: Universidad Adventista del Plata, 2013), 199–213. This writer's adaptations have been utilized with the consent and general approval of Rodríguez.

43. Robert Brinsmead, *Man Born to Be King* (Australia: Prophetic Research, 1966), 109.

44. Ibid., 109, 110.

45. Brinsmead, *God's Eternal Purpose* (Brisbane: Jackson and O'Sullivan, 1959), 199, quoted in *History and Teaching of Robert Brinsmead* (Washington, DC: Review and Herald®, 1962), 18.

46. See, for instance, the following articles by Herbert E. Douglass: "Ellen White's Eschatological Principle," *Review and Herald*, May 23, 1974, 12; "A Special Truth and a Special Work," *Review and Herald*, June 6, 1974, 14; "Truth Understood Only by Men of Faith," *Review and Herald*, June 20, 1974, 11; "God Stakes His Honor on a Victorious People," *Review and Herald*, July 4, 1974, 15, 16; "Fitness for Heaven, Now," *Review and Herald*, July 18, 1974, 11; "Not Entrapped by Cheap Grace," *Review and Herald*, August 1, 1974, 17, 18; "Sanctification Not Imputed," *Review and Herald*, August 15, 1974, 13, 14; "Heaven Waits for Human Channels," *Review and Herald*, August 29, 1974, 13, 14.

47. Herbert E. Douglass, "Men of Faith—the Showcase of God's Grace," in *Perfection: The Impossible Possibility*, ed. Herbert E. Douglass (Nashville, TN: Southern Pub. Assn., 1975), 20.

48. Ibid., 22.

49. Ibid., 15. See also his article "Why God Waits," *These Times*, July 1, 1975, 8–11, where he has written, "The evidence that vindicates God's patience, mercy, and justice rests in the lives of men and women who have proved that God's way is best."

50. Douglass, "Men of Faith," 19.

51. Ibid., 43.

52. Ibid., 52.

53. Ibid., 53.

54. Ibid., 13.

55. See Douglass's earlier books, *Why Jesus Waits* (Washington, DC: Review and Herald®, 1976); *The End: Unique Voice of Adventists About the Return of Jesus* (Mountain View, CA: Pacific Press®, 1979), 132–140; and then compare these earlier works with his later *A Fork in the Road: "Questions on Doctrine"; The Historic Adventist Divide of 1957* (Coldwater, MI: Remnant Publications, 2008), 108–111 and, to a more subtle degree, in one of his last books—a compilation interlaced with questions and some succinct commentary—*The Heartbeat of Adventism: The Great Controversy Theme in the Writings of Ellen G. White* (Nampa, ID: Pacific Press®, 2010). His LGT themes even managed to delicately permeate a very evangelically Arminian-flavored book on the subject of the personal assurance of salvation that was entitled *Should We Ever Say, "I Am Saved"?* (Nampa, ID: Pacific Press®, 2003), see 138–143 and 157, 158, where LGT themes emerge.

56. C. Mervyn Maxwell, "Ready for His Appearing," in Douglass, *Perfection*, 149.

57. Ibid.

58. Ibid., 151.

59. Ibid.

60. Ibid., 152.

61. Ibid., 159.

62. Ibid., 166.

63. Ibid., 171.

64. Ibid., 196.

65. See particularly Hans K. LaRondelle's book *Perfection and Perfectionism: A Dogmatic-Ethical Study of Biblical Perfection and Phenomenal Perfectionism* (Berrien Springs, MI: Andrews University Press, 1971).

66. Edward Heppenstall, " 'Let Us Go On to Perfection,' " in Douglass, *Perfection*, 63.

67. Ibid., 64.

68. Ibid., 67.

69. Ibid., 77.

70. Ibid., 82. Heppenstall's position on sanctification is very similar to that of Jean R. Zurcher, *Christian Perfection: A Bible and Spirit of Prophecy Teaching* (Washington, DC: Review and Herald®, 1967). Zurcher argues that in the Bible perfection "seems to be fundamentally a matter of the quality of one's devotion to God, rather than an absolute possession. But as relative as it may be, God sets it up as the goal of a Christian life" (9). He adds that "living without sinning is not possible, but that triumph over sin is the

final goal of our combat" (22). But that "victory is never more than partial. The Christian's victory lies in believing in Christ's victory and in appropriating the benefits of His triumph. For, in our present situation, 'the victory that overcometh the world,' is 'our faith' (1 John 5:4)" (24). But he finds in Ellen G. White a call for the last generation to grow into the likeness of Christ. Those individuals who will live through the time of trouble "have reached character perfection and are guarded from all sin by the Lord's all-powerful grace" (59). That victory is not their achievement but the result of God's protection over them.

71. Hans K. LaRondelle, "The Biblical Idea of Perfection," in Douglass, *Perfection*, 105, 108.

72. Ibid., 119, 120.

73. Ibid., 122.

74. Ibid., 130. LaRondelle's views on perfection influenced George R. Knight, who at the turn of the twenty-first century wrote extensively on the subject; see, for instance, his book *I Used to Be Perfect: A Study of Sin and Salvation*, 2nd ed. (Berrien Springs, MI: Andrews University Press, 2001), 72–82; and *The Pharisee's Guide to Perfect Holiness: A Study of Sin and Salvation* (Nampa, ID: Pacific Press®, 1992), 149–166.

75. LaRondelle, "Biblical Idea of Perfection, 134.

76. Ibid., 136.

77. Russell R. Standish and Colin D. Standish, *Adventism Vindicated* (Rapidan, VA: Hartland Publications, 1980), 123. It should be clarified that the Standish brothers believed that "the sacrifice of Jesus removed from the universe all doubt concerning the character of God. At the cross, Satan's lies were laid bare for all to see. At the cross, the true rightful ownership of the world was determined. At the cross, the depth of the love of God was totally revealed to mankind." Colin D. Standish and Russell R. Standish, *The Evangelical Dilemma* (Rapidan, VA: Hartland Publications, 1994), 141. It is not clear in their writings in what sense the last generation contributes to the vindication of God.

78. Ibid., 138.

79. Donald K. Short, *Why the Delay? Integrity Explains Why Christ Has Not Yet Returned* (Paris, OH: Glad Tidings, 1996), 37.

80. Robert J. Wieland, *The 1888 Message: An Introduction*, rev. and enl. (Paris, OH: Glad Tidings, 1997), 159.

81. Ibid., 161. See also Donald K. Short, *"Made Like... His Brethren"* (Paris, OH: Glad Tidings, 1991), 131–134.

82. For instance, Ron Spear, *Adventism in Crisis* (Eatonville, WA: Hope International, 1987), 1. Spear has argued that the purpose for the final generation's victory over every sin is that God wants "to make the final demonstration of their perfect characters before the world." *What Is the Church?* (Eatonville, WA: Hope International, 1994,) 70.

83. What follows is based on a presentation by Larry Kirkpatrick that appeared October 23, 2007, on the now-defunct website Great Controversy.org, under the title "A Response to 'The Crucial Role of M. L. Andreasen and His Last Generation Theology,' From George R. Knight's Book, *A Search for Identity*, pp. 144-152." This writer located a hard copy of this presentation at the Center for Adventist Research, James White Library, Andrews University. The ensuing response is more particularly focused on pages 9–11 of Kirkpatrick's presentation.

3

What Shall We Say About Sin?

A Study of *Hamartia* in Paul's Letter to the Romans

Martin Hanna

Introduction: The semantic complexity of sin

The topic of this chapter is derived from the following questions that Paul asks about sin (*hamartia*) in his letter to the Roman Christians. "What shall we say then? Shall we continue in sin?" (Romans 6:1).[1] "What shall we say then? Is the law sin?" (Romans 7:7). The subject of sin is also implied when Paul asks, "Has then what is good [the law] become death to me?" (verse 13); and "Who will deliver me from this body of death?" (verse 24). It is evident that these also are questions about sin, because Paul writes that "sin . . . was producing death in me through what is good" (verse 13). Paul's attention to these questions indicates that his letter to the Romans is an important resource for clarifying the biblical teaching on sin. Romans is "the sum and crown of the Pauline gospel,"[2] and it is "arguably the single most important work of Christian theology ever written."[3]

The most important New Testament Greek word translated as "sin" is *hamartia* (nearly 175 times).[4] The word appears most frequently in Paul's letters,[5] and among these letters, the word appears most frequently in the letter to the Romans (48 times). In Romans 1–4,[6] Paul uses the word *hamartia* less frequently (4 times) than in Romans 5–8 (42 times).[7] In the first section of the letter, the focus is on salvation from sin (Romans 3:9, 20; 4:7, 8) through justification (Romans 3:21–26; 4:5, 6). In the second section of the letter, the focus is on salvation from sin in terms of the relation of justification to sanctification and to glorification (Romans 5:1, 2, 5; 6:20, 22; 8:21, 30).[8]

It is important to appreciate the semantic complexity of Paul's teaching on sin. Otherwise, as Peter writes in a different context, we will "twist" Paul's statements in a way that facilitates spiritual "destruction" (2 Peter 3:16). The teaching that we are "set free from sin" (Romans 6:22) is destructively twisted (1) when Christians are spiritually discouraged, because they notice that they continue to struggle with sin, (2) when Christians are spiritually presumptuous in concluding that they no longer commit any sins, and (3) when Christians no longer resist sin because of spiritual discouragement or presumption.[9]

The semantic complexity of Paul's teaching on sin is evident in his reference to three dimensions of sin: involuntary corruption,[10] voluntary carnality,[11] and legal condemnation.[12] These dimensions of sin are presented here in an order that reflects the different dimensions of the meaning of the word *hamartia* that are presented in Paul's writings.

First, Paul uses the word *hamartia* when he refers to sin as "the bondage of corruption" (Romans 8:21) whereby even "if Christ is in you, the body is dead because of sin [*hamartia*]" (verse 10). This meaning of the word—taken from archery—involves missing the mark or target that one aims at.[13] As such, sin is an involuntary activity as is illustrated in Paul's personal testimony: "For the good that I will to do, I do not do; but the evil I will not to do, that I practice. Now if I do what I will not to do, it is no longer I who do it, but sin that dwells in me" (Romans 7:19, 20).[14]

Second, Paul uses another dimension of the biblical meaning of *hamartia* when he refers to those who are "carnally minded" (Romans 8:6; cf. verse 7), "who live according to the [sinful] flesh," thus Jesus "condemned sin [*hamartia*] in the flesh" (verses 5, 3). This dimension of the word's meaning involves voluntary sin through intentionally aiming at the wrong mark as is evident in the following rhetorical question: "Do you not know that to whom you present yourselves slaves to obey, you are that one's slaves whom you obey, whether of sin leading to death, or of obedience leading to righteousness?" (Romans 6:16).[15]

Third, Paul uses another dimension of the biblical meaning of *hamartia* when he describes God's legal judgment of "condemnation" (Romans 3:8; 5:16; 8:1, 3) on those who have missed the mark. As such, sin is a status of condemnation under the law of "God [who is] judge [of] the world" (Romans 3:6). Paul judges that "all [are] under sin" in that "whatever the law [of God] says, it says to those who are under the law, that ... all the world may become guilty before God" (verses 9, 19). As Paul writes in his letter to the Galatians, "Scripture has confined all under sin," so they are "kept under guard by the law" (Galatians 3:22, 23; cf. Galatians 3:10; 4:4, 5, 21; 5:18).[16]

Paul's teaching on these three dimensions of the sin problem will be described more completely in subsequent sections of this study.[17] My goal is not to explain away "the mystery of lawlessness [sin]" (2 Thessalonians 2:7; cf. 1 John 3:4)[18] since an explanation of sin would be an excuse for sin—and sin is inexplicable and inexcusable. "Could excuse for it be found, or cause be shown for its existence, it would cease to be sin."[19] Rather, my goal is to clarify Paul's way of presenting the mystery of the sin problem in his letter to the Romans. Other biblical perspectives will also be mentioned where they are helpful in clarifying the content of Paul's teaching on the mystery of sin in Romans 1–4 and Romans 5–8.[20]

Part 1: Sin in Romans 1–4

Romans 1: The good news about sin. The word *hamartia* is not used in Romans 1. Instead, Paul refers to "ungodliness," "unrighteousness" (verse 18), "uncleanness," and "lusts" (verse 24). But these terms are connected with *hamartia* in other chapters of the letter (Romans 4:5–8; 5:6–12; 6:12, 13, 18–20). Through this variety of words for sin, Paul presents the sin problem in relation to its solution through the good news of "the gospel of God" and "Christ," which "is the power of God to salvation" from sin (Romans 1:1, 16). In the gospel, "the righteousness [justification] of God is revealed from faith to faith;[21] as it is written, 'The just [the righteous] shall live by faith' " (verse 17; cf. Romans 3:19, 20);[22] and "whatever is not from faith is sin" (Romans 14:23).

The connection between the gospel and the sin problem is also indicated when Paul devotes the entire second half of the first chapter of his letter to presenting an extensive catalog of specific sins (Romans 1:17–32).[23] All sinners who read this chapter will find at least some of their sins listed here. We may regard some of these as small sins. But Paul's point is that all sins, large or small,[24] put us in need of salvation because "the wrath of God is revealed from heaven against all ungodliness and unrighteousness of men" (verse 18). The good news is that those who have been "justified . . . shall be saved from [God's] wrath" against sin (Romans 5:9).

Romans 2: Sin and the law. As with Romans 1, the noun *hamartia* does not appear in chapter 2. Instead, Paul uses the verb *hamartano*, which he connects with *hamartia* in other chapters (Romans 3:20–23; 5:12–16; 6:14–16). Paul uses *hamartano* to teach that the need for salvation is present among all people since "as many as have sinned [*hamartano*] without law will also perish without law, and as many as have sinned in the law will be judged [as condemned] by the law" (Romans 2:12; cf. Romans 3:19, 20). Here Paul refers to the law that was revealed to the nation of Israel since the Gentiles "are a law to themselves" and "show the work of the law written in their hearts" (Romans 2:14, 15). The relation between the law (in its various forms)[25] and the sin problem is further described in the next chapter of Romans.

Romans 3: Under sin and under law. Paul makes explicit in chapter 3 what is implied in the first two chapters of his letter—all have sinned, and all are condemned as sinners. "For we have previously charged both Jews and Greeks that they are all under sin [*hamartia*]. As it is written: 'There is none righteous, no, not one' " (Romans 3:9, 10). "We know that whatever the law says, it says to those who are under the law, that every mouth may be stopped, and all the world may become guilty [condemned] before God" (verse 19).[26] Therefore, everyone needs God's justification from the condemnation of sin. We cannot accomplish this for ourselves because "by the deeds of the law no flesh will be justified in His [God's] sight, for by the law is the knowledge of sin [*hamartia*]" (verse 20; cf. Romans 4:15). In addition, everyone needs God's glorification because "all have sinned [*hamartano*] and fall short of the glory of God" (Romans 3:23). Paul further discusses the condemnation of sin in Romans 4.

Romans 4: Case studies on sin—Abraham and David. As described above, beginning in the first chapter of his letter, Paul presents God's righteousness and justification as a solution to the sin problem. This is illustrated through two case studies concerning Abraham and David. Abraham has nothing "to boast about" "according to the flesh" because he is not "justified by works." Instead, "his faith is accounted for righteousness [justification]" (verses 1–5).[27]

This justification and righteousness is a solution to the sin problem as Paul indicates in his second case study where "David also describes the blessedness of the man to whom God imputes righteousness [justification] apart from works: 'Blessed are those whose lawless [*anomia*] deeds are forgiven, and whose sins [*hamartia*] are covered; blessed is the man to whom the LORD shall not impute sin [*hamartia*]' " (verses 6–8).[28] Here the meaning of the word *sin* includes the legal status of condemnation. As is discussed further below, those who are "freed [*dekaioo*, "justified"] from sin" (Romans 6:7) and "set free [*eleutheroo*] from sin" (verse 22) have been set free from the condemnation of sin. Similarly, they also need to be set free from the other dimensions of the sin problem.

Sin segue: Unjust, uncircumcised, and inglorious. In the previous paragraphs of this study, I have focused largely on Paul's teaching concerning *hamartia* (sin) as condemnation that stands in contrast to justification. At the same time, additional elements from Romans 1–4 provide a suitable segue and transition to Paul's discussion of the different dimensions of sin in Romans 5–8. These dimensions of sin are anticipated in both explicit and implicit references to God's solution to the sin problem through justification, sanctification, and glorification. First, sinners "will be justified" (Romans 2:13).[29] Second, sinners are uncircumcised "in the Spirit" (verse 29)—meaning that they need to be "sanctified by the Holy Spirit" (Romans 15:16).[30] Third, "all have sinned and fall short of the glory of God" (Romans 3:23; cf. Romans 2:7, 10). Therefore, God responds to this with the "promise" that "Abraham" and "his seed" would be "the [heirs] . . . of the world" (Romans 4:13)—a promise that includes glorification since those who are "heirs of God and joint heirs with Christ" will "also be glorified together" with Him (Romans 8:17).[31]

In part 2 of his letter, Paul shows that the solution to the sin problem (through justification, sanctification, and glorification) is a response to three dimensions of the sin problem (legal condemnation, voluntary carnality, and involuntary corruption).

Part 2: Sin in Romans 5–8

Romans 5: The ancestry of sin—Adam and his descendants. In this second part of his letter, Paul presents three dimensions of salvation from sin as follows: "Having been justified by faith [justification]," "we . . . rejoice in hope of the glory of God [glorification]" "because the love of God has been poured out in our hearts by the Holy Spirit [sanctification]" (Romans 5:1, 2, 5; cf. Romans 15:16).[32] The three dimensions of salvation are also indicated when Paul writes in another letter that we "wait for the hope [glorification] of righteousness [justification] by faith" "working through love [sanctification]" (Galatians 5:5, 6). Paul's discourse of these three dimensions of salvation prepares the way for his extensive presentation of the ancestry of the sin problem in Adam and his descendants and its solution through Christ (Romans 5:6–21). For the purposes of this study, I will focus on what Paul writes about the sin problem.

Paul introduces the ancestry of the sin problem by pointing out that "sinners" (verse 8) are "without strength," "ungodly" (verse 6), not "righteous," not "good" (verse 7), under "wrath" (verse 9), and are "enemies" of God (verse 10). Then, using a vivid personification of sin and death,[33] Paul describes how "through one man [Adam] sin entered the world, and death through sin, and thus death spread to all men, because all sinned" (verse 12; cf. verses 15, 17);[34] so "sin reigned in death" (verse 21) and "death reigned from Adam to Moses, even over those who had not sinned according to the likeness of the transgression of Adam" (verse 14).

Adam's first sin was voluntary; but after this, he and his descendants possess a corrupt nature[35] and, therefore, we sin both voluntarily and involuntarily. The involuntary dimension is indicated in the fact that "by one man's disobedience many were made sinners" (verse 19). This results in sin as a legal condemnation since "the judgment [of God] which came from one offense [by Adam] resulted in condemnation" "to all" (verses 16, 18). "Adam's legacy was not simply physical mortality" "but also spiritual depravity."[36] Sin is "a lack of conformity to the will of God, either in act or state" "into which we are born (original corruption)."[37] "The inheritance of children is that of sin. . . . As related to the first Adam, men receive from him nothing but guilt and the sentence of death."[38]

Both the awareness of involuntary sin and the voluntary activity of sin increases when there is an increasing revelation of God's law. "Until [or before] the law [came through Moses] sin was in the world, but sin is not imputed when there is no law" (verse 13; cf. verse 14). This harmonizes with Paul's teaching that there was a revelation of law to the Gentile nations before the revelation of the law of Moses to the nation of Israel (verses 14, 15). This discussion of sin and law prepares the way for Paul's presentation (in Romans 6) of conscious and voluntary sin in relation to God's grace. At the end of chapter 5, Paul writes that "the law entered that the offense might abound. But where sin abounded, grace abounded much more" (verse 20; cf. Romans 6:1).

Romans 6: Voluntary sin. Paul's teaching in chapter 5 leads to two questions presented at the start of chapter 6: "What shall we say then? Shall we continue in sin that grace may abound?" (verses 1, 2). The answer to these questions contains a description of how we are saved (1) from the legal status of sin (condemnation) through justification, (2) from the voluntary carnality of sin through sanctification, and (3) from the involuntary corruption of sin through glorification.

These dimensions of salvation from sin are grounded in the death and resurrection of Christ (verses 3–11).[39] "Our old man was crucified with Him [Christ], that the body of sin might be done away with, that we should no longer be slaves of sin.[40] For he who has died has been freed [*dekaioo*, "justified"] from sin" (verses 6, 7). "But now having been set free from sin [justification],[41] . . . you have your fruit to holiness [sanctification],[42] and the end, everlasting [eternal] life [glorification]" (verse 22; cf. verse 23).

Paul's reference to the fruit of holiness (sanctification) is closely connected with his teaching that sin is sometimes voluntary in the life of a believer. This is evident in the following appeal by Paul. "Therefore do not let sin reign in your mortal body,[43] that you should obey it in its lusts.[44] And do not present your members as instruments of unrighteousness to sin. . . . For sin shall not have dominion over you" (verses 12–14). "Just as you presented your members as slaves of uncleanness, and of lawlessness leading to more lawlessness, so now present your members as slaves of righteousness for holiness" (verse 19).[45]

Romans 7: Involuntary sin. While Paul sometimes describes sin as voluntary, he also describes sin as involuntary. This is the case in Romans 7, which many Bible students have concluded is the most difficult chapter in the entire letter. The chapter begins by using marriage to illustrate the differences between the law and Christ (Romans 7:1-6). "When we were in the flesh, the sinful passions[46] which were aroused by [marriage to] the law were at work in our members to bear fruit to death. But now[47] we have been delivered from [marriage to] the law [by marriage to Christ] . . . so that we should serve in the newness of the Spirit [sanctification] and not in the oldness of the letter [of the law]" (verses 5, 6; cf. Romans 2:25-29; 8:9).[48]

This prepares the way for Paul to answer some questions that reflect misunderstandings of sin in relation to the law as follows. "What shall we say then? Is the law sin? Certainly not! On the contrary, I would not have known [been conscious of] sin except through the law" (Romans 7:7). We can be "unconscious" of our "sinful state,"[49] and sin "includes unconscious acts" that are identified by the law as sin.[50] At the same time, sin misuses the law to produce not only voluntary sin but also involuntary sin. As Paul writes, "Sin, taking opportunity by the commandment, produced in me all manner of evil desire. For apart from the law sin was dead [unconscious and/or involuntary]. . . . But when the commandment came, sin revived" (verses 8, 9); sin "deceived me, and . . . killed me" (verse 11). Even when we become conscious of our sin, we cannot remove it through any

voluntary power within ourselves.

Paul's description of the involuntary corruption of sin is not intended to minimize the seriousness of sin. Instead, his goal is to highlight the superlative sinfulness of sin in contrast to "the law [which] is holy, . . . just and good" (verse 12; cf. 1 Timothy 1:8).[51] This leads him to ask, and answer, another question about sin and the law. "Has then what is good become death to me? Certainly not! But sin, that it might appear sin, was producing death in me through what is good, so that sin through the commandment might become exceedingly sinful" (Romans 7:13).[52] Those who limit sin to the sins that they consciously and voluntarily choose are the ones who are minimizing the problem of sin!

As indicated at the start of Romans 7, the problem of sin is increased if we are *married* to the law instead of to Christ (verses 1-6). This contrast between marriage to the law and to Christ clarifies how Paul uses the present tense (in verses 14-25) to describe his Christian perspective on his relationship to the law and sin apart from Christ.[53] This is similar to the use of the present tense in another letter to indicate who Paul is apart from Christ—as one among "sinners, of whom I am chief" (1 Timothy 1:15). Paul's presentation of who he is apart from Christ is outlined in Romans 7 as follows.

In Christ, "we know that the law is spiritual, but [apart from Christ] I am carnal, sold under sin" (verse 14)—I am an involuntary captive to sin (verses 14-25). What "I will" in Christ, apart from Christ, "I do not practice" (verse 15). "But now, it is no longer I who do it, but sin that dwells in me" (verse 17; cf. Romans 3:21, 26; 7:20).

"For I know that in me (that is, in my flesh) nothing good dwells" (Romans 7:18) since "evil is present with me" (verse 21).[54] "I delight in the law of God according to the inward man [in Christ]. But [apart from Christ] I see another law in my members, warring against the law of my mind, and bringing me into captivity to the law of sin which is in my members. O wretched man that I am [apart from Christ]! Who will deliver me from this body of death? I thank God—through Jesus Christ our Lord![55] So then, [in Christ] with the mind I myself serve the law of God, but [apart from Christ] with the flesh [I serve] the law of sin" (verses 22–25).[56]

Romans 8: Sin as condemnation, carnality, and corruption. The three dimensions of freedom from sin are mentioned in Romans 8. The first two dimensions are mentioned right at the start of the chapter. Present freedom from the legal status of sin and guilt is indicated in that "there is therefore now no condemnation" (Romans 8:1); this is justification from sin. In addition, present freedom from voluntary activity of sin is indicated in that "those who are in Christ Jesus . . . do not walk according to the flesh, but according to the Spirit [sanctification from sin]. For the law of the Spirit of life in Christ Jesus has made me free from the law of sin and death" (verses 1, 2; cf. verse 4).[57] Note that this freedom is not the result of the removal of the flesh with its involuntary sin. Instead, this freedom results from choosing to walk according to "the Spirit [who] is [the source of] life because of righteousness" (verse 10).[58]

Voluntary walking according to the flesh is voluntary sin because the flesh is "sinful flesh" due to involuntary "sin in the flesh" (verse 3). Those who "live according to the flesh [are those who voluntarily] set their minds on the things of the flesh" (verse 5). As such, they are "carnally minded," which is spiritual "death" (verse 6) "because the carnal mind is enmity against God; for it is not subject to the law of God, nor indeed can be.[59] So then, those who are in the flesh cannot please God" (verses 7, 8). Even "if Christ is in you, the body is [spiritually] dead [mortal] because of sin" (verse 10).[60] As a result, there are involuntary sinful "deeds of the body," which Christians are to "put to death" (verse 13).[61]

This process of "sanctification is not a work of a day or a year, but of a lifetime."[62] It continues until glorification: "we suffer with Him [Christ], that we may also be glorified together [with Him]. . . . The sufferings of this present time are not worthy to be compared with the glory which shall be revealed in us" (verses 17, 18). This glorification takes place when "the creation itself also will be delivered from the bondage of corruption [the involuntary activity of sin] into the glorious liberty [freedom] of the children of God" (verse 21).[63] This glorious freedom is described as "the adoption" and "the redemption of our body" (verse 23). Until then, "the Spirit . . . helps in our weaknesses" (verse 26). "Are you ready for a lifetime of daily change?"[64]

Conclusion: I'm pressing on the upward way

In this study, I have surveyed Paul's teaching on sin in his letter to the Romans, which contains the most extensive teaching on sin in the New Testament. Paul teaches that, with the exception of Christ, all humans are sinners though not all have sinned in the same way. There are three dimensions of sin: (1) legal condemnation, (2) voluntary carnality, and (3) involuntary corruption. This study of the various dimensions of the sin problem prepares the way for the studies of justification, sanctification, and glorification in subsequent chapters.

The different dimensions of sin and salvation are implicit in Paul's testimony about "the righteousness [justification] which is from God by faith"[65] through which "I may attain to the resurrection from the dead [glorification]" (Philippians 3:9, 11). "Not that I have already attained, or am already perfected [*teleioo*]; but I press on.... One thing I do, ... I press toward the goal for the prize of the upward call of God in Christ Jesus [sanctification]. Therefore let us, as

many as are mature [*teleios* ("perfect," KJV) in Christ], have this mind" (verses 12–15).[66]

The essence of Paul's testimony is wonderfully captured in the words of a favorite hymn by Johnson Oatman entitled "Higher Ground." The hymn begins with the words "I'm pressing on the upward way." The last verse is especially expressive of the truth that those who are justified from the legal condemnation of sin will be sanctified from the carnality of voluntary sin and will receive God's "finishing touch"[67] of glorification from the corruption of involuntary sin.

I want to scale the utmost height,
And catch a gleam of glory bright;
But still I'll pray till heaven I've found,
"Lord, lead me on to higher ground."[68]

Endnotes

1. In this study, all Bible texts are quoted from the NKJV unless otherwise noted.

2. Peter Stuhlmacher, "The Purpose of Romans," in *The Romans Debate*, ed. Karl P. Donfried (Edinburgh: T & T Clark, 1991), 242, quoted in J. R. Dodson, "The 'Powers' of Personification: Rhetorical Purpose in the *Book of Wisdom* and the Letter to the Romans" (PhD thesis, University of Aberdeen, 2008), 106.

3. James D. G. Dunn, "Romans, Letter to the," in *Dictionary of Paul and His Letters*, ed. Gerald F. Hawthorne and Ralph P. Martin (Downers Grove, IL: IVP, 1993), 838, quoted in Dodson, " 'Powers' of Personification," 106.

4. John M. Fowler, "Sin," in *Handbook of Seventh-day Adventist Theology*, ed. Raoul Dederen (Hagerstown, MD: Review and Herald®, 2001), 238.

5. Erin Roberts, "Reconsidering Hamartia as 'Sin' in 1 Corinthians," *Method and Theory in the Study of Religion* 26, nos. 4–5 (2014): 356.

6. Some textual links between the beginning and ending of this section of Paul's letter (Romans 1–4) are indicated by Edward Adams in "Abraham's Faith and

Gentile Disobedience: Textual Links Between Romans 1 and 4," *Journal for the Study of the New Testament* 19, no. 65 (July 1, 1997): 47–66.

7. *Hamartia* is used two more times in Romans 11:27 and 14:23. (Cf. Dodson, " 'Powers' of Personification," 109).

8. These actions of God in setting us free from sin will be described more comprehensively by other authors in later chapters of this book. The study I present here will discuss these issues only as far as is necessary to clarify Paul's teaching on sin.

9. See Keith Miller, *Sin: Overcoming the Ultimate Deadly Addiction* (San Francisco: Harper and Row, 1987).

10. See also Paul T. Berghaus and Nathan L. Cartagena, "Involuntary Sins, Social Psychology, and the Application of Redemption," *Heythrop Journal* 56, no. 4 (July 1, 2015): 593–603.

11. Here the word *carnal* (fleshly) does not refer to physical flesh but to voluntary choices in harmony with the sinful tendencies of the flesh. Christians may be, but ought not to be, carnally minded—living or walking according to the flesh (Romans 8:1–9; cf. 1 Corinthians 3:1). The concept of involuntary and

voluntary sins is similar yet distinct from Ellen G. White's references to "inherited" and "cultivated tendencies to wrong-doing." Ellen G. White, *Christ's Object Lessons* (Washington, DC: Review and Herald®, 1941), 330. Inherited tendencies are involuntary, but they can lead to voluntary as well as involuntary sins, which then cultivate further tendencies to sin. Ellen G. White also refers to "voluntary or involuntary violation of Nature's laws" ("Importance of Preserving Physical Health," *Health Reformer*, November 1, 1877) and to "involuntary commandment breakers" ("Our Children—Importance of Early Training," *Health Reformer*, February 1, 1878).

12. This threefold summary of the sin problem has some similarity to the fourfold summary proposed by Arthur W. Pink, *A Fourfold Salvation: Rescue From the Pleasure, Penalty, Power, and Presence of Sin* (North Charleston, SC: CreateSpace, 2014). There is overlap between my categories and Pink's categories as follows: condemnation/penalty, voluntary/power, and involuntary/presence. I choose different terminologies for the categories because sin is present and powerful in all three dimensions and because it is important to highlight justification as God's solution to the problem of sin as condemnation (Romans 5:16, 18; 8:33, 34).

13. Fowler, "Sin," 238. In contrast with common assumptions, sin is not limited to acts "such as not telling the truth, or failing to love our neighbour. Paul is much more concerned with the *corporate or communal* state of humanity, and its alienation from God and from one another." Anthony C. Thiselton, *The Living Paul: An Introduction to the Apostle and His Thought* (London: SPCK, 2009), 75. See also Ryan Lamothe, "Missing the Mark: Sin and Potential Space in Pastoral Counseling," *American Journal of Pastoral Counseling* 7, no. 4 (2004): 3–24; Charles C. Ryrie, *Basic Theology: A Popular Systematic Guide to Understanding Biblical Truth* (Chicago: Moody Publishers, 1999), 241.

14. This concept of sin as involuntary corruption reflects an understanding of the depth of the sin problem that is also reflected in the biblical teaching on God's provision of atonement for sins of ignorance (Ezekiel 45:20; Hebrews 9:7). See Roy Gane, *Leviticus, Numbers*, The NIV Application Commentary (Grand Rapids, MI: Zondervan, 2004).

15. See Chris L. de Wet, "Sin as Slavery and/or Slavery as Sin? On the Relationship Between Slavery and Christian Hamartiology in Late Ancient Christianity,"

Religion & Theology 17, nos. 1–2 (January 1, 2010): 26–39. There is an interrelationship between voluntary and involuntary sin since a voluntary yielding to sin makes us involuntary slaves to sin. Therefore, it is only by the grace of God that our freedom to choose is preserved. W. Brian Shelton, *Prevenient Grace: God's Provision for Fallen Humanity* (Anderson, IN: Francis Asbury Press, 2014).

16. See Martin Hanna, "The Servant-Master Roles of the Laws of Christ, of Scripture, and of Nature," *Journal of the Adventist Theological Society* 9, nos. 1–2 (1998): 278–309.

17. "The word *hamartia* is used in the NT predominantly to refer to sin as an act of wrongdoing (typically in the plural, e.g., Matt 9:2; 12:31). It may also be used, however, to refer to a state of guilt that results from an act of sin or general sinfulness (1 John 3:4). In John 1:29, John the Baptist's proclamation of Jesus as the 'Lamb of God who takes away the sin (*hamartia*) of the world' presents sin as a phenomenon, or syndrome, of guilt that affects all humankind rather than describing the 'sins' of humanity. Similarly, *hamartia* is used to describe a state of guilt that remains after sin in John 9:41. The idea of a sin (*hamartia*) being held against someone represents guilty status in Acts 7:60, and counting sin (*hamartia*) against a person is likewise a determination of guilty status in Rom 4:8. In Romans 5, *hamartia* is described as a force of evil, a personified power that rules and reigns and enslaves humankind before Christ. After faith in Christ, the believer is freed from bondage to sin, i.e., a guilty state before God (Rom 6)." L. DiFransico, "Guilt," *Lexham Theological Wordbook*, ed. D. Mangum, D. R. Brown, R. Klippenstein, and R. Hurst (Bellingham, WA: Lexham Press, 2014).

18. Like Paul, the apostle John refers to different dimensions of sin, as is evident in the following examples. "Whoever commits sin also commits lawlessness, and sin is lawlessness" (1 John 3:4). "The blood of Jesus Christ . . . cleanses us from all sin. If we say that we have no sin, we deceive ourselves, and the truth is not in us. . . . He is faithful and just to forgive us our sins and to cleanse us from all unrighteousness. If we say that we have not sinned, we make Him a liar, and His word is not in us" (1 John 1:7–10). "I write to you, so that you may not sin. And [yet] if anyone sins, we have an Advocate with the Father, Jesus Christ the righteous. And He Himself is the propitiation for our sins, and not for ours only but also for the

whole world" (1 John 2:1, 2; cf. 1 John 4:10). "Your sins are forgiven you for His name's sake" (1 John 2:12). "He was manifested to take away our sins, and in Him there is no sin. Whoever abides in Him does not sin. Whoever sins has neither seen Him nor known Him" (1 John 3:5, 6). "He who sins is of the devil. . . . For this purpose the Son of God was manifested, that He might destroy the works of the devil. Whoever has been born of God does not sin, for His seed remains in him; and he cannot sin" (verses 8, 9).

John resolves the tension through making a distinction between "a sin which does not lead to death" and a "sin leading to death" (1 John 5:16; cf. verse 17). "All unrighteousness is sin, and there is sin not leading to death. We know that whoever is born of God does not sin [unto death]; but he who has been born of God keeps himself, and the wicked one does not touch him" (verses 17, 18). See also Donald W. Mills, "The Concept of Sinlessness in 1 John in Relation to Johannine Eschatology" (PhD diss., Westminster Theological Seminary, 1998).

19. Ellen G. White, *The Great Controversy* (Mountain View, CA: Pacific Press®, 1950), 493.

It is impossible to explain the origin of sin so as to give a reason for its existence. Yet enough may be understood concerning both the origin and the final disposition of sin to make fully manifest the justice and benevolence of God in all His dealings with evil. Nothing is more plainly taught in Scripture than that God was in no wise responsible for the entrance of sin; that there was no arbitrary withdrawal of divine grace, no deficiency in the divine government, that gave occasion for the uprising of rebellion. Sin is an intruder, for whose presence no reason can be given. It is mysterious, unaccountable; to excuse it is to defend it. (Ibid., 492, 493).

20. Paul grounds his teaching in the Old Testament Scripture (Romans 1:1, 2; 16:25, 26). A survey of the biblical teaching on sin shows that, while there is some difference in terminology and emphasis, there is a harmony between Paul's teaching and the rest of the Bible. See the comprehensive survey in Fowler, "Sin," and the discussion of the relations between views of sin and salvation in Ivan T. Blazen, "Salvation," in Dederen, *Handbook of Seventh-day Adventist Theology*, 274, 275.

21. Terry Wardlaw, "A Reappraisal of 'From Faith to Faith' (Romans 1:17)," *European Journal of Theology* 21, no. 2 (October 1, 2012): 107–119.

22. Paul makes explicit the connection between righteousness, justification, and sin as condemnation and guilt in Romans 3:19, 20—as I discuss later in this section of my study. See Ronald Damholt, "*Rightwiseness* and Justice, a Tale of Translation," *Anglican Theological Review* 97, no. 3 (June 1, 2015): 413–432.

23. Here is a partial list of the sins mentioned in Romans 1, 2, and 3: ungodliness (Romans 1:18, 21); unrighteousness (verses 18, 29); resistance of truth (verses 18–20, 25, 28, 32); vain imagination (verse 21); foolish and darkened hearts (verses 21, 22); idolatry (verses 23, 25); uncleanness, lust, dishonorable use of bodies (verse 24), vile affections (verse 26), lustful sexuality contrary to nature (verses 26, 27); fornication, wickedness, covetousness, maliciousness; envy, murder, debate, deceit, malignity; whisperers (verse 29); backbiting, hating God, spite, pride, boasting, inventing of evil things, disobedience to parents (verse 30); lacking understanding, natural affection, and mercy; covenant breaking; being implacable (verse 31); doing evil, neglecting good (Romans 2:9, 10; 3:12); hearing the law without doing it (Romans 2:13, 23, 25); unbelief (Romans 14:23); deceit, cursing, bitterness, murder, destruction, misery, having no fear of God (Romans 3:13–18); and being without peace (verse 17). See also Alec J. Lucas, *Evocations of the Calf? Romans 1:18–2:11 and the Substructure of Psalm 106 (105)* (Boston: De Gruyter, 2015).

24. Daniel Gomes Silveira, "Is Every Sin Equal in God's Sight? An Anthropological, Historical, and Biblical Outlook on the Problem of Sin," *Puritan Reformed Journal* 7, no. 1 (January 1, 2015): 69–87.

25. See Hanna, "Servant-Master Roles."

26. Todd A. Wilson, " 'Under Law' in Galatians: A Pauline Theological Abbreviation," *Journal of Theological Studies* 56, no. 2 (October 1, 2005): 362–392.

27. "What then shall we say that Abraham our father has found according to the flesh? For if Abraham was justified by works, he has something to boast about, but not before God. For what does the Scripture say? 'Abraham believed God, and it was accounted to him for righteousness.' Now to him who works, the wages are not counted as grace but as debt. But to him who does not work but believes on Him who justifies the ungodly, his faith is accounted for righteousness" (Romans 4:1–5).

28. God does not impute to us the righteousness

of Christ apart from Christ. When we are united with Christ by faith, then His righteousness is imputed to us. See Michael F. Bird, "Incorporated Righteousness: A Response to Recent Evangelical Discussion Concerning the Imputation of Christ's Righteousness in Justification," *Journal of the Evangelical Theological Society* 47, no. 2 (June 2, 2004): 263–275; Sibylle Rolf, "Luther's Understanding of *Imputatio* in the Context of His Doctrine of Justification and Its Consequences for the Preaching of the Gospel," *International Journal of Systematic Theology* 12, no. 4 (October 1, 2010): 435–451; Oliver D. Crisp, "Federalism vs Realism: Charles Hodge, Augustus Strong and William Shedd on the Imputation of Sin," *International Journal of Systematic Theology* 8, no. 1 (January 1, 2006): 55–71; Oliver D. Crisp, "Scholastic Theology, Augustinian Realism and Original Guilt," *European Journal of Theology* 13 (2004): 17–28.

29. "The doers of the law will be justified" (Romans 2:13), but not by their doing of the law (Romans 3:20). They will be justified "in the day when God will judge the secrets of men by Jesus Christ, according to my gospel" (Romans 2:16), which includes justification by faith (Romans 1:16, 17). The doing of the law (Romans 2:13) by those who are saved is the result of the sanctifying work of God's Spirit (verses 25–29).

30. Lyle J. Story, "Pauline Thoughts About the Holy Spirit and Sanctification: Provision, Process, and Consummation," *Journal of Pentecostal Theology* 18, no. 1 (May 1, 2009): 67–94.

31. Caroline Schleier Cutler, "New Creation and Inheritance: Inclusion and Full Participation in Paul's Letters to the Galatians and Romans," *Priscilla Papers* 30, no. 2 (May 1, 2016): 21–27.

32. "Sanctification is the process by which Christians become progressively more loving." George R. Knight, *I Used to Be Perfect* (Boise, ID: Pacific Press®, 1994), 46. "Perfect love is *not* perfect performance, perfect skill, or perfect human nature." Ibid., 71.

33. Paul personifies sin as a power that is external and internal to humanity. Among the ancient documents available to us, this may be the most extensive personification of sin ever done up to the time of Paul. Sin is personified as an external ruler reigning in death (Romans 5:12–21), as a slave master from whom we have been set free to whom we can return (Romans 6:12–23), and as a deceiver and murderer that rules from within a person who is unconsciously and/or involuntarily complicit (Romans 7:7–25). Dodson, " 'Powers' of Personification," 109–111. "In Romans 1, sin is a

false assumption and an evil deed, here Sin and Death are personified as alien intruders." Ibid., 111, 112.

34. Paul's statement here indicates that the power of sin over humanity is not unilateral. Instead, humanity is "a willing instrument in its system of domination." Robert Jewett, *Romans,* Hermeneia (Minneapolis: Fortress Press, 2007), 409, quoted in Dodson, " 'Powers' of Personification," 115.

35. John W. Mahony, "Why an Historical Adam Matters for a Biblical Doctrine of Sin," *Southern Baptist Journal of Theology* 15, no. 1 (2011): 60–78; A. B. Caneday, "The Language of God and Adam's Genesis & Historicity in Paul's Gospel," *Southern Baptist Journal of Theology* 15, no. 1 (2011): 26–59; Larry Kreitzer, "Christ and Second Adam in Paul," *Communio Viatorum* 32 (1989): 55–101.

36. See Gerhard Pfandl, "Some Thoughts on Original Sin," Seventh-day Adventist Biblical Research Institute, https://www.adventistbiblicalresearch.org /sites/default/files/pdf/sinoriginal-web.pdf, 17.

37. See ibid., 21, 22.

38. Ellen G. White, *Child Guidance* (Nashville, TN: Southern Pub. Assn., 1954), 475.

39. "Likewise you also, reckon yourselves to be dead indeed to sin, but alive to God in Christ Jesus our Lord" (Romans 6:11). "Or do you not know that as many of us as were baptized into Christ Jesus were baptized into His death? Therefore we were buried with Him through baptism into death, that just as Christ was raised from the dead by the glory of the Father, even so we also should walk in newness of life. For if we have been united together in the likeness of His death, certainly we also shall be in the likeness of His resurrection" (verses 3–5; cf. Romans 3:24).

40. Different Bible students have proposed one or more of the following conclusions. Crucifying the old man and doing away with the body of sin is (1) justification from legal condemnation, and/or (2) sanctification from voluntary carnality, and/or (3) glorification from involuntary corruption. See J. Sidlow Baxter, *A New Call to Holiness: A Restudy and Restatement of New Testament Teaching Concerning Christian Sanctification* (London: Marshall, Morgan, and Scott, 1968).

41. Paul connects the words *freedom* and *slavery* with the words *righteousness* and *sin* as follows: (a) those who are slaves of sin are free from righteousness; and (b) those who are slaves of righteousness are free from sin (Romans 6:16–22). See Geoffrey Turner, "The Christian Life as Slavery: Paul's Subversive Met-

aphor," *Heythrop Journal* 54, no. 1 (January 1, 2013): 1–12.

42. In contrast, "What fruit did you have then in the things of which you are now ashamed? For the end of those things is death" (Romans 6:21).

43. Dodson capitalizes the word *Sin* in order to highlight Paul's use of personification to focus on one dimension of the sin problem. "Here for the first time in Romans, Sin is referred to as something internal as well as external; the apostle commands the believers to reject the reign of Sin *in* their bodies, to refuse to stand alongside of Sin and no longer to place themselves at the disposal of this slave master." " 'Powers' of Personification," 114, 115.

> Within this passage, the stress moves from the action of Sin with humanity (5.12-21) to the re-action of the believer to Sin (6.12-23). In other words, there is a shift of agency in Romans 6. In Rom. 5.12-21, Paul emphasises the agency of Sin, Death and the Law over against that of God, Grace and the Christ; here however, Paul focuses more on human agency—the believer's obligation to reject Sin and stop sinning....
>
> Therefore, whereas 5.12-21 focuses more on the past—what Christ has done in spite of the cooperation between Sin and sins—6.12-23 focuses more on the present cooperation between the believer and Sin in spite of their participation in Christ's death to Death. According to Paul then, Sin will reign only if the believers do not reckon themselves to be dead to it. In other words, if Sin dominates the believer, it is only because the Christian has accepted, or even embraced, that reign (Ibid., 115).

44. "Walk in the Spirit, and you shall not fulfill the lust of the flesh" (Galatians 5:16).

45. Paul's references to yielding to the reign and slavery of sin show the interrelationship between voluntary and involuntary sin. See earlier comment on this in note 13.

46. Anthony N. S. Lane, "Lust: The Human Person as Affected by Disordered Desires," *Evangelical Quarterly* 78, no. 1 (January 1, 2006): 21–35.

47. When Paul contrasts flesh and spirit, he is indicating the difference between what we are in Adam (who represents the old age) and what we are in Christ (who represents the new age) (1 Corinthians 15). The

tension between the two ages is evident in the statement of Jesus that "the hour is coming, and now is" (John 5:25). See Lane A. Burgland, "Eschatological Tension and Existential *Angst*: 'Now' and 'Not Yet' in Romans 7:14-25 and 1QS11 (Community Rule, Manual of Discipline)," *Concordia Theological Quarterly* 61, no. 3 (July 1997): 163–176.

48. "You also have become dead to [your marriage to] the law through the body of Christ, that you may be married to another—to Him [Christ] who was raised from the dead, that we should bear fruit to God" (Romans 7:4). See Keith Augustus Burton, " 'So That You May Be With Another': The Status of Nomos in the Mystical Life of the Believer in the Rhetoric of Analogy in Romans 7:1-6" (PhD diss., Northwestern University, 1994).

49. "The lost coin represents those who are lost in trespasses and sins, but who have no sense of their condition. They are estranged from God, but they know it not. Their souls are in peril, but they are unconscious and unconcerned." White, *Christ's Object Lessons*, 193, 194. If one child "is unconscious of his sinful state, parents should not rest" but should "see if the lost piece of silver cannot be found." Ellen G. White, Manuscript 118, 1898. "It was possible for Adam, before the fall, to form a righteous character by obedience to God's law. But he failed to do this, and because of his sin our natures are fallen and we cannot make ourselves righteous. Since we are sinful, unholy, we cannot perfectly obey the holy law. We have no righteousness of our own with which to meet the claims of the law of God." Ellen G. White, *Steps to Christ* (Washington, DC: Review and Herald®, 1956), 62.

50. Knight, *I Used to Be Perfect*, 76.

51. "We know that the law is good if one uses it lawfully" (1 Timothy 1:8).

52. "Ego claims to be a victim of Sin. That is to say, for Ego, Sin is not [simply] an act committed, nor [simply] a sphere in which he dwells; rather, it is [in addition] an evil force dwelling in him, working every illicit desire." Dodson, " 'Powers' of Personification," 118.

"Sin used the good Law to work death so that the sinfulness of Sin might be shown—Sin is a murderer and Ego a victim." Sin is "a slave master" and Ego is "a prisoner of war." Ibid.

"Paul makes Sin a law of her own and substitutes the word 'Sin' with the phrase 'Law of Sin.' " Ibid., 119.

"Rather than entering into the world as in 5.12, Sin

enters into the body of Ego. However, whereas in Romans 6 the believer has power over Sin, here Sin is invasive, working desires inside of Ego whether Ego wants her to or not." Ibid.

"Nevertheless, there is a part of Ego that resists and regrets the work of Sin." Ibid., 119, 120.

For a comprehensive treatment of this subject, see Michael Paul Middendorf, *The "I" in the Storm: A Study of Romans 7* (Saint Louis, MO: Concordia Academic Press, 1997).

53. Outstanding Bible students make strong arguments for time-based, preconversion and postconversion interpretations of Romans 7:14–25 that seem to cancel each other out. This suggests that Paul is expressing his *in Christ* perspective on an aspect of who he is—*in himself apart from Christ.* This conclusion is supported by the fact that in Greek the shift from augmented tenses (verses 7–13) to the present tense (verses 14–25) may indicate a shift from a narrative of how Paul came to understand the true function of the law through Christ to a description of the condition of Paul in himself as viewed from the perspective of that new understanding. See Stanley E. Porter, *Verbal Aspect in the Greek of the New Testament, With Reference to Tense and Mood,* Studies in Biblical Greek 1 (New York: Peter Lang, 1989); referenced by Mark A. Seifrid, "The Subject of Rom 7:14-25," *Novum Testamentum* 34, no. 4 (1992): 317, 321. See also Hae-Kyung Chang, "The Christian Life in a Dialectical Tension? Romans 7:7-25 Reconsidered," *Novum Testamentum* 49, no. 3 (July 1, 2007): 257–280.

54. Paul's references to sin that dwells in us and in our flesh identify the fact and state of our sinful nature. See Jiří Moskala, "Genesis 3 as a Model for Understanding the Nature of Sin and Salvation," *Journal of the Adventist Theological Society* 27, nos. 1–2 (2016): 132, 133.

55. Ellen G. White applies this text to the experience of Christians.

Those in positions of responsibility in God's work, who have been wrought upon by the Holy Spirit, have seen their nothingness, as from the depths of penitence they have cried for mercy and the love of Christ. As the great apostle to the Gentiles looked at his sinful condition, he exclaimed, "O wretched man that I am, who shall deliver me from the body of this death?" [Romans 7:24.] Did Paul love Jesus? Read his letters—full of intense ardor and deep yearning for the churches. His words are weighted with a burning desire to love his Redeemer with greater love.

The depth of our love for God and Christ is revealed by the clearness and fulness of our conviction of what constitutes sin. And our love is shown also by the genuine faith we have in the offering made in our behalf. I repeat: the degree of our love for Jesus depends on the clearness and fulness of our conviction of sin, our realization of the need of simple, living faith, and our dependence on Christ's power and grace (Ellen G. White, Manuscript 104, 1901).

56. "The inadequacy of the law is only revealed as Peter and Paul discover that they are sinners *in a way that previously they were unaware of.*" Timothy Ashworth, *Paul's Necessary Sin: The Experience of Liberation* (Burlington, VT: Ashgate, 2006), 9. "Mere determination on the part of the Christian will never control the flesh or produce the fruit of the Spirit. Paul amplifies this theme in Rom. 7, where he shows that the believer's determined attempts to please God in his own strength are destined to fail." Warren W. Wiersbe, *Wiersbe's Expository Outlines on the New Testament* (Colorado Springs, CO: Victor, 1992), 529.

57. "But if you are led by the Spirit, you are not under the law" (Galatians 5:18). "If we live in the Spirit, let us also walk in the Spirit" (verse 25). In another letter to the Corinthians, Paul makes a similar distinction in terms of natural and spiritual humanity (1 Corinthians 2).

58. As Paul instructs later in his letter, "Put on the Lord Jesus Christ, and make no provision for the flesh, to fulfill its lusts" (Romans 13:14). Nevertheless, Christians remain limited by the flesh as Paul indicates in a similar statement in his letter to the Galatians. Paul writes, "Walk in the Spirit, and you shall not fulfill the lust of the flesh. For the flesh lusts against the Spirit, and the Spirit against the flesh; and these are contrary to one another, so that you do not do the things that you wish" (Galatians 5:16, 17). Therefore, "believers, so long as they are in this life, whatever may be the earnestness of their endeavours, do not obtain such a measure of success as to serve God in a perfect manner. The highest result does not correspond to their wishes and desires." J. Calvin, *Commentaries on*

the Epistles of Paul to the Galatians and Ephesians, trans. W. Pringle (Bellingham, WA: Logos, 2010), 163, 164. "The dynamic 'line' of character development is infinite. 'Perfect Christians' always become more and more like Jesus without ever becoming just like Him." Knight, *I Used to Be Perfect*, 66. Being a perfect Christian does not mean (1) that every choice you make is inspired by the Spirit, (2) that you will not experience sickness or tragic accidents, (3) that you practice a legalistic obedience to the external requirements of the law, or (4) that you do not need to grow in perfection since you are already perfect in Christ. Ibid., 67, 68. Even those who "love God with all their heart . . . dwell in a shattered body, and . . . cannot always exert themselves as they would, by thinking, speaking, and acting, precisely right." John Wesley, quoted in Knight, *I Used to Be Perfect*, 77. See also Steven L. Porter, "The Gradual Nature of Sanctification: Σάρξ as Habituated, Relational Resistance to the Spirit," *Themelios* 39, no. 3 (November 2014): 470–483; and Turner, "Christian Life as Slavery."

59. "The believer can have two 'dispositions' (minds): he can lean toward the things of the flesh and be a carnal Christian ("carnal" means "of the flesh") who is at enmity with God; or he can incline toward the things of the Spirit, be a spiritual Christian, and enjoy life and peace. The carnal mind cannot please God; only the Spirit working in and through us can please God." Wiersbe, *Wiersbe's Expository Outlines*, 388.

60. As noted earlier, in Romans 6 and 7 Paul asks, and answers, a number of questions about sin. In chapter 8, Paul introduces seven more questions about the sin problem and its solution through Christ. "What then shall we say to these things? If God is for us, who can be against us? He who did not spare His own Son, but delivered Him up for us all, how shall He not with Him also freely give us all things? Who shall bring a charge against God's elect? It is God who justifies. Who is he who condemns? It is Christ who died, and furthermore is also risen, who is even at the right hand of God, who also makes intercession for us. Who shall separate us from the love of Christ? Shall tribulation, or distress, or persecution, or famine, or nakedness, or peril, or sword?" (Romans 8:31–35).

61. "To pass from the self-centered spirit that is natural to humanity to the spirit of Christ is not a matter of gentle growth or natural evolution. Rather, claims H. H. Farmer, 'it is an uprooting, rending, tearing, splitting and breaking, surgical-operation kind of thing.' It is a crucifixion." Knight, *I Used to Be Perfect,* 60.

62. Ellen G. White, *Testimonies for the Church* (Mountain View, CA: Pacific Press®, 1948), 3:325.

63. Laurie J. Braaten, "All Creation Groans: Romans 8:22 in Light of the Biblical Sources," *Horizons in Biblical Theology* 28, no. 2 (December 1, 2006): 131–159; Beverly Roberts Gaventa, "The Cosmic Power of Sin in Paul's Letter to the Romans: Toward a Widescreen Edition," *Interpretation* 58, no. 3 (July 2004): 229–240.

64. Tim Chester, *You Can Change: God's Transforming Power for Our Sinful Behavior and Negative Emotions* (Wheaton, IL: Crossway, 2010), 167.

65. Even the good works of "true believers" involve "the corrupt channels of humanity" and are therefore "defiled" and "not acceptable to God" "unless purified by blood"—i.e., "by His righteousness." See Ellen G. White, *Selected Messages* (Washington, DC: Review and Herald®, 1958), 1:344.

66. Christ "is our pattern. . . . He is a perfect and holy example, given for us to imitate. We cannot equal the pattern; but we shall not be approved of God if we do not copy it and, according to the ability which God has given, resemble it." Ellen G. White, *Testimonies for the Church* (Mountain View, CA: Pacific Press®, 1948), 2:549.

67. "If we are true to the promptings of the Spirit of God, we shall go from grace to grace, and from glory to glory, until we have received the finishing touch of immortality." Ellen G. White, *Gospel Workers* (Battle Creek, MI: Review and Herald®, 1892), 421. "The science of salvation and godliness . . . will prepare the sons and daughters of God to be finally transformed by the finishing touch of immortality." Ellen G. White, Manuscript 41a, 1896.

68. "Higher Ground," hymn no. 625, *Seventh-day Adventist Hymnal* (Washington, DC: Review and Herald®, 1985).

4

How Shall a Person Stand Before God?
What Is the Meaning of Justification?

Richard M. Davidson

I. Importance of the Issue

In what is likely the earliest book of the Bible, the patriarch Job asks the penetrating question, "How can a mortal be just before God?" (Job 9:2, NRSV).[1] Down through the centuries, this question of one's standing before God, how one is justified by Him, has been viewed as the most crucial question faced by human beings, foundational to all other questions.

Martin Luther asserted that "if we lose the doctrine of justification, we lose simply everything."[2] Luther believed that justification is "the article with and by which the church stands, without which it falls."[3] In the preface to his forty-five theses drawn up in 1537, Luther makes this impassioned plea: "The article of justification is the master and prince, the lord, the ruler, and the judge over all kinds of doctrines; it preserves and governs all Church doctrine and raises up our conscience before God. Without this article the world is utter death and darkness."[4]

John Calvin considered the doctrine of justification to be "the main hinge upon which religion turns." He explained further: "For unless you understand first of all what your position is before God, and what the judgment which he passes upon you, you have no foundation on which your salvation can be laid, or on which piety towards God can be reared."[5]

Ellen G. White wrote, in the wake of the 1888 General Conference Session, "The light given me of God places this important subject [justification by faith] above any question in my mind."[6] At the same time, she warned that this subject is liable to be confused and is the object of Satan's attack: "The danger has been presented to me again and again of entertaining, as a people, false ideas of justification by faith. I have been shown for years that Satan would work in a special manner to confuse the mind on this point."[7] Luther had earlier given similar warnings: "Whoever falls from the doctrine of justification is ignorant of God and is an idolater.... For once this doctrine is undermined, nothing more remains but sheer error, hypocrisy, wickedness and idolatry, regardless of how great sanctity that appears on the outside."[8] "No error is so insignificant, so clumsy, so outworn as not to be supremely pleasing to human reason and to seduce us if we are without the knowledge and the contemplation of this article [of justification]."[9] We must clearly understand the truth about justification by faith, in view of its central importance in our lives and in view of Satan's special work to undermine and to confuse minds on this foundational biblical teaching.

II. The Debate Over Justification: Differing Views

The traditional Protestant view[10]

The Protestant Reformation occurred largely in protest against the Catholic understanding of justification, which Protestant theologians considered to be a gross distortion of the biblical teaching.

Building upon the writings of Paul, especially Romans and Galatians, and the roots in the Old Testament, Martin Luther presented justifying righteousness as "the alien righteousness of Christ."[11] This was in opposition to the Augustinian understanding in which justifying righteousness, although completely through the grace of God, was something that inhered in the human recipient.

Luther affirmed that the justified Christian was *simul justus et peccator.* R. C. Sproul explains,

> Luther's famous dictum *simul justus et peccator* goes to the heart of the issue regarding forensic justification. The Latin phrase means "at the same time just and sinner." This simultaneous condition refers to the situation wherein the sinner is counted just forensically by virtue of the imputation of Christ, while he remains in and of himself, yet a sinner.
>
> Luther did not mean that the sinner who is still a sinner is an unchanged person. The sinner who has saving faith is a regenerate person. He is in-

dwelt by the Holy Spirit. But he is still unjust in himself. Nor does it mean that the sinner is not in a real process of sanctification by which he is becoming just. Those who possess saving faith necessarily, inevitably, and immediately begin to manifest the fruits of faith, which are works of obedience. However, the *grounds* of that person's justification remain solely and exclusively the imputed righteousness of Christ. It is by His righteousness and His righteousness alone that the sinner is declared to be just.[12]

For Luther, justification was not before the onlooking eyes of men, but *coram Deo,* "before the face of God," or as his theological colleague Philip Melanchthon put it, "before the heavenly divine tribunal." Grace was not a holy substance that came down from God and inhered in the human being; it was an attitude of divine favor.

Melanchthon further worked out Luther's concepts using more precise language of imputation. Justification was presented as the divine act of *declaring* sinners righteous, based upon the extrinsic, imputed righteousness of Christ. This was in contrast with Augustine, who saw justification as God's *making* sinners righteous by a conversion of their wills.[13]

Calvin's doctrine of justification was deeply indebted to the concepts developed by Luther and Melanchthon.[14] Calvin eloquently emphasizes the forensic nature of justification by the imputed righteousness of Christ as he clearly summarizes the doctrine in his *Institutes*: "A man will be [is] justified by faith when, excluded from the righteousness of works, he by faith lays hold of the righteousness of Christ and clothed in it appears in the sight of God not as a sinner, but as righteous. Thus we simply interpret justification as the acceptance with which God receives us into His favor as if we were righteous. And we say that this justification consists in the forgiveness of sins and the imputation of the righteousness of Christ."[15]

"To *justify*, therefore, is nothing else than to acquit from the charge of guilt, as if innocence were proved. Hence, when God justifies us through the intercession of Christ, he does not acquit us on a proof of our own innocence, but by an imputation of righteousness, so that though not righteous in ourselves, we are deemed righteous in Christ."[16]

"Christ's righteousness . . . must appear in court on our behalf, and stand surety for us in judgment. Received from God, this righteousness is brought to us and imputed to us, just as if it were ours."[17]

For Calvin, justification is not separated from union with Christ. In fact, "Calvin speaks of a mystical union with Christ wrought by the Holy Spirit, the Author of faith, the Creator of this community of righteousness, and from this union arises a double grace: justification and sanctification. They are simultaneous, and although they can be distinguished, they cannot be separated."[18] Calvin writes, "I acknowledge that we are devoid of this incomparable gift [of justification] until Christ becomes ours. Therefore, to that union of the head and members, the residence of Christ in our hearts, in fine, the mystical union, we assign the highest rank, Christ when he

becomes ours making us partners with him in the gifts with which he was endued."[19]

Calvin understood that justification and sanctification occur simultaneously and are inseparable but must be distinguished:

> As Christ cannot be divided into parts, so the two things, justification and sanctification, which we perceive to be united together in him, are inseparable. Whomsoever, therefore, God received into his favour, he presents with the Spirit of adoption, whose agency forms them anew into his image. But if the brightness of the sun cannot be separated from its heat, are we therefore to say that the earth is warmed by light and illumined by heat? Nothing can be more apposite to the matter in hand than this simile. The sun by its heat quickens and fertilises the earth; by its rays enlightens and illumines it. Here is a mutual and undivided connection, and yet reason itself prohibits us from transferring the peculiar properties of the one to the other.[20]

While the Magisterial Reformers (we refer especially to Martin Luther, John Calvin, and Philip Melanchthon) emphasized different aspects of the doctrine and experienced their own personal growth in understanding its meaning,[21] by 1540 there was general consensus regarding its essential contours. Alister McGrath summarizes the main points of the consensus:

1. Justification is the forensic declaration that the Christian is righteous,

rather than the process by which he or she is made righteous. It involves a change in *status* rather than in *nature*.

2. A deliberate and systematic distinction is made between justification (the external act by which God declares the believer to be righteous) and sanctification or regeneration (the internal process of renewal by the Holy Spirit).

3. Justifying righteousness as the alien righteousness of Christ, imputed to the believer and external to him, not a righteousness that is inherent within him, located within him, or in any way belonging to him.

4. Justification takes place *per fidem propter Christum* [through faith on account of Christ], with faith being understood as the God-given means of justification and the merits of Christ as the God-given foundation of justification.[22]

This basic understanding of justification was accepted by later Reformers, such as Arminius[23] and John Wesley,[24] and became embodied in the major Protestant creeds in their treatment of justification.[25]

Protestant versus Catholic view of justification

The Magisterial Reformers (including Luther, Calvin, and Melanchthon, and we can add Arminius and Wesley) rejected the Roman Catholic view of justification. R. C. Sproul summarizes the basic issues at stake in the Reformation's rejection of Catholic doctrine regarding justification: "In simple terms the issue boils down to this: Are we justified by a *process* by which we become *actually just* or are we justified by a *declarative* act by which we are *counted* or *reckoned* to be just by God? Are we *declared* just or are we *made* just in justification?"[26]

"The conflict over justification by faith alone boils down to this: Is the ground of our justification the righteousness of Christ imputed *to us* [the Reformation view], or the righteousness of Christ working *within* us [the Catholic view]? For the Reformers the doctrine of justification by faith alone meant justification by Christ and His righteousness alone."[27]

"Inseparably connected to the doctrine of forensic justification is the concept of imputation. The issue of the Reformation focused on the distinction between infused righteousness and imputed righteousness. For Roman Catholicism, justification occurs via the infusion of the grace of Christ, which makes righteousness possible if the believer assents to and cooperates with this grace."[28]

"The Reformers did not exclude the infusion of grace. Grace is poured into the soul. The issue was the grounds of our justification. For the Reformers the sole grounds are the imputed righteousness of Christ, not the inherent righteousness of the believer or the infused righteousness of Christ.... It is the inherent righteousness of Christ, not the inherent righteousness of the believer that is the ground of our justification."[29]

At the Council of Trent (1545–1563), the Roman Catholic Church, in its Decree on Justification (1547), not only systematically rejected the distinctive tenets of justification by faith alone as espoused by the Reformers but also anathematized anyone who believed or taught such beliefs.[30]

Thomas Schreiner summarizes the major conclusions regarding justification decided at Trent: "At Trent, justification is understood to be a process and is defined in terms of inherent righteousness. Justification by faith alone is categorically rejected, and justification is based in part on human works. Hence, the notion that righteousness is imputed to us is also repudiated, along with the notion that one can have assurance of final salvation."[31]

John Gerstner highlights the major difference between Protestant and Catholic thinking regarding justification from the perspective of the relationship between faith and works. He points out how for the Protestant justification is by faith alone, but it is never without works. As he puts it, " 'Justification is by faith alone, but NOT by a faith that is alone.' Justification is by a WORKING faith."[32] "Justification is ultimately by works—the works of Jesus Christ! They are received by the justified sinner as his own works. Christ justified His people by His works as their works; works done *by them* in their Substitute."[33] "Justification comes by faith, *to which is immediately and inseparably added works.*"[34]

Gerstner uses three formulas to illustrate the views of (1) Protestants, (2) Catholics, and (3) the common Roman Catholic caricature of Protestantism:[35]

1. Reformation view:
   FAITH → JUSTIFICATION + WORKS
2. Roman Catholic error:
   FAITH + WORKS → JUSTIFICATION
3. Common Roman caricature
   of Protestantism:
   FAITH → JUSTIFICATION - WORKS

He summarizes, "Justification by faith alone, but not by a faith that is alone, is the teaching of the Reformation."[36]

Recent Protestant rapprochement with Catholics

In recent years, there has been a trend, at least in America, for a number of evangelicals to engage in dialogue with Roman Catholics; and in a surprising turn of events, many evangelicals are now returning to Rome, reaching consensus with Catholic scholars and proclaiming that the Reformation was a misunderstanding that should have never happened. Some evangelical scholars have actually returned to Roman Catholicism.

For example, Scott Hahn is a former Presbyterian turned Catholic. He tells of his journey back to Catholicism in his book *Rome Sweet Home.*[37] He now teaches in the theology department at Franciscan University in Steubenville, Ohio, and is an articulate spokesman for the Catholic view on justification.

Others who have not left Protestantism now argue that the concept of imputation of Christ's righteousness in justification is not biblical. For example, Robert Gundry, biblical scholar at Westmont College, writes that "the doctrine that Christ's righteousness is imputed to believing sinners needs to be abandoned."[38]

In 1994, a group of evangelicals and Roman Catholics under the leadership of Charles Colson and Richard John Neuhaus crafted a document entitled "Evangelicals and Catholics Together: The Christian Mission in the Third Millennium."[39] The document affirms that "we are justified by grace through faith because of Christ." But it says nothing about justification by faith alone, nothing about the imputed righteousness of Christ, nothing about forensic (only) justification. Those upholding the traditional view of justification are convinced that this document basically "trivialized the Reformation."[40]

In 1997, the signatories of this document, after a year of study, issued a clarifying statement entitled "The Gift of Salvation."[41] While claiming that "what we here affirm is in agreement with what the Reformation traditions have meant by justification by faith alone (*sola fide*)," in fact the essential contours of the Roman Catholic teaching are still embraced.[42]

Martin Luther posted his Ninety-Five Theses on October 31, 1517. On October 31, 1999, in Augsburg, Germany (the city that gave its name to the first Lutheran confession of faith), leading officials from the Lutheran World Federation and the Roman Catholic Church issued a "Joint Declaration on the Doctrine of Justification,"[43] in which it was affirmed that the differences that remain between Lutherans and Catholics no longer warrant any ecclesiastical division. The Joint Declaration claims to have reached "a consensus on basic truths" and "a shared understanding of justification" (paragraph 14) regarding justification, while disclaiming having reached full agreement on the entire doctrine. Many Lutheran churches, both within and outside the federation, rejected the declaration, and the chairperson of the Missouri Synod of Lutherans, A. L. Barry, denounced the document as "a betrayal of the Gospel of Jesus Christ."[44] More than 150 theologians

signed a protest against the declaration. A close reading of the declaration reveals that the distinctive differences between the Protestant and Catholic positions have not been abandoned.[45]

The new perspective on Paul and justification

Spearheaded by the triumvirate of E. P. Sanders,[46] James Dunn,[47] and N. T. Wright[48] in the late 1970s and early 1980s and continuing till the present, a new perspective on Paul does not claim to present a position on justification that is fundamentally antithetical to the concerns of the Reformers, but rather it claims to offer additional and corrective perspectives to the traditional Reformation position.

There are major points where the new perspective gives support to the traditional Protestant view,[49] and other emphases provide a broader (but still harmonious) context for understanding justification than is often considered in the traditional view.[50]

In some crucial areas, however, the new perspective seems to depart from the traditional Protestant understanding of justification and related concepts.[51] First, it builds on a new understanding of first-century Judaism, which rejects the Reformation view that Judaism was a legalistic religion in which one earned salvation by works of the law. Rather, as Sanders summarizes, the Jewish religion is seen to be one of "covenant nomism"; "*salvation is by grace . . . ; works are the condition of remaining 'in,' but they do not earn salvation.*"[52] Paul's objection was not to this "covenant nomism" but to Judaism's rejection of Jesus Christ as the sole path of salvation.

Second, according to Dunn and Wright, Paul's reference to the "works of the law" does not deal with the attempt on the part of Jews to keep the law in order to be saved (as in the traditional Reformation understanding) but rather refers to the particular laws of Judaism, such as circumcision, Sabbath keeping, and dietary regulations that functioned as "ethnic badges" of Judaism, marking the boundary between Jews and Gentiles.[53]

Third, the "righteousness of God" is defined as His faithfulness to the covenant promises made to Abraham and not as moral virtue or conformity to a norm that is His own character, as understood by the Reformers.[54]

Fourth, in contrast to the Reformers who viewed justification as soteriological (how one is made right with God), Wright sees justification as primarily ecclesiological. He writes, "Justification is not how someone *becomes* a Christian. It is the declaration that they *have* become a Christian." "What Paul means by justification, in this context, should therefore be clear. It is not 'how you become a Christian,' so much as 'how you can tell who is a member of the covenant family.' "[55]

Fifth, proponents of the new perspective state that "Israel's fundamental problem was its failure to bless the world" (an instrumental problem), in contrast to the Reformer's understanding of Paul, which emphasizes "Israel's inherent sinfulness" (an ontological problem).[56]

Sixth, proponents of the new perspective on Paul deny that the Reformation concept of imputation is biblical. Wright states categorically, "If we use the language of the law court, it makes no sense whatever to say that the judge imputes, imparts, bequeaths, conveys or otherwise transfers his righteousness either to the plaintiff or the defendant."[57] No righteousness is imputed by God to the believer.[58]

Finally, the new perspective proponents regularly understand the phrase *pistis Christou* as a reference to "Christ's faith or faithfulness," not as referring to the believer's "faith in Christ," as the Reformers took it.[59]

To what extent are these divergences from the traditional view of various aspects of justification faithful to Scripture, and to what extent do they veer away from the mark of biblical truth?

Seventh-day Adventist alternatives to the traditional Reformation view[60]

In the last few decades, there have been a number of Adventist voices who oppose the Reformation view of forensic justification, including the imputation of the righteousness of Christ. They see the whole legal model of justification either as not biblical or as a culturally conditioned expression of the atonement that spoke to the primitive mind-set in biblical times but now is transcended by a larger view of the atonement that eliminates this forensic imputation.

Other Adventists accept forensic justification in principle but go on to state that justification means more than imputation of Christ's righteousness; it also includes the process by which Christ actually makes us righteous. According to this view, justification is primarily to "make righteous," not just to "declare righteous," or else it would be only a legal fiction. Despite protests to the contrary, proponents of this view seem to adopt major Catholic arguments against the Reformers in the sixteenth century. Justification is both imputed and imparted righteousness, in the view of these Seventh-day Adventist interpreters.

Some Adventists maintain that justification means only the forgiveness of past sins when one first comes to Christ; but after one's initial justification, acceptance by God is based on Christ's infused righteousness that makes one righteous and thereby acceptable in God's sight. Linked to this position is the understanding that there is a necessity for absolute victory over sinfulness by God's people in the end time, which will in effect make objective justification no longer needed, because God's people have reached a state of sanctification in which objective (imputed) justification is wholly replaced by the imparted righteousness of Christ.

After this brief survey of differing views on justification, we need to ask ourselves, Is the Reformation view of justification solid, or should we be going back to Rome or in some other direction as suggested by other views mentioned above? The only way to answer this question is to test the various views by the Word of God. What is the biblical teaching about justification? Let's go to the Scriptures!

III. The Biblical Teaching on Justification by Faith

Most biblical studies on justification focus almost entirely upon the Pauline writings, but Paul himself goes to the Old Testament to base his doctrine of justification! Paul explicitly states, "But now the righteousness of God apart from the law is revealed, *being witnessed by the Law and the Prophets*" (Romans 3:21; emphasis added). In this study, following the lead of Paul (who was arguably the greatest Old Testament theologian!), we go directly to the Old Testament, concentrating especially on those passages used by Paul. In the process, we will see how Paul and other New Testament writers develop their teaching on justification based upon the Old Testament witness.[61] But first, let's examine the meaning of the basic terms *righteousness* and *justify* in both the Old and the New Testaments.

Word study

Righteousness. In the Hebrew Bible, the basic idea of *ts-d-q* and its derivatives (410 times) is "conformity to a norm" (see, e.g., Genesis 38:26; Job 9:15, 20).[62] The Greek root *dikaio-* and its derivatives in the Septuagint and the New Testament (147 times in the New Testament) are largely determined by the Hebrew concept of *ts-d-q*. In the case of God, His "righteousness" centers in His "covenant faithfulness" (as emphasized by the new perspective on Paul). The biblical terms for "righteousness" often denote God's mighty acts in fulfilling the promises and threats of the covenant made with His people (e.g., Judges 5:10, 11; 1 Samuel 12:7; Nehemiah 9:8; Psalm 98:9; Micah 6:5; Zephaniah 3:5). Since the covenant consists of both blessings and curses (Deuteronomy 27; 28), it follows that God's righteousness will include both punitive justice (e.g., Psalms 11:6; 129:4; 2 Chronicles 12:6; Isaiah 28:17) and salvation (e.g., Psalms 112:6; 116:5; Proverbs 8:18; Isaiah 45:23; 56:1), depending upon the human response to the covenant.

The term "righteousness of God" can also be used in a wider ethical sense denoting a general attribute of God's moral character of right-doing—that is, doing what is consistent with (in conformity to) His character of love, which involves both justice and mercy (Exodus 34:6, 7; cf. Psalms 31:1; 36:10; 40:10; 71:2; 88:11, 12; 143:1; Isaiah 45:8; 46:13; 51:4–8; Romans 3:5, 25, 26). This "righteousness of God" may also denote God's own righteous moral character, which is imputed to believers as a free gift (Romans 1:17; 3:21, 22; 10:3; Philippians 3:9; cf. Romans 5:17; 1 Corinthians 1:30; 2 Corinthians 5:21).

When used in connection with the conduct of persons, the biblical terms for "righteousness" denote conformity to norms or demands of a particular relationship. Righteousness is entire conformity of attitude and action to the will of God within the covenant relationship (e.g., Psalm 82:3; Isaiah 51:7; Jeremiah 22:3; Ezekiel 18:5–9; Amos 5:24). Christ, as fully God and fully human, combined both the "righteousness of God" (mighty saving acts and acts of judgment upon sin consistent with His character) and human righteousness (perfect obedience to God's law), as illustrated in Isaiah 59:17–19 (cf. Isaiah 53:11; Romans 5:18, 19; Philippians 2:8; Hebrews 5:8). Christ imputes this righteousness to believers (Romans 5:17; 2 Corinthians 5:21).

To justify. The Hebrew word for "justify," *tsadaq*, in the Hifil stem (*hitsdiq*), consistently means "to declare righteous," not "to make righteous" (see Exodus 23:7; Deuteronomy 25:1; Job 27:5; Proverbs 17:15; Isaiah 5:23).[63] The Septuagint word that translates this term, *dikaioō*, which is also the New Testament word for "justify," also

has as its primary meaning "to declare in the right"; it does not mean "to make righteous."[64] It is a legal courtroom term to describe the pronouncement of the judge that the one on trial is acquitted, declared in the right.

Part of the confusion over the meaning of this verb for "justify" in the history of the Christian church came because in the Latin Vulgate, which became the dominant Bible translation in Western Christianity, the Greek and Hebrew verbs for "justify" are translated by the Latin term *iustificare*, which in its etymology drawn from Roman culture meant "to *make* just," and which Augustine interpreted to mean "to make righteous."[65] Contrary to the Latin translation in the Vulgate, as articulated by Augustine, the original Hebrew and Greek words for "justify" (both in the Old and the New Testaments) do not mean "make righteous" but "declare righteous"; they do not speak about the moral *condition* of the person in question but speak about the *declaration* of the judge that the defendant is acquitted (declared in the right).

What is the basis upon which the judge can declare the defendant acquitted? For the biblical answer, we go first to the Old Testament material, to the opening chapters of Genesis, to the Abrahamic narratives (especially Genesis 15:6 in its wider context), and to other Old Testament passages upon which the apostle Paul built his doctrine of justification.

Old Testament passages regarding justification (especially those cited by Paul)

Genesis 1–3: Adam-Christ typology. In Paul's sustained treatment of the Adam-Christ typology concerning justification in Romans 5:12–21, he ultimately refers back to the Genesis account of Creation and the Fall (Genesis 1–3). In what follows, we go directly to the opening chapters of Scripture to see how Moses introduces the concepts that compose the message of justification by faith[66] and then examine the truths that Paul draws from these chapters.

Reading Genesis 1–3 in Hebrew, one is struck with the sustained wordplay involving the word 'adam (or, with the article, ha'adam). In Genesis 1:26, 27, the word (once with the article and once without) means "humankind." In Genesis 2:18–23, ha'adam (with the article) indicates an individual person, "the man." In the succeeding verses of Genesis 2 and opening verses of Genesis 3, it is not clear whether to translate the term (with the article) as "the man" or by the name Adam (see the different practices of various modern versions). But by Genesis 3:17, the term (without the article) clearly constitutes the proper name Adam. In Genesis 5:1, 2, which recaps human creation at the beginning of the second major section of the book, the same term 'adam (without the article) denotes both the name Adam (verse 1a) and "humankind," the name of the human race, including both male and female (verses 1b, 2). Significantly, throughout the rest of Scripture, no one else is named Adam.

By the usage of the term 'adam in the opening chapters of Genesis, it seems apparent that Adam is presented as the representative Head in solidarity with the entire human race.[67] Adam bears the name that is also the name of humankind. Only Adam in Old Testament salvation history is given this name. Adam, the person, is in corporate solidarity with the 'adam that is humanity as a whole. This concept of Adam's solidarity with the human race is developed by Paul in Romans 5 and 1 Corinthians 15.[68] When Adam sinned, the whole human race ("the many") were "constituted sinners" (Romans 5:19).[69] Adam and all subsequent humanity received a sinful nature and legally stood guilty before God.[70]

If Genesis 1–3, in general, presents Adam as the representative man in corporative solidarity with the human race, the proto-evangelium (first gospel promise) of Genesis 3:15, in particular, presents One who is to come as the representative "Seed" of the woman and who is in corporate solidarity with the corporate "seed" of the woman. Genesis 3:15 appears in a judgment setting, in which God comes for a "legal process," a "trial," a "court process."[71] Genesis 3:15 forms the chiastic center of Genesis 3 and introduces the first gospel promise in the midst of judgment. The final clauses of the verse go to the heart of this promise and show that it is centered in a Person. God tells the serpent: "He"—the ultimate representative (individual) masculine Seed of the woman and her descendants, later to be revealed as the Messiah—"shall bruise your head, [Satan,] and you [Satan] shall bruise His [the Messiah's] heel."[72]

The Messianic Seed will take off His sandal, as it were, bare His heel, and step voluntarily on the venomous viper. Christians have rightly viewed this as a picture of the Seed voluntarily giving up His life to slay the serpent, which Revelation 12:9 identifies as Satan. The Messiah would volunteer to consciously step on the head of the deadliest viper in the universe, the serpent Satan himself, knowing full well that it would cost Him His life. This is a powerful portrait of the substitutionary sacrifice of Christ on behalf of sinful humanity. The implication is that the guilt of Adam and Eve and their seed (descendants) will be imputed to their representative Seed, the Messiah, and He will bear their penalty on their behalf.[73]

The prediction in Genesis 3:15 is clarified and amplified a few verses later. In Genesis 3:21, the record states that God clothed Adam and Eve with skins—implying the sacrifice of animals. In the context of this chapter, the "nakedness" being clothed was not just physical exposure. Adam and Eve had tried to cover their nakedness by the works of their hands, putting on fig-leaf garments that they had made (verse 7). But according to verse 10, when God came to the Garden, Adam still regarded himself as "naked," even though clothed with the fig-leaf garments. The nakedness involved a sense of "being unmasked,"[74] a consciousness of guilt and shame, a "nakedness of soul."[75] Therefore, God's act of "clothing" Adam and Eve was not just a covering of their physical nudity but a covering of their guilt and shame. The blood of an innocent victim was shed instead of theirs.[76] Here is intimated the Messiah's substitutionary sacrifice on behalf of guilty humanity who deserved the penalty of death (Genesis 2:17). "The instant man accepted the temptations of Satan, and did the very things God had said he should not do, Christ, the Son of God, stood between the living and the dead, saying, 'Let the punishment fall on Me. I will stand in man's place.' "[77]

Instead of the fig leaves of their own works with which they unsuccessfully tried to cover their nakedness (Genesis 3:7–10), God covered them with animal skins, symbolizing the Messiah's "robe of righteousness" (Isaiah 61:10), righteousness which He imputes to repentant sinners who believe in Him.[78]

In Romans 5:12–21, Paul's recognition of Jesus Christ as the new representative Head of the seed of the woman, the antitypical Adam, is ultimately rooted in Genesis 1–3, especially Genesis 3:15, 21 (as well as echoing Isaiah 53, which we examine later). By means of four typological comparisons and contrasts, Paul accurately draws the implications for justification by faith: (1) as "the many" died through one man's sin, so "the many" have grace available to them through the One Man, Jesus Christ (Romans 5:15); (2) just as judgment and condemnation came through the one who sinned, the "free gift" of acquittal and justification is available to all through the righteous act of the One Man (verses 16, 18); (3) as sin and death reigned through one man's offense, so those who receive the gift of righteousness through the One Man, Jesus Christ, will reign to eternal life (verses 17, 21); and (4) as "the many" were "constituted" sinners through one man's disobedience, so "the many" (who will receive, verse 17b) will be "constituted" righteous (i.e., justified) through One Man's obedience imputed to them (verse 19).[79]

The opening chapters of Genesis and the Pauline exposition of these passages affirm crucial truths about the nature of justification:

- Justification is a judicial declaration of acquittal, the opposite of condemnation (Genesis 3:15; Romans 5:16), and not an ethical condition.
- Justification is based upon the external righteousness of Christ, not the inherent righteousness of the individual (Genesis 3:21; Romans 5:17, 18).
- The sole ground of justification is the substitutionary death of Christ and the imputed merits of His righteousness, not the imparted righteousness of Christ (i.e., sanctification) (Genesis 3:15, 21; Romans 5:15, 17–19).
- Justification is a free gift, not a matter of human works (Genesis 3:15, 21; Romans 5:16, 17).

Genesis 15:6 and its antecedent contexts. There is probably no more potent biblical statement on justification by faith than that found in Genesis 15:6: "And he [Abram] believed in the Lord, and He [the Lord] accounted [imputed; Hebrew: *khashab*[80]] it to him for righteousness."[81] In the New Testament, Paul cites this verse as one of the primary biblical foundations of his doctrine of justification by faith (Romans 4:3, 9, 22).

Abraham is accepted and accounted by Yahweh as righteous as he believes in the Lord. In this verse, we have a clear statement of the basic features of the biblical doctrine of justification by faith. First, Abraham was not *made* righteous but was *accounted* righteous; righteousness was imputed to him, not imparted to him. Abraham was not reckoned righteous because of an inherent righteousness. In the chapters that follow Genesis 15, it becomes clear

that Abraham is no model of righteousness (see his sin in Genesis 16; 20; 21 of taking Hagar as a wife and deceiving Abimelech that Sarah was his sister). Immediately after citing Genesis 15:6, Paul boldly states that God "justifies the ungodly" when "his faith is accounted for righteousness" (Romans 4:5). Fleming Rutledge has captured the radical nature of this divine "reckoning": "Abraham, far from being a model of righteousness, is first and foremost the original justified sinner, the original 'ungodly' person who is reshaped by God into godliness, not because of his own deeds but because of the God who does the unimaginable thing—the God who justifies, rectifies, redeems, and remakes the *least* acceptable, most *un*-godly person."[82]

Second, Abraham was accounted righteous *not because of his works.* After citing Genesis 15:6, Paul rightly points out that "now to him who works, the wages are not counted as grace but as debt" (Romans 4:4). Paul also notes the chronology of the narrative flow, that Abraham was accounted righteous (justified) in Genesis 15 before he performed the work of circumcision described in Genesis 17 (Romans 4:9–12). Abraham was justified before he worked!

Third, Abraham appropriated righteousness *by faith* alone. The Hebrew construction in Genesis 15:6 (*a'aman* in the Hifil plus the preposition *be*) indicates that Abraham did not just give intellectual assent to Yahweh and His promises but that he relationally "put his trust in" the Lord.[83] He entered into a personal, intimate trust relationship with God. Abram's trust in Yahweh was not meritorious. Note the fragility of Abram's faith. Immediately after Abram's lofty statement of faith in God's promise that he will inherit the land (Genesis 15:6), Abram asks God, "How shall I know that I will inherit it?" (verse 8). In this chapter, he is still Abram, not Abraham. His name change, signifying his development of character, has not taken place; he has yet several striking experiences ahead of him that reveal his lack of mature faith. But God accepts him where he is. His faith, feeble though it may have been, was the instrument, the "empty hands," that grasped the promises Yahweh had made about his future seed.

With grammatical precision, the New Testament writers later confirm, in discussion of this and related Old Testament passages, that faith is only the means or instrument, not the ground or agent, of justification.[84]

Some proponents of the new perspective on Paul argue that the Pauline phrase *pistis Christou* (literally, the faith of Christ) should not be taken as an objective genitive (the believer's "faith in Christ") with regard to justification, as the Reformers took it, but rather as a subjective genitive (a reference to Christ's faith or faithfulness). While this is a possible translation in some passages (e.g., Romans 3:22; Galatians 2:16; cf. NET), it is nonetheless clear from these very verses that the believer's own "faith in Christ" is the instrument of justification.[85] Genesis 15:6 leaves no doubt that it is Abram himself who believes in God and that his faith is counted as righteousness; and Paul's commentary on this passage in Romans 4:5 is unambiguous: "But to him who does not work but believes on [present active participle of *pisteuō* + *epi*] Him who

justifies the ungodly, his faith is accounted for righteousness."

Fourth, that which was imputed to Abram for righteousness is focused on the *object* of Abram's faith—Yahweh's promise of the coming Messianic Seed who would die a substitutionary death for the sins of the world and impute His righteousness to penitent sinners who receive the gift in faith.[86] In the grammar of Genesis 15:6, there is no antecedent noun for the pronoun "it" in the clause, "He accounted [imputed] it to him for righteousness." The "it" encompasses the object of Abraham's faith: the promise of seed (Hebrew: *zera'*) mentioned in the previous verse (verse 5), which, according to earlier chapters of Genesis, as we have seen above, includes the substitutionary death of the promised Messianic Seed on behalf of the sinful race and the imputation of His righteousness to repentant sinners. Based upon the *protoevangelium* of Genesis 3:15, 21, the promise of the coming Seed extends throughout the Genesis narratives dealing with the life of Abraham, revealing the basis upon which God can count Abraham's faith as righteousness. It is already intimated in Genesis 12:3 ("And in you all the families of the earth shall be blessed") but made more explicit in Genesis 15.

After Abram believed in the Lord and His promises (Genesis 15:6) but then wavered in His faith (verse 8), Yahweh graciously condescended to enter into a covenant with Abram of the kind that was understood in Abraham's day so that he could understand the message of the gospel of justification in the sacrificial imagery.[87] Picture a scene somewhat repulsive to us of modern minds, yet fraught with deep significance. A heifer three years old, a three-year-old goat, a three-year-old ram, a turtledove, and a young pigeon—all in the peak of health, slain with a stroke of the slaughter knife. The larger animals are cut in two down the middle, and each half is laid beside the other. The birds, left whole, are laid opposite one another, with room for someone to pass through the rows of paired carcasses.

The vultures come down to eat the pieces, but Abram drives them away. The sun sets. A deep sleep settles upon the man who has slain the animals and separated their parts. The sleep is followed by a dread and great darkness. All is silence and blackness. Suddenly out of the darkness appear a smoking firepot and a flaming torch. The firepot and torch slowly pass between the pieces of the dead animals. The ceremony is complete. (See Genesis 15:9–18.)

What does it all mean? Moses explicitly states in Genesis 15:18 that on this day "the Lord made [Hebrew: *karat*] a covenant with Abram." Throughout the Bible, when it is stated that God "made" a covenant, the Hebrew word for "made" is generally *karat*, literally, "cut." This expression of "cutting" a covenant refers to the common practice in ancient Near Eastern times of making a covenant by cutting a sacrifice and walking between the pieces. In Jeremiah 34:18–20, we find a reference to this practice still in use in Jeremiah's day. God says to those in Judah who broke the covenant they made with the Lord, "And I will give the men who have transgressed My covenant, who have not performed the words of the covenant which they made [*karat*] before Me, when

they cut [*karat*] the calf in two and passed between the parts of it—the princes of Judah, the princes of Jerusalem, the eunuchs, the priests, and all the people of the land who passed between the parts of the calf—I will give them into the hand of their enemies."

In the ancient Near Eastern treaties, when a suzerain (overlord) entered into a treaty or covenant with a vassal (servant state), he would have them cut a sacrifice and pass through the pieces. What is important for us to note here is what the vassal was in effect acknowledging by passing through the pieces: "May it be done to me as was done to this animal if I am unfaithful to the covenant." We have numerous illustrations of this practice in the ancient Near East, with the king saying in effect to the vassal, "If you do not remain faithful to the covenant, it will happen to you as to this animal."[88] The one passing through the pieces, by so doing, indicates that he will undergo similar dismemberment if he is unfaithful to the covenant.

It was expected that the vassal would pass through the pieces and in effect make this kind of dismemberment oath. Note that in Jeremiah 34 the people passed through the pieces. But in the ceremony described in Genesis 15, there is no mention that Abram passed through the pieces.[89] The point emphasized is that, radically contrary to ancient Near Eastern practice, where only the vassal and not the suzerain moved through the pieces, God Himself, the divine Suzerain, or Overlord, passed through the pieces! The reference to the smoking oven and the burning torch are symbols of the divine presence, reminiscent of the smoking fire on Mount Sinai.

The same two Hebrew words connoting the divine presence link these two events together: 'ashan (smoke; Genesis 15:17; Exodus 19:18; 20:18) and lapid (lamp; Genesis 15:17; Exodus 20:18).

Why two symbols of the divine presence in Genesis 15? I believe it is significant that both a smoking oven and the burning torch passed through—two divine light sources, symbolizing the Father and the Son. Over and over in the narratives recorded in Genesis and Exodus, we find the Angel of the Lord who is sent from Yahweh yet saying of Himself, "I am Yahweh."[90] There is the implication of two Divine Beings in the Godhead who are involved in these narratives. Likewise, both the Father and Son appeared at Mount Sinai,[91] and we can conclude that both Father and Son were involved in the covenant-making ceremony with Abraham. The poignant truth of Genesis 15 is that as the Father and the Son pass through the pieces of the sacrifices, Divinity is saying, in effect, "If We break Our promise of the covenant, then let the Godhead be dismembered, let Divinity be ripped from Divinity, as these pieces." In effect, the Father and Son were placing Their very existence and unity on the line in this oath of covenant loyalty! That's how sure is the gospel promise of the covenant!

What is even more amazing is that Abram and his descendants did break the covenant, and instead of their being dismembered, the Godhead stepped into their place and took the covenant curses in their stead (Galatians 3:10–13). The choice of the animals that Abram was to sacrifice is instructive, as these are the very animals that were at the heart of the sacrificial

system in Leviticus. They point to the substitutionary sacrifice of the Messiah taking the place of us sinners.

The linkage of Genesis 15 with the Servant Song of Isaiah 53 is revealed in a striking way. The Hebrew word for the "[cut off or separated] pieces [of a slaughtered animal]" that the divine Presence passed through in Genesis 15:17 is from the root gzr, and this root appears again in the Hebrew Bible in a sacrificial context only in Isaiah 53:8: "For he was cut off [gzr] from the land of the living; for the transgressions of My people He was stricken." By using this rare word for being sacrificially "cut [off]," Isaiah links the divine passing through the pieces in Genesis 15 with the death of the Messiah. Thus is revealed the substitutionary atonement and the imputation of the guilt of the world to the Suffering Servant.

Daniel 9:26, 27 further links the Messiah's death with the cutting of the covenant portrayed in Genesis 15. According to the prophecy, the Anointed One (Messiah) would be "cut off" in the midst of the week. The Hebrew verb karat (in the Niphal passive), "to be cut off," is the technical term in the Pentateuch for the death penalty and, even more, implies a death penalty with no prospect of a future life[92]—that is, the equivalent of the "second death." As previously noted, karat, the same Hebrew verb, also is the technical term in Scripture for the making (literally, cutting) of a covenant. The Hebrew word here means "cut off" in (the second) death and also implies the making (cutting) of a covenant. The Messiah was "cut off" (died the equivalent of the second death because He could not see through the portals of the tomb) to ratify the new, everlasting covenant with His blood (Matthew 26:28; Hebrews 13:20). This is the same word found in Genesis 15:18 for God's making (literally, cutting) of the covenant.

To see the ultimate depth of the gospel—for the ultimate fulfillment of this covenant-making service in Genesis 15, alluded to also in Isaiah 53 and Daniel 9—we must go to Calvary. At the cross, we hear Jesus' anguished words as He takes upon Himself the covenant curses that we deserve: "My God, My God, why have You forsaken Me?" (Matthew 27:46). In light of God's implied oath of self-dismemberment in Genesis 15, this takes on incredible meaning. Ellen G. White points out that on the cross, as Jesus became the Sin Bearer, the unity of the Father and Son was broken up, and Jesus felt the anguish of eternal separation from His Father.[93]

In terms of Genesis 15, God, as it were, was ripped from God! Deity was torn from Deity! Divine dismemberment took place so that we might live! Christ took our curses (Galatians 3:13) as our Representative, Substitute, and Surety, suffering the agony of eternal separation between God and man that we deserved so that we might have the covenant blessings of eternal life that He deserved. That is the heart of justification by faith: the imputed guilt of the world placed upon Christ, and the imputed gift of righteousness offered to all repentant sinners who will reach out and take it with the hand of faith.

So in Genesis 15, when Yahweh promises to multiply Abram's seed like the stars of the heavens and illustrates it by making a covenant with Abram, implicit in that promise and covenant was the prediction of the Messianic Seed from Genesis 3:15, 21. When Abram "believed in Yahweh" and it was imputed to him for righteousness, Abram's faith grasped the promise of the coming of the Messiah to bear the sins of humanity by penal substitution and to impute to the believer His righteousness.

This is made even more explicit in Genesis 22, a passage to which Paul also refers.

Genesis 22. The narrative of Genesis 22, describing the divine test of Abraham in asking him to offer up his son, Isaac, on Mount Moriah, may be the very apex of Old Testament gospel prefigurations, revealing in advance how both the Father and Son were to be involved in the anguish of the atoning sacrifice. Jesus remarked that "Abraham rejoiced to see My day, and he saw it and was glad" (John 8:56). When did Abraham see Jesus' day? Paul records that "Scripture . . . preached the gospel to Abraham" (Galatians 3:8), and the text cited by the apostle to prove this point is from Genesis 22:18: "In your seed all the nations of the earth shall be blessed."

In Genesis 22:16–18, we encounter the same movement as in Genesis 3:15, narrowed from the collective "seed" of Abraham's many descendants (Genesis 22:17a, NASB) to the singular Seed, the coming Messiah, who will "possess the gate of *his* enemies" in whom "all nations of the earth shall be blessed" (verses 17b, 18, ESV; the pronoun modifying "seed" here is singular—"his"—although some versions have mistranslated by a plural "their"). By this paralleling of Isaac with the Messiah (verses 16, 18) the narrator, Moses, makes it clear that Isaac is a prefiguration of Christ. Thus, the whole incident in this chapter is a depiction in advance of the Father's offering up of His "only" Son, His beloved Son (verse 2), Jesus, to die for the world.[94] Bruce Waltke summarizes some of the typological correspondences:

> Within the canon of Scripture, the story of Abraham's willingness to obediently sacrifice his son of promise typifies Christ's sacrifice. Abraham's decision that "God himself will provide the Lamb" (22:8) resonates with God's offer of the Lamb to save the world (Mark 10:45; John 1:29, 36; 2 Cor. 5:17–21; 1 Peter 1:18, 19). God's provision of the ram on Mount Moriah typifies his sacrifice of Jesus Christ. Ultimately God provides the true Lamb without blemish that stands in humanity's place. . . .
>
> . . . Like Isaac, Christ is a Lamb led to the slaughter, yet he does not open his mouth. Just as Isaac carries his own wood for the altar up the steep mount, Christ carries his own wooden cross toward Golgotha (see John 19:17). . . . Abraham's devotion ("You have not withheld from me your son, your only son") is paralleled by God's love to us in Christ as reflected in John 3:16 and Rom. 8:32, which may allude to this verse. Symbolically, Abraham receives Isaac back from death, which typifies Christ's resurrection from the death of the cross (Heb. 11:19).[95]

Abraham was willing to sacrifice his son, and his son, Isaac, was willing to die. The anguish depicted in this scene gave those in Old Testament times "with eyes to see" a faint glimpse of the anguish to be experienced by the Father in not sparing His Son, and of the Son in dying the death that we deserve. But in this passage, the angel's voice spares Abraham from actually carrying out this sacrifice, and Abraham saw "a ram caught in a thicket by its horns" (Genesis 22:13a). This verse contains the *first explicit mention in Scripture of a substitutionary sacrifice of one life for another*: "So Abraham went and took the ram, and offered it up for a burnt offering instead of [Hebrew: *takhat*] his son" (verse 13b).

The apostle Paul seems to have lingered long over Genesis 22 when he wrote, "What then shall we say to these things? If God is for us, who can be against us? *He who did not spare His own Son, but delivered Him up for us all,* how shall He not with Him also freely give us all things?" (Romans 8:31, 32; emphasis added). The Greek word for "spared" (*pheidomai*) here in Romans 8 is the same one used in the Septuagint of Genesis 22:12: "Now I know that you fear God, since you have not withheld [spared] your son, your only son."[96]

Here is the basis for our justification. Here is a typological picture of the sinner Isaac, representing all of us, deserving to die, but the sacrificial Lamb or Ram is offered in his place. Isaac figuratively is raised from the dead (Hebrews 11:19) by virtue of the innocence of the Sacrifice who died in his place. Indeed, on Mount Moriah Abram saw the gospel of justification by faith!

All of this foundational material from the early chapters of Genesis lies behind Paul's doctrine of justification by faith. Informed by these chapters and later Old Testament materials, Paul systematically argues for the penal substitutionary death of Christ for the sins of the world (e.g., Romans 3:21–26; 4:24, 25 [echoing Isaiah 53:6, 11, 12]; Romans 5:8–10; 8:1–3; Galatians 3:10–13),[97] and the imputation of His righteousness to those who believe (e.g., Romans 4 [especially verse 3]; 5:12–21 [especially verse 19]; and 2 Corinthians 5:12–21 [especially verse 21]).[98] We will return to these Pauline passages again later.

The typology of the sanctuary. The precincts, furnishings, and services of the sanctuary, as described in the Pentateuch, teach the truths of justification by faith in numerous ways.[99] We can give only some representative examples. According to Leviticus 4,[100] the repentant sinner comes with his sin offering, lays or leans his hands on the head of the innocent animal, and confesses his sin. Symbolically his sin is transferred to the sacrifice. Then the sinner kills the animal with his own hand. The blood is carried by the priest to the Holy Place and sprinkled before the veil—or a part of the sacrifice is eaten by the priest and the blood is sprinkled upon the horns of the altar of burnt offering. The sacrifice is burned upon the altar of burnt offering. After the priest has made atonement for him concerning his sin, "it shall be forgiven him" (Leviticus 4:31). Thus, the blood of the substitute has made atonement (Leviticus 17:11). The sinner is forgiven, pardoned, declared righteous by God by virtue of the substitute that has been offered and in harmony with his heartfelt repentance and confession of sin.[101] Here is taught in type the glorious truth of justification by

faith—God's acceptance of the repentant sinner just as if he had not sinned by virtue of the Substitute.

Again, the altar of burnt offering[102] reveals central truths of justification by faith. On this altar, the Substitute, in type, is burned as a sweet savor to God—Christ is typified as satisfying divine justice as He pays the penalty for sin, enduring the fires of God's wrath in the sinner's stead. God can therefore be both just and the justifier of the believing, repentant sinner (Romans 3:25, 26). The ashes signify a final end—the acceptance of the offering.[103]

The foundational sacrifice of the Levitical system was the "continual" (or "regular"; Hebrew: *tamid*) burnt offering,[104] the offering for which the altar in the sanctuary courtyard was named (Exodus 31:9; Leviticus 4:30; etc.). A one-year-old male lamb was offered every morning and every evening (Numbers 28:3–8). Not only was this daily offering of two lambs to be done *regularly* (verse 3), but the offering was to be kept burning *continually* night and day upon the altar (Leviticus 6:9–13).[105] The regular, or continual, burnt offering is a vivid portrayal of Israel's "constant dependence upon the atoning blood of Christ."[106] No matter how advanced was the worshiper's sanctification, that person was never beyond need of the atoning blood of Christ to cover his or her sinfulness. Thus is taught the Reformation truth of *simul justus et peccator*—at the same time justified and a sinner.

Justification is not merely something to be experienced at the beginning of the Christian life but is constantly retained by Christians as the basis of their salvation.

Christ as high priest within the veil so immortalized Calvary that though He liveth unto God, He dies continually to sin. . . .

. . . Christ Jesus is represented as continually standing at the altar, momentarily offering up the sacrifice for the sins of the world. . . .

. . . All incense from earthly tabernacles must be moist with the cleansing drops of the blood of Christ.[107]

We can never this side of eternity get above the necessity for the continual justifying atonement provided by Jesus' blood.

In the Holy Place, the altar of incense[108] occupied a position nearest the Most Holy Place, directly before the veil. The incense itself points unmistakably to the "merits and intercession of Christ, His perfect righteousness, which through faith is imputed to His people, and which can alone make the worship of sinful beings acceptable to God."[109]

If one views the court of the sanctuary as the dimensions of two squares, each square contains an altar—the eastern square has the altar of burnt offering, and the western square, the altar of incense. Two altars, one of "perpetual intercession," the other of "continual atonement."[110] Blood and incense—one presents the efficacy of Christ's death as the Substitute for man, the other presents the efficacy of Christ's merits (or righteousness) that is imputed to the believing sinner. Both are interconnected. The horns of the altar of incense are stained with the blood of the sin offering. The altar of incense gives off its fragrance that infuses the smoke from the brazen altar and perfumes the camp for miles around.[111] Only by virtue of Christ's substitutionary death can He be qualified to apply His merits in our behalf. And at the same time, only by virtue of His spotless, incense-filled life of righteousness was He qualified to die in our stead.

As a final example from sanctuary typology, we refer to the ark covered by the mercy seat in the Most Holy Place. The ark, the "most sacred object" of the sanctuary,[112] contained the Decalogue, the basis of the covenant between God and man. The law was the expression of God's character; it was love codified. But it pronounced death upon the transgressor. The consequence of sin is separation from God, nonexistence, death. Above the ark was the Shekinah glory, the visible manifestation of the presence of God.[113] Humans, as transgressors of God's law, could never stand in the presence of God. The justice of God in dealing with sin could be satisfied only by the death of the sinner. But the ark reveals the way in which God, in His infinite wisdom and love, can be both "just and justifier" of repentant sinners (Romans 3:26). The mercy seat (*kapporet*) came between the law and the presence of God. Christ, by virtue of the atonement, can grant pardon to the repentant sinner and still be just.[114] Here at the mercy seat, in symbol, "mercy and truth have met together; righteousness and peace have kissed [each other]" (Psalm 85:10). Paul grasped the profound meaning of this typology and proclaimed Christ as our "mercy seat"—our *hilastērion* (the Greek translation of *kapporet*)—put forward by God to reveal His righteousness in dealing with sin and to make it possible for Him to be both "just and the justifier of the one who has faith in Jesus" (Romans 3:26).[115]

Psalm 32:1, 2, and related passages. Another major Old Testament passage used by Paul to teach justification by faith is Psalm 32:1, 2: "Blessed is he whose transgression is forgiven, whose sin is covered. Blessed is the man to whom the Lord does not impute [charge his account with] iniquity ["does not hold guilty," NJPS Jewish Bible], and in whose spirit there is no deceit."

The Hebrew word for "impute" in Psalm 32:2 is the same word used in Genesis 15:6—*khashab*—which means "to impute, reckon to." Psalm 32 indicates that God does not impute iniquity or guilt but rather covers our sin, implying that God imputes righteousness to us apart from our works. Paul cites this verse in Romans 4:5–8, highlighting this very understanding:

But to him who does not work but believes on Him who justifies the ungodly, his faith is accounted for righteousness, just as David also describes the blessedness of the man *to whom God imputes righteousness apart from works*:

"Blessed are those whose lawless
    deeds are forgiven,
And whose sins are covered;
Blessed is the man to whom the Lord
    shall not impute sin" (emphasis
    added).

In Romans 3:10–18, Paul cites a whole chain of Old Testament passages to show that all humanity stands "under sin" and "guilty before God" (verses 9, 19), and thus there is no way that their justification can be based upon their works of the law:

As it is written:

"There is none righteous, no, not
    one;
There is none who understands;
There is none who seeks after God.
They have all turned aside;
They have together become unprof-
    itable;
There is none who does good, no, not
    one" [Psalms 14:1–3; 53:1–3].
"Their throat is an open tomb;
With their tongues they have prac-
    ticed deceit" [Psalm 5:9];
"The poison of asps is under their
    lips" [Psalm 140:3];
"Whose mouth is full of cursing and
    bitterness" [Psalm 10:7].
"Their feet are swift to shed blood;
Destruction and misery are in their
    ways;
And the way of peace they have not
    known" [Proverbs 1:16; Isaiah 59:7,
    8].
"There is no fear of God before their
    eyes" [Psalm 36:1].

Paul's citation in Romans 1–3 of these passages, and other references to the sins of both Jews and Gentiles, is not primarily ecclesiological (as claimed by the new perspective on Paul) but profoundly ontological and soteriological: "both Jews and Greeks . . . are all under sin" (Romans 3:9). Although there are ecclesiological implications, the fundamental problem of the people of Israel was not their failure to bless the world but their inherent sinfulness (an ontological problem). All humanity stands guilty before God because they have failed to obey God and keep His law.[116]

While the new perspective on Paul rightly points to elements of grace in first-century Judaism, nonetheless, the evidence is strong both within the Pauline corpus and other extant literature of the period that Judaism, despite its "covenant nomism," commonly involved a legalistic strain in which one earned salvation by works of law.[117] Likewise, the references to "works" (Romans 4:2, 4, 6; 11:6; Ephesians 2:9; 2 Timothy 1:9; Titus 3:5) and "works of the law" (Romans 3:27; 9:32; Galatians 2:16; 3:10) in the Pauline writings dealing with justification are not limited to the particular "ethnic markers" of Judaism (boundaries between Jews and Gentiles), as claimed by proponents of the new perspective, but refer to all attempts on the part of humanity to keep the law in order to be saved.[118]

Finally, these and other Old Testament passages, and their New Testament counterparts, also make clear that true believers, justified persons, are still sinners and can never have a standing before God based upon their own works of righteousness or even after conversion through those works wrought in them by the Holy Spirit. In the words of Martin Luther, we are ever *simul justus et peccator* (at the same time just and sinner).

Many additional biblical passages make this abundantly evident. Yahweh states after the Flood: "The inclination of the human heart is evil from youth" (Genesis 8:21, NRSV). David exclaims, "Behold, I was brought forth in iniquity, and in sin my

mother conceived me" (Psalm 51:5). Again, David confesses, "No one living is righteous before you" (Psalm 143:2, ESV). In his prayer at the dedication of the temple, Solomon acknowledged, "There is no one who does not sin" (2 Chronicles 6:36). He reiterates this same point in Ecclesiastes 7:20: "There is not a righteous man on earth who does good and never sins" (ESV). Isaiah states regarding all humanity, even the faithful ones in Israel: "But we are all like an unclean thing, and all our righteousnesses are like filthy rags" (Isaiah 64:6). Regarding human nature, Jeremiah states, "The heart is deceitful above all things, and desperately wicked; who can know it?" (Jeremiah 17:9). Examples of godly individuals in the Old Testament, such as Noah, Job, and Daniel, who are called "righteous" or "blameless" (Ezekiel 14:14, 20; cf. Genesis 7:1; Job 1:1), are described as either having committed sin or as confessing sin (Genesis 9:21; Job 40:4; 42:2–6; Daniel 9:4–19).[119] In the New Testament, Paul asserts that "all have sinned [aorist punctiliar = sins of the past] and fall short [present continuous, "continue to fall short"] of the glory of God" (Romans 3:23). No matter how advanced one's character development may be, one is still a sinner. Paul frankly acknowledged, "This is a faithful saying and worthy of all acceptance, that Christ Jesus came into the world to save sinners, of whom I am [present tense] chief" (1 Timothy 1:15).

Isaiah 53. We return once more to Isaiah 53, where arguably one finds the most profound statement on justification by faith in the Old Testament; a chapter to which the New Testament writers, including Paul, return again and again.[120]

At the heart of Isaiah 53 are the intertwined themes of penal substitution and forensic justification—that the Messianic Servant paid the legal penalty of our transgressions to make atonement for us so that we might escape punishment and to justify us (declare us righteous) by bearing our sins.[121] All of the major elements involved in the biblical doctrine of justification are found in this chapter: (1) the Servant was sinless and righteous (verses 7, 9, 11); (2) all of us are sinners, having gone astray and turned to our own way (verse 6); (3) the guilt and punishment of our sins was imputed to Him, as the Lord laid on Him the iniquity (Hebrew: 'awon; "guilt," NJPS) of us all and numbered (Septuagint: logizomai, "reckoned") Him with the transgressors (verses 4–6, 8, 11, 12); (4) He suffered and died for "all," an unlimited atonement making justification available to everyone (verse 6; cf. Isaiah 52:12); (5) God the Father Himself acted to lay our iniquity and guilt upon the Servant and to punish Him for those sins, according to the principle of lex talionis (just retribution), thus satisfying His justice (Isaiah 53:6, 10); (6) the Righteous Servant suffered willingly and deliberately (verses 4, 11, 12); (7) He became a guilt offering (Hebrew: 'asham) to make atonement for our guilt (verse 10; cf. Leviticus 5–7); (8) the voluntary suffering and death of the Righteous Servant "will justify the many, as He will bear their iniquities" (Isaiah 53:11, NASB); His righteousness will be imputed to them; (9) the need for the response of faith is highlighted in Isaiah's rhetorical question at the beginning of the chapter: "Who has believed our report?" (thus also implying that not everyone would believe; verse 1); and (10) the work of the Servant in justifying sinners is accompanied by the work of sanctification ("healing") in the believer, although this is distinct from and not part of justification (verse 5).

Several of the preceding points call for further comment. Note especially point 8. After Isaiah's focus upon the Messiah's substitutionary sacrifice, he indicates in the final stanza of the song that the substitutionary sacrifice of the Messiah forms the basis of His work of justification, by placing the two items in poetic synonymous parallelism:

> By His knowledge [Hebrew: da'at, "His personal experience"] the Righteous One,
> My Servant, will justify [Hebrew: hitsdiq; Hifil of tsadaq, "declare, or pronounce, righteous"] the many,
> As He will bear their iniquities (verse 11, NASB).

The reference to "the Righteous One, My Servant" in this verse also implies that the Servant's righteousness is imputed to sinful humanity. Paul alludes to this verse in Romans 5:19, and several other verses in Isaiah 53 (verses 5, 6, 8, 10, 12) "provide a compelling and meaningful backdrop to Paul's thought" in Romans 5:12–21.[122]

In 2 Corinthians 5:12–21 (especially verse 21), Paul alludes to these verses in Isaiah 53 and also ultimately to the Creation, Fall, and Redemption in Genesis 1–3. The Creation connection is found in 2 Corinthians 5:17: "Therefore, if anyone is in Christ, he is a new creation." We saw at the beginning of our biblical study that according to Genesis 1 and 2, Adam was the representative Head of creation, and when he fell, all humanity was constituted sinners. Likewise, Genesis 3:15, 21 implicitly teach that Christ is the New Adam, the representative Head of the new creation, who took upon Himself the sins of humanity, died in our place, and imputes His righteousness to the contrite sinner.

These ideas, already nascent in the opening chapters of Scripture, are crystalized in Isaiah 53 and developed further by Paul in 2 Corinthians 5:12–21. In verse 14, Paul states that "if One died for all, then all died." Christ died as our Representative, as our Substitute, having our sins imputed to Himself. Further, He became our righteousness, imputing His righteousness to us: "For He made Him who knew no sin to be sin for us, that we might become the righteousness of God in Him" (verse 21).[123] Murray Harris succinctly summarizes, "It is not inappropriate to perceive in this verse a double imputation: sin was reckoned to Christ's account (v. 21a), so that righteousness is reckoned to our account (v. 21b). . . . As a result of God's imputing to Christ something extrinsic to him, namely sin, believers have something imputed to them that was extrinsic to them, namely righteousness."[124]

N. T. Wright, representing the new perspective on Paul, rejects the imputation of Christ's righteousness as unbiblical, largely because he contends "that in a courtroom when the judge declares the defendant to be righteous, he doesn't give his righteousness to the defendant."[125] But Wright is judging the divine courtroom by what he

knows of human courtrooms! As Schreiner states regarding the heavenly courtroom, "But we see the distinctiveness of the biblical text and the wonder and glory of the gospel precisely here. God is not restricted by the rules of human courtrooms. This is a most unusual courtroom indeed, for the judge delivers up his own Son to pay the penalty. That doesn't happen in human courtrooms! And the judge gives us his own righteousness—a righteousness from God (Phil 3:9)."[126]

Note also point 9 regarding Isaiah 53. At the beginning of the chapter, the prophet implies the need to respond to His "report" of the Messiah's work by "faith." "Who has believed our report?" (verse 1). Thus, at the end and at the beginning of Isaiah 53, like bookends, we have "justification" and "faith."

In regard to points 8 and 9, some have questioned whether our justification is only a legal fiction, if it always is based on an "alien" righteousness of the Messiah and is granted only by faith to those who are still sinners. This is a major argument of Roman Catholic theology against forensic (only) justification.[127] After all, it is pointed out, the Old Testament strongly condemns those who "justify" (Hebrew: *hitsdiq*) the wicked: "He who justifies the wicked, and he who condemns the just, both of them are alike an abomination to the LORD" (Proverbs 17:15; cf. Exodus 23:7; Deuteronomy 25:1).

But to speak of God's acquittal of the guilt of sinners in justification is not a legal fiction for two crucial reasons. First, the term *hitsdiq*, "to declare righteous," speaks of the declaration of the judge, not the moral state of the one being judged. It is a real declaration of acquittal or pardon, not a fictional one. Second, it is not a legal fiction nor opposed to the biblical statements quoted in the previous paragraph, because it is a real righteousness (that of Christ), not a fictional one, that is imputed to the believer. As R. C. Sproul puts it,

> The forensic declaration of justification is not a legal fiction. It is real and authentic because the imputation upon which it is based is no fiction. It is a real imputation of real righteousness of a real Christ. Christ is our righteousness.... He gives us His righteousness before the tribunal of God. Our righteousness remains as filthy rags. We must be adorned or cloaked by His righteousness, a cloak which covers the nakedness of our sin. This is the truly good news of the Gospel that by grace God counts or reckons the very righteousness of Christ to us.[128]

Because Christ has taken our iniquities, the covenant curses that we deserved, He, the Righteous One, can truly put to our account His infinite righteousness, and as we, "the many," accept Him in faith, He justifies (accounts, or declares, righteous) "the many" (i.e., all who trust in Him)! Christ is indeed the embodiment of Jeremiah 23:6: "THE LORD OUR RIGHTEOUSNESS."

Finally, we must comment further on point 10 in our discussion of Isaiah 53. The atoning work of Christ brings not only justification (a judicial declaration of pardon, receiving Christ's imputed righteousness)

but also healing (verse 5)—an internal transformation (the imparted righteousness of Christ, which the New Testament calls sanctification). Both of these gifts from Christ the Righteous One flow to the repentant sinner who "believes" the report of Christ's work and accepts Him as his Savior. While these two gifts of grace cannot be separated, they must be distinguished. Many passages in Scripture illustrate this point: Isaiah 53:1–5, 11; Habakkuk 2:4; Romans 1:17; 5:1–5; 1 Corinthians 6:11; Ephesians 2:8–10; and Titus 3:5–8.

When one accepts Christ by faith and is united to Him, that person is both justified (legally pardoned) and sanctified (regenerated) at the same time (with sanctification also an ongoing process). But the two actions of justification and sanctification must be distinguished. The basis of our justification is always the *imputed* righteousness of Christ (what Christ has done for us, outside of us), which is perfect and acceptable to God, not His *imparted* righteousness (what Christ is doing in us; sanctification), which is always partial, always "falls short" of the glory of God, and can never commend us to God. Only on the basis of the imputed righteousness of Christ can we have peace—the assurance of salvation.

Paul makes this clear in Romans 5. According to verse 1, "Therefore, having been justified by faith, we have peace with God through our Lord Jesus Christ." Justification is by faith alone, and peace is based upon this legal declaration of God that is accepted by faith. At the same time, verses 2–5 are also true, describing the work of sanctification in our lives that flows from this justification: "The love of God has been poured out in our hearts by the Holy Spirit who was given to us" (verse 5).

The biblical doctrine of justification by faith alone is sometimes viewed with suspicion because if it is by faith alone, it seems like one is opening the door to antinomianism. But the Bible never teaches that justification is a form of "cheap grace," removing the importance of obedience to God's law. Justification is not opposed to, nor to be separated from, sanctification in terms of experience. Isaiah 53 makes clear that the Servant both "justifies" (justification) and "heals" (sanctification) those who believe in Him. John Gerstner aptly remarks, "Faith is not a work, but it is never without work. . . . If a believer is not changed, he is not a believer. No one can have Christ as Savior for one moment when he is not Lord as well! We can never say too often: 'Justification is by faith alone, but NOT by the faith that is alone.' Justification is by a WORKING faith."[129]

In his epistles, especially Romans and Galatians, Paul clearly affirms the points described above—that justification describes the imputed righteousness of Christ based on His sinless life that is placed to our account by faith alone, not by works (see especially Romans 3:20–31; 4:3–5, 22–25; 5:1, 12–21; 10:3–10; Galatians 2:16, 17; 3:5–14, 24; Titus 3:5–7). Yet Paul also makes clear that this justifying faith is a deep and active faith that is demonstrated by how we live (Galatians 5:6; cf. Colossians 1:4; 1 Thessalonians 1:3; 2 Thessalonians 1:11; Romans 1:5; 5:1, 5; 16:26; Titus 3:7, 8). It is this latter point that the apostle James emphasizes (James 2:21–25) when he writes that "faith without works is dead" (verse 20). Paul and James are not opposed to each other. Paul is emphasizing that justification is by faith alone, while James is emphasizing that justifying faith is never alone![130] Both apostles agree that our faith includes our disposition to be willing to act in accordance with God's will. Jesus also teaches the doctrine of justification by faith, providing the same balance between faith and works that is found in Paul and James (see Luke 18:9–14; Matthew 12:36, 37).[131] There are numerous biblical texts throughout Scripture showing that humans are justified by faith alone but also that works of faith provide evidence to the universe in the final eschatological judgment of acquittal (sometimes called "final justification") that the faith of those justified is genuine.[132]

Habakkuk 2:4. In his introduction to the epistle to the Romans, Paul cites Habakkuk 2:4: "The just shall live by faith" (Romans 1:17). Scholars have struggled to understand whether Paul intends this quotation to refer only to his treatment of justification by faith (concentrated in the first half of his epistle) or also to sanctification (the focus of the last half of his epistle). The Hebrew word for "faith" in Habakkuk 2:4 is *'emunah*, which can mean "faith" or "faithfulness."[133] Recent study has shown from the immediate context in Habakkuk that the Old Testament prophet intended to include both meanings in his statement.[134] The Old Testament passage teaches justification by faith *and* that the justified are faithful. Paul no doubt grasped this twofold implication of the passage and used this verse to be the introduction to his entire epistle to encompass both the concept of justification by faith (first half of his book) and sanctifying faithfulness on the part of those who are justified (the second half of the book), and probably also ultimately to underscore the Messiah's own faith and/or faithfulness as the basis of both our justification and sanctification.[135]

The great doctrine of justification by faith is a message that brings peace and hope and eternal life to those who are justified. When contrite sinners reach out and receive the gift of justification by faith, they find peace and hope (Romans 5:1, 2) and can have full assurance of faith that they have eternal life (Romans 10:9, 10; Titus 3:7; cf. John 6:47; 1 John 5:13). It is indeed the "justification of life" (Romans 5:18)!

IV. Conclusions and Implications

This brief survey of the biblical materials reveals that the doctrine of justification by faith, as taught by the Reformers, has a solid basis in Scripture, both the Old Testament and the New Testament.[136] The following conclusions and implications emerge from our biblical study.[137]

Justification by faith is of crucial importance as "the article of our true standing in the sight of God" (Job 9:2; Romans 3:21–26).[138] The question of one's standing before God, how one is justified by Him, is the most crucial question faced by human beings; it is foundational to all other questions.

Justification may be defined as a judicial declaration of acquittal or pardon (Isaiah 53:11; Luke 18:9–14; Romans 4:3–5; 5:16; cf. Exodus 23:7; Deuteronomy 25:1; Job 27:5; Proverbs 17:15; Isaiah 5:23).[139] *It does not include the process of ethical transformation.*

Justification is accounting or reckoning a person righteous (Genesis 15:6; Romans 4:3–6), not *making* a person righteous.

Justification is based upon an external ("alien") righteousness, not internal (inherent) righteousness in the believer (Genesis 3:21; Isaiah 53:11; Luke 18:9–14; Romans 4:5, 6; 5:17, 18; 2 Corinthians 5:21). Justification does not include an actual righteousness inhering in the believer because of which he or she is declared righteous.[140]

The only ground of justification is the imputed merits of Christ's righteousness, based upon His sinless life and His substitutionary death for our sins (Genesis 3:15, 21; 15:6, 9–18; 22:13; Leviticus 4; 6:9–13; Isaiah 53:4–12; Romans 3:21–26; 4:3–6, 11, 23–25; 5:8–10, 15, 17–19; 8:1–3; 2 Corinthians 5:12–21; Galatians 3:10–13; Philippians 3:9). The law demands perfect righteousness (obedience to the law), and the only way sinners can meet the law's requirements is through the perfect righteousness of Christ that is imputed to them.[141]

Justification is not a legal fiction (Genesis 3:15; Isaiah 53:11; 61:10; Jeremiah 23:6; 2 Corinthians 5:12–21). Christ really died as our Representative and as the Substitute for the sins of the world. The real righteousness of Christ is truly imputed to the repentant and believing sinner, and that sinner is really declared justified (pardoned).[142]

Justification is by faith alone, not by faith plus works (Genesis 15:6; Isaiah 53:1; Romans 3:10–18, 28; 4:4, 9–12, 25; 10:10; Galatians 2:16, 17; 3:5–14, 24; Titus 3:5–7); *but faith is never alone* (Romans 1:5; 5:1, 5; 16:26; Galatians 5:6; Colossians 1:4; 1 Thessalonians 1:3; 2 Thessalonians 1:11; Titus 3:5–8; James 2:21–25). While justification is by faith alone, the faith by which one is justified is never alone; it is a working faith. Justifying faith is not merely intellectual assent to Christ and His promises but placing one's trust in Him. It is a deep and active faith that is demonstrated by how we live.[143] At the same time, no works that we perform, even our most fervent obedience wrought through the power of the Holy Spirit, can in any way become the basis of our acceptance with God.[144]

The faith by which we are justified is itself a gift of God and earns no creaturely merit (Genesis 15:6; Romans 3:28; 4:1–8; 12:3; Ephesians 2:8, 9). Faith is simply the "empty hands"[145] that receive the gift of Christ's righteousness.[146] It is in no way meritorious.

Justification and sanctification cannot be separated, but must be distinguished (Isaiah 53:1–5, 11; Habakkuk 2:4; Romans 1:17; 5:1–5; 1 Corinthians 6:11; Ephesians 2:8–10; Titus 3:5–8).[147] Numerous biblical passages speak of justification and sanctification in virtually the same breath, but the inspired biblical writers nonetheless clearly distinguish between the two.

The righteousness by which one is justified is imputed (Genesis 15:6; Psalm 32:1, 2; Isaiah 53:11; Romans 4:3, 7–9, 22; 5:1, 12–21; 2 Corinthians 5:12–21), *whereas the righteousness by which we are sanctified is imparted* (Exodus 31:13; Leviticus 22:9, 16; Ezekiel 20:12; 37:28; Romans 5:2–5; 6:13–19; Ephesians 4:24; Philippians 1:9–11; 1 Thessalonians 4:3–8). Justification, as the judicial verdict of acquittal before God, is the believer's legal claim or title to heaven (Romans 5:9, 21; Ephesians 2:8), while sanctification is the ever-developing, ever-incomplete fitness for heaven (1 Thessalonians 5:23).[148]

The obedience of faith (sanctification) is evidence to the universe in the end-time judgment (sometimes called "final justification") that the faith of those justified is genuine (Matthew 12:36, 37; Romans 2:13). But our sanctification is always progressive, always partial; it always "falls short" of the glory of God (Romans 3:23) and can never commend us to God.

Both justification and sanctification flow from the sinner's union with Christ, by placing one's trust in Him, giving oneself to Him, accepting Him as one's Savior (Genesis 15:6; Romans 6; 2 Corinthians 5:17; Ephesians 1:13; 2:4–9; Colossians 1:27; cf. John 15:1–8; 1 John 5:11–13).[149] Justification is not a forensic heavenly verdict that is disconnected from an intimate union with Christ; rather, justification flows from that mystical union with Christ established by faith.[150] Neither is sanctification separated from one's union with Christ but flows spontaneously from the believer's connection with the Savior.

Those who are justified by faith may have continued full assurance of salvation in Christ their Substitute as they maintain their connection with Him (Romans 5:1, 18; 10:9, 10; Ephesians 1:6; Titus 3:7; cf. John 6:47; 1 John 5:13). "We are not to be anxious about what Christ and God think of us, but about what God thinks of Christ, our Substitute. Ye are accepted in the Beloved."[151] We may "give ourselves to Christ and know that He accepts us."[152]

Since we are simul justus et peccator (*at the same time just and sinners*) *till our glorification* (2 Chronicles 6:36; Psalms 14:1–3, 7; 36:1; 140:3; 143:2; Ecclesiastes 7:20; Isaiah 53:5, 6; 59:7, 8; 64:6; Romans 3:10–22; 4:5;

1 Timothy 1:15), *we are in constant need of justification for our pardon and atonement in our sinful state* (Exodus 30:1–10; 25:10–22; Leviticus 6:9–13; Zechariah 3:1–5; Romans 3:23, 25, 26; 8:34; Hebrews 7:25). Justification is not a one-time event, taking care only of past, preconversion sins, but is retained throughout our lives as we continually receive pardon or acquittal from God for our sins (based upon Christ's merits) as the only basis for our acceptance by God, and reveal the genuineness of our justifying faith by the (real but always incomplete) sanctified fruit of obedience.[153] There will never be a time this side of glorification when we will not be in "constant dependence upon the atoning blood of Christ"[154] and in constant need of the merits of Christ's righteousness to cover for our sinfulness:

> The religious services, the prayers, the praise, the penitent confession of sin ascend from true believers as incense to the heavenly sanctuary, but passing through the corrupt channels of humanity, they are so defiled that unless purified by blood, they can never be of value with God. They ascend not in spotless purity, and unless the Intercessor, who is at God's right hand, presents and purifies all by His righteousness, it is not acceptable to God. All incense from earthly tabernacles must be moist with the cleansing drops of the blood of Christ. He holds before the Father the censer of His own merits, in which there is no taint of earthly corruption. He gathers into this censer the prayers, the praise, and the confessions of His people, and

with these He puts His own spotless righteousness. Then, perfumed with the merits of Christ's propitiation, the incense comes up before God wholly and entirely acceptable.[155]

Without mentioning either the word *justification* or the word *faith*, Ellen G. White beautifully summarizes the essence of justification by faith in the following (my favorite!) quotation from her entire corpus:

> It was possible for Adam, before the fall, to form a righteous character by obedience to God's law. But he failed to do this, and because of his sin our natures are fallen and we cannot make ourselves righteous. Since we are sinful, unholy, we cannot perfectly obey the holy law. We have no righteousness of our own with which to meet the claims of the law of God. But Christ has made a way of escape for us. He lived on earth amid trials and temptations such as we have to meet. He lived a sinless life. He died for us, and now He offers to take our sins and give us His righteousness. If you give yourself to Him, and accept Him as your Saviour, then, sinful as your life may have been, for His sake you are accounted righteous. Christ's character stands in place of your character, and you are accepted before God just as if you had not sinned.[156]

Addendum: Personal Experience

Growing up as a fourth-generation Seventh-day Adventist in a time of our denominational history when the doctrine of justification by faith was often not clearly understood, it was not easy for me to grasp or accept this beautiful teaching of the gospel. I was taught by well-meaning Bible teachers that justification was not by faith alone in Christ's imputed righteousness, but that it somehow also included my works as part of the basis of my acceptance by God. I viewed justification as forgiving my past sins; but after conversion, I felt I needed to depend upon my sanctification as the basis of my continued acceptance by God. Since my works of obedience always seemed to fall short of the divine standard, I had no assurance of salvation.

I believed that Christ, the Lamb of God, my Substitute, had died for my sins. But somehow I could not grasp the fact that as I received Christ, I was covered with the robe of His righteousness. It was too good to believe that as I gave myself to Him and accepted Him as my Savior, God said to the great accuser, "The Lord rebuke you, Satan!" (Zechariah 3:2). I did not dare to believe with assurance that I was acquitted, pardoned, and cleansed. I failed to understand that I did not need to be "anxious about what Christ and God think of us, but about what God thinks of Christ, our Substitute."[157]

I dared not believe it even as a theology major in college, as a seminary student, and as a young pastor. Inspired statements such as the following kept ringing in my ears: "Those who accept the Saviour, however sincere their conversion, should never be taught to say or to feel that they are saved."[158] I didn't understand that Ellen White was refuting the erroneous belief of "once saved, always saved." I thought she

meant that one could never have present assurance of salvation. How tragic that I did not continue to read in the very same paragraph God's assurance that we can "give ourselves to Christ and know that He accepts us"! For several years as a young pastor, I preached sermons about Christ, yet they were devoid of assurance of salvation through an experiential knowledge of justification by faith. But finally, through a chain of marvelous providential leadings, the beauty and simplicity of the gospel truth of justification began to dawn before my eyes.

The sublime promises jumped out at me from Scripture: "Truly, truly, I say to you, he who believes *has* eternal life" (John 6:47, RSV; emphasis added). "I write this to you who believe in the name of the Son of God, that you may *know* that you *have* eternal life" (1 John 5:13, RSV; emphasis added; cf. verses 11, 12).

The marvelous news that I am "accepted in the Beloved" (Ephesians 1:6), that Christ is my righteousness, brought to my soul a joy and peace like that described by the ones who heard the message of justification by faith in the wake of the 1888 General Conference Session. Ellen G. White captured my own feelings as she depicted the experience of many at the Ottawa, Kansas, camp meeting in 1889: "Light flashed from the oracles of God in relation to the law and the gospel, in relation to the fact that Christ is our righteousness, which seemed to souls who were hungry for the truth, as light too precious to be received."[159] I felt like the young pastor at that Kansas camp meeting who "saw that it was his privilege to be justified by faith; he had peace with

God, and with tears confessed what relief and blessing had come to his soul."[160]

Since that experiential introduction to gospel assurance while I was a young pastor, the beauty of justification by faith has grown ever more precious. I must confess that sometimes it still seems almost too good to be true! I catch myself unconsciously falling back into old habit patterns of trying to be good enough to deserve salvation and have to discover anew the joyous truth of "laying the glory of man in the dust"[161] and trusting wholly in Christ's righteousness imputed to me as the basis of my acceptance with God. How precious, then, has the doctrine of justification by faith become to me!

Justification by faith is even more precious as I consider that we are living during the antitypical day of atonement, facing the close of probation and last-day events. In ancient Israel throughout the Day of Atonement, the "daily" (*tamid*) sacrifice continued to burn on the bronze altar (Numbers 28:2–7; 29:7–11), and the incense continued to waft over the inner veil and cover the holy ark (Exodus 30:7–10). Throughout the antitypical day of atonement, even after the close of probation and the time of trouble, on to the time of glorification, we can have assurance of being accepted by God solely on the basis of the atoning blood and intercessory merits of Christ's righteousness! Justification by faith is, and will remain till the end, the most precious truth that answers the age-old question of questions: "How can a mortal be just with God?" (Job 9:2, Emphasized Bible).

Endnotes

1. Scripture quotations in this chapter are from the NKJV unless otherwise noted (as in this case).

2. Martin Luther, *Luther's Works*, ed. Jaroslav Pelikan, vol. 26, *Lectures on Galatians, 1535, Chapters 1–4* (Saint Louis, MO: Concordia, 1963), 26.

3. Martin Luther, *What Luther Says: An Anthology*, comp. Ewald M. Plass (Saint Louis, MO: Concordia, 1959), 2:704n5. Though these words were not coined by Luther himself, it is widely recognized that they well represent his thought. See Paul Rhodes Eddy, James K. Beilby, and Steven E. Enderlein, "Justification in Historical Perspective," in *Justification: Five Views*, ed. James K. Beilby and Paul Rhodes Eddy (Downers Grove, IL: IVP Academic, 2011), 24.

4. Luther, *What Luther Says*, 2:703.

5. John Calvin, *Institutes of the Christian Religion*, 1559 ed., trans. Henry Beveridge (Grand Rapids, MI: Eerdmans, 1966), 3.11.1.

6. Ellen G. White, *Faith and Works* (Nashville, TN: Southern Pub. Assn., 1979), 20.

7. Ibid., 18.

8. Luther, *Lectures on Galatians*, 395, 396.

9. Luther, *What Luther Says*, 2:703.

10. This represents the understanding of the Magisterial Reformers, especially Martin Luther, John Calvin, and Philip Melanchthon, whose views on justification were for the most part followed by Arminius (Arminianism), John Wesley (Methodism), and many other Protestant theologians and traditions. For recent treatment of the traditional Reformation doctrine, see Thomas Schreiner, *Faith Alone: The Doctrine of Justification: What the Reformers Taught . . . and Why It Still Matters* (Grand Rapids, MI: Zondervan, 2015). For discussion (with bibliography) of the history of other views on justification, such as that of the early church (e.g., Origen, Augustine), Latin Middle Ages (e.g., Anselm and Aquinas), Anabaptists and the "Radical Reformation" (e.g., Menno Simons), liberal Protestantism (e.g., Albrecht Ritschl), existential reinterpretations (Paul Tillich, Rudolf Bultmann, and Karl Barth), liberation and feminist theology (e.g., Elsa Tamez), Pentecostal theologies (Frank Macchia), and Finnish Lutheran theology (Tuomo Mannermaa, Veli-Matti Kärkkäinen) see, e.g., Eddy, Beilby, and Enderlein,

"Justification in Historical Perspective," 13–52.

11. The "Finnish school" of Luther interpretation, in dialogue with Russian Orthodox theology, claims that Luther's view was closer to the orthodox understanding of *theosis*, "deification," and that for Luther justifying righteousness was not solely an alien righteousness: "In line with Catholic theology, justification means both declaring righteous and making righteous." Veli-Matti Kärkkäinen, "Deification View," in Beilby and Eddy, *Justification: Five Views*, 222. For a critique of this view from the perspective of the traditional interpretation of Luther, see Michael S. Horton's response "Traditional Reformed" to Kärkkäinen's chapter in Beilby and Eddy, *Justification: Five Views*, 244–249.

12. R. C. Sproul, "The Forensic Nature of Justification," in *Justification by Faith Alone: Affirming the Doctrine by Which the Church and the Individual Stands or Falls*, ed. John Kistler, rev. ed. (Morgan, PA: Soli Deo Gloria Publications, 2003), 33, 34.

13. The mature Melanchthon also grasped the concept of the human free will in which salvation was truly available to all human beings, unlike Calvin and Luther who held on to a doctrine of predestination. See Gregory B. Graybill, *Evangelical Free Will: Philipp Melanchthon's Doctrinal Journey on the Origins of Faith* (New York: Oxford University Press, 2010).

14. For a summary of Calvin's views on justification and his indebtedness to Luther and Melanchthon, see Karla Wübbenhorst, "Calvin's Doctrine of Justification: Variations on a Lutheran Theme," in *Justification in Perspective: Historical Developments and Contemporary Challenges*, ed. Bruce L. McCormack (Grand Rapids, MI: Baker, 2006), 99–118.

15. Calvin, *Institutes* (1559 ed.), 3.11.2.

16. Ibid., 3.11.3.

17. Calvin, *Institutes* (1536 ed.), 1.32.

18. Wübbenhorst, "Calvin's Doctrine of Justification," 115.

19. Calvin, *Institutes* (1559 ed.), 3.11.10.

20. Ibid., 3.11.6. The mature Calvin wants to emphasize this point so much that in his final 1559 edition of the *Institutes* he reverses the order of his treatment of justification and sanctification, putting the latter first.

21. For more details and substantiation, see, e.g., McCormack, *Justification in Perspective*, passim; and Schreiner, *Faith Alone*, 37–63.

22. Alister McGrath, *Justification by Faith* (Grand Rapids, MI: Zondervan, 1988), 61.

23. See Arminius's own statement: "It is a justification by which a man, who is a sinner, yet a believer, being placed before the throne of grace which is erected in Christ Jesus the Propitiation, is accounted and pronounced by God, the just and merciful Judge, righteous and worthy of the reward of righteousness, not in himself but in Christ, of grace, according to the gospel, to the praise of the righteousness and grace of God, and to the salvation of the justified person himself. (Rom. iii. 24-26; 3, 4, 5, 10, 11.)" Arminius, "Disputation 19: On the Justification of Man Before God," in *Works of James Arminius*, vol. 1, http://www.ccel.org/ccel/arminius/works1.v.xx.html. Cf. Arminius, "A Declaration of the Sentiments of James Arminius," 2.13, in *Arminius Speaks: Essential Writing on Predestination, Free Will, and the Nature of God*, ed. John D. Wagner (Eugene, OR: Wipf and Stock, 2011): "I am not conscious to myself, of having taught or entertained any other sentiments concerning the justification of man before God, than those which are held unanimously by the Reformed and Protestant Churches, and which are in complete agreement with their expressed opinions." Arminius, however, as did the mature Melanchthon, widened justification to include all who chose to accept it (and not just the elect as for Luther and Calvin).

24. For a summary of the views of Jonathan Edwards and John Wesley on justification, see, e.g., Schreiner, *Faith Alone*, 80–94.

25. See, e.g., the Westminster Confession of Faith (1647) 11.1, 2, conveniently cited in Joel Beeke, "Justification by Faith Alone (The Relation of Faith to Justification)," in Kistler, *Justification by Faith Alone*, 85. For this and other major Protestant creeds, see John H. Leith, ed., *Creeds of the Churches: A Reader in Christian Doctrine From the Bible to the Present* (Garden City, NY: Doubleday, 1963).

26. Sproul, "The Forensic Nature of Justification," 25.

27. R. C. Sproul, *Faith Alone: The Evangelical Doctrine of Justification* (Grand Rapids, MI: Baker, 1995), 73 (bracketed material added).

28. Sproul, "The Forensic Nature of Justification," 34.

29. Ibid., 36, 37.

30. Here are some sample statements from the Council of Trent's Decree on Justification. See Henry J. Schroeder, *Canons and Decrees of the Council of Trent* (London: Herder, 1941). Regarding justification *by faith alone*: "If anyone says that the sinner is justified by faith alone meaning that nothing else is required

to cooperate in order to obtain the grace of justification, and that it is not in any way necessary that he be prepared and disposed by the action of his own will, let him be anathema." Session 6, canon 9; Schroeder, *Canons*, 43. Canon 10 rejects the forensic nature of justification: "If anyone says that men are justified without the justice of Christ whereby He merited for us, or by that justice are formally just, let him be anathema." Ibid. Canon 11 insists that justification takes place via the infused righteousness of Christ, not His imputed righteousness: "If anyone says that men are justified either by the imputation of the righteousness of Christ alone or by the remission of sins alone, to the exclusion of the grace and love that is poured forth in their hearts by the Holy Spirit, and is inherent in them; or even that the grace by which we are justified is only the favor of God, let him be anathema." Cited in modern translation in John M. MacArthur, "Long Before Luther (Jesus and the Doctrine of Justification)," in Kistler, *Justification by Faith Alone*, 12. In chapter 7 of Trent's sixth session, justification is conflated with sanctification: "This disposition or preparation is followed by justification itself, which is not only a remission of sins but also the sanctification and renewal of the inward man through the voluntary reception of the grace and gifts whereby an unjust man becomes just." Schroeder, *Canons*, 33. In chapter 3, justification is seen as God not only pronouncing a man just but making him just: "If they were not born again in Christ, they would never be justified, since in that new birth there is bestowed upon them, through the merit of His passion, the grace by which they are made just." Schroeder, *Canons*, 30, 31. Finally, in chapter 9 of the Decree of Justification in the council, assurance of salvation is denied: "No one can know with the certainty of faith, which cannot be subject to error, that he has obtained the grace of God." Cited in Klaas Runia, "Justification and Roman Catholicism," in *Right With God: Justification in the Bible and the World*, ed. D. A. Carson (Eugene, OR: Wipf and Stock, 1992), 215.

31. Schreiner, *Faith Alone*, 66.

32. John H. Gerstner, "The Nature of Justifying Faith," in Kistler, *Justification by Faith Alone*, 114.

33. Ibid., 118.

34. John H. Gerstner, "Rome NOT Home," in Kistler, *Justification by Faith Alone*, 150.

35. Ibid., 150, 151.

36. Ibid., 151.

37. Scott Hahn and Kimberly Hahn, *Rome Sweet Home: Our Journey to Catholicism* (San Francisco: Ignatius Press, 1993).

38. Robert Gundry, "Why I Didn't Endorse the Gospel of Jesus Christ: An Evangelical Celebration," *Books and Culture* 7, no. 1 (January/February 2001), 9.

39. "Evangelicals and Catholics Together: Christian Mission in the Third Millennium," *First Things* 43 (May 1994): 15–22, https://www.firstthings.com/article/1994/05/evangelicals-catholics-together-the-christian-mission-in-the-third-millennium.

40. Sproul, "The Forensic Nature of Justification," 49.

41. "The Gift of Salvation," *First Things* 79 (January 1998): 20–23, http://www.leaderu.com/ftissues/ft9801/articles/gift.html.

42. Here are the relevant paragraphs from the document:

> Justification is central to the scriptural account of salvation, and its meaning has been much debated between Protestants and Catholics. We agree that justification is not earned by any good works or merits of our own; it is entirely God's gift, conferred through the Father's sheer graciousness, out of the love that he bears us in his Son, who suffered on our behalf and rose from the dead for our justification. Jesus was "put to death for our trespasses and raised for our justification" (Romans 4:25). In justification, God, on the basis of Christ's righteousness alone, declares us to be no longer his rebellious enemies but his forgiven friends, and by virtue of his declaration it is so.
>
> The New Testament makes it clear that the gift of justification is received through faith. "By grace you have been saved through faith; and this is not your own doing, it is the gift of God" (Ephesians 2:8). By faith, which is also the gift of God, we repent of our sins and freely adhere to the Gospel, the good news of God's saving work for us in Christ. By our response of faith to Christ, we enter into the blessings promised by the Gospel. Faith is not merely intellectual assent but an act of the whole person, involving the mind, the will, and the affections, issuing in a changed life. We understand that what we here affirm is in agreement with what the Reformation traditions have meant by justification by faith alone (*sola fide*).
>
> In justification we receive the gift of the

Holy Spirit, through whom the love of God is poured forth into our hearts (Romans 5:5). The grace of Christ and the gift of the Spirit received through faith (Galatians 3:14) are experienced and expressed in diverse ways by different Christians and in different Christian traditions, but God's gift is never dependent upon our human experience or our ways of expressing that experience.

43. "Joint Declaration on the Doctrine of Justification" may be accessed at http://www.vatican.va/roman_curia/pontifical_councils/chrstuni/documents/rc_pc_chrstuni_doc_31101999_cath-luth-joint-declaration_en.html. For discussion of this joint declaration, see, e.g., Henri A. Blocher, "The Lutheran-Catholic Declaration on Justification," in McCormack, *Justification in Perspective*, 197–217.

44. From the "Lutheran Church–Missouri Synod press release," October 15, 1999, quoted in Raoul Dederen, "The Joint Declaration on the Doctrine of Justification: One Year Later," *Ministry*, November 2000, 13, https://www.ministrymagazine.org/archive/2000/11/the-joint-declaration-on-the-doctrine-of-justification-one-year-later.

45. For a demonstration of how Catholics have not changed their views since Trent, see Schreiner, *Faith Alone*, 209–230; and Runia, "Justification and Roman Catholicism," 197–215. Most of the sections of the declaration differentiate between the Lutheran and the Catholic positions on respective points, even though there is an attempt to reconcile these differences. So, e.g., section 4.2 is entitled "Justification as Forgiveness of Sins and Making Righteous," the first part ("Forgiveness of Sins") being the Lutheran view, and the second ("Making Righteous") the Catholic view. *Notice again what is not affirmed by both: by faith alone, the imputed righteousness of Christ and forensic (only) justification, and personal assurance of salvation.* For a collection of all the main documents in the recent Protestant-Catholic rapprochement over the doctrine of justification and a sympathetic assessment, see, e.g., Anthony N. S. Lane, *Justification by Faith in Catholic-Protestant Dialogue: An Evangelical Assessment* (London: T & T Clark, 2002).

46. E. P. Sanders, *Paul and Palestinian Judaism: A Comparison of Patterns of Religion* (Philadelphia: Fortress Press, 1977).

47. James D. G. Dunn, "The New Perspective on Paul," *Bulletin of the John Rylands Library* 65 (1983): 95–

122. See his later works, especially *The New Perspective on Paul*, rev. ed. (Grand Rapids, MI: Eerdmans, 2008) and "New Perspective View," in Beilby and Eddy, *Justification: Five Views*, 176–201.

48. N. T. Wright, "The Paul of History and the Apostle of Faith," *Tyndale Bulletin* 29 (1978): 61–88. For his most comprehensive study, see N. T. Wright, *Justification: God's Plan and Paul's Vision* (Downers Grove, IL: IVP Academic, 2009).

49. Examples include (1) justification is forensic (a divine legal declaration) and not transformative (making someone righteous); (2) perfect obedience is needed to be right with God; and (3) God's wrath is propitiated by Jesus' death.

50. These emphases include, especially (1) the divine law court setting; (2) the big picture of the covenant and God's purpose for the descendants of Abraham; and (3) the eschatological dimension of justification (the final verdict is announced in advance). Schreiner provides good evidence for the conclusion that these "larger perspectives" of the new perspective harmonize with and enrich the Reformation view. *Faith Alone*, 239–264.

51. For this section, I am indebted not only to the writings of Sanders, Dunn, and Wright but also to those who have provided constructive critique of their views. See, in particular, Schreiner, *Faith Alone*, 239–261; John Piper, *The Future of Justification: A Response to N. T. Wright* (Wheaton, IL: Crossway, 2007); Mark A. Seifrid, *Christ, Our Righteousness: Paul's Theology of Justification*, New Testament Studies in Biblical Theology 9 (Downers Grove, IL: InterVarsity, 2000); Guy Prentiss Waters, *Justification and the New Perspectives on Paul: A Review and Response* (Phillipsburg, NJ: P & R, 2004); and Stephen Westerholm, *Justification Reconsidered: Rethinking a Pauline Theme* (Grand Rapids, MI: Eerdmans, 2013).

52. Sanders, *Paul and Palestinian Judaism*, 543 (emphasis in original).

53. See, e.g., Dunn, "New Perspective View," in Beilby and Eddy, *Justification: Five Views*, 189–195; Wright, *Justification*, 116–118. Cf. the critique by Schreiner, *Faith Alone,* 249–252.

54. See Dunn, "New Perspective View," 182, 183; Wright, *Justification*, 64–71.

55. N. T. Wright, *What Saint Paul Really Said: Was Paul of Tarsus the Real Founder of Christianity?* (Grand Rapids, MI: Eerdmans, 1997), 129, 125.

56. Summary by Schreiner, *Faith Alone*, 244. See also Wright, *Justification*, 195.

57. Wright, *What Saint Paul Really Said*, 98. For critique, see Schreiner, *Faith Alone*, 253–261.

58. Instead of imputation, Wright argues for the concept of representation: the Messiah *"represents* his people, now appropriately *standing in for them*, taking upon himself the death which they deserved, so that they might not suffer it themselves." *Justification*, 105.

59. See, e.g., Dunn, "New Perspective View," 196–198.

60. I have purposely not identified by name specific individuals or groups within this section of the chapter, because it is hoped that the focus will be upon the issues and not individuals or "camps" within Adventism. In this chapter, we do not address the view of some Adventists called "corporate" or "objective" or "universal" justification, which is seen to have taken place at the cross. This position calls for extended separate treatment and evaluation in another venue.

61. For an example of the rare instances where a biblical study on justification does give considerable emphasis to the Old Testament roots of Paul's doctrine of justification, see Edmond P. Clowney, "The Biblical Doctrine of Justification by Faith," in Carson, *Right With God*, 19–37.

62. I have developed and shown the biblical support for the conclusions in this section in an unpublished paper, "Righteousness—a Word Study." See also Willem A. VanGemeren, ed., *New International Dictionary of Old Testament Theology and Exegesis* (Grand Rapids, MI: Zondervan, 1997), s.v. "ts-d-q"; Moisés Silva, *New International Dictionary of New Testament Theology and Exegesis*, 2nd ed. (Grand Rapids, MI: Zondervan, 2014), s.v. *"dikaiosynē"*; Gerhard Kittel and Gerhard Friedrich, eds., *Theological Dictionary of the New Testament* (Grand Rapids, MI: Eerdmans, 2006), s.v. *"dik-"*; Edmond Jacob, *Theology of the Old Testament* (New York: Harper & Row, 1958), 94–102; and Schreiner, *Faith Alone*, 144–152, 158–178.

63. Ludwig Köhler et al., *The Hebrew and Aramaic Lexicon of the Old Testament* (New York: E. J. Brill, 1994), s.v. *"tsadaq"*; B. Johnson, in G. Johannes Botterweck and Helmer Ringgren, *Theological Dictionary of the Old Testament*, vol. 12 (Grand Rapids, MI: Eerdmans, 1974), s.v. *"tsadaq."*

64. Silva, *Dictionary of New Testament Theology*, s.v. *"dikaiosynē,"* 725, 735.

65. Sproul, "Forensic Nature of Justification," 28, 29; and Alister E. McGrath, *Justitia Dei* (Cambridge: Cambridge University Press, 1986), 1:30, 31.

66. Treatments of justification by faith generally do not focus attention upon the opening chapters of Genesis as already providing the essential contours of the message of justification by faith (albeit without the technical terminology). An exception is MacArthur, "Jesus and the Doctrine of Justification," 20, 21, although his comments are limited to one brief paragraph.

67. This solidarity indicated by the singular-collective fluidity of the term *'adam* also seems underscored by its explicit etymological linkage with the "ground." In Genesis 2:5, 7, the term [*ha*]*'adam* (once with and once without the article) denotes the human being who is at first not present to till and then is formed from the "ground" (*ha'adamah*). The linkage between [*ha*]*'adam* (human) and [*ha*]*'adamah* (ground) highlights corporative solidarity because in Genesis 2:6, 7 "ground" also refers to both localized "dust of the ground" from which Adam was made (verse 7) and to the universalized "whole face of the ground" (verse 6; cf. Genesis 7:23). Ellen G. White supports this interpretation of Adam's position with regard to humanity. She writes, "Under God, Adam was to stand at the *head* of the earthly family." *Counsels to Parents, Teachers, and Students* (Mountain View, CA: Pacific Press®, 1913), 33; and "The Sabbath was committed to Adam, the father and *representative* of the whole human family." *Patriarchs and Prophets* (Battle Creek, MI: Review and Herald®, 1890), 48.

68. For a succinct and insightful summary of Paul's usage of the concept of corporate solidarity, see C. H. Dodd, *The Epistle of Paul to the Romans* (London: Hodder and Stoughton, 1954), 78–83; and Herman Ridderbos, *Paul: An Outline of His Theology* (Grand Rapids, MI: Eerdmans, 1975), 57–64.

69. Many modern versions translate this phrase as "made sinners," but the Greek verb here is *kathistēmi* (aor. pass. 3pl), which in this context means "to be constituted." See John Murray, *The Epistle to the Romans*, New International Commentary on the New Testament (Grand Rapids, MI: Eerdmans, 1963), 204–206. Adam and all subsequent humanity receive a sinful nature and legally stand guilty before God.

70. See White, *Patriarchs and Prophets*, 61: "Their [Adam's and Eve's] nature had become depraved by sin"; and Ellen G. White Comments, in *The Seventh-day Adventist Bible Commentary*, ed. Francis D. Nichol, vol. 6 (Washington, DC: Review and Herald®, 1957), 1074: "As related to the first Adam, men receive from him nothing but guilt and the sentence of death."

71. Claus Westermann, *Creation*, trans. John J. Scullion (London: SPCK, 1974), 96.

72. In a penetrating doctoral dissertation, Afolarin Ojewole shows how in this central verse of the chapter the conflict narrows from many descendants (a collective "seed"; Hebrew: *zera'*) in the first part of the verse to a masculine singular pronoun in the last part of the verse: "He"—fighting against the serpent. Elsewhere in Scripture, whenever the term *seed* has a singular pronominal referent, it is a single "seed" (i.e., a single individual) who is in view. Afolarin Ojewole, "The Seed in Genesis 3:15: An Exegetical and Theological Study" (PhD diss., Andrews University, 2002), 190–207.

73. For support of these conclusions, see Ojewole, "The Seed in Genesis 3:15," 207–213.

74. Westermann, *Creation*, 95.

75. White, *Patriarchs and Prophets*, 57. It is not often recognized that Genesis 2 and 3 utilize two different Hebrew words for "naked." In Genesis 2:25, the word for "naked" is *'arom*, which elsewhere in Scripture frequently refers to someone not *fully* clothed or not clothed in the *normal* manner. In 1 Samuel 19:24, e.g., the term is "used of one who, having taken off his mantle, goes only clad in his tunic." Wilhelm Gesenius, *Gesenius' Hebrew and Chaldee Lexicon to the Old Testament Scriptures*, trans. Samuel P. Tregelles (Grand Rapids, MI: Eerdmans, 1949), 653. Again, in Isaiah 20:2, the reference is to one "dressed with *śaq* only." Ludvig Koehler and Walter Baumgartner, *Lexicon in Veteris Testamenti Libros*, 2nd ed. (Grand Rapids, MI: Eerdmans, 1958), 735; cf. John 21:7. Other passages employ the term in the sense of "ragged, badly clad" (Job 22:6; 24:7, 10; Isaiah 58:7). Gesenius, *Lexicon*, 653. Genesis 2:25 does not explicitly indicate in what way Adam and Eve were without clothes in the normal sense ("normal" from the post-Fall perspective), but the parallel Creation passage in Psalm 104 gives a hint. Psalm 104 follows exactly the same order as the Genesis Creation account and analyzes the point-by-point parallels between the two passages. In Psalm 104, along with the poetic description of God's creative *work*, there appears to be at least one indication of His *appearance*, or rather, His "clothing" (verses 1, 2): "You are clothed with honor and glory, who cover Yourself with light as with a garment." If God is portrayed as clothed with "garments" of light and glory, it is not unreasonable to deduce that man, created in the image and likeness of God both in outward resemblance and in character (as implied by the two terms "image," *tselem*, and "likeness," *demut*, in Genesis 1:26), is similarly clothed; namely, that Adam and Eve were originally "clothed" with "garments" of light and glory. If such is the case in Genesis 2:25, then the contrast with Genesis 3 becomes clear. In Genesis 3:7, 10, 11, the Hebrew word for "naked" is *'erom*, which elsewhere in Scripture always appears in a context of total (and usually shameful) exposure, describing someone as "utterly naked" or "bare" (cf. Ezekiel 16:7, 22, 39; 18:7, 16; 23:29; Deuteronomy 28:48). Gesenius, *Lexicon*, 625; Francis Brown, S. R. Driver, and Charles A. Briggs, *The Brown-Driver-Briggs Hebrew and English Lexicon* (Chicago: Snowball Publishing, 2010), 735, 736; Koehler and Baumgartner, *Lexicon in Veteris Testamenti Libros*, 702. As a result of sin, the human pair find themselves "utterly naked," bereft of the garments of light and glory, and they seek to clothe themselves with fig leaves.

76. In parallel with the burnt offering of Leviticus 1:5, 11 and the sin offering of Leviticus 4:29, the human sinners probably slaughtered the sacrificial animal themselves.

77. Ellen G. White Comments, in *The Seventh-day Adventist Bible Commentary*, ed. Francis D. Nichol, vol. 1 (Washington, DC: Review and Herald®, 1976), 1085.

78. See, e.g., Francis A. Schaeffer, *Genesis in Space and Time* (Downers Grove, IL: InterVarsity, 1975), 105, 106.

79. For further discussion of these points, see Richard M. Davidson, *Typology in Scripture: A Study of Hermeneutical Typos Structures*, Andrews University Seminary Doctoral Dissertation Series 2 (Berrien Springs, MI: Andrews University Press, 1981), 299–304; Seifrid, *Christ, Our Righteousness*, 70–74; Murray, *Romans*, 178–210. Some (such as Wright in the new perspective) would see in this Pauline passage (and its parallels such as 2 Corinthians 5:12–21) only representation and human solidarity and not imputation. But Murray rightly points out how representation and solidarity and imputation go together in Romans 5:19: "Our involvement cannot be that of personal voluntary transgression on our part. It can only be that of imputation, that by reason of representative unity the sin of Adam is reckoned to our account and therefore reckoned as ours. . . . The same principle of solidarity that appears in our relation to Adam, and by reason of which we are involved in his sin, obtains in our relation to Christ. And just as the relation to Adam means the imputation to us of his disobedience, so the relation to Christ means the imputation to us of his obedience." *Romans*, 205, 206.

80. Köhler et al., *Hebrew and Aramaic Lexicon*, s.v. "*khashab*."

81. Some scholars have suggested that Abraham is the subject throughout this entire verse; i.e., "Abraham believed the Lord and [Abraham] reckoned it [i.e., what the Lord had promised] to him [a manifestation of his] righteousness" (author's translation). But as pointed out by Johnson, "Elements militating against this view include especially the consecutive verb form and the divine name immediately before the verb 'and he reckoned,' where 'he' can more naturally refer to God." Botterwick and Ringgren, *Theological Dictionary of the Old Testament*, vol. 12, s.v. "*tsadaq*."

82. Fleming Rutledge, *Not Ashamed of the Gospel: Sermons From Paul's Letter to the Romans* (Grand Rapids, MI: Eerdmans, 2007), 115.

83. In the Hebrew Bible, the expression *'aman* (Hifil) plus the preposition *le*, "believe [to]," often implies only giving intellectual assent to something or someone, "regarding something [or someone] as trustworthy." Köhler et al., *Hebrew and Aramaic Lexicon*, s.v. "'*aman*" (cf. Exodus 4:8, 9; 1 Kings 10:7; Isaiah 53:1; Psalm 106:24; Proverbs 14:15; 2 Chronicles 9:6), whereas the same verb with the preposition *be*, as we have in Genesis 15:6, usually expresses the added relational idea of "having trust in." Ibid. (Cf. Exodus 14:31; Numbers 14:11; 20:12; Deuteronomy 1:32; 2 Kings 17:14; Jonah 3:5; Psalm 78:22; 2 Chronicles 20:20.)

84. See especially the discussion by Beeke, "Justification by Faith Alone," 53–105. Regarding Genesis 15:6, Paul (in Romans 4 and Galatians 3:6–14) makes clear that this verse does not support the notion that God reckons righteousness to Abraham because of some kind of creaturely merit in his faith (as we find claimed in Catholic theology) but as a free gift of God. When Paul states that God reckoned his faith "for [Greek: *eis*] righteousness" (Romans 4:5, 9, 22), the preposition *eis* does not denote "in the stead of" (implying it is the ground of righteousness) but "with a view to" or "toward" (implying it was the occasion and means of receiving the free gift of God's righteousness). Ibid., 55, 56. The three different Greek expressions in Paul's writings on justification translated as "by faith" also do not ever imply that faith is the ground of receiving righteousness. Romans 3:28 uses *pistei* (*pistos* in the dative) speaking of the "necessity and importance of faith." Romans 5:1 has *ek* [from, out of, by] *pisteos*, which "describes faith as the *occasion* of justification" but not its ultimate cause. Ephesians 2:8 uses *dia* [in the dative; through, by means of] *pisteos*, which "describes faith as the *instrument* of justifica-

tion." The Bible writers never use *dia* with the accusative (*dia ten pistin*) to describe faith, which would mean "on the ground of" or "on account of" and imply that faith was the ground of the righteousness. Ibid., 58–60. Beeke concludes, "Yet such is the precision of the Holy Spirit's oversight of the New Testament Scriptures that nowhere does any writer slip into using this prepositional phrase." Ibid., 60.

85. These verses not only use the phrase *pistis Christou* but also clearly speak of a person's faith in Christ as the instrument of justification: "We have believed in [*pisteuō* + *eis*] Christ Jesus, so that we may be justified" (Galatians 2:16, NASB); "to all . . . who believe" (Romans 3:22). For a discussion on whether to translate *pistis Iēsou Christou* (faith of Jesus Christ) as an objective genitive (faith in Jesus Christ) or as a subjective genitive (faithfulness of Jesus Christ) with the main arguments on either side, see Schreiner, *Faith Alone*, 124–132, who favors the traditional reading of "faith in Jesus Christ." Both readings are grammatically possible, and Paul may mean one in one context and the other in a different context, or even both may be implied in some cases. It need not be an either-or; both Christ's faithfulness and the believer's faith are involved in justification. But the overall Pauline message is unambiguous that the gospel calls for faith on the part of the believer in Jesus Christ for justification (e.g., Galatians 2:16).

86. See also how for Paul (e.g., Romans 4:17), "what makes faith salvific is the *object* of faith" (Schreiner, *Faith Alone*, 122), specifically focusing upon God's promises of salvation in the Messiah, faith in Jesus Christ. Ibid., 124–132.

87. See White, *Patriarchs and Prophets*, 137.

88. Note, e.g., the covenant made by the Assyrian king Assur-nerari V with the vassal Mati'-ilu. After Mati'-ilu divides a lamb, Assur-nerari V says, "This head is not the head of a spring lamb, it is the head of Mati'-ilu; it is the head of his sons, his nobles [and] the people of the land. If Mati'-ilu should sin against this treaty, just as the head of this ram is cut off, . . . so may the head of Mati'-ilu be struck off." Kenneth A. Kitchen and Paul J. N. Lawrence, *Treaty, Law and Covenant in the Ancient Near East, Part I: The Texts* (Wiesbaden: Harrassowitz Verlag, 2012), 940, 941; cf. James Pritchard, ed., *Ancient Near Eastern Texts Relating to the Old Testament*, 3rd ed. (Princeton: Princeton University Press, 1969), 532–534. For discussion and further examples, see Victor P. Hamilton, *The Book of*

Genesis: Chapters 1–17, New International Commentary on the Old Testament (Grand Rapids, MI: Eerdmans, 1990), 430–434.

89. Even though this is not explicitly mentioned, the possibility of Abram's passing through the pieces is not totally eliminated by the text. The vassal's vow of obedience was expected in the ancient Near Eastern covenant pattern, and Abram's action would also be parallel with Israel's vow to be obedient in the making of the Mosaic covenant (Exodus 19:5–8; 24:6, 7). If Abram passed through the pieces, this would not negate Paul's argument (Galatians 3:15–18) that the covenant of promise given to Abraham (which was really the content of Genesis 12, coming before Genesis 15, and was totally promissory!) preceded the covenant of obligation given to Israel through Moses some 430 years later. God's original intention was simply to give ten (covenant) promises to Abraham (eight are found in Genesis 12:1–3, and two more in Genesis 17:6, 7), based upon the eternal covenant between the Father and the Son in eternity (cf. Genesis 3:15; Isaiah 42:6; Zechariah 6:13; Revelation 13:8). But because of Abram's lack of faith (see Genesis 15:8), "the Lord condescended to enter into a covenant with His servant, employing such forms as were customary among men for the ratification of a solemn engagement. By divine direction, Abraham sacrificed a heifer, a she-goat, and a ram, each three years old, dividing the bodies and laying the pieces a little distance apart. To these he added a turtledove and a young pigeon, which, however, were not divided. This being done, he reverently passed between the parts of the sacrifice, making a solemn vow to God of perpetual obedience." White, *Patriarchs and Prophets*, 137. By focusing only upon the mysterious climax to the covenant making, with Yahweh's passing through the pieces, the text emphasizes the action of Yahweh as Suzerain, which was utterly unique among ancient Near Eastern covenants.

90. Cf. Genesis 16:7–11 with verse 13; Genesis 18:1 with verses 2, 33, and with Genesis 19:1; Genesis 31:11 with verse 13; Genesis 32:24, 30 with Hosea 12:3–6; Genesis 48:15 with verse 16; Exodus 3:2 with verses 4, 6, 7; and Exodus 13:21 with Exodus 14:19.

91. Ellen G. White, *Evangelism* (Washington, DC: Review and Herald®, 1946), 616.

92. See Donald J. Wold, "The Meaning of the Biblical Penalty *kareth*" (PhD diss., University of California, Berkeley, 1978).

93. See especially Ellen G. White, *The Desire of Ages*

(Mountain View, CA: Pacific Press®, 1940), 686, 753, 754; Ellen G. White, *The Faith I Live By* (Washington, DC: Review and Herald®, 1958), 101; Ellen G. White, *God's Amazing Grace* (Washington, DC: Review and Herald®, 1973), 170, 171.

94. See Richard M. Davidson, "New Testament Use of the Old Testament," *Journal of the Adventist Theological Society* 5, no. 1 (1994): 30, 31.

95. Bruce K. Waltke, *Genesis: A Commentary* (Grand Rapids, MI: Zondervan, 2001), 310, 311.

96. For more detailed analysis of this potent narrative, see Jo Ann Davidson, "Eschatology and Genesis 22," *Journal of the Adventist Theological Society* 11, nos. 1, 2 (2000): 232–247; and Jacques Doukhan, "The Center of the 'Aqedah: A Study of the Literary Structure of Genesis 22:1–19," *Andrews University Seminary Studies* 31, no. 1 (1993): 17–28.

97. For exegesis of the major biblical passages supporting penal substitution, see especially Steve Jeffery, Michael Ovey, and Andrew Sach, *Pierced for Our Transgressions: Rediscovering the Glory of Penal Substitution* (Wheaton, IL: Crossway, 2007); Norman R. Gulley, *Christ, Our Substitute* (Washington, DC: Review and Herald®, 1982), and Ángel Rodríguez, *Substitution in the Hebrew Cultus* (Berrien Springs, MI: Andrews University Press, 1982). For a particular treatment of Pauline passages, see Simon Gathercole, *Defending Substitution: An Essay on Atonement in Paul* (Grand Rapids, MI: Baker Academic, 2015).

98. For exegesis of these Pauline passages supporting imputation, see especially Brian Vickers, *Jesus' Blood and Righteousness: Paul's Theology of Imputation* (Wheaton, IL: Crossway, 2006); John Piper, *Counted Righteous in Christ: Should We Abandon the Imputation of Christ's Righteousness?* (Wheaton, IL: Crossway, 2002); Schreiner, *Faith Alone*, 182–189; and D. A. Carson, "The Vindication of Imputation: On Fields of Discourse and Semantic Fields," in *Justification: What's at Stake in the Current Debate?* ed. Mark A. Husbands and Daniel J. Treier (Downers Grove, IL: InterVarsity, 2004), 46–78.

99. Note the insightful comment by Clowney: "There are not two alternate ways of being accepted by God, but there are two figures by which acceptance is expressed: the verdict of God and the blessing of the priest. Both are found in the New Testament. In Romans, the language of the law-court is used to describe our justification; in Hebrews the language of the sanctuary includes the same truth." "Biblical Doctrine of Justification by Faith," 28, 29. In this chapter,

we focus upon the law court imagery (especially in our treatment of New Testament material); but in this section, we focus upon examples of sanctuary typology that teach the same truths.

100. For further discussion of Leviticus 4, see, e.g., Richard M. Davidson, *Song for the Sanctuary* (Berrien Springs, MI: Andrews University Press, forthcoming), chap. 12; and Roy E. Gane, *Cult and Character: Purification Offerings, Day of Atonement, and Theodicy* (Winona Lake, IN: Eisenbrauns, 2005), 45–213.

101. For a discussion of the accounted, declared righteousness involved here, refer to Hans K. LaRondelle, *Perfection and Perfectionism* (Berrien Springs, MI: Andrews University Press, 1971), 127, 128. See also Gerhard von Rad, *Old Testament Theology*, trans. D. M. G. Stalker (New York: Harper & Row, 1962), 1:247, 248, 261, 262. Instead of these "declaratory formulae" being recited by the priest, however, as LaRondelle and von Rad suggest, the Niphal (passive) verb suggests that these were "divine passives" declared by Yahweh Himself.

102. For details of construction, see Exodus 27:1–8; 38:1–7.

103. See Psalm 73:17. The psalmist sees the "end" of the wicked in the ashes. Psalm 20:3 has the offering "accepted," literally "reduced to ashes."

104. Ellen G. White, *Selected Messages*, bk. 1 (Washington, DC: Review and Herald®, 1958), 343, 344.

105. The word *tamid* can mean either "regular" or "continual," depending upon the context. In Numbers 28:3, it seems to emphasize the regularity of the burnt offering, thus translated in the NKJV as "regular [*tamid*] burnt offering." In Leviticus 6:13, the term seems to imply the continual burning of the sacrifice on the fire, thus translated by the NKJV as "perpetual [*tamid*] fire."

106. White, *Patriarchs and Prophets*, 352.

107. White, *Selected Messages*, bk. 1, 343, 344.

108. For details of construction and use, see Exodus 30:1–10; 37:25–28.

109. White, *Patriarchs and Prophets*, 353. Revelation 5:8; 8:3; and Psalm 141:2 reveal the mingling of this incense with the prayers of the saints. Numbers 16:47 adds the insight that incense provided atonement for the people.

110. White, *Patriarchs and Prophets*, 353.

111. Ibid., 348.

112. Ellen G. White, "The Sanctuary," *Signs of the Times*, June 24, 1880, 277. The ark was the first article of furniture mentioned in God's instructions to Moses regarding the sanctuary (Exodus 25:10–22).

113. The word *Shekinah* is a rabbinic term not used in Scripture, though often employed by Ellen G. White (*Patriarchs and Prophets*, 349; *Prophets and Kings* [Mountain View, CA: Pacific Press®, 1917], 18, etc.). It is the "glory of the Lord" that was enthroned above the mercy seat between the cherubim (Psalm 80:1). It filled the sanctuary after it was completed and set up by Moses (Exodus 40:34, 35), as it later filled the temple of Solomon (2 Chronicles 5:13, 14). But the glory departed during the apostasy of Zedekiah's reign (Ezekiel 11:22, 23) and never returned as a visible presence till Christ, the true Shekinah (White, *Prophets and Kings*, 18; Ellen G. White, *Christ's Object Lessons* [Washington, DC: Review and Herald®, 1941], 288), by entering the second temple five centuries later, brought greater glory to it than was enjoyed by the Solomonic temple (Haggai 2:9).

114. Note the blood of the Lord's goat that on the Day of Atonement was sprinkled on the mercy seat (Leviticus 16:15).

115. For substantiation of this interpretation of *hilasterion* in Romans 3:25 as "mercy seat," following the Septuagint translation of the Hebrew *kapporeth* and exposition of Romans 3:25, see Valentin Zywietz, "Representing the Government of God: Christ as the *Hilasterion* in Romans 3:25" (master's thesis, Andrews University, 2016).

116. For further discussion with biblical evidence, see especially Schreiner, *Faith Alone*, 244–249.

117. See especially D. A. Carson, Peter T. O'Brien, and Mark A. Seifrid, eds., *Justification and Variegated Nomism*, 2 vols. (Grand Rapids, MI: Baker Academic, 2001, 2004). "It would be naïve, however, to think that in mainstream Jud., and particularly in the popular imagination, good deeds were not regarded as meritorious. . . . Although there was no well-defined and consistent doctrine on the subject among the rabbis, the evidence suggests that, in the minds of many, merits were indeed weighed against demerits, and that those who had accumulated a preponderance of the former were deemed righteous." Silva, *Dictionary of New Testament Theology and Exegesis*, s.v. "*dikaiosynē*."

118. See, e.g., Schreiner, *Faith Alone*, 249–252; Waters, *Justification and the New Perspective*, 158–170. Waters shows how, e.g., in Romans 11:5, 6, Paul "contrasts grace and works in such a way that they are mutually exclusive" so that "works" cannot be taken in an

ethnic sense but must mean "anything that human beings do." *Justification and the New Perspective*, 159. Waters also examines other Pauline passages regarding "works" in relation to justification (Romans 4:4–6; 9:30–32; 10:5; Philippians 3:2–11; Titus 3:5; Ephesians 2:9; 2 Timothy 1:9; Galatians 3:10–13; 5:3, 4) with the same conclusion that "works" in these passages do not refer to Jewish identity markers, as claimed by proponents of the new perspective, but to "human activity," and in the Jewish context, "Jews' efforts to achieve a state of righteousness by the activity of obedience to the law." Ibid., 158, 159.

119. See also the typology of the high priest's miter or turban in Exodus 28:38, where the high priest is said to "bear the iniquity of the holy things which the children of Israel hallow in all their holy gifts." As Tim Arena comments,

> It is not willful sin or acts of rebellion against God that the high priest is said to be bearing (though of course these are included elsewhere) when he יָשָׂא אָשֹׁן [bears the iniquities] of the Israelites. It is rather said to occur when they are offering their "holy gifts"—that is, in all of their participation in the sanctuary service—there is iniquity which must be borne and atoned for even when they are doing what God has asked them to do. All human beings are sinful even when they are doing what God has asked them to do, because all have sinful, defiled natural depravity from birth that taints everything (Ps. 51:5; Eph. 2:3; Gen. 8:21; Prov. 22:15; Jer. 17:9; Rom. 7:14–23) ("The Holy Attire of the High Priest and His Role in Bearing Guilt: An Exegetical Examination of Exodus 28:29–38" [unpublished paper, Andrews University Theological Seminary, 2016], 12).

120. For the New Testament references to Isaiah 53, see especially Michael J. Wilkins, "Isaiah 53 and the Message of Salvation in the Four Gospels," in Darrell L. Bock and Mitch Glaser, eds., *The Gospel According to Isaiah 53: Encountering the Suffering Servant in Jewish and Christian Theology* (Grand Rapids, MI: Kregel Academic, 2012), 109–132; and Craig A. Evans, "Isaiah 53 in the Letters of Peter, Paul, Hebrews, and John," in Bock and Glaser, *The Gospel According to Isaiah 53*, 145–170. Quotations and echoes of Isaiah 52:13–53:12 by Paul include Romans 15:21 and 1 Corinthians 2:9 (Isaiah 52:15;

64:4); Romans 10:15, 16 (Isaiah 53:1; 52:7); Romans 4:25 (Isaiah 53:4, 5); 1 Corinthians 5:7 (Isaiah 53:7); 1 Corinthians 15:3 (Isaiah 53:8, 9); and Romans 5:19 (Isaiah 53:11). Besides those listed by Evans, we note in particular the allusions to Isaiah 53:6, 9, in 2 Corinthians 5:21, which will be discussed more later.

121. For a deeper study of the aspects of substitutionary atonement and components of the doctrine of justification in this Servant Song, see especially Bock and Glaser, *The Gospel According to Isaiah 53*; KyeSang Ha, "Cultic Allusions in the Suffering Servant Poem (Isaiah 52:13–53:12)," (PhD diss., Andrews University, 2009); Jeffery, Ovey, and Sach, *Pierced for Our Transgressions*, 52–67; F. Duane Lindsey, *The Servant Songs: A Study in Isaiah* (Chicago: Moody, 1985); J. Alec Motyer, *The Prophecy of Isaiah: An Introduction and Commentary* (Downers Grove, IL: InterVarsity Press, 1993), 442, 443; and Edward J. Young, *The Book of Isaiah*, vol. 3 (Grand Rapids, MI: Eerdmans, 1972), 334–359.

122. Evans, "Isaiah 53 in the Letters of Peter, Paul, Hebrews, and John," 161.

123. For further discussion of 2 Corinthians 5:12–21 and its teaching of the imputation of sin to Christ and of His righteousness to the believer, see, e.g., Piper, *Counted Righteous in Christ*, 68, 69; Schreiner, *Faith Alone*, 186–188, 258, 259; Waters, *Justification and the New Perspective*, 177–179.

124. Murray J. Harris, *The Second Epistle to the Corinthians: A Commentary on the Greek Text*, The New International Greek Testament Commentary (Grand Rapids, MI: Eerdmans, 2005), 455.

125. Schreiner, *Faith Alone*, 180. Wright writes, "If Paul uses the language of the law court, it makes no sense whatever to say that the judge imputes, imparts, bequeaths, conveys or otherwise transfers his righteousness either to the plaintiff or the defendant." *What Saint Paul Really Said*, 98. Again, "The judge has not clothed the defendant with his own 'righteousness.' That doesn't come into it. Nor has he given the defendant something called 'the righteousness of the Messiah'—or, if he has, Paul has not even hinted at it. What the judge has done is to pass judicial sentence on sin, in the faithful death of the Messiah, so that those who belong to the Messiah, though in themselves 'ungodly' and without virtue or merit, now find themselves hearing the law court verdict, 'in the right.'" Wright, *Justification*, 206.

126. Schreiner, *Faith Alone*, 260. Schreiner aptly points out that

Wright leads us astray when he says that because justification is a legal declaration, it is not based on one's moral character.... Wright fails to state clearly the role that moral character plays in justification, and because he separates moral character from the law court, he fails to see the role that Christ's righteousness plays in imputation. When a judge in Israel declared a person to be innocent or guilty, he did so on the basis of the moral innocence or guilt of the defendant [Deuteronomy 25:1]....

... The fundamental question is how God can declare sinners to be righteous.... The answer of Scripture is that the Father because of his great love sent his Son, who willingly and gladly gave himself for sinners, so that the wrath that sinners deserved was poured out upon the Son (cf. Romans 3:24–26). God can declare sinners to be in the right because they are forgiven by Christ's sacrifice. God vindicates his *moral righteousness* in the justification of sinners since Christ takes upon himself the punishment and wrath sinners deserve (Ibid., 259).

Wright claims that his view of "representation" is adequate to accomplish what the traditional view of imputation seeks to express, but these need not be exclusive, as we have noted in our earlier comments on Romans 5:21 and 2 Corinthians 5:21. Christ's work encompasses both representation and imputation.

127. Sproul summarizes the Catholic view: "Rome rejects this notion of imputed forensic justification on the grounds that it involves God in a 'legal fiction.' This casts a shadow on the integrity of God and His justice. They claim that for God to consider someone just who is not inherently just is for God to be involved in some sort of fictional deceit. Rome cannot tolerate Luther's dictum, *simul justus et peccator*. For Rome a person is either just or sinner, one cannot be both at the same time. For Rome only the truly just can ever be declared to be just by God." "The Forensic Nature of Justification," 37, 38.

128. Ibid., 39.

129. Gerstner, "The Nature of Justifying Faith," 114.

130. See especially Ronald Y. K. Fung, " 'Justification' in the Epistle of James," in Carson, *Right With God*, 146–162.

131. See especially MacArthur, "Jesus and the Doctrine of Justification," 1–22. MacArthur states that

"although Christ made no *formal* explication of the doctrine of justification (such as Paul did in his epistle to the Romans), justification by faith under lay and permeated all His gospel preaching. While Jesus never gave a discourse on the subject, it is easy to demonstrate from Jesus' evangelistic ministry that He taught *sola fide*." Ibid., 15. MacArthur points to Jesus' statements that "he who hears My word and believes ... has passed out of death unto life" (John 5:24), and the experience of the thief on the cross (Luke 23:24) who did no work to procure justification. He further points to Jesus' various healings where He states that "your *faith* has made you well" (Matthew 9:22; cf. Mark 5:34; 10:52; Luke 8:48; 17:19; 18:42). But there is one passage—Luke 18:9–14—where "Jesus actually declared some 'justified' and this passage provides the best insight into the doctrine as He taught it." Ibid., 16. MacArthur shows how the basic features of the doctrine of justification by faith are present in this parable of the Pharisee's and tax collector's prayers. These are my own arranging of his points: (1) it is by faith alone, as the Pharisees "trusted in themselves that they were righteousness" (verse 9), while the penitent tax collector simply threw himself upon God's mercy and went away justified without performing any works; (2) it is an instantaneous judicial pronouncement of God, not a process; (3) the tax collector acknowledged his unrighteousness and that even his best works were sin; (4) he went home justified, implying that the righteousness of Another had been imputed to him (as in Philippians 3:9; Romans 4:9–11); and (5) justification was essentially forgiveness or pardon of the sinner. Ibid., 16–20. At the same time, Jesus also uses the term *justification* for the time of the final judgment when all will be justified according to their works (see especially Matthew 12:36, 37 and the next endnote). For further discussion of the role of faith in salvation according to Jesus, the Gospel writers, and Acts, see Schreiner, *Faith Alone*, 113–120.

132. There is not space in this study to deal extensively with the role of obedience as an evidence of the genuineness of one's faith in the final eschatological judgment. I have dealt with this in a paper entitled "Final Justification According to Works: Is N. T. Wright Right?" presented at the ETS Annual Convention, November 19, 2010. There are some Pauline passages that seem to refer to the acquittal at the final judgment using the term *justification*, and this "final justification" is according to works (see especially Romans 2:13: "For it is not the hearers of the Law who are

just before God, but the doers of the Law will be justified" [*dikaiōthēsontai*, from the verb *dikaioō*; NASB). Jesus also speaks of the final judgment as "justification": "But I tell you that every careless word that people speak, they shall give an accounting for it in the day of judgment. For by your words you will be justified [*dikaiōthēsē*], and by your words you will be condemned" (Matthew 12:36, 37, NASB). Scores of passages in Pauline writings and elsewhere in Scripture indicate that the final judgment will be "according to works" (see Davidson, "Final Justification According to Works," 4–10, where I cite some thirty passages in the writings of Paul, some twenty passages elsewhere in the New Testament, and some twenty-five representative Old Testament passages). Ivan Blazen summarizes well my own conclusion:

> The Bible teaches that justification belongs to the "last things," for it brings the hoped-for verdict of acquittal in the last judgment into the present. . . . Though the blessing of acquittal in the future judgment indeed becomes operative even now, Scripture is clear that what God desires to see in the final judgment is justified believers who through His grace have borne fruit to His glory. . . . The new history God gives each believer is not over when he comes to Christ and is justified; it is just begun. At the end God asks for justification with its fruit—*not in the sense of the formula "Faith plus works saves,"* but in the sense that justification is the source of sanctified fruit. . . . The cross is the means by which justification is effected; faith is the means by which justification is accepted; and good works are the means by which justification is manifested. Works of righteousness [in the final judgment] testify to the reality and vitality of justification (Ivan T. Blazen, "Justification and Judgment," in *The Seventy Weeks, Leviticus, and the Nature of Prophecy*, ed. Frank B. Holbrook [Washington, DC: Biblical Research Institute, 1986], 339–388nn364, 387).

In the final judgment, works of faith in the life of the Christian provide the evidence that one's faith is genuine. But the ultimate ground of one's acceptance in the judgment is not the believer's Spirit-enabled works but the righteousness of Christ. Blazen emphatically concludes, "While the character of Christ can

be imitated and approximated, the infinite character of His goodness can never be equaled. Consequently, two things must remain true for the [final] judgment: (1) the sanctified fruit of justification must be present, but (2) justification itself must continue its function of pardon." Ibid., 367.

133. Köhler et al., *Hebrew and Aramaic Lexicon of the Old Testament*, s.v. "*'emunah.*"

134. R. M. Moody, "The Habakkuk Quotation in Romans 1:17," *Expositor Times* 92, no. 7 (1981): 205–208.

135. See Rahel Schafer and Paul Petersen, *Habakkuk*, Seventh-day Adventist International Bible Commentary (Nampa, ID: Pacific Press®, forthcoming). The citation of Habakkuk 2:4 by Paul does not precisely follow either the Hebrew text or the Septuagint. It appears that Paul not only wishes to capture the two meanings just mentioned—justification by faith and the faithfulness of the justified—but also to indicate that according to the original meaning of Habakkuk, it is the Messiah's own faith and faithfulness that is ultimately the basis of both our justification and our sanctification.

136. We have seen that the traditional view of justification upheld by the Reformers has in general been confirmed by examining the biblical evidence. Ellen G. White attests, "The great doctrine of justification by faith" was "clearly taught by Luther." *The Great Controversy*, 253. This is not to deny that new insights into this doctrine have been forthcoming since the sixteenth-century Reformation. In this chapter, we have had occasion to interact briefly with the claims of the new perspective on Paul, specifically concerning the aspects of the traditional Reformation view on justification that are rejected by proponents of this perspective. In sum, we have found that the new perspective rightly provides a broader context to the doctrine of justification, but we have also seen that this perspective is often problematic in what is rejected from the traditional view, which usually results from "false polarities" that are drawn. See especially Schreiner's summary of Wright's three main false polarities (*Faith Alone*, 244): "First, he wrongly says that justification is primarily about ecclesiology instead of soteriology. Second, he often introduces a false polarity when referring to the mission of Israel by saying that Israel's fundamental problem was its failure to bless the world whereas Paul focuses on Israel's inherent sinfulness. Third, he insists that justification is a declaration of God's righteousness but does not include the imputation of God's righteousness." Each of these "false

polarities" has been briefly treated in our discussions. See ibid., 243–261.

137. In the endnotes (and occasionally in the main text) of this conclusion, we cite sample passages from Ellen G. White's writings that emphasize the various points that have emerged from the Scriptures regarding justification.

138. Ellen G. White, MS 91, 1899.

139. Ellen G. White often defines justification in terms of "pardon." Of the more than fifty references, here is a sample: "As the penitent sinner, contrite before God, discerns Christ's atonement in his behalf and accepts this atonement as his only hope in this life and the future life, his sins are pardoned. This is justification by faith." *Faith and Works*, 103. "Justification is a full, complete pardon of sin. The moment a sinner accepts Christ by faith, that moment he is pardoned. The righteousness of Christ is imputed to him, and he is no more to doubt God's forgiving grace." *The Faith I Live By*, 107, quoted in Nichol, *Seventh-day Adventist Bible Commentary*, 6:1071; "Faith and Good Works," *Signs of the Times*, May 19, 1898). "When God pardons the sinner, remits the punishment he deserves, and treats him as though he had not sinned, He receives him into divine favor, and justifies him through the merits of Christ's righteousness." Ellen G. White, *A New Life* (Washington, DC: Review and Herald®, 1972), 20. "Pardon and justification are one and the same thing." In Nichol, *Seventh-day Adventist Bible Commentary*, 6:1070. Ellen G. White also defines justification in more general terms: "What is justification by faith? It is the work of God in laying the glory of man in the dust, and doing for man that which it is not in his power to do for himself. When men see their own nothingness, they are prepared to be clothed with the righteousness of Christ." *The Faith I Live By*, 111. Again, "The great work that is wrought for the sinner who is spotted and stained by evil is the work of justification. By Him who speaketh truth he is declared righteous. The Lord imputes unto the believer the righteousness of Christ and pronounces him righteous before the universe. He transfers his sins to Jesus, the sinner's representative, substitute, and surety. Upon Christ He lays the iniquity of every soul that believeth. 'He hath made him to be sin for us, who knew no sin; that we might be made the righteousness of God in him.' 2 Corinthians 5:21." Ibid., 112.

140. "Pardon and justification are one and the same thing. Through faith, the believer passes from the position of a rebel, a child of sin and Satan, to the position of a loyal subject of Christ Jesus, *not because of an inherent goodness*, but because Christ receives him as His child by adoption. The sinner receives the forgiveness of his sins, because these sins are borne by his Substitute and Surety. The Lord speaks to His heavenly Father, saying: 'This is My child. I reprieve him from the condemnation of death, giving him My life insurance policy—eternal life—because I have taken his place and have suffered for his sins. He is even My beloved son.' Thus man, pardoned, and clothed with the beautiful garments of Christ's righteousness, stands faultless before God." Ellen G. White, *Reflecting Christ* (Hagerstown, MD: Review and Herald®, 1985), 74; Ellen G. White, *Manuscript Releases*, vol. 9 (Silver Spring, MD: Ellen G. White Estate, 1990), 301 (emphasis added).

141. "Righteousness is obedience to the law. The law demands righteousness, and this the sinner owes to the law; but he is incapable of rendering it. The only way in which he can attain to righteousness is through faith. By faith he can bring to God the merits of Christ, and the Lord places the obedience of His Son to the sinner's account. Christ's righteousness is accepted in place of man's failure, and God receives, pardons, justifies, the repentant, believing soul, treats him as though he were righteous, and loves him as He loves His Son. This is how faith is accounted righteousness." White, *Selected Messages*, bk. 1, 367. "It is the Father's prerogative to forgive our transgressions and sins, because Christ has taken upon Himself our guilt and reprieved us, imputing to us His own righteousness. His sacrifice satisfies fully the demands of justice." White, *Faith and Works*, 103, 104. "It is the righteousness of Christ that makes the penitent sinner acceptable to God and works his justification. However sinful has been his life, if he believes in Jesus as his personal Saviour, he stands before God in the spotless robes of Christ's imputed righteousness." Ibid., 106.

Through the imputed righteousness of Christ, the sinner may feel that he is pardoned, and may know that the law no more condemns him, because he is in harmony with all its precepts. It is his privilege to count himself innocent when he reads and thinks of the retribution that will fall upon the unbelieving and sinful. By faith he lays hold of the righteousness of Christ. . . . Knowing himself to be a sinner, a transgressor of the holy law of God, he looks to the perfect obedience of Christ, to His death upon Calvary for the sins of the world; and he has the assurance that he is justified by faith in the merit and sacrifice of Christ. He realizes that the law was obeyed in his behalf by the Son of God, and that the penalty of transgression cannot fall upon the believing sinner. The active obedience of Christ clothes the believing sinner with the righteousness that meets the demands of the law (Ellen G. White, *Sons and Daughters of God* [Washington, DC: Review and Herald®, 1955], 240).

142. It is true that there is language of "as if" and "as though." "Sinners can be justified by God only when He pardons their sins, remits the punishment they deserve, and treats them *as though* they were really just and had not sinned, receiving them into divine favor and treating them *as if* they were righteous." Ellen G. White, *Our High Calling* (Washington, DC: Review and Herald®, 1961), 52 (emphasis added). But this does not make justification a "legal fiction." "Having made us righteous through the imputed righteousness of Christ, God pronounces us just, and treats us as just. He looks upon us as His dear children." White, *The Faith I Live By*, 112. We are truly "made righteous," even though not inherently, because Christ's righteousness has truly been imputed to us, and God treats us as righteous "in Christ." "For He made Him who knew no sin to be sin for us, that we might become the righteousness of God in Him" (2 Corinthians 5:21).

143. Some interpret the following statement to mean that justification includes transformation of heart as well as a declaration of acquittal or pardon: "God's forgiveness is not merely a judicial act by which He sets us free from condemnation. It is not only forgiveness *for* sin, but reclaiming *from* sin. It is the outflow of redeeming love that transforms the heart." Ellen G. White, *Thoughts From the Mount of Blessing* (Oakland, CA: Pacific Press®, 1896), 114 (emphasis in original). But the context of this passage is Jesus' sermon on the mount, and Ellen G. White comments on Jesus' statement "forgive us our sins; for we also forgive everyone who is indebted to us" (Luke 11:4), making the point that "we can receive forgiveness from God only as we forgive others." Ibid., 113. White is not saying that justification includes faith plus works but only that justifying faith is a working faith. One cannot receive forgiveness (jus-

tification) without at the same time receiving a forgiving spirit (sanctification).

God's justification (pardon) is not cheap grace, leading to antinomianism or a life of cherished sin. Ellen G. White is clear: "But while God can be just, and yet justify the sinner through the merits of Christ, no man can cover his soul with the garments of Christ's righteousness while practicing known sins, or neglecting known duties. God requires the entire surrender of the heart, before justification can take place; and in order for man to retain justification, there must be continual obedience, through active, living faith that works by love and purifies the soul." White, *Selected Messages*, bk. 1, 366.

144. "Let the subject be made distinct and plain that it is not possible to effect anything in our standing before God or in the gift of God to us through creature merit. Should faith and works purchase the gift of salvation for anyone, then the Creator is under obligation to the creature. Here is an opportunity for falsehood to be accepted as truth. If any man can merit salvation by anything he may do, then he is in the same position as the Catholic to do penance for his sins. Salvation, then, is partly of debt, that may be earned as wages. If man cannot, by any of his good works, merit salvation, then it must be wholly of grace, received by man as a sinner because he receives and believes in Jesus. It is wholly a free gift. Justification by faith is placed beyond controversy. And all this controversy is ended, as soon as the matter is settled that the merits of fallen man in his good works can never procure eternal life for him." White, *Faith and Works*, 19, 20.

145. For the phrase "empty hands of faith," see Ellen G. White, "Feeding the Five Thousand," *Signs of the Times*, August 19, 1897, para. 14. This phrase is also used often by the Reformers.

146. "There is nothing in faith that makes it our saviour. Faith cannot remove our guilt. Christ is the power of God unto salvation to all them that believe. The justification comes through the merits of Jesus Christ—He has paid the price for the sinner's redemption. Yet it is only through faith in His blood that Jesus can justify the believer." White, *The Faith I Live By*, 107. "Faith is the condition upon which God has seen fit to promise pardon to sinners; not that there is any virtue in faith whereby salvation is merited, but because faith can lay hold of the merits of Christ, the remedy provided for sin. Faith can present Christ's perfect obedience instead of the sinner's transgres-

sion and defection. When the sinner believes that Christ is his personal Saviour, then, according to His unfailing promises, God pardons his sin, and justifies him freely. The repentant soul realizes that his justification comes because Christ, as his substitute and surety, has died for him, is his atonement and righteousness." White, *Selected Messages*, bk. 1, 366, 367.

147. Ellen G. White writes that "many commit the error of trying to define minutely the fine points of distinction between justification and sanctification. Into the definitions of these two terms they often bring their own ideas and speculations. Why try to be more minute than is Inspiration on the vital question of righteousness by faith?" *The Faith I Live By*, 116, quoted in Nichol, *Seventh-day Adventist Bible Commentary*, 6:1072. Some take this quotation as supporting a definition of justification that includes sanctification, thus blurring the distinction between the two. But the context of this passage (found in its entirety in MS 21, 1891, published in *Manuscript Releases*, 9:293–302) is Ellen G. White's caution directed toward those who had not attended the full ministerial Bible School session in 1891 and who expressed "fear that there was danger of carrying the subject of justification by faith altogether too far, and of not dwelling enough on the law." *Manuscript Releases*, 9:293. In response to these fears, White wrote, "Judging from the meetings that I had been privileged to attend, I could see no cause for alarm; and so I felt called upon to say that this fear was cherished by those who had not heard all the precious lessons given, and that therefore they were not warranted in coming to such a conclusion." Ibid. Immediately after stating her caution against some trying to "define minutely the fine points of distinction between justification and sanctification," Ellen G. White proceeds to give one of her most profound portrayals of the nature of justification and its relation to sanctification:

As the penitent sinner, contrite before God, discerns Christ's atonement in his behalf, and accepts this atonement as his only hope in this life and the future life, his sins are pardoned. This is justification by faith. Every believing soul is to conform his will entirely to God's will, and keep in a state of repentance and contrition, exercising faith in the atoning merits of the Redeemer, and advancing from strength to strength, from glory to glory.

Pardon and justification are one and the same thing. Through faith, the believer passes from the position of a rebel, a child of sin and Satan, to the position of a loyal subject of Christ Jesus, not because of an inherent goodness, but because Christ receives him as His child by adoption. The sinner receives the forgiveness of his sins, because these sins are borne by his Substitute and Surety. The Lord speaks to His heavenly Father, saying: "This is My child. I reprieve him from the condemnation of death, giving him My life-insurance policy—eternal life—because I have taken his place and have suffered for his sins. He is even My beloved son." Thus man, pardoned, and clothed with the beautiful garments of Christ's righteousness, stands faultless before God.

The sinner may err, but he is not cast off without mercy. His only hope, however, is repentance toward God and faith in the Lord Jesus Christ. It is the Father's prerogative to forgive our transgressions and sins, because Christ has taken upon Himself our guilt and reprieved us, imputing to us His own righteousness. His sacrifice satisfies fully the demands of justice.

Justification is the opposite of condemnation. God's boundless mercy is exercised toward those who are wholly undeserving. He forgives transgressions and sins for the sake of Jesus, who has become the propitiation for our sins. Through faith in Christ, the guilty transgressor is brought into favor with God and into the strong hope of life eternal (Ibid., 9:301, 302).

148. "The righteousness by which we are justified is imputed; the righteousness by which we are sanctified is imparted. The first is our title to heaven, the second is our fitness for heaven." White, *The Faith I Live By*, 116; Ellen G. White, "Qualifications for the Worker," *Advent Review and Sabbath Herald*, June 4, 1895, 353. Some have taken the following statement from Ellen G. White as implying that part of the grounds for our salvation is Christ's imparted righteousness: "Our only ground of hope is in the righteousness of Christ imputed to us, and in that wrought by His Spirit working in and through us." Ellen G. White, *Steps to Christ* (Washington, DC: Review and Herald®, 1956), 63. But the context is describing justification and sanctification, and the preceding paragraphs make clear that the only basis for our justification is Christ's imputed

righteousness: "If you give yourself to Him, and accept Him as your Saviour, then, sinful as your life may have been, for His sake you are accounted righteous. Christ's character stands in place of your character, and you are accepted before God just as if you had not sinned." White, *Steps to Christ*, 62. The next paragraph describes the work of sanctification: "More than this, Christ changes the heart." Ibid. The work of the Holy Spirit in transforming our lives is evidence that our justification by faith is real and thus gives us hope (see Romans 5:1, 2), but it is never the basis of our justification, because our works, even done in the power of the Holy Spirit, always "fall short of the glory of God" (Romans 3:23) and need the covering blood of Christ's atonement mingled with the incense of His righteousness. White, *Selected Messages*, bk. 1, 344.

149. Note how Ellen G. White's classic statement on justification and sanctification (without using those terms), begins: "If you give yourself to Him, and accept Him as your Saviour, then . . ." *Steps to Christ*, 62. This is language describing the union with Christ, from which union flows both justification and sanctification, described in the succeeding paragraphs after this introductory statement. Ibid., 62, 63.

150. "Through the provision Christ has made by taking the punishment due to man, we may be reinstated in God's favor, being made partakers of the divine nature. If we repent of our transgression, and receive Christ as the Life-giver, our personal Saviour, we become one with him, and our will is brought into harmony with the divine will. We become partakers of the life of Christ, which is eternal. We derive immortality from God by receiving the life of Christ for in Christ dwells all the fulness of the Godhead bodily. This life is the *mystical union* and cooperation of the divine with the human." Ellen G. White, "The Life and Light of Men," *Signs of the Times*, June 17, 1897, 5 (357) (emphasis added); cf. Ellen G. White, *Maranatha* (Washington, DC: Review and Herald®, 1976), 302.

151. Ellen G. White, *Selected Messages*, bk. 2 (Washington, DC: Review and Herald®, 1958), 32, 33. We may "give ourselves to Christ and *know* that He accepts us." White, *Christ's Object Lessons*, 155 (emphasis added).

Through the imputed righteousness of Christ, the sinner *may feel that he is pardoned*, and may

know that the law no more condemns him, because he is in harmony with all its precepts. It is his privilege to *count himself innocent* when he reads and thinks of the retribution that will fall upon the unbelieving and sinful. By faith he lays hold of the righteousness of Christ. . . . Knowing himself to be a sinner, a transgressor of the holy law of God, he looks to the perfect obedience of Christ, to His death upon Calvary for the sins of the world; and he has the *assurance that he is justified by faith in the merit and sacrifice of Christ*. He realizes that the law was obeyed in his behalf by the Son of God, and that the penalty of transgression cannot fall upon the believing sinner. The active obedience of Christ clothes the believing sinner with the righteousness that meets the demands of the law (White, *Sons and Daughters of God*, 240; emphasis added).

152. White, *Christ's Object Lessons*, 155 (emphasis added).

153. "When He sees men lifting the burdens, trying to carry them in lowliness of mind, with distrust of self and with reliance upon Him, He adds to their work His perfection and sufficiency, and it is accepted of the Father. We are accepted in the Beloved. The sinner's defects are covered by the perfection and fullness of the Lord our Righteousness. Those who with sincere will, with contrite heart, are putting forth humble efforts to live up to the requirements of God, are looked upon by the Father with pitying, tender love; He regards such as obedient children, and the righteousness of Christ is imputed unto them." Ellen G. White, *In Heavenly Places* (Washington, DC: Review and Herald®, 1967), 23.

154. White, *Patriarchs and Prophets*, 352.

155. White, *Selected Messages*, bk. 1, 344.

156. White, *Steps to Christ*, 62.

157. White, *Selected Messages*, bk. 2, 32, 33.

158. White, *Christ's Object Lessons*, 155; cf. *Selected Messages*, bk. 1, 314.

159. White, *Selected Messages*, bk. 1, 356.

160. Ibid.

161. Ellen G. White, *Testimonies to Ministers and Gospel Workers* (Mountain View, CA: Pacific Press®, 1923), 456.

5

Sanctification and Perfection Are the Work of a Lifetime

Denis Fortin

> *And the very God of peace sanctify you wholly; and I pray God*
> *your whole spirit and soul and body be preserved blameless*
> *unto the coming of our Lord Jesus Christ.*
> —1 Thessalonians 5:23, KJV[1]

When the concept of sanctification is discussed among Seventh-day Adventists, one brief statement of Ellen G. White usually comes in fairly quickly. As early as 1875, and repeated numerous times in other writings afterward, she stated, "Sanctification is not a work of a day or a year, but of a lifetime."[2]

The Seventh-day Adventist understanding of sanctification is briefly mentioned in the last half of Fundamental Belief 10, "The Experience of Salvation."

In infinite love and mercy God made Christ, who knew no sin, to be sin for us, so that in Him we might be made the righteousness of God. Led by the Holy Spirit we sense our need, acknowledge our sinfulness, repent of our transgressions, and exercise faith in Jesus as Saviour and Lord, Substitute and Example. This saving faith comes through the divine power of the Word and is the gift of God's grace. Through Christ we are justified, adopted as God's sons and daughters, and delivered from the lordship of sin. Through the Spirit we are born again and sanctified; the Spirit renews our minds, writes God's law of love in our hearts, and we are given the power to live a holy life. Abiding in Him we become partakers of the divine nature and have the assurance of salvation now and in the judgment.[3]

The statement enumerates a number of key concepts linked together in one's personal experience of salvation; concepts that are important in order to understand the theological context of the Adventist view of sanctification. The experience of salvation originates first in the love and mercy of God, who in Christ graciously saves humanity. The Holy Spirit initiates the first steps of salvation by bringing about a conviction of sin, then a response of repentance and faith—all of these are the gifts of God's grace and not by any means meritorious human works. The next concepts refer to the experience of salvation: repentant sinners are justified, adopted into God's family, delivered from the power of sin, born again, sanctified, and renewed in the Spirit. Although statement 10 lacks precision and clarity in this respect, sanctification can be understood as subsequent to justification and adoption. With the experience of the new birth, one begins the lifelong process of sanctification, which includes the spiritual renewing of our minds, the writing of God's law of love in our hearts, the reception of a spiritual power to live a holy life, and the process of becoming partakers of Christ's divine nature. The statement is silent about perfection.

Although this statement appears to be simple and clear, Seventh-day Adventists are often confused in their understanding of the importance and place of sanctification in one's salvation; and like many in other denominations, Adventists often misunderstand the relationship between salvation, justification, sanctification, and perfection. Some are closer to a Lutheran understanding, others are Wesleyan, and some are very close to a Catholic expression of the relationship between justification and sanctification.[4]

Admittedly, much of the confusion among Seventh-day Adventists stems also from an emphasis on keeping the commandments of God as a demonstration of one's love for God (see John 14:15). One end-time scenario in Adventist eschatology clearly states that the seal of God (Revelation 7:3, 4) is given only to those who keep the Sabbath and all of God's commandments.[5] Hence, is obedience a requisite for one's salvation? Are we saved by faith *and* obedience? What level of good must such obedience attain in order to qualify as a condition for salvation? How "perfect" and faultless must one's obedience and sanctification be in order for a person to be saved? Much confusion about obedience, sanctification, and perfection arises from a perspective that is called last generation theology (LGT).

Last generation theology teaches that perfect obedience is necessary to ensure one's salvation and that salvation is forfeited without this kind of obedience. "Obedience is both a condition for salvation and an ongoing requirement of salvation."[6] The role of human free will is crucial in this scheme and dominates the narrative, but it is an understanding of free will seemingly unbridled and untainted by the sinful nature, or at least so robust that one can will oneself to overcome sinfulness. Last generation theology teaches that just as Jesus was able to make all the right decisions in His life, a repentant sinner can also make all the right decisions and perfectly obey God's will. While "we cannot possibly keep the commandments of God without the regenerating grace of Christ," a true Christian "must be obedient in order to be saved, but my obedience is not in itself sufficient to save me. Jesus died for me on the cross, and He made a sacrifice of sufficient value to save me, but I must actively embrace His sacrifice. The question of salvation is not alone about the sufficiency of the sacrifice but also about my willingness to embrace it."[7] Notice carefully the subtleties in this argumentation. The sacrifice of Jesus on the cross is not sufficient to save a person unless that person fully embraces it by living a life of perfect obedience. The sacrifice of Jesus is said to be of "sufficient value to save me," but it is not said to be of complete sufficiency and merit. In subtle ways, LGT affirms the insufficiency of Christ's sacrifice and the added value of one's obedience to the experience of salvation. Such obedience is unmistakably meritorious. In no uncertain terms, LGT upholds a Pelagian view of the human condition and the nature of sin, and it denies the complete sufficiency of Christ's sacrifice to save humanity and effectively win the great controversy. This view teaches that human beings must do something, even though it is claimed to be by God's grace and by faith, in order to be saved and for the universe finally to be redeemed from sin. In fact, as the title of Herbert Douglass's book *God at Risk* suggests, humans are saving God from failure; Christ's sacrifice on the cross is not sufficient to declare victory over the forces of evil.

The LGT perspective is clear about the role of obedience, sanctification, and perfection in one's salvation: without perfect obedience, there cannot be salvation. Sanctification and obedience are not so much the *fruit* of justification and salvation as they are the *cause* of salvation—as much as is God's forgiveness of sin. The implications of this view lead directly to a Pelagian legalism that, in time in one's spiritual journey, destroys all hope and assurance of salvation. In my pastoral ministry, I have seen this over and over in the lives of faithful Christians to whom I have ministered.

This chapter will elaborate a more balanced and coherent Seventh-day Adventist understanding of sanctification and perfection in the context of other key doctrines, such as the human condition, justification by grace through faith, and the role of obedience in sanctification and perfection. We will also address some of the distortions advocated by LGT.

God's love and the human condition[8]

As we have seen already, the Christian doctrine of salvation begins with the concept of God's love. A well-known passage of John's Gospel, during the dialogue between Jesus and Nicodemus, has given the context of humanity's salvation: "For God so loved the world, that He gave His only begotten Son, that whoever believes in Him shall not perish, but have eternal life" (John 3:16). God's primary disposition of love in Christ is to save humanity, and all who believe will be saved by grace through faith.[9]

Yet things are not simple. The human condition since the fall of Adam and Eve has complicated things, and human beings cannot save themselves. Paul in his epistle to the Romans portrays a grim picture of humanity's predicament in its natural state:

> "There is none righteous, not even one;
> There is none who understands,
> There is none who seeks for God;
> All have turned aside, together they have become useless;
> There is none who does good,
> There is not even one." . . .

For all have sinned and fall short of the glory of God (Romans 3:10–12, 23).

Ellen G. White states that at creation humanity "was originally endowed with noble powers and a well-balanced mind. . . . But through disobedience, his [Adam's] powers were perverted. . . . His nature became so weakened through transgression that it was impossible for him, in his own strength, to resist the power of evil."[10] What was said of Adam immediately after the Fall became much more dire for his descendants. "It is impossible for us, of ourselves, to escape from the pit of sin in which we are sunken. Our hearts are evil, and we cannot change them."[11]

Consequently, only God's grace can intervene and make salvation possible. Adventists refer to God's intervention in human life in ways similar to Wesley's concept of prevenient grace.[12] Prevenient grace is God's universal work of grace upon all human beings to draw or call them to Him (cf. John 1:9; 12:32). It is God who, taking the first step in humanity's salvation, yearns over lost humanity and desires to bring people back to Him. As Ellen G. White stated in a similar way, God's "grace alone can quicken the lifeless faculties of the soul, and attract it to God, to holiness."[13] The Adventist theology of original sin, or sinful nature, is similar to that of Wesley and other Arminian theologians who affirm a universal total depravity of human nature inherited since the fall of Adam and Eve[14] and the total inability to save oneself. The sinful nature, with its inherent power of sin, alienates and separates human beings from God—all human beings are born lost and in need of a Savior.[15] God's initial step of prevenient grace is given to all human beings to restore in them a measure of free will, enough to respond to God's invitation to salvation (see Jeremiah 31:3; John 1:9).

Justification by grace through faith

As with God's primary disposition of love, the human sinful condition, and the concept of prevenient grace, Adventist thought on salvation also reflects a Wesleyan-Arminian perspective when it comes to justification and sanctification. Adventists understand justification to be God's forgiveness of the penalty for sins because Christ's sacrifice paid this penalty and changes the sinner's status from sinner to righteous on account of Christ's righteousness that is imputed to the forgiven sinner when he or she believes this promise of God. This is Paul's thought in Romans 3:21–4:8, where he explicitly joins together the concepts of justification, faith, forgiveness, and the imputation (or crediting) of Christ's righteousness.

In 1890, Ellen G. White stated, "Justification is wholly of grace and not procured by any works that fallen man can do,"[16] and added a year later, "As the penitent sinner, contrite before God, discerns Christ's atonement in his behalf and accepts this atonement as his only hope in this life and the future life, his sins are pardoned. This is justification by faith."[17] With words reminiscent of Wesley's thought in one of his sermons, White also declared, "Pardon and justification are one and the same thing. Through faith, the believer passes from the position of a rebel, a child of sin and Satan, to the position of a loyal subject of Christ Jesus, not because of an inherent goodness, but because Christ receives him as His child by adoption. The sinner receives the forgiveness of his sins, because these sins are borne by his Substitute and Surety. . . . Thus man, pardoned, and clothed with the beautiful garments of

Christ's righteousness, stands faultless before God."[18] For her, "justification is the opposite of condemnation,"[19] and "however sinful has been his life, if he [the sinner] believes in Jesus as his personal Saviour, he stands before God in the spotless robes of Christ's imputed righteousness."[20] Ellen G. White had no hesitation to accept the forensic nature of justification by faith and the imputation of Christ's merits to the repentant sinner: "Christ's character stands in place of your character, and you are accepted before God just as if you had not sinned."[21] Furthermore, she categorically affirmed the all-sufficiency of Christ's sacrifice on the cross, to which nothing can be added to save a human being.

Sanctification by grace through faith

With these preliminary concepts in mind, we can now discuss sanctification. While justification is a divine declaration of forgiveness, graciously given to repentant sinners on the basis of the imputation of Christ's righteousness, sanctification is the work of God's grace in repentant sinners to restore in them the image of God.[22] This work of sanctification is not instantaneous; it is "the work of a lifetime."[23] In *The Acts of the Apostles*, White also stated,

> Sanctification is not the work of a moment, an hour, a day, but of a lifetime. It is not gained by a happy flight of feeling, but is the result of constantly dying to sin, and constantly living for Christ. Wrongs cannot be righted nor reformations wrought in the character by feeble, intermittent efforts. It is only by long, persevering effort, sore discipline, and stern conflict, that we shall overcome. We know not one day how strong will be our conflict the next. So long as Satan reigns, we shall have self to subdue, besetting sins to overcome; so long as life shall last, there will be no stopping place, no point which we can reach and say, I have fully attained. Sanctification is the result of lifelong obedience.[24]

The distinction and link between justification and sanctification are important: one is either justified or not, while one is being progressively sanctified. Wesley explains that at the time a person is justified, "in that very moment, sanctification begins. . . . From the time of our being 'born again' the gradual work of sanctification takes place."[25] Justification and sanctification are thus considered in relation to the righteousness of Christ and one's readiness for heaven; justification is imputed righteousness and entitles one to heaven, while sanctification is imparted righteousness and prepares one for heaven.[26]

The English words *saint*, *sanctification*, *sanctify*, *holy*, and *holiness* come from the same root words: from the Hebrew *qadoš* and from the Greek *hagios*. The basic biblical meaning of *qadoš* and *hagios* is "to set apart," "to be separate," and "belonging to God." Thus, in this sense, the Old Testament speaks of a "holy day" (Isaiah 58:13), "holy bread" (1 Samuel 21:4, NKJV), and God's "holy mountain" (Ezekiel 20:40). The primary reference point is God, who is holy and from whom other things get their holiness (cf. Leviticus 11:44; 20:3; Hosea 11:9; Isaiah 6:3; 1 Peter 1:16).

When applied to God's people, sanctification is the continuing work of God in the life of the believer, making the person actually holy, separated from the world, more and more dedicated and consecrated to the service of God. First Peter 2:9 speaks of the believer's separation from the world: "But you are a chosen people, a royal priesthood, a holy nation, God's special possession" (NIV). In John 17:17, Jesus alludes to growth in knowledge and obedience to God's word as the work of sanctification: "Sanctify them by Your truth. Your word is truth" (NKJV). Entire consecration to God and spiritual growth are the intent of Paul's words to the Thessalonians: "And the very God of peace sanctify you wholly; and I pray God your whole spirit and soul and body be preserved blameless unto the coming of our Lord Jesus Christ" (1 Thessalonians 5:23, KJV). And in the epistle to the Galatians, Paul reminds his readers of their lifelong commitment to growth: "But I say, walk by the Spirit, and you will not carry out the desire of the flesh. . . . If we live by the Spirit, let us also walk by the Spirit" (Galatians 5:16, 25). Sanctification is thus a process by which one's life is brought into conformity with one's legal status before God. It is a continuation of what has begun at the new birth (or regeneration)—at the moment of justification when one's sins are forgiven.

Thus, according to Millard Erickson, there are four significant contrasts between justification and sanctification: (1) justification is an instantaneous occurrence, complete in a moment, whereas sanctification is a process requiring an entire lifetime for completion; (2) one is either justified or not, whereas one is progressively sanctified; (3) justification is a forensic declaration of forgiveness and imputation of Christ's righteousness, whereas sanctification is an actual lifelong transformation of the character of the person through the impartation of Christ's righteousness and character; and (4) justification is an objective work affecting our standing before God, whereas sanctification is a subjective work affecting our inner person.[27]

The lingering presence of sin

In order to prevent an unhealthy focus on obedience and legalism, the Christian doctrine of sanctification must be articulated in the context of a crucial aspect of the human condition: the lingering presence of inherited sin and its power inhabiting the human heart and mind (i.e., the self or the ontological nature of human beings). Luther had a statement for this concept: *simul justus et peccator*, "at once justified and sinner." The inclination to sin we have inherited, with which we struggle, remains in the human nature of believers; and the regenerated Christian continues to live with a sinful nature that can cause, and is the source of, temptations until Christ changes the human nature at the moment of glorification (1 Corinthians 15:50–57). As we will see next, the new birth provides a spiritual power that enables us to no longer be controlled by this sinful power.

A number of passages in Paul's epistles explain this relationship between justification in Christ and regeneration, between still being sinful human beings and yet not being controlled by the old self. The Holy Spirit is given to renew our minds and bodies to live according to our new status in Christ, but the struggles with the old nature remain, and one can never speak of total sinlessness or of being without sin (1 John 1:8). In Ellen G. White's words, "We cannot say, 'I am sinless,' till this vile body is changed and fashioned like unto His glorious body."[28]

Paul admonishes the Philippians to "do nothing from selfishness or empty conceit, but with humility of mind regard one another as more important than yourselves" (Philippians 2:3). Selfishness, the basic element of sinful human nature, is still present in a Christian's life but need not control or direct one's life. In the epistle to the Galatians, Paul states, "I say, walk by the Spirit, and you will not carry out the desire of the flesh." "If we live by the Spirit, let us also walk by the Spirit" (Galatians 5:16, 25). The implication of Paul's understanding of human nature is clear: the inner sinful desires of human nature are still present in the believer and are battling for supremacy.[29]

Three other passages similar to Galatians 5 confirm that our human self is still affected by a sinful, selfish, and perverted nature that is battling against the things of God, but that the regeneration of the Holy Spirit brings a transformation and new disposition. In Colossians, Paul states, "Therefore consider the members of your earthly body as dead to immorality, impurity, passion, evil desire, and greed, which amounts to idolatry. For it is because of these things that the wrath of God will come upon the sons of disobedience, and in them you also once walked, when you were living in them. But now you also, put them all aside: anger, wrath, malice, slander, and abusive speech

from your mouth" (Colossians 3:5–8). A similar thought is expressed in Ephesians 4: "In reference to your former manner of life, you lay aside the old self, which is being corrupted in accordance with the lusts of deceit, and that you be renewed in the spirit of your mind, and put on the new self, which in the likeness of God has been created in righteousness and holiness of the truth" (verses 22–24).

In Romans 8 as well, we read of the lingering presence of sin in the believer's nature:

> However, you are not in the flesh but in the Spirit, if indeed the Spirit of God dwells in you. . . . If Christ is in you, though the body is dead because of sin, yet the spirit is alive because of righteousness. But if the Spirit of Him who raised Jesus from the dead dwells in you, He who raised Christ Jesus from the dead will also give life to your mortal bodies through His Spirit who dwells in you.
>
> So then, brethren, we are under obligation, not to the flesh, to live according to the flesh—for if you are living according to the flesh, you must die; but if by the Spirit you are putting to death the deeds of the body, you will live (verses 9–13).[30]

It is explicit in these statements that this side of heaven, our human nature remains ontologically sinful and depraved. A proper understanding of the human condition prevents the adoption of teachings that encourage human obedience as a necessary condition for one's salvation. Nothing that we do is holy or perfect enough to merit or even cause our salvation. All that human beings do, however good and righteous it may be, is tainted by selfishness and sin, and therefore stands before God "as filthy rags" (Isaiah 64:6, KJV).

But Paul mentions in a number of his letters that believers are not left on their own to struggle with the lingering presence of sin. The Holy Spirit renews our minds and gives us the power to live holy lives.

The Holy Spirit and regeneration to new life

In His conversation with Nicodemus, Jesus said emphatically, "You must be born again" (John 3:7). This new birth is the result of the action of the Holy Spirit in a person's life (verses 5–8). Regeneration, or new birth, is the salvific strength of God made available to all who believe. It is the empowerment by the Holy Spirit to obey God's will. This spiritual empowerment partially undoes the total inability we are born with; it provides spiritual vigor to allow us to overcome the human selfishness and desire for supremacy that we inherited and which are at the root of all human sins. The inclination to sin we have inherited, the inner man of Romans 7 with which we struggle, remains in the hearts of believers in Christ, but its power is no longer controlling them. As this statement in *Steps to Christ* highlights, a new spiritual power is given at the new birth: "If the heart has been renewed by the Spirit of God, the life will bear witness to the fact. While we cannot do anything to change our hearts or to bring ourselves into harmony with God; while we must not trust at all to ourselves or our good works, our lives will reveal whether the grace of God is dwelling within us. A change will be seen in the character, the habits, the pursuits. The contrast will be clear and decided between what they have been and what they are."[31]

We are reminded that justification does something *for* us. Our sins are forgiven; Christ's righteousness is imputed (or credited) to us; we are restored to divine favor and adopted into God's family; and we have a new status in the eyes of God. On a day-to-day basis, the justifying grace of God continues to cover us with Christ's robe of righteousness, and we receive forgiveness of the sins we repent of as the Holy Spirit continues to convince us of sin, mistakes, and weaknesses in our lives. We continue to stand before God as if we had never sinned. On the other hand, sanctification does something *in* us. At the moment of justification, we begin a new life in Christ. The Holy Spirit gives an inward power to overcome temptations and the lingering presence of sin through the impartation of Christ's righteousness. This is the beginning of the restoration of the image of God. Speaking of Wesley's understanding of regeneration, Kenneth Collins states, the "new birth marks the beginning not simply of an incremental change, not merely one of degree, but a qualitative change that issues in a distinct kind of life, a life that men and women cannot bring about by themselves."[32] Writing about the relationship between justification and sanctification, Adventist theologian Hans K. LaRondelle spoke of an effective justification—our justification in Christ naturally leads to the indwelling of Christ in the heart of the believer.[33]

The fruits of this regeneration are evidences of the work of the Holy Spirit. There is love of God and love of neighbor (Luke 10:26, 27) and obedience to the commandments of God (1 John 5:3). Regeneration is a reorientation of human nature. While original sin orients us toward sin and rebellion, the new birth reorients us toward obedience and holiness. The new birth is an inward change, not an outward one. It is a spiritual change, not a natural one. It is not the entirety of sanctification but only its beginning.

In the chapter "Growing Up Into Christ" in *Steps to Christ*, Ellen G. White presents her understanding of sanctification and how one grows in Christ after being justified. Christian growth and sanctification are comparable to the life of a plant. As God first gives life to a plant when the seed germinates, it is also God who continues to give life to the plant as it grows. Never is the plant capable of making itself grow. So it is only through the gift of God that spiritual life is formed in our lives, and thus growth results.[34] In order to grow, Christians are invited to "abide in Christ," for it is only as one is dependent on Christ that one receives power to resist temptation or to grow in grace. "You are just as dependent upon Christ, in order to live a holy life, as is the branch upon the parent stock for growth and fruitfulness. Apart from Him you have no life."[35]

To those who misunderstand that justification is by faith but that sanctification is dependent on human obedience, White states categorically that such an approach to spiritual growth will fail. "Many have an idea that they must do some part of the work alone. They have trusted in Christ for the forgiveness of sin, but now they seek by their own efforts to live aright. But every such effort must fail."[36] Once we remind ourselves of Jesus' words "without me ye can do nothing" (John 15:5, KJV), we understand that all aspects of Christian growth are dependent on our union with Christ and, as such, are by faith. We are justified by faith, and we are sanctified by faith. "It is by communion with Him, daily, hourly,—by abiding in Him,—that we are to grow in grace. He is not only the Author, but the Finisher of our faith. It is Christ first and last and always. He is to be with us, not only at the beginning and the end of our course, but at every step of the way."[37] Such a moment-by-moment dependence on Christ for continued spiritual growth excludes the value of human effort. In fact, in harmony with her view of the depravity of human nature, which still remains a hindrance to spiritual life and growth even after conversion and justification, Ellen G. White remarks, "The religious services, the prayers, the praise, the penitent confession of sin ascend from true believers as incense to the heavenly sanctuary, but passing through the corrupt channels of humanity, they are so defiled that unless purified by blood, they can never be of value with God."[38]

One of White's best expressions of this spiritual regeneration to new life is from an article she wrote in 1901, shortly after arriving back in the United States after living for nine years in Australia:

There are those who listen to the truth. . . . [A]nd they repent of their transgressions. Relying upon the merits of Christ, exercising true faith in Him, they receive pardon for sin. As they cease to do evil and learn to do well, they grow in grace and in the knowledge of God. . . . The warfare is before them, . . . fighting against their natural inclinations and selfish desires, bringing the will into subjection to the will of Christ. Daily they seek the Lord for grace to obey Him, and they are strengthened and helped. This is true conversion. In humble, grateful dependence he who has been given a new heart relies upon the help of Christ. He reveals in his life the fruit of righteousness. He once loved himself. Worldly pleasure was his delight. Now his idol is dethroned, and God reigns supreme. The sins he once loved he now hates. Firmly and resolutely he follows in the path of holiness.[39]

Obedience and good works

While it is clear in Scripture that works, even righteous works, do not merit salvation for anyone, there is still a valid biblical teaching about obedience and good works. It is faith in the merits of Christ's sacrifice that leads to justification, and justification must and will invariably and effectively produce good works in the life of the new person. Paul affirms this to the Ephesians: "For by grace you have been saved through faith; and that not of yourselves, it is the gift of God; not as a result of works, so that no one may boast. For we are His workmanship, created in Christ Jesus for good works, which God prepared beforehand so that we would walk in them" (Ephesians 2:8–10). And in Philippians, "So then, my beloved,

just as you have always obeyed, not as in my presence only, but now much more in my absence, work out your salvation with fear and trembling; for it is God who is at work in you, both to will and to work for His good pleasure" (Philippians 2:12, 13).

In the Old Testament, we are told that Abraham obeyed God and kept His commandments, statutes, and laws (Genesis 26:5). Even the Ten Commandments were spoken to the people of Israel in the context of God's love and deliverance from Egypt. God first delivered His people and then gave them His commandments (Exodus 20:1, 2). This command to obey God is repeated many times in the New Testament by Jesus (John 14:15, 21; 15:10, 12; 1 John 5:3), the apostle Paul (Romans 13:8–10; Galatians 5:14), and James (James 2:8–12). Believers are therefore certainly asked to obey God's will for their lives as revealed in Scripture, yet such obedience is never the *condition* of their salvation, which rests only in the sacrifice of Jesus. But obedience is always the undeniable and evident fruit of salvation.

The most evident transformation in the life of a person is the work of the Holy Spirit. In Galatians, Paul paints a vivid contrast between life lived in the Spirit and life lived in the flesh: "For the flesh sets its desire against the Spirit, and the Spirit against the flesh; for these are in opposition to one another, so that you may not do the things that you please. . . . Now the deeds of the flesh are evident, which are: immorality, impurity, sensuality, idolatry, sorcery, enmities, strife, jealousy, outbursts of anger, disputes, dissensions, factions, envying, drunkenness, carousing, and things like these, of which I forewarn you, just as I have forewarned you, that those who practice such things will not inherit the kingdom of God" (Galatians 5:17–21). The absence of the work of the Holy Spirit is manifested in the various works of the flesh (the natural human being), but in contrast, the fruit of the Spirit brings new dispositions, qualities, and character virtues (the regenerated human being):

> But the fruit of the Spirit is love, joy, peace, patience, kindness, goodness, faithfulness, gentleness, self-control; against such things there is no law. Now those who belong to Christ Jesus have crucified the flesh with its passions and desires.
>
> If we live by the Spirit, let us also walk by the Spirit (verses 22–25).

Ellen G. White affirmed this Protestant understanding of the relationship between faith and obedience. She stated in a sermon in Switzerland in 1885, "Faith and works go hand in hand; they act harmoniously in the work of overcoming. Works without faith are dead, and faith without works is dead [James 2:26]. Works will never save us; it is the merit of Christ that will avail in our behalf. Through faith in Him, Christ will make all our imperfect efforts acceptable to God. The faith we are required to have is not a do-nothing faith; saving faith is that which works by love and purifies the soul."[40]

Two other statements from White's writings are worth noticing at this point in our study. In a manuscript written at the time of a pastors' meeting in Battle Creek

in 1890, she discussed the dangers of false ideas about justification by faith. Obedience and good works will always remain important, but never enough to be necessary for our salvation. Note carefully her thoughts and how it is dangerous to even insinuate that our obedience proves anything:

> Should faith and works purchase the gift of salvation for anyone, then the Creator is under obligation to the creature. Here is an opportunity for falsehood to be accepted as truth. If any man can merit salvation by anything he may do, then he is in the same position as the Catholic to do penance for his sins. Salvation, then, is partly of debt, that may be earned as wages. If man cannot, by any of his good works, merit salvation, then it must be wholly of grace, received by man as a sinner because he receives and believes in Jesus. It is wholly a free gift. Justification by faith is placed beyond controversy. And all this controversy is ended, as soon as the matter is settled that the merits of fallen man in his good works can never procure eternal life for him.[41]

The Lord Jesus imparts all the powers, all the grace, all the penitence, all the inclination, all the pardon of sins, in presenting His righteousness for man to grasp by living faith—which is also the gift of God. If you would gather together everything that is good and holy and noble and lovely in man and then present the subject to the angels of God as acting a part in the salvation of the human soul or in merit, the proposition would be rejected as treason. . . .

Christ for our sakes became poor, that we through His poverty might be made rich. And any works that man can render to God will be far less than nothingness. My requests are made acceptable only because they are laid upon Christ's righteousness. The idea of doing anything to merit the grace of pardon is fallacy from beginning to end. . . .

Man can achieve no praiseworthy exploits that give him any glory.[42]

The conclusions are clear that obedience to God, although required of the believer, is never to be considered a condition for one's salvation. Such an argument insinuates that human obedience adds something to Christ's all-sufficient sacrifice. All human obedience, however good and wholesome it may be, is tainted by human selfishness and merits nothing in the eyes of God.

Character development and perfection

Christian perfection is also a biblical teaching to be discussed with sanctification, but it is one that Greek philosophy has undoubtedly twisted. There is an inherent view of perfection that owes much to Aristotelian philosophy, with its objective understanding of perfection as something totally and absolutely free of errors, mistakes, mishaps, or anything short of an idealist and faultless view of perfect behavior and attitudes.[43] Christian teaching about perfection easily makes the mistake of adopting a

view of perfection that is more Aristotelian than biblical—a view that teaches sinless behavior (free from all moral errors, faultless) and even sinless nature (an ontological human nature so sanctified by regeneration that it no longer has any traces of the lingering presence of sin).[44]

In the Sermon on the Mount, Jesus affirmed the concept of perfection. At the end of a forthright discussion of how a believer's personal relationships ought to be shaped by the law of God, He concluded with a far-reaching statement: "Therefore you are to be perfect, as your heavenly Father is perfect" (Matthew 5:48). This statement has often been interpreted within an Aristotelian framework to say that human behavior ought to be exactly as perfect and faultless as God's behavior. Such an interpretation is misguided and not contextual. In Matthew 5, Jesus discusses the deeper meaning and intent of the law of God and how it ought to direct people's lives. And the last example He gives is about love for one's neighbor (verses 43–47). God's love for people, whether they deserve it or not, is the example for people to follow. In this sense, Jesus invites His listeners to love others as perfectly as the Father does. How God relates to people is the ideal for Jesus' disciples to follow, and this ideal is to be adapted to different cultures and customs.

The Greek word *telos*, translated as "perfect" in most Bible translations, also means "mature," "fulfilled," and "complete." This biblical meaning of perfection is far from the Aristotelian perspective; rather it is about loving others and having human relationships that exemplify maturity and completeness within our sphere as God does in His sphere.[45] Never are we to try to live our lives within God's sphere or domain. That is totally unrealistic. Yet many people interpret the passage in this way and, as another chapter in this book discusses, this causes many people to suffer from unrealistic expectations leading to discouragement. We are not asked to be faultless, but we are asked to be mature in our relationships with others and to seek more maturity and completeness in ways that reflect how God relates to humanity. A focus on perfect and faultless behavior leads to an unhealthy preoccupation with oneself as well.[46]

Paul also discusses the concept of perfection in his letter to the Philippians. Is biblical perfection a state of being we attain in this life, or, like sanctification, is it a process of Christian growth? Is perfection about perfect and faultless behavior, or is it about mature character?

> More than that, I count all things to be loss in view of the surpassing value of knowing Christ Jesus my Lord, for whom I have suffered the loss of all things, and count them but rubbish so that I may gain Christ, and may be found in Him, not having a righteousness of my own derived from the Law, but that which is through faith in Christ, the righteousness which comes from God on the basis of faith, that I may know Him and the power of His resurrection and the fellowship of His sufferings, being conformed to His death; in order that I may attain to the resurrection from the dead.
>
> Not that I have already obtained it or have already become perfect, but I press on so that I may lay hold of that for which also I was laid hold of by Christ Jesus. Brethren, I do not regard myself as having laid hold of it yet; but one thing I do: forgetting what lies behind and reaching forward to what lies ahead, I press on toward the goal for the prize of the upward call of God in Christ Jesus. Let us therefore, as many as are perfect, have this attitude; and if in anything you have a different attitude, God will reveal that also to you; however, let us keep living by that same standard to which we have attained (Philippians 3:8–16).

Note the active verbs Paul uses in this passage. Clearly, he had not yet attained perfection; he was striving toward that goal in Christ Jesus. For Paul, perfection is a process just like sanctification, because the concept he teaches is about maturity and growth in the Christian's life. It is about character development, which is a process that also goes on throughout one's lifetime. Woodrow Whidden comments on this passage: "Paul's definition is that if any believer is growing in grace, advancing in union with Christ, he or she can be declared to be perfect."[47]

Since the process of sanctification is often invisible and imperceptible in one's life; it is therefore misguided to speak of perfectionism or of the possibility of attaining a sinless life on this earth. In fact, Ellen G. White gave a caution to those who teach perfectionism: "The closer you come to Jesus, the more faulty you will appear in your own eyes."[48] "Christ is our pattern, the perfect and holy example that has been given us to follow. We can never equal the pattern; but we may imitate and resemble it according to our ability."[49] She also clearly declared, "We cannot say, 'I am sinless,' till this vile body is changed and fashioned like unto His glorious body."[50]

Yet White spoke of the possibility of character perfection in one's life, which is to be carefully distinguished from perfectionism.[51] Commenting on the parable of the talents in Matthew 25, she wrote,

A character formed according to the divine likeness is the only treasure that we can take from this world to the next. . . .

The heavenly intelligences will work with the human agent who seeks with determined faith that perfection of character which will reach out to perfection in action.[52]

In fact, that perfection of character is a reflection of the loving character of God. As servants of God become more and more like Christ, they receive "the Spirit of Christ—the Spirit of unselfish love and labor for others." As a result, she concluded, "your love [will] be made perfect. More and more you will reflect the likeness of Christ in all that is pure, noble, and lovely."[53] George Knight comments that Ellen G. White thus "ties her discussion of Christian perfection to the internalization of God's loving character in daily life."[54]

Another crucial step in growth is to daily surrender to Christ's will and to keep our eyes fixed upon Christ.[55] In other words, we are to live daily in the presence of Christ, by the power of His Holy Spirit. Such a life brings about transformation of character and obedience. White is careful to balance the work of God's grace in justification and sanctification with the role of human effort in the process of growth. As a result of the work of God's grace in our lives, characters are transformed into the likeness of Christ's character, and obedience to God's law and to the gospel become part of our inner redeemed nature.

If the heart has been renewed by the Spirit of God, the life will bear witness to the fact. While we cannot do anything to change our hearts or to bring ourselves into harmony with God; while we must not trust at all to ourselves or our good works, our lives will reveal whether the grace of God is dwelling within us. A change will be seen in the character, the habits, the pursuits. The contrast will be clear and decided between what they have been and what they are. The character is revealed, not by occasional good deeds and occasional misdeeds, but by the tendency of the habitual words and acts.[56]

As one's character is developed into the likeness of Christ's character, obedience becomes a natural aspect of growth and of one's faithful response to the gift of the grace of God. "Instead of releasing man from obedience, it is faith, and faith only, that makes us partakers of the grace of Christ, which enables us to render obedience. We do not earn salvation by our obedience; for salvation is the free gift of God, to be received by faith. But obedience is the fruit of faith."[57] White stated to believers in Sweden in 1886, "True sanctification will be evidenced by a conscientious regard for all the commandments of God" and "a careful improvement of every talent, by a circumspect conversation, by revealing in every act the meekness of Christ."[58]

Given this understanding set forth by Ellen G. White and in the pages of Scripture, any talk of perfectionism is really a moot point if we properly understand the warnings and encouragements in 1 John. "If we say that we have no sin, we are deceiving ourselves and the truth is not in us.... If we say that we have not sinned, we make Him a liar and His word is not in us" (1 John 1:8, 10). The solution is only in Christ and not in ourselves. "If we confess our sins, He is faithful and righteous to forgive us our sins and to cleanse us from all unrighteousness" (verse 9).[59] According to Richard Rice, "Even perfectionists agree that no one should ever claim to be sinless. In fact, a truly sinless person wouldn't even be aware of the fact. There are good reasons, therefore, not to insist that we should expect to reach sinlessness in this life."[60] And George Knight summarizes well what biblical perfection intends to teach: "Being 'perfect' for Paul in Philippians and being 'sinless' for John in his first epistle did not mean either absolute perfection or absolute sinlessness. But it did involve being free from an attitude of rebellion toward the Father and His principles set forth in the law of love."[61]

Conclusion

The Adventist understanding of sanctification and perfection teaches that by faith, we are in Christ, and He in us. Sanctification and perfection are the work of the Holy Spirit in our lives, and first and foremost they are about character and the maturity of one's relationship with God and others, not behavior (although behavior is a fruit of the Holy Spirit's work in one's life). Both are progressive and never end. Jesus' life and character is to be contemplated; He is our example to follow, yet Jesus' example will never completely be reproduced in our lives. The closer we get to Him, the more sinful we see ourselves. By faith and union with Christ, power to live a life of obedience is given to those who surrender their lives to God.

A biblical and balanced view of sanctification and perfection avoids some dangerous pitfalls. On the one hand, some think that Christian growth in grace and obedience to God and His will are optional, since justification forgives sins past, present, and future. This attitude can easily lead into antinomianism and a life lived without Christ. On the other hand, some think that obedience causes one's salvation and that without it one will be eternally lost. Such an understanding is misleading, because it denies the lingering presence of sin in human nature and unconsciously adds to Christ's all-sufficient sacrifice. This attitude easily leads to legalism and perfectionism. Both pitfalls are to be avoided.

Christians should rest secure in the love of God and be assured of their acceptance, in Christ, by the Father. In Christ, we are justified, sanctified, and perfected. In Christ, and by faith, we receive the power of the Holy Spirit to live a life to the glory of God.

Endnotes

1. Scripture quotations in this chapter are from the NASB unless otherwise noted (as in this case).

2. Ellen G. White, *Testimonies for the Church*, (Mountain View, CA: Pacific Press®, 1948), 3:325.

3. The statement includes the following Bible references at the end of the statement: "Gen. 3:15; Isa. 45:22; 53; Jer. 31:31-34; Ezek. 33:11; 36:25-27; Hab. 2:4; Mark 9:23, 24; John 3:3-8, 16; 16:8; Rom. 3:21-26; 8:1-4, 14-17; 5:6-10; 10:17; 12:2; 2 Cor. 5:17-21; Gal. 1:4; 3:13, 14, 26; 4:4-7; Eph. 2:4-10; Col. 1:13, 14; Titus 3:3-7; Heb. 8:7-12; 1 Peter 1:23; 2:21, 22; 2 Peter 1:3, 4; Rev. 13:8." "Beliefs," Seventh-day Adventist Church, https://www.adventist.org/en/beliefs/.

4. I likely simplify things too much in this statement, but by a Lutheran understanding of the relationship between justification and sanctification I refer to an emphasis on justification to the detriment of the importance and necessity of good works, and to the Catholic understanding I refer to the understanding that justification and sanctification are comingled and that good works are necessary for justification, and even meritorious.

5. Herbert E. Douglass, *God at Risk: The Cost of Freedom in the Great Controversy* (Roseville, CA: Amazing Facts, 2004), 338–342.

6. Larry Kirkpatrick, *Cleanse and Close: Last Generation Theology in 14 Points* (Highland, CA: GCO Press, 2005), 62.

7. Ibid., 65, 66.

8. Some of the concepts discussed in the next few sections of this chapter are adapted from the essays "The Theology of Ellen G. White," in Denis Fortin and Jerry Moon, eds., *The Ellen G. White Encyclopedia* (Hagerstown, MD: Review and Herald®, 2013), 241–286; and "Historical Introduction," in Ellen G. White, *Steps to Christ* (Berrien Springs, MI: Andrews University Press, 2017), 21–68, with historical introduction and notes by Denis Fortin.

9. See Don Thorsen, *Calvin Vs Wesley: Bringing Belief in Line With Practice* (Nashville, TN: Abingdon Press, 2013), 1–15.

10. Ellen G. White, *Steps to Christ* (Mountain View, CA: Pacific Press®, 1956), 17. Page references to *Steps to Christ* are to the standard edition. One should note that she refers to the weakening of Adam's human nature, not to a total depravity. Another statement often referred to is this one: "But the Fall and its ef-

fects have perverted these gifts. Sin has marred and well-nigh obliterated the image of God in man." Ellen G. White, *Patriarchs and Prophets* (Oakland, CA: Pacific Press®, 1890), 595. From this, many have said that her view of human nature is more optimistic than the Augustinian doctrine of the Magisterial Reformers. But White rejects any thought of Pelagianism or semi-Pelagianism, which are views of human nature that teach human beings are not infected with some of the consequences of Adam's fall. More specifically, semi-Pelagianism teaches that the fall of Adam and Eve has weakened all aspects of human nature, but not all the effects of their sin are transferred to their descendants. Each person is born with an unaltered free will and can choose to abstain from sin even if inclinations to sin are inherited. The personal guilt of Adam is not transferred, and people will be lost only after they have committed a willful sin.

11. White, *Steps to Christ*, 18. In contrast to the ideals of the Enlightenment, White also affirms that "Education, culture, the exercise of the will, human effort, all have their proper sphere, but here they are powerless." These human efforts "cannot purify the springs of life." The only power that can operate a change in human hearts must come from Christ. "His grace alone can quicken the lifeless faculties of the soul, and attract it to God." Ibid. Many years before publishing *Steps to Christ*, in a sermon given at the General Conference Session in November 1883, White emphasized that "we must not think that our own grace and merits will save us; the grace of Christ is our only hope of salvation." Ellen G. White, *Faith and Works* (Nashville, TN: Southern Pub. Assn., 1979), 36.

12. John Wesley's sermon "The Scripture Way of Salvation," which is believed to be his "most successful summary of the Wesleyan vision of the 'way of salvation,'" includes a section on prevenient grace and the universal work of God on human hearts. Wesley uses a few synonyms to refer to prevenient, or "preventing," grace: "all the 'drawings' of 'the Father,' the desires after God . . . all the 'light' wherewith the Son of God 'enlighteneth everyone that cometh into the world' [John 1:9], . . . all the convictions which his Spirit from time to time works in every child of man." John Wesley, *John Wesley's Sermons: An Anthology*, ed. Albert Cook Outler and Richard P. Heitzenrater (Nashville: Abingdon Press, 1991), 371–380.

13. White, *Steps to Christ*, 18.

14. By total depravity I do not mean that each human is as bad as he or she could possibly be, but rather that the entirety of human nature is infected by sin, including the will and the ability to make decisions.

15. The Adventist view of human nature is semi-Augustinian: Like Augustine and the Protestant Reformers, Adventists hold that the fall of Adam and Eve has corrupted all aspects of human nature, including the will and ability to respond to God and that the human race is lost apart from the death of Christ that makes provision for the salvation of everyone who believes. In distinction from Augustine, however, the Adventist-Arminian view understands the Holy Spirit's prevenient grace to work on all human beings to restore a measure of free will to allow for a free response to the gift of salvation. Both views teach that propensities to sin and the consequences of Adam's fall are inherited: every human being comes into the world as a sinner separated from God. Yet when it comes to inherited guilt, the Adventist view is not entirely Augustinian; it does not share the view that humans inherit Adam's personal guilt for transgressing God's command (see Ezekiel 18:19, 20). While Ellen G. White did state in a number of places, e.g., that "the children of Adam share his guilt and its consequences" ("Obedience Is Sanctification," *Signs of the Times*, May 19, 1890, para. 8) and that "children received from Adam an inheritance of disobedience, of guilt and death" (Letter 8, 1895, in *Manuscript Releases*, vol. 13 [Silver Spring, MD: Ellen G. White Estate, 1990], 14), I understand these statements to discuss the imputation of the objective consequences of sin, and not the inheritance of the guilt of Adam and Eve's personal act of disobedience, a perspective she categorically denied in page 306 of *Patriarchs and Prophets*. (See also *Patriarchs and Prophets*, 61; and Ellen G. White, *Child Guidance* [Washington, DC: Review and Herald®, 1954], 475.) White's understanding of original sin comes close to the federalist view that Adam and Eve's sin, in their role as our representatives, imputed guilt (probably best seen as liability to punishment) to every human being—everyone is de facto born a sinner separated from God and lost without Christ.

16. White, *Faith and Works*, 20.

17. Ibid., 103.

18. Ibid., 103. In the sermon "The Scripture Way of Salvation," John Wesley states, "Justification is another word for pardon. It is the forgiveness of all our sins, and (what is necessarily implied therein) our acceptance with God." Wesley, *John Wesley's Sermons*, 373.

19. White, *Faith and Works*, 104.

20. Ibid., 106; see also Ellen G. White, *Selected Messages*, bk. 1 (Washington, DC: Review and Herald®, 1958), 389.

21. White, *Steps to Christ*, 62. See Woodrow W. Whidden, *Ellen White on Salvation: A Chronological Study* (Hagerstown, MD: Review and Herald®, 1995), 151. See also Whidden's article, "Wesley on Imputation: A Truly Reckoned Reality or Antinomian Polemical Wreckage?" *Asbury Theological Journal* 52, no. 2 (Fall 1997): 63–70.

22. Ellen G. White, *Thoughts From the Mount of Blessing* (Mountain View, CA: Pacific Press®, 1956), 114.

23. Ellen G. White, *Christ's Object Lessons* (Battle Creek, MI: Review and Herald®, 1900), 65.

24. Ellen G. White, *The Acts of the Apostles* (Mountain View, CA: Pacific Press®, 1911), 560, 561.

25. Wesley, *John Wesley's Sermons*, 373, 374. It is important to note that while Wesley talked of the theoretical possibility of entire sanctification in one's lifetime, Ellen G. White did not espouse this view and spoke of sanctification as the work of a lifetime that will never end until Jesus comes again.

26. Ibid., 562; Ellen G. White, "Qualifications for the Worker," *Advent Review and Sabbath Herald*, June 4, 1895, 353.

27. Millard J. Erickson, *Christian Theology*, 2nd ed. (Grand Rapids, MI: Baker Academic, 1998), 982.

28. Ellen G. White, *Selected Messages*, bk. 3 (Washington, DC: Review and Herald®, 1980), 355.

29. This might also be why Paul exhorts his readers to "reckon" or "consider" themselves dead to sin but alive to God in Christ (Romans 6:11). One would not need to "reckon" oneself as such if we were actually, completely, dead to sin.

30. John Calvin understood Paul's discussion of the struggling man in Romans 7 to be a metaphor for Paul himself and a confirmation that sin remains in the ontological nature of human beings even after conversion. "Now, because that depravity of nature does not so readily appear in secular man (who indulges his own desires without fear of God), Paul takes his example from a regenerated man, that is, himself. He therefore says that he has a perpetual conflict with the vestiges of his flesh, and that he is

held bound in miserable bondage, so that he cannot consecrate himself wholly to obedience to the divine law [Romans 7:18–23]. Hence, he is compelled to exclaim with groaning: 'Wretched man that I am! Who will deliver me from this body subject to death?' [Romans 7:24]." John Calvin, *Institutes of the Christian Religion*, trans. Henry Beveridge (Grand Rapids, MI: Eerdmans, 1989), 4.15.12.

31. White, *Steps to Christ*, 57.

32. Kenneth J. Collins, *The Scripture Way of Salvation: The Heart of John Wesley's* Theology (Nashville: Abingdon Press, 1997), 113. In his explanation of regeneration, John Wesley made a thoughtful distinction between the guilt, the power, and the being of sin in the believer's life after justification and during the sanctification process. "That believers are delivered from the *guilt* and *power* of sin we allow; that they are delivered from the *being* of it we deny." John Wesley, "On Sin in Believers," *John Wesley's Sermons*, 366.

33. Hans K. LaRondelle, "The Seventh-day Adventist View of the Relationship of Justification, Sanctification, the Final Judgment," in *Lutherans and Adventists in Conversation* (Silver Spring, MD: General Conference of Seventh-day Adventists; Geneva: Lutheran World Federation, 2000), 122–133; also in Woodrow W. Whidden, *E. J. Waggoner: From the Physician of Good News to the Agent of Division* (Hagerstown, MD: Review and Herald®, 2008), 384–397.

34. White, *Steps to Christ*, 67. She also states, "The plants and flowers grow not by their own care or anxiety or effort, but by receiving that which God has furnished to minister to their life. The child cannot, by any anxiety or power of its own, add to its stature. No more can you, by anxiety or effort of yourself, secure spiritual growth." Ibid., 68.

35. Ibid., 69.

36. Ibid.

37. Ibid.

38. White, *Selected Messages*, bk. 1, 344.

39. Ellen G. White, *Messages to Young People* (Washington, DC: Review and Herald®, 1930), 73, 74.

40. White, *Faith and Works*, 48, 49.

41. Ellen G. White, "Danger of False Ideas on Justification by Faith," Manuscript 36, 1890.

42. Ibid.

43. Up to the Renaissance, the Aristotelian view of cosmology understood that the orbits of planets around the earth formed a perfect circle and prevented the beginning of modern astronomy from

thinking in terms of orbits as ellipses. An ellipse was thought to be an imperfect circle and could not reflect God's perfect creation.

44. See George R. Knight, *Sin and Salvation: God's Work for and in Us* (Hagerstown, MD: Review and Herald®, 2008), 140.

45. I recommend Hans K. LaRondelle's two books on this topic: *Perfection and Perfectionism: A Dogmatic-Ethical Study of Biblical Perfection and Phenomenal Perfectionism* (Berrien Springs, MI: Andrews University Press, 1971) and *Christ Our Salvation: What God Does for Us and in Us* (Mountain View, CA: Pacific Press®, 1980).

46. Richard Rice, *Reign of God: An Introduction to Christian Theology From a Seventh-day Adventist Perspective*, 2nd ed. (Berrien Springs, MI: Andrews University Press, 1997), 280, 281. See also Knight, *Sin and Salvation*, 143.

47. Woodrow W. Whidden, *The Judgment and Assurance: The Dynamics of Personal Salvation* (Hagerstown, MD: Review and Herald®, 2012), 91. See his entire discussion of Philippians 3 on pages 89–91.

48. White, *Steps to Christ*, 64.

49. Ellen G. White, "Conquer Through the Conqueror," *Advent Review and Sabbath Herald*, February 5, 1895, 81.

50. Ellen G. White, " 'Abide in Me,' " *Signs of the Times*, March 23, 1888, 178.

51. In his sermon "The Scripture Way of Salvation," Wesley defines *perfection* as "perfect love." "It is love excluding sin; love filling the heart, taking up the whole capacity of the soul." Wesley, *John Wesley's Sermons*, 373. For a more extensive summary of Ellen G. White's thought on perfection, see Whidden, *Ellen White on Salvation*, 119–156, and Knight, *Sin and Salvation*, 146–153.

52. White, *Christ's Object Lessons*, 332.

53. Ibid., 68.

54. George R. Knight, *Meeting Ellen White* (Hagerstown, MD: Review and Herald®, 1996), 126. See also Knight's summary of Ellen G. White's theology of perfection and sinlessness in *Sin and Salvation*, 156–169.

55. White, *Steps to Christ*, 70–72.

56. Ibid., 57, 58.

57. Ibid., 60, 61. See also White, *Selected Messages*, bk. 1, 398; *Faith and Works*, 85–87.

58. White, *Faith and Works*, 53. See also *Faith and Works*, 95; *Steps to Christ*, 62.

59. Yet we are encouraged to persist in obedience: "By this we know that we love the children of God,

when we love God and observe His commandments. For this is the love of God, that we keep His commandments; and His commandments are not burdensome" (1 John 5:2, 3).

60. Rice, *Reign of God*, 282.

61. Knight, *Sin and Salvation*, 148. Knight adds, "Perfection in the Bible, in terms of human beings in their moral bodies, is perfection of the spiritual orientation and attitude rather than total perfection in all its aspects." Ibid., 149.

6

Inhabiting the Kingdom:
On Apocalyptic Identity and Last Generation Lifestyle

Ante Jerončić

Introduction

Swimming is a big "No" on Sabbath. You can take a dip in the sea, but make sure that your feet do not leave the ground lest you begin exercising. Skiing is equally out. You can hike, although it demands more energy than skiing, but skiing seems more like doing what you please on God's holy day (Isaiah 58:13). You can sail on the Sabbath, but don't exert yourself by pulling the mainsheet; that would be "working." Shave before sundown on Friday, and don't shower on the Sabbath; avoid rock music (especially those tricky Beatles and their satanic backmasking); and be suspicious of laughter. After all, Ellen G. White exhorts, "God is dishonored by the frivolity and the empty, vain talking and laughing that characterize the life of many of our youth."[1] Always place your Bible on top of other books; avoid Coke like the plague; wash your dishes after sundown on Sabbath; do colporteur evangelism at least once a week; and by all means, don't do any window shopping if you happen to walk through town after the Sabbath morning church service.

These lifestyle precepts were just some of the rules and practices that defined my Adventist teenage and young adult years. As a new convert, I embraced them with a relish and seriousness that matched my zeal for my newfound faith. After all, becoming a Seventh-day Adventist, at least in the context of my home church, amounted to more than simply encountering God and finding forgiveness and grace; this was not a religion of mere sin management. Instead, nothing less than a complete transmutation of identity was called for. You didn't just start praying, read devotional literature, and attend communal worship, you changed what you ate, watched, and listened to. In other words, you accepted and immersed yourself into a completely new lifestyle. You began to view the world as an arena of the great controversy and the urgency of "today" (Hebrews 3:7)[2] and aimed to live accordingly. No choice was trivial, and no moment was to be wasted for anyone readying himself or herself to stand "without blemish" during the "time of trouble." So if that meant reading your pocket Bible while walking through town—bumping into people and lampposts in the process—or other efforts to become a complete overcomer, well, that was what one did.

Now it might appear that I am recalling such practices with a tinge of dismissal or sarcasm; I certainly am not. Granted, some of them were perhaps a bit too inflexible, too arbitrary—shaving on Sabbath as "work" (!)—but they were mostly done in good conscience and with a desire to honor God. With that in mind, I am leery of slapdash dismissals of "traditional Adventism"; those forms of reactionary zeal that mask a certain laziness of imagination and thought. Instead, my guiding desire is to probe the marrow of the Adventist way(s) of life in order to illuminate its architectonic beauty, to highlight its cohesive holism of doctrine and practice, and to celebrate its prodigious relevance to contemporary existence. One of the essential tasks of theology, after all, is to ferret out vital elements of the Christian faith from their overuse (and underuse) in order to imaginatively and critically resharpen them for both the life and the mission of the church. The same applies to the issue of "last generation lifestyle"; that is, those copious attitudes and opinions of how Adventist believers ought to rearrange the totality of their lives—mentally, bodily, spiritually, socially, economically, and so on—in light of the imminent return of Christ. But how should one go about doing that? How can we meaningfully and coherently articulate what it means to truly worship God with all our heart, soul, strength, and mind? What does it mean for our generation to live out the three angels' messages? In sum, whither *apocalyptic identity*?

Clearing: Naming malfunctions

Dictionary treatments of *lifestyle* usually define the term almost redundantly as "a particular way of living" or as the way an individual or a group decides to live, including convictions, attitudes, and emotional investments.[3] Thus, for example, when we say that Helen lives a "green lifestyle," we have in mind a sense of identity expressed through specific practices over a period of time. But once we move away from such generic definitions and inquire into the specifics of an Adventist lifestyle, things become trickier. Be it questions of sexual ethics, diet, patriotism, choice of non-Adventist reading material, entertainment practices, Sabbath observance, jewelry, or spending money on status symbols in general—on these and other matters, one faces a deluge of opinions. That is particularly true in an age in which the immediacy of social media at times accentuates the basest aspects of human nature. Indeed, a simple Web search of matters Adventist will project one into a world of ministries or advocacy groups that elevate one or another lifestyle matter to *status confessionis* (confessional status)—an issue by which the church supposedly stands or falls. (Paul's sarcastic jab in Galatians 5:15 about believers consuming one another is altogether apropos in this regard.) And how could it be otherwise in a religious movement in which disagreements habitually rise to the pitch of an apocalyptic "to be or not to be'"? Such a burden of ultimacy is never an easy one to carry, neither for Hamlet nor for the Adventist believer.

As tempting as it might be to prance my way through these issues by advancing a personal "Here I stand" list, in this chapter I will instead take a step back and look at some of the foundational principles and beliefs that might aid us in approaching these matters in a faithful and coherent manner. For starters, we need to be transparent about various lifestyle malfunctions that routinely plague our community of faith, including the tendency to approach last generation lifestyle matters in a reductionist sense. By that, I have in mind situations in which various communal rules and mores are wielded inconsistently at best, and disingenuously at worst. In fact, a habitual part of the Adventist folklore is to spoof the adroit ways in which we have mastered the craft of "straining out a gnat and swallowing a camel" (Matthew 23:24). One does not have to be a pastor or church leader to realize that jadedness among Adventist young adults often stems from exposures to such sanctimonious standards. We have all heard statements such as, "But Mom, Elder So-and-So just bought a nine hundred and seventy-five thousand dollar home and drives an Audi A8, and you're telling me that I cannot have these twenty-five dollar earrings?" Examples like that abound, and many a family's Sabbath lunch has been visited by such riveting disputations.

In addition to the problem of *inconsistency*, we, as Adventist believers, are frequently affected by the issue of *segmentation* (which, indeed, is another type of inconsistency). It is always tempting to approach issues of last generation lifestyle in a thoroughly fragmented manner, in which one fixates on prayer but not on money; on missions but not on social justice (as defined in the Bible); on the dinner plate but not on speech; or perhaps on sexual purity but not on practices of nonviolence—and vice versa.[4] Of course, such selectivity seldom results from an intentional decision to become imbalanced; our interests, religious environment, and cultural trends do their skewing work in

our lives without asking for our permission.[5] And yet, we need to guard against such bifurcations, whatever their spurious rationale. Simply saying, "This is not my thing," or "It does not concern me" just won't cut it, irrespective of the garnish we bestow on our complacent apathies. Thus, it is usually a good all-around policy to distrust our preferred inclinations. We would do well to ask ourselves, Why do I find this unimportant? Who or what has influenced me in that regard? What emotions drive my resistance? What unpleasant experiences, bad examples, or personal slights lie at the bottom of my reservations? Even a modicum of self-honesty will usually help us discover a reactionary motive behind our misgivings.

In that regard, the Adventist pioneers, such as Joseph Bates, provide an enviable model. As we read Bates's life vignettes, we are struck by the extent to which they exhibit, for lack of a better word, a deeply organic or integrative *spirituality*. Quite honestly, I am grappling for words to express my utter astonishment in that regard, especially if we consider the common denominator of most apocalyptic movements, both Christian and non-Christian—the separation of the "children of light" from everything that is dark and impure.[6] You break off contact and build your little communes; you don't soil your hands with pesky matters of this world. Not so with Bates. In 1842, while believing that Jesus Christ, the great Abolitionist, would come within a year or so, Bates continued to walk the trenches of social justice. To wit, this is a man who in 1846, in the context of the Mexican-American

War, readily condemned the United States as a "land of blood and slavery," a "heaven-daring, soul-destroying, slave-holding, neighbor-murdering country."[7] How about chewing on that for a morning devotional while sipping a cup of tea?

My point here does not concern the exact wording that Bates chose but rather the question, What was it about his understanding of the coming of Christ that made such a prophetic indictment both possible and necessary? He himself answers this question in his diary, where he writes: "All who embraced this doctrine [of the Second Advent] would and must necessarily be advocates of temperance and the abolition of slavery; and those who opposed this doctrine of the second advent would be not very effective laborers in moral reform."[8] So, whatever we mean by living in the light of the First Advent, it has to include such a broadened scope of discipleship; it has to include spiritual practices and ethical integrity, the indicative (proclamation) and the interrogative (critique), the personal and the social, our deeds and our hearts. All of these elements will be present in a Spirit-filled community; a community that lives out its apocalyptic calling in a holistic way. Therefore, let us not put asunder what the Spirit of God seeks to put together.

Then on top of everything else, we have the malfunction of *misapplication.* We must caution against the tendency to view various lifestyle matters, including treasured spiritual practices such as prayer and Bible study, as barometers of spirituality. It is at this point that Jonathan Edwards, arguably the most significant American theologian, offers a treasure trove of spiritual insights—his stringent Calvinism notwithstanding.[9] In his *Religious Affections* (1746) and other works, he deals with the following conundrums: What are the true signs of Christian conversion? How can we know that an experience of revival is genuine? What principles should we use "to discern the spirits"? In an effort to respond to these tricky concerns, Edwards helpfully points to the "signs of nothing," that is, to all those practices and manifestations of spirituality that might or might not point to a genuinely converted life. Things such as long prayers, passionate worship, rigorous morality, avoidance of entertainment practices, frequent quoting of Scripture, and service to others could indeed be a testament that someone has a relationship with Jesus but not necessarily so. Are we not all familiar with instances when this or some other "sign" in ourselves or in others proved to be a mirage, a cover for a cavernous soul devoid of spiritual vitality? Even altar calls can easily turn into ritualized protocols whose long-lasting effect just about rivals the length of those minor key choruses we love to employ on such occasions.

But if we cannot trust these things per se, what else could possibly serve as a measuring stick for self-evaluation (Ezekiel 40:3)? Quite importantly, Edwards reminds us that we should always turn the index finger in our direction and not play the game of guessing the motives of others, including their altar call responses. In the end, his answer is not surprising: "positive signs" of genuine conversion concern living according to the law of the Spirit and exhibiting His fruits: "love, joy, peace, patience, kindness, goodness, faithfulness, gentleness, self-control" (Galatians 5:22, 23)—not the external observance of the "law," including the Adventist "law" of lifestyle rules. Without a progressive growth in such character traits, I am but an annoying quack, irrespective of my denominational status, YouTube reputation, or sense of self-righteousness. Such laser-focused attention on the core of genuine conversion is desperately needed, particularly at a time when passion for truth among the saints increasingly functions as a license for meanness. We would do well to heed Ellen G. White's counsel in this regard: "There can be no more conclusive evidence that we possess the spirit of Satan than the disposition to hurt and to destroy those who do not appreciate our work, or who act contrary to our ideas."[10]

That is why we need to be watchful lest our religion morph into a perfidious means of God evasion—our fourth malfunction, that of *delusion*. Remember David, for instance, on the heels of the Bathsheba affair (see 2 Samuel 12). Just observe him sliding into religious talk during his tête-à-tête with the prophet Nathan, now that morality concerns others and not his own ignoble actions. In 2 Samuel 11, we see him acting with a moral conscience befitting a Mafia don, sending people left and right as it pleases him, including to their death. When it comes to condemning someone else, the word *God* glides dexterously over his lips while amounting to little more than a type of religious accoutrement. Miraculously, moral obtuseness is now nowhere to be found, so that his ethical judgment dazzles us with its swiftness and severity. In that sense, religion, for David, fulfills a conscience-placating role. Its fervency only masks the absence of a genuine devotion, which is a tendency readily observed in the Gospels as well. A lot of religious hot air gets generated—tears are shed, healings take place, pamphlets are delivered, prayer hugs dished out—but in the end, the person does not really know the Lord and is not known by Him. The religious carnival "has left town," so to speak, and all you have is someone building his house on sand, because he refuses to listen to the words of Jesus and put them into practice (Matthew 7:24).

These, then, are some of the potential pitfalls that threaten to sabotage the faith of Christ's followers: inconsistency (selective application of principles), segmentation (focusing on certain lifestyle issues at the expense of others), misalignment (forgetting the function and purpose of discipleship), and delusion (turning religion into a means of disobedience). Of course, all of that is clearly addressed in the Bible. Whether one takes a passage such as Isaiah 58 or perhaps delves into the Sermon on the Mount, the urgency to avoid such forms of inauthenticity are pressed upon us with particular vigor and insistence. How could they not, when so much is at stake; when the deceptiveness of the human heart exerts such a blinding vigor? In truth, the plea of Bartimaeus often comes to my mind as I think of these issues, sometimes despairingly: "Rabbi, I want to see!" (Mark 10:51, NIV).

Deepening: On "seeing," "standing," and "being"

At one point in The Chronicles of Narnia, C. S. Lewis's famed collection of children stories, the narrator offhandedly reminds his audience that "what you see and what you hear depends a great deal on where you are standing. It also depends on what sort of person you are."[11] Lewis hints here at the obvious truism that our "way of seeing" depends on our "standing" and "being."[12] To appropriate an image from a well-known cultural critic, it is one thing to see the city of Chicago from the top of the Willis Tower; it is quite another to do so while standing in an alley on Chicago's South Side.[13] The position and orientation of your standing is significant in determining your perception—the extent, intensity, perspective, impact, angle, and proportion of it—as well as your potential actions and accompanying attitudes and emotions.

To develop this a bit more, let us say that "seeing," or *perception* in the Lewis quote above, includes the following elements: attunement (predisposition to notice), understanding (interpretation), judgment (valuation), and imagination (envisioning possibilities). It leads to statements such as, "Notice this!" or "It means this," or "This matters!" or perhaps, "We could do that!" The Bible is saturated with examples of perception, so defined, playing a determining role in the lives of believers. Take the case of Jesus describing the extravagant act of His anointing as "beautiful"—the amazing connection of self-sacrifice and aesthetics here warrants a deeper exploration—while others dismiss the spilling of the fragrance as wasteful or self-promoting (Mark 14:4-6). Or when Paul becomes "greatly distressed" (Acts 17:16, NIV) upon entering the city of Athens and seeing the city littered with pagan symbols, while others

walking next to him are either at peace or greatly impressed with the city's splendor. In both of these occasions, we have a clash of perceptions—with Jesus and Paul on one side, and the disciples and the crowd on the other. To repeat, Jesus and Paul did not just act in opposition to others; they perceived things differently. They were predisposed to notice certain things when the people around them were oblivious to them (attunement); they understood them correctly (interpretation); they attached a different level of significance to these things than did their followers or adversaries (valuation); and they were alert to a range of potentialities (imagination) that others were not aware of. In that sense, the foundational question for Christ's disciples is not simply, What would Jesus do? but rather, What and how would Jesus see? This often boils down to, What would Jesus care about?

Given that our actions are always a response to how we see things, it is easy to see why the question of perception is so important for ethics and Christian discipleship in general. As the ethicist Stanley Hauerwas rightly notes, ethics "is not first of all concerned with 'thou shalt' or 'thou shalt not.' Its first task is to help us rightly envision the world."[14] Such an observation, of course, applies to a multiplicity of life spheres. A doctor reading MRI and CT scans for diagnostic purposes, an art connoisseur noticing compositional elements of a Vermeer painting, a musicologist marveling at the mathematical brilliance of Bach's Chaconne for solo violin, an activist sensitized to subtle patterns of institutional injustice—these and countless other examples illustrate how competencies, life experiences, character, interests, psychological and physiological states, and beliefs influence our seeing or failure to see and how that in turn determines the range of our potential actions, emotional responses, and cares.[15] (There is actually a whole discipline that studies the nature and causes of ignorance called *agnotology*, but that, too, must be left for another context.[16])

And it is on this last point that the significance of Lewis's insight comes fully to the fore—the idea that perception is connected with our "standing" and "being." The former, I suggest, refers to our *orienting beliefs*, which include everything from basic worldview commitments—what James Sire refers to as ideas about the "basic constitution of reality"—to more ordinary, everyday beliefs.[17] All beliefs matter! In fact, by using the term *orienting beliefs* I mean to avoid the natural impulse to accord foundational worldview commitments a greater life-orienting weight than other, seemingly mundane, beliefs. After all, most people in the United States today deem Black Fridays more existentially pressing than black holes—used here as a metonym for questions of cosmology—and virtual reality fantasies more enticing than concerns over the nature of ultimate reality. And I don't mean this in any snide or demeaning sense. On the contrary, I simply credit the way in which minuscule tenets sometimes disproportionately affect the way we *live* our lives. For instance, Don might firmly believe in the glory of God—certainly a claim about the "basic constitution of reality"—but when it comes to mentally processing, let's say, a failed work promotion, it is his

peeve about the dysfunctionality of bureaucratic institutions that assumes the ultimate orienting force. (Or he might be just an incorrigible quibbler!) Accordingly, describing a person in terms of his worldview, such as theist, deist, or monist, represents only a portion of who that person is and the choices he makes while working, commuting, socializing, relaxing, and so on. The question, therefore, is not which of his beliefs are important in some ultimate sense but rather which of them orients or directs his decision-making.

Adding to this problematic situation is the vexed role of the cognitive unconscious that frequently overrides orienting beliefs without our conscious awareness.[18] A person who ardently sings and preaches about the love of God might nurture, at a more fundamental level, the image of an unpredictable and arbitrary deity whose providential interventions border on the schizophrenic. Yes, a theology of the love of God is intact and loquaciously defended— as we impassionedly seek to do in this book—but hidden uncertainties shape the person's decision-making, self-perception, and basic life orientation. To compound the problem, the presence and substance of the cognitive unconscious eludes superficial introspection. Along those lines, A. W. Tozer suggests that "our real idea of God may lie buried under the rubbish of conventional religious notions and may require an intelligent and vigorous search before it is finally unearthed and exposed for what it is. Only after an ordeal of painful self-probing are we likely to discover what we actually believe about God."[19] Therefore, much ardent prayer needs to be offered to God asking Him to reveal to us the true state of our hearts and minds.

That being said, as important as are orienting beliefs ("where we stand") for perception—and here we are moving to the other element of the Narnia quote above— what we see also depends on "who we are." Obviously, we *are* in some ways our beliefs; how could it be otherwise? At the same time, we are so much more. That is, there is a more encompassing, *existential* dimension to us as human beings in general (and specifically as last generation believers) that at the bare minimum includes the following aspects:

Affective investments comprise *desires* for objects, experiences, states of mind, God, or people; *passions* for causes, that is, things we feel strongly about; *loyalties* toward God, individuals, life roles, communities, institutions, traditions, the nation-state, and so on; and *priorities* in time and allocation of resources. Such affective investments might be either acute or protracted; they inextricably shape who we are as human persons. In fact, given their obstreperous character, these allegiances frequently exert a determinate influence on where and how we land on various moral issues. They not only supercharge our responses but also fundamentally direct them; they incline us to certain actions and affections.

Embodied sensibilities include automatic responses expressed through a "sense" or "feeling" about an issue, leading us either to recoil from it or to cling to it—often automatically. By functioning as the basis of our emotions, these embodied sensibilities manifest themselves through deep-seated feelings of like or dislike, attraction or repulsion, and delight or aversion and are often at work long before cogent, intellectual reasoning arrives on the scene. We are attracted by that which we find beautiful, pleasing, hip, and aspiring on the one hand and repulsed by that which we perceive as hypocritical, odious, passé, and limiting on the other. In other words, much of our being in the world is determined by these aesthetic sensibilities; sensibilities that in conjunction with the cognitive unconscious provide a covert mechanism of decision-making. This has enormous implication for pastoral practice and missions because most people do not reject Christianity because they see it as wrong; they reject it because they find it unseemly— they are in some way repulsed by it. To a large extent, their rationales are aesthetic, not epistemological. In other words, their response involves judgments of taste and not statements of truth. For the most part, this blinding does not result from unearthing some faith-shattering axiom; instead, it sprouts from a slow, almost imperceptible shift of aesthetic sensibilities where fragments of God alienation coalesce into alloys of religious indifference imperceptibly over time. In the end, the spark and luster are gone, and God just does not do it for the person anymore. (Of course, as the story of the Fall illustrates, such changes can happen more suddenly. Adam and Eve's about-face had nothing gradual about it; the shift in their aesthetic sensibilities seemingly happened with remarkable speed.)

Character, as the very term implies, refers to dispositions or tendencies to act, feel, and think in a certain way over an extended period of time. According to the

Bible, it is impossible to talk about human identity, including the pursuit of truth, without focusing on character, which is that internal network of good habits and bad habits, virtues and vices. Namely, we may arrive at wrong judgments about something or someone—we "see" or "read" wrongly—not only because we possess inadequate information or misguided beliefs but also because we are plagued by character faults. A selfish person will see the world differently than a person who is generous, and the "fool," as depicted in Proverbs, will remain impervious to words of wisdom despite their rational appeal (cf. Proverbs 23:9). Put differently, both the pursuit and articulation of truth inevitably rides the jagged topography of virtues and vices, emotions and experiences, influences and presuppositions. There is always more to knowing than simply knowing; inevitably, all kinds of motives, character traits, tastes, and emotions also get thrown into the mix in a way that often eludes our clear comprehension. That is why training in truthfulness requires "training in godliness." Peter says as much when he exhorts us to supplement our "faith with virtue, and virtue with knowledge, and knowledge with self-control, and self-control with steadfastness, and steadfastness with godliness, and godliness with brotherly affection, and brotherly affection with love." He then concludes by stressing that these virtues have an epistemic, or truth, weight in that they keep us "from being ineffective or unfruitful in the knowledge of our Lord Jesus Christ" (2 Peter 1:5–8).

Personal particularities, finally, pertain to matters such as *context* (cultural, economic,

sociohistorical, etc.), *narrative* (forces of socialization, formative experiences, conversions, traumatic markers, etc.), *memories* (including suppressed ones), and *self-markers* (personality, gender, ethnicity, mental and physiological health, intelligence, etc.).

As a summary, we could now rephrase Lewis's words from the beginning of this section—about how our seeing depends on where we stand and who we are—as follows: what you *perceive* (as attunement, understanding, judgment, and imagination) depends on your *orienting beliefs* (worldview, doctrines, cognitive unconscious, etc.) and *existential situation* (investments, sensibilities, character, and particularities). And that leads us to the core claim in this chapter: personal *identity* is an emergent property, a gestalt (composite whole) that arises from the interaction happening among perception ("seeing"), beliefs ("standing"), and situation ("being"). Let us unpack this bit more.

What has been clear so far is that our account does not find much sympathy for an intellectualized reduction of human beings to "thinking things," that is, to disembodied cognitive machines churning out worldview blueprints or fundamental beliefs that are then more or less acted upon.[20] But neither do I think that our core identity is just a sublimation of existential situations; that human persons are nothing but a patchwork of reactive emotions or mindless passions. Rather, human identity understood in an existential sense is a type of gestalt—a protean, continually malleable pattern of interaction between beliefs and situations affecting, as we have argued all along, both our perceptual horizons (attunement) and acts (understanding, judgment, and imagination).[21] The Bible abounds with examples that speak to how identity, so defined, shapes the actions of individuals. Some see the resurrection of Lazarus as a miracle of God; others see it as a reason to condemn Jesus to death. One thief on the cross perceives Jesus to be the Messiah, while the other mocks Him. Some discern John the Baptist to be a great prophet, while others dismiss him as a religious fanatic and a usurper of established power arrangements. In all these instances, we have a clash of perceptions, because people possess different identities and different perceptual horizons and cares.

As expected, the precise anatomy of identity differs not only from person to person but also within an individual in different moments of that individual's life; the exact shape of our identity changes and fluctuates—sometimes less and sometimes more—as we go through life. We acquire new friendships, suffer tragedies, grow older, become victims of conflicts, see miracles, battle addictions, experience conversions, and grow in wisdom. In other words, we experience life in its ungraspable and baffling complexity. All these events, internal states, aspirations, and concerns, combined with our deepest-held beliefs, shape each configuration of identity, and with it, our relation to truth. We could even say that at any given point in our lives our identity tends to coalesce around one or more *centrations* or concerns.[22] In everyday language, we sometimes refer to such centrations as "consciousness." Thus, when we say that "Hannah has a strong social consciousness" or "Andy's patriotic consciousness is quite pronounced," we have precisely such centrations in mind. In both instances, identity centration stands for everything about these individuals that explains Hannah's and Andy's attitudes toward social issues and the nation-state respectively at that moment in their lives.

What the notion of centration points to, therefore, is that various events, states of mind, personality, and insights can function as catalysts to either stress or neglect certain faith commitments in the way environmental factors, analogically speaking, might lead to gene silencing or activation in human cells. For instance, a church member coming from a war-torn region where religious symbols fueled nationalistic jingoism might feel differently about national flags in houses of worship than would a proud mother of a newly minted Marine in the pew behind. To wit, the former might even see such flags as "the mark of the beast on the Christian body."[23] As it happens, both individuals believe in the sovereignty of God, the creation of humanity in the image of God, the Sermon on the Mount as the charter for Christian discipleship, respect for authorities, the three angels' messages, and a host of other beliefs. But the disparity in their affective investments and their life centrations alters the way they interpret, emphasize, or apply those faith commitments.[24] These two individuals might have identical orienting beliefs on paper—there is no denial of the objectivity of truth here—but their configurations of identity result in certain beliefs becoming accentuated while others are muted; they simply care about different things in different ways. In other words, their identity gestalt determines their *inhabitation* of truth, which can be either authentic or inauthentic or biblically faithful or not.

While granting that the word *authentic* is a slippery one that means different things to different people, in this context it does indeed pull a hefty polemical punch. Namely, if you recall our discussion from the previous section (*Clearing*), you will remember that we examined some of the common faith malfunctions that plague our community of believers: inconsistency, segmentation, misalignment, and delusion. All these represent different forms of incongruity or inauthenticity that last generation Christians need to confront. In this section, we have covered the same territory from a different angle by taking a more specific look at the notion of human identity and the various elements that compose it. It will not be lost on the attentive reader that the notion of congruency, and thus authenticity, has been the driving force here as well. After all, isn't that our most urgent need? To bring *all* our orienting beliefs into harmony with the Word of God (authenticity 1)? To make sure that *all* our loyalties and priorities reflect those Christ-centered beliefs? (authenticity 2)? To prayerfully examine *all* our sensibilities to see whether they mirror the timbre of Christ's mind and spirit (authenticity 3)? And to petition the Spirit to instill in us His "fruits" or "kingdom virtues" that they might sustain us in our loyalty to Christ and provide the soil in which right sensibilities might flourish (authenticity 4)? The fusion of these four facets of authenticity is what

I have in mind in the preceding paragraph as I refer to the authentic "inhabitation of truth." For the last generation remnant, such an authentic Christian identity is by definition an apocalyptic one.

Broadening: Inhabiting the apocalyptic "space"

For the Adventist pioneers, the confession "Jesus is coming soon" was so much more than a vacuous gesture. Their apocalyptic focus on the imminent return of Christ, the conviction that eternity was right at the door, led them to craft a lifestyle that would reflect the gravity of the times in which they were living. As they saw it, you could not profess such a cosmic announcement and continue to stroll around as if nothing had happened. "The King is coming; be ready!" A radical change of identity and practice was the only proper response to God's ensuing interruption of history. Priorities had to be rearranged and resources reallocated; "life as usual" was no longer possible. To their credit, their response was one of verve, and then some. They were ready to assiduously upend their existence and reject all forms of cultural and religious normality to an extent that we today find both inspiring and slightly unnerving. Any brief visit to the Adventist Village in Battle Creek, Michigan, or perusing early Adventist literature will make such an air of self-sacrifice and commitment virtually palpable. One feels dwarfed in the presence of such a spiritual dedication. And I don't mean this in a hagiographic, melodramatic sense; their blind spots and character defects can hardly be hidden from any semicritical historiography. But whatever their shortcomings, and there were many, no one can question our pioneers' pursuit of congruence between faith and practice, between the proclamation of the final judgment and an unreserved commitment to God. They not only believed in the Second Coming, they lived it.

So what happens when that focus diminishes? What happens to an apocalyptic movement when it becomes progressively unapocalyptic—note the shift here in identity centrations as discussed above—a fact only partially masked by the requisite "Jesus is coming soon" affirmations populating our collective gatherings? George Knight addresses these questions with some intensity in his widely received book *Apocalyptic Vision and the Neutering of Adventism.*[25] I remember how much I was taken in by this book's title the first time I saw it. It was the word *neutering* that did it for me and still does. I like the way it conveys the image of Adventism being drained of its vitality; the process of making it more placid, more insipid, and ultimately barren. There are many ways, of course, in which such an *unadventizing* of Adventism might and does happen: institutionalism, authoritarianism, lack of missionary focus, and doctrinal infighting are just some of the potential forces that might contribute to it. But for Knight, and I would concur with him on this point, many of these problems are simply symptomatic of a deeper issue, namely, the loss of the apocalyptic identity central to Adventist pioneers.

Admittedly, that is a somewhat contentious claim because it is not at all self-evident that "apocalyptic" should be the central organizing idea of our Christian identity. Even our own community of faith faces significant disenchantments with apocalyptic discourse, particularly on a grassroots level. While the reasons for such disaffection vary, they usually fall back on some of the following: unease concerning Christ's delay, antagonism toward Adventist "particulars"; rejection of a sectarian, contemptus mundi (contempt of the world) mentality; disillusionment with "beasts and charts" evangelism; alternative conceptions of Christ's Parousia, or visible arrival; stress on the humanitarian and world-affirming dimensions of Adventism; and aversion toward a religiosity that fuels fear or promotes violence. As a corollary, many view apocalypticism as synonymous with loopy hysteria or uncouth exclusivism.

In response, I would say that the true character of Adventist apocalyptic identity is of an entirely different sort. It is *not* unduly obsessed with cataclysmic events in the near future, although its view of history is rather bleak. It is *not* conspiratorial, although it is often mistrustful of that which passes for "normality" or "common sense." It is *not* world denying, although it is not naïve about the ways in which structured unbelief permeates most facets of our life or world. And most important, it is *not* just one aspect of biblical revelation; the Bible is apocalyptic through and through. In fact, we cannot make any sense of the ministry of Jesus, including such basic items as the Lord's Prayer, without an apocalyptic framework. As Jürgen Moltmann famously and rightly puts it, "From first to last, and not merely in the epilogue, Christianity is eschatology, is hope, forward looking and forward moving, and therefore also revo- lutionizing and transforming the present. The eschatological is not one element of Christianity, but it is the medium of Christian faith as such, the key in which everything in it is set, the glow that suffuses everything here in the dawn of an expected new day. For Christian faith lives from the raising of the crucified Christ, and strains after the promises of the universal future of Christ."[26]

In this quote, the word *medium* is key because it pushes Adventist apocalyptic identity beyond a narrow preoccupation with final events and issues of character perfection, important as these topics are, to include fundamental questions of human existence such as philosophy of history, divine action, tragedy, truth, power, and the common good. In that sense, Adventist apocalyptic identity mirrors the scope of the great-controversy narrative, both in terms of its historical span and its thematic inclusivity. It functions as a lens by which last generation Christians ought to conduct their lives in obedience to Christ.

As it is quite impossible to fully unpack these issues here given our space limitations, let me highlight but a few selected and rather compressed theses on apocalyptic identity and its key centrations (or consciousness, as I will use the term synonymously here):

1. The benevolence of the self-giving God is the foundation of all reality. "Anyone who does not love does not know God, because God is love" (1 John 4:8). Everything stands and falls with that. No theology, practice, doctrine, policy, tradition, or anything else is ever—simply *must not be!*—allowed

to impinge on this fundamental truth, this animating force of the universe. We are not waiting for just any God; some generic deity whose intentions are spurious or unclear. The coming of God—in Creation, Redemption, and final glorification—speaks of a God of covenant faithfulness, of unmitigated and fierce love, of boundless grace, and of overwhelming compassion. The self-emptying (*kenosis*) of Jesus that Paul so movingly portrays in Philippians 2 is a dramatic enactment of divine humility, a revelation of who God always was, and is, and always will be throughout all eternity. Such a *God consciousness* frames the apocalyptic lifestyle.

2. To have apocalyptic hope is to live under the sense of the "now." "I tell you, now is the time of God's favor, now is the day of salvation" (2 Corinthians 6:2, NIV). *Therefore,* we conduct our lives under the sign of the *terminus,* the end. The very idea of imminence puts pressure on time; it compresses it, and with it shortens the horizon of our expectations. Apocalyptic Christians do not envision a historical horizon of perpetual postponement—a sense of slow, evolutionary development of humanity. They experience the urgency of time, and with it, the restlessness of hope. They are awake and alert, prayerfully attending to the "signs of the times." Such a *time consciousness* frames the apocalyptic lifestyle.

3. God's transcendence, or otherness, bursts through human expectations. " 'For my thoughts are not your thoughts, neither are your ways my ways,' declares the LORD" (Isaiah 55:8, NIV). *Therefore,* we affirm God as the God of "breaking in" and rupture. He unsettles as much as He pacifies; He interrupts as much as He heals. We cannot control Him, nor can we confine Him within our arbitrary standards. He shatters all our religious efforts to turn Him into a manageable deity, into a god of our projections, wishes, and needs. Thus, to live in response to the coming of God means to live in repentance of all our idols, fetishes, and disguised forms of ego worship; it means to live in the light of truth that strips us of all falsehood and protective shields, especially religious ones. That God would confront us so is an act of grace, an act of "apocalyptic rupture" par excellence.[27] Such a *truth consciousness* frames the apocalyptic lifestyle.

4. The cross of Christ is the essence of our faith and identity. "For I decided to know nothing among you except Jesus Christ and him crucified" (1 Corinthians 2:2). *Therefore*, we side with Martin Luther's words: "*Crux probat omnia*" (the cross tests everything). In so doing, we confess that apocalyptic identity is a cruciform identity. It imitates the crucified God in at least two key aspects: *kenosis* (self-emptying) and solidarity with others in their needs and sufferings. In other words, it recognizes that "the law of self-renouncing love is the law of life for earth and heaven."[28] Who then is the coming God for us today? He is the one who continually invites us to the *via crucis* (the way of the cross), to a life of self-emptying benevolence and true freedom. Such a *cross consciousness* frames the apocalyptic lifestyle.

5. An apocalyptic philosophy and theology of history is a form of remembrance. "They called out in a loud voice, 'How long, Sovereign Lord, holy and true, until you judge the inhabitants of the earth and avenge our blood?'" (Revelation 6:10, NIV). *Therefore*, we spurn bids to view historical developments and current societal arrangements through the eyes of the victors and their ideologies of "exception" by which they justify the necessity of exploitation, oppression, and destruction of human life. Instead, apocalyptic identity presents a form of counter-memory; an orientation attentive to the underside of history and the muted voices of victims, the multitude of slain souls under the altar (verse 9).[29] It refuses to sentimentalize their deaths, to abandon them to the logic of historical necessity and ideologies of collateral damage, and thus protests an "unalterable bias toward inhumanity and destruction in the drift of the world."[30] Such a *solidarity consciousness* frames the apocalyptic lifestyle.

6. God's high regard for human and angelic freedom accounts for the provisional tragic dimension of human existence. "For we know that the whole creation has been groaning together in the pains of childbirth until now" (Romans 8:22). *Therefore*, we reject easy identifications of Divine Providence and history. We see God's purposes repeatedly thwarted by the mendaciousness and folly of both human and angelic freedom—the hubris of Lucifer, the rebellion of Adam who was "sufficient to have stood, though free to fall,"[31] the apotheosis of Babylon, and the surreptitiousness of the lamblike beast of Revelation 13. There is a certain sense in which it is fitting, therefore, to speak of "the weakness of God," as Dietrich Bonhoeffer put it, not in order to make God impotent or complicit vis-à-vis human suffering, but rather to account for God's sovereign self-limitation in the face of human freedom. Such a *tragic consciousness* frames the apocalyptic lifestyle.

7. *In imitating the way of Jesus Christ, we pursue a life of peaceable witness.* "Blessed are the peacemakers, for they shall be called sons of God" (Matthew 5:9). *Therefore*, we consider peacemaking as essential to the "ministry of reconciliation" (2 Corinthians 5:18) that God has given to us in this world. Following the lead of the Adventist pioneers who considered "all participation in acts of war and bloodshed as being inconsistent with the duties enjoined upon us by our divine Master toward our enemies and toward all mankind,"[32] we, too, seek to engage in peacemaking efforts in all spheres of life. Such a *peace consciousness* frames the apocalyptic lifestyle.

8. *The whole cosmos is alienated from God and under the provisional rule of principalities and powers.* "When we were underage, we were in slavery under the elemental spiritual forces of the world" (Galatians 4:3, NIV). *Therefore*, we profess that such fallenness extends beyond individual sinfulness; it infects all human institutions and endeavors, including corporations and governments, ideologies and philosophies. Principalities and powers, in whatever form they manifest themselves, always seek to make God weird and the "world" normal. With that in mind, apocalyptic Christians will be skeptical of powers of normalization. They will continually ask, How did such-and-such become a problem? Who defines the parameters of the "acceptable" and the "normal"? What reigning mythologies or ideologies seek to capture our imagination and actions? What liturgies or repeated practices have been established to achieve

such outcomes? What symbols and rituals do they contain? How do they employ threats and promises as mechanisms of control? Such a *critical consciousness* frames the apocalyptic lifestyle.

9. *In a world opposed to the gospel of Christ, our remnant identity will be one of cosmopolitan exiles.*

> Peter, an apostle of Jesus Christ,
> To those who are elect exiles . . . according to the foreknowledge of God the Father, in the sanctification of the Spirit, for obedience to Jesus Christ and for sprinkling with his blood (1 Peter 1:1, 2).

Therefore, apocalyptic speaks of a nomadic existence, a sense that in this world, even in the best of circumstances, we are never fully "at home." The Adventist movement as a religion of hope unsettles societal norms, continually breaking camp and extinguishing existing campfires. The very notion of a tribal allegiance to an ideology or the state flies in the face of the cosmopolitan character of the people of God who refuse any form of "adjectival subversion" in which "black," "white," "American," "libertarian," "progressive," or any other label would serve as a modifier of the noun "Adventist" instead of the other way around. Our kingdom is not of this world. Such an *exilic consciousness* frames the apocalyptic lifestyle.

10. *The Spirit awakens us to the presence of the kingdom in all of its manifold manifestations.* "Seek the welfare of the city where I have sent you into exile, and pray to the LORD on its behalf, for in its welfare you will find your welfare" (Jeremiah 29:7).

Therefore, we readily affirm the sprouts of God's kingdom as we encounter them in different dimensions of life—art, nature, science, the political sphere, and so on. Because apocalyptic Christians recognize the sovereignty of God in all things, they are free to recognize and support the common good wherever they encounter it. Such a *kingdom consciousness* frames the apocalyptic lifestyle.

These theses, while being borderline cryptic, at least partially limn, I hope, the contours of an apocalyptic lifestyle. Or rather, they outline foundational truths that ought to function as orienting beliefs for last generation Christians so that Christ may reign supreme over our existence. Because in the end, isn't that at the heart of it all? Isn't it of utmost importance that Jesus Christ be the Alpha and Omega, the key identity centration encompassing all of our lives? As Dietrich Bonhoeffer movingly puts it,

[Christ] is in the middle. He has deprived those whom he has called of every immediate connection to those given realities. He wants to be the medium; everything should happen only through him. He stands not only between me and God, he also stands between me and the world, between me and other people and things. *He is the mediator*, not only between God and human persons, but also between person and person, and between person and reality. Because the whole world was created by him and for him (John 1:3; 1 Cor. 8:6; Heb. 1:2), he is the sole mediator in the world. Since Christ there has been no more unmediated relationship for the human person, neither to God nor to the world. Christ intends to be the mediator.[33]

Indeed, everything needs to go through Christ; all our words, deeds, and beliefs have to pass through Him as the Center, as do all facets of our existential situation. He is the norm, the measure, the example, and it is in obedience to Him, the soon-coming King, that we are called to live out our apocalyptic identity.

Endnotes

1. Ellen G. White, *Messages to Young People* (Hagerstown, MD: Review and Herald®, 2002), 367.

2. Unless otherwise indicated, Scripture quotations in this chapter are from the ESV.

3. *Merriam-Webster Dictionary*, s.v. "lifestyle," http://www.merriam-webster.com/dictionary/lifestyle.

4. A theme that cannot be explored here concerns how preoccupations with personal or communal purity regulated through idioms of disgust and fear of defilement might lead to ill effects such as social disengagement and negative self-image. For a provocative treatment of these issues, see Richard Allan Beck, *Unclean: Meditations on Purity, Hospitality, and Morality* (Eugene, OR: Cascade, 2011). On a related note, see George R. Knight, *I Used to Be Perfect: A Study of Sin and Salvation*, 2nd ed. (Berrien Springs, MI: Andrews University Press, 2001).

5. We will take a closer look at this issue in the following section.

6. While the term *apocalyptic* is rather difficult to define, in this context I am employing it as a general designation for groupings that subscribe to some expectation of a cataclysmic future on the one hand and the idea of an end-time "remnant" on the

other. For a helpful discussion of different meanings of apocalypticism, see Stephen L. Cook, *Prophecy and Apocalypticism: The Postexilic Social Setting* (Minneapolis: Fortress Press, 1995), 1–84.

7. George R. Knight, *Joseph Bates: The Real Founder of Seventh-day Adventism* (Hagerstown, MD: Review and Herald®, 2004), 54.

8. Ibid., 59.

9. Most readers will be familiar with Edwards's notorious sermon, "Sinners in the Hands of an Angry God." What is less known is that Edwards was not a typical "fire and brimstone" preacher but, instead, focused primarily, perhaps like no other thinker in the history of Christian thought, on the beauty of God. See, e.g., Roland André Delattre, *Beauty and Sensibility in the Thought of Jonathan Edwards* (New Haven, CT: Yale University Press, 1968).

10. Ellen G. White, *The Desire of Ages* (Mountain View, CA: Pacific Press®, 1964), 487.

11. C. S. Lewis, *The Magician's Nephew* (New York: Scholastic, 1995), 136.

12. The relationship of truth and virtue has been a major concern in the relatively recent field of virtue epistemology. One aspect of this discussion focuses on the definition of intellectual virtues, i.e., whether they refer to reliable cognitive faculties (memory, introspection, etc.) or to character traits (open-mindedness, thoroughness, etc.). For elements of virtue epistemology at work in the Narnia Chronicles, see Kevin Kinghorn, "Virtue Epistemology: Why Uncle Andrew Couldn't Hear the Animals Speak," in *The Chronicles of Narnia and Philosophy: The Lion, the Witch, and the Worldview*, ed. Gregory Bassham and Jerry L. Walls (Chicago: Open Court, 2005). For a more technical discussion of these issues, see Ernest Sosa, *Knowledge in Perspective: Selected Essays in Epistemology* (Cambridge: Cambridge University Press, 1991); Jason S. Baehr, *The Inquiring Mind: On Intellectual Virtues and Virtue Epistemology* (Oxford: Oxford University Press, 2011); and Michael R. DePaul and Linda Trinkaus Zagzebski, *Intellectual Virtue: Perspectives From Ethics and Epistemology* (New York: Oxford University Press, 2003).

13. See Michel de Certeau, *The Practice of Everyday Life* (Berkeley, CA: University of California Press, 1984), 91–110.

14. Stanley Hauerwas, *The Peaceable Kingdom: A Primer in Christian Ethics* (Notre Dame: University of Notre Dame Press, 1983), 29.

15. For an interesting, personal take on this problem, see Alexandra Horowitz, *On Looking: Eleven Walks With Expert Eyes* (New York: Scribner, 2013). Writing from an autobiographical perspective, she notes, "I would find myself at once alarmed, delighted, and humbled at the limitations of my ordinary looking. My consolation is that this deficiency of mine is quite human. We see, but we do not see: we use our eyes, but our gaze is glancing, frivolously considering its object. We see the signs, but not their meanings. We are not blinded, but we have blinders." Ibid., 8.

16. Robert Proctor and Londa L. Schiebinger, *Agnotology: The Making and Unmaking of Ignorance* (Stanford, CA: Stanford University Press, 2008).

17. James W. Sire, *The Universe Next Door: A Basic Worldview Catalog*, 5th ed. (Downers Grove, IL: InterVarsity, 2009), 20.

18. For a classic treatment of the cognitive unconscious, see John F. Kihlstrom, "The Cognitive Unconscious," *Science* 237 (September 1987): 1445–1452. Kihlstrom notes, "Consciousness is not to be identified with any particular perceptual-cognitive functions such as discriminative response to stimulation, perception, memory, or the higher mental processes involved in judgment and problem-solving. All these functions can take place outside of phenomenal awareness." Ibid., 1450.

19. A. W. Tozer, *The Knowledge of the Holy: The Attributes of God, Their Meaning in the Christian Life* (New York: HarperSanFrancisco, 1961), 2.

20. In that regard, I am in agreement with James K. A. Smith, *Desiring the Kingdom: Worship, Worldview, and Cultural Formation* (Grand Rapids, MI: Baker Academic, 2009).

21. For Christians, identity also has an ontological dimension entailed in the concept of the *imago Dei* that in turn includes both *capacities* for personhood (capacity for self-determination, sociality, etc.) and a *status* conferred upon us in creation (rights, sacredness of human life, etc.) and redemption (election, justification, "children of God," etc.). Unfortunately, due to space limitations, these themes cannot be adequately addressed here.

22. Jürgen Moltmann, *God in Creation: An Ecological Doctrine of Creation* (San Francisco: Harper & Row, 1985), 261.

23. Douglas K. Harink, *Paul Among the Postliberals: Pauline Theology Beyond Christendom and Modernity* (Grand Rapids, MI: Brazos, 2003).

24. Charles Taylor's concept of "social imaginaries"

would be quite helpful for describing some of those differences in perception. He writes, "By social imaginary, I mean something much broader and deeper than the intellectual schemes people may entertain when they think about social reality in a disengaged mode. . . . I am thinking, rather, of the ways people imagine their social existence, how they fit together with others, how things go on between them and their fellows, the expectations that are normally met, and the deeper normative notions and images that underlie these expectations." *Modern Social Imaginaries* (Durham, NC: Duke University Press, 2004), 23.

25. George R. Knight, *The Apocalyptic Vision and the Neutering of Adventism* (Hagerstown, MD: Review and Herald®, 2008).

26. Jürgen Moltmann, *Theology of Hope: On the Ground and the Implications of a Christian Eschatology* (London: SCM, 1967), 25.

27. Nathan Kerr, *Christ, History, and Apocalyptic: The Politics of Christian Mission* (Eugene, OR: Cascade, 2009), 66.

28. White, *The Desire of Ages*, 20.

29. For a helpful discussion of Christian apocalyptic as a form of counter-memory and counter-history, see David Toole, *Waiting for Godot in Sarajevo: Theological Reflections on Nihilism, Tragedy, and Apocalypse* (Boulder, CO: Westview, 1998), chap. 7.

30. George Steiner, *The Death of Tragedy* (New Haven, CT: Yale University Press, 1996), 291.

31. John Milton, *Paradise Lost*, 3.95–9.

32. "Report of the Third Annual Session of the General Conference of S. D. Adventists," *Advent Review and Sabbath Herald*, May 23, 1865, 197.

33. Dietrich Bonhoeffer, *Discipleship* (Minneapolis: Fortress Press, 2001), 93, 94 (emphasis in original).

7

Inside the Mind of a Struggling Saint: The Psychology of Perfection

H. Peter Swanson

Perfection perplexities

Very daunting imperatives, aren't they? "You must be perfect—just as your Father in heaven is perfect" (Matthew 5:48, GNT). "Higher than the highest human thought can reach is God's ideal for His children. Godliness—godlikeness—is the goal to be reached."[1] Awe-inspiring ideals, indeed, and the most admirable of aspirations!

The trouble is, people who are perfect in every way are incredibly rare. Even when individuals are confident that they are doing really, really well, others may clearly see their personally unrecognized imperfections and dispute their claims of faultlessness.

So, if we are unable to convince others that we are perfect—"Every fact is to be confirmed by the testimony of two or three witnesses" (2 Corinthians 13:1, NASB)—what assurance can we have that we are indeed perfect and that our perfection will not be tarnished by lapses? And even if we persuade ourselves that we have achieved infallibility, how unshakable is our certainty? How can we be absolutely sure that we aren't self-deceived? After all, "the human mind is the most deceitful of all things. It is incurable. No one can understand how deceitful it is" (Jeremiah 17:9, GW).

Can we be completely certain that what we think is true is actually true and not a misperception on our part? And if we aren't sure, if doubt creeps in, does that undermine our standing with God? And what shall be done with the deep-down unsettledness that comes with lingering disquiet over past wrongs, with forgotten, and therefore unconfessed, sins? And what can be done with persistent apprehensions about the tempestuous testing time when "everything that can be shaken will be shaken"?[2]

These tenacious, anxiety-provoking concerns trouble many and unsettle their peace of mind and heart. Worse still, when confronted with these disturbing issues, there are some who are tempted to abandon Adventism and even to turn their backs on Christianity because they cannot reconcile their personal understanding about perfection with their demonstrated inability to achieve it.

We obviously need to critically examine error-based assumptions, groundless fears, and distorted expectations. And we need to understand what is attainable and what is not. As we take these steps, we must guard against despair and cynicism, because we shall discover, as we go along, that there are effective antidotes for doubts and fears and uncertainties.

Let us begin by examining the assumption that a person can know, with certainty, when he or she has reached perfection. Isn't it logical that believers need to know their condition so that, if they aren't quite there yet, they can take the necessary steps to remedy the deficiency?[3]

Quest for certainty

So how can we know how perfect we are? How assured can we be that our self-knowledge is accurate? What can we do to prove that what we believe about our condition is actually true?

Individuals generally use different approaches to reach a settled conviction about what they know. For some, the first step is to listen to what their *senses* tell them. The information that reaches the brain through the avenues of sensation is what is most meaningful to them. If, like Thomas, they can see it and handle it, then they know that it is real (see John 20:25).[4]

It is very important to take seriously what our senses tell us. If we hear a fire alarm, we must quickly evacuate the building. If we see a speeding car coming toward us, we need to jump out of the way. If something smells putrid and tastes awful, it probably isn't good to eat.

And yet, there are times when we cannot trust our senses to be right. A student pilot is taught to be very alert to what she can see outside the aircraft. But the time comes when the flight instructor places a hood over the student's head so that she cannot see out of the windows. The student has to learn how to "fly blind" and to fully trust the instruments, even when her senses are screaming that the instruments are wrong.

So our senses are often right about what they reveal, but sometimes the knowledge they convey is like an optical illusion—a distortion of the truth.

Trust your gut?

Others rely on their gut instinct. They choose their path to knowledge impulsively. Whatever seems right to them in the moment is what they go with. The most impetuous of these impulsive persons relish risk taking and spine-tingling excitement. High energy, adventurous, and intrepid, they thrive on danger. Tragically, all too many of these adrenaline junkies die young because their false faith fools them into believing the dubious "truth" that they are invincible. How much better it would have been for them if only they had heeded the Good Book's words of caution, "What you think is the right road may lead to death" (Proverbs 16:25, GNT).

Impulsiveness, however, should not be mistaken for intuition. Some of the world's greatest advances in knowledge have come about as a result of intuition. It is the ability to leap over the ponderous steps that logic takes to reach the solution to a problem. Subjectively, a person may say, "Don't ask me how I know; I just know." Quite often, intuitive people will remember with great clarity the times when their intuitions proved correct but overlook or forget the times their hunches were dead wrong.

Fickle feelings

For still others, feeling precedes knowing. In fact, for them, feeling and knowing are practically indistinguishable. Feeling is the lens through which they perceive the world. Their hearts tell their heads what to believe. What is true for the senses is also true for the emotions. Feelings can alert us when things are going wrong, when life is out of kilter. And emotions can be very effective in motivating us to get things done.

Unfortunately, feelings are notoriously changeable. One moment they can be consistent with reality; and the next instant the person may feel, and therefore believe, that the exact opposite is true. Though feelings can urge us forward, they can also set up major roadblocks on the path toward accurate knowledge.

Logic's limits

For philosophically inclined individuals, logical reasoning is the sure means of arriving at indisputable conclusions. It is undeniable that the use of logical reasoning in the diagnosis and treatment of illness has led to astounding health benefits. And programming logic has resulted in astonishing breakthroughs in computer technology. But put a group of logicians in a room together to critique each other's work, and they will delight in detecting the logical fallacies and other errors in one another's declarations. And there are mysteries a plenty that defy logic.

Closely aligned to logic is the scientific method of determining the veracity of claims and hypotheses. If you come up with a theory about something, that idea will not be given credence until it is tested using rigorous procedures. And when you have collected the data and presented the evidence in support of what you believe to be so, your findings will be closely scrutinized, and you will be expected to reveal

the degree of confidence you have in what you claim. Are you more than 95 percent convinced that you are right? Can you be 99.9 percent sure that your discovery is what you have demonstrated it to be? On the other hand, could it be that what you observed happened by chance or coincidence or was caused by some overlooked, intervening variable?

Even if you present solid evidence that makes a watertight case, skeptical scientists will not accept what you claim to be so until your experiment has been replicated repeatedly by other researchers and their findings are shown to be consistent with yours. Still other investigators may seek to prove you wrong by developing competing hypotheses and using differing methods to show that the opposite of what you found is actually true.

It can be confidently asserted that the stupendous advances in knowledge in the last hundred years are largely due to the amazing discoveries made using the scientific method. But even when researchers working for pharmaceutical manufacturers follow extremely exacting protocols to prove that a new medicine is safe, and even after the Food and Drug Administration has scrutinized rigorous studies prior to issuing its approval for the use of the new drug, subsequent evidence can emerge showing that users of the medicine have suffered unexpected and harmful effects. So even the use of the scientific method to verify a truth is not exempt from the possibility of error or from unintended consequences, and those who have great faith in science can sometimes reach false conclusions.

Imperious pronouncements

Lastly, many people form their convictions based on what authorities declare to be so. They take their physician's word at face value. They believe what their teachers tell them. They do what those in authority say they should do. If they want to know what something means, they consult an expert, open a dictionary, or simply Google it. Then they put their trust in whatever the so-called authority assures them is so, even though it is obvious that all supposedly dependable authorities are not equally credible.

When it comes to religious beliefs, those who make authority their guide typically accept the teachings of the founders of their faith community and revere the writings that the faithful hold in high regard. And this is all well and good if the authorities are actually right in what they say and if the listener is not simply going along blindly without giving any thought to what he hears. Truth be told, not all religious authorities are trustworthy, and falsehoods long believed to be true are still wrong.

So people use a variety of means such as sensation, impulse, intuition, emotion, logic, scientific observation, and authority to move beyond uncertainty to assurance about what they believe to be authentic knowledge. As has been shown, each of these methods can assist one to draw conclusions about what is really true. It is also evident that a claim of infallibility for any one of these methods is suspect; for while each method has its strengths, each also has its limitations.

Best methods

How, then, can one decide which of these methods to trust? That depends, of course, on the specific task and on the kind of conclusion to be reached. Under normal circumstances, if a person is blindfolded and a white granulated substance is placed on her tongue and she is asked to decide whether it is sugar or salt, logic and authority must defer to her sensation of taste to make that determination. Similarly, intuition and emotion must bow to logic when a mathematical proof is required for a complex calculation. Having a feeling that an answer is correct just won't do.

So which methods are best suited to establish whether we have reached perfection? We can easily rule out sensation, impulse, intuition, emotion, and the scientific method as the most trustworthy means of achieving well-founded confidence about our salvation and sanctification because they are the wrong tools for the job. That leaves us with authoritative revelation[5] and sanctified reasoning as the safest paths toward a correct understanding of our salvation status and of ultimate truths.

These two approaches are the established means of accessing solid evidence and of discerning the veracity of substantiating arguments. An additional safeguard that can counteract our human proclivity to err when we draw conclusions is reliance on true-hearted, fact-checking colleagues to confirm or call into question the results of our quest for an untainted understanding of truth (see Acts 17:11).[6]

Certainty is illusive

But even when we have done our utmost to establish the accuracy of our knowledge of truth and our conformity to it, we can have only a partial understanding, for "now we see a blurred image in a mirror. Then we will see very clearly. Now my knowledge is incomplete. Then I will have complete knowledge as God has complete knowledge of me" (1 Corinthians 13:12, GW).

In the here and now, and in the absence of absolute certainty, faith and doubt will inevitably contend for the right to make the final ruling when issues of truth and error are in question. And be assured, "God will never remove every occasion for doubt. He gives sufficient evidence on which to base faith."[7] Therefore, "there is no excuse for doubt or skepticism. God has made ample provision to establish the faith of all [people] . . . if they will decide from the weight of evidence. But if they wait to have every seeming objection removed before they believe, they will never be settled, rooted, and grounded in the truth."[8] "With distorted vision they will see many causes for doubt and unbelief in things that are really plain and simple."[9]

So, in the end, the decision is left up to us. Will we consult our doubts, or will we exercise our faith when momentous issues are in the balance?

One of the important issues that can unsettle faith is the belief that we should know, with certainty, when we have reached perfection. But if, as we have seen, all the standard means of knowing are subject to error and misunderstandings, then perfect knowledge about one's state of perfection is unattainable and that underlying assumption is false.[10]

And if absolute certainty about whether we have attained perfection is beyond our reach, then presumptuous claims of personal perfection are illusory and without merit. "When the conflict of life is ended, when the armor is laid off at the feet of Jesus, when the saints of God are glorified, then and then only will it be safe to claim that we are saved and sinless. True sanctification will not lead any human being to pronounce himself holy, sinless, and perfect."[11]

It is comforting to realize that it is *not* essential for us to know how perfect we are. Instead of anxiously worrying about whether we have reached an accurate appraisal of our attainments, we can confidently declare, "I believe and am sure, that it is Christ's righteousness alone that counts in the judgment—not mine." And we can rely on Him to reveal to us what we need to know about how we can cooperate with Him as *He* goes to work to sanctify and purify our lives *for His glory alone.*[12]

Progressive perfection

Another misconception is that perfection is a destination, a state, a discernible end point of a process. But "there can be no life without growth. The plant must either grow or die. As its growth is silent and imperceptible, but continuous, so is the growth of character. At every stage of development our life may be perfect; yet if God's purpose for us is fulfilled, there will be constant advancement."[13] "We are never to rest in a satisfied condition, and cease to make advancement, saying, 'I am saved.' . . . No sanctified tongue will be found uttering these words till Christ shall come, and we enter in through the gates into the city of God." "Never can we safely put confidence in self or feel, this side of heaven, that we are secure against temptation."[14] "So long as Satan reigns, we shall have self to subdue, besetting sins to overcome; so long as life shall last, there will be no stopping place, no point which we can reach and say, I have fully attained."[15] "I am certain that God, who began the good work within you, will continue *his* work until it is finally finished *on the day when Christ Jesus returns*" (Philippians 1:6, NLT; emphasis added).

We can, and must, pray every day,[16] "Examine me, God! Look at my heart! Put me to the test!" (Psalm 139:23, CEB). "Know what I'm thinking" (verse 23, NIrV). "Point out anything in me that offends you, and lead me along the path of everlasting life" (verse 24, NLT). Then we can confidently depend on Him to accomplish in us what we can never do for ourselves. "For it is God Himself whose power creates within you the desire to do His gracious will and also brings about the accomplishment of the desire" (Philippians 2:13, Weymouth). And while the Holy Spirit is at work motivating, empowering, and transforming us, we must strive to do everything we are able to do to fully cooperate with Him (see Luke 13:24).

Ordinary overcomers

Another assumption that deserves scrutiny is the idea that only an elite class of believers will make it through the end-time crises. Right here it is important to recognize that "God treats everyone on the same basis" (Acts 10:34, GNT); "God doesn't show partiality to one group of people over another" (verse 34, CEB). In other words, we should not expect that those who live victoriously through the trials of last-day events will be a superelite group of the most intellectually astute and exceptionally gifted Christians on earth.

If the last generation were not ordinary, everyday people who access the overcoming power that is available to everyone,[17] God could rightly be accused of favoritism, of hand-selecting only those who possess extraordinary capabilities for demonstrating their loyalty to Him under unprecedented and extremely harsh circumstances. But this, apparently, is not the case. "The unlearned as well as the educated are to comprehend the truths of the third angel's message."[18] "At the loud cry of the third angel, these agents will have an opportunity to receive the truth, and some of them will be converted, and endure with the saints through the time of trouble."[19] These "unlearned" believers will "endure," even though there will be very little time left for sanctification ("the work of a lifetime"[20]) to accomplish its purpose. "The strength of Jesus will be imparted to every soul who strives lawfully for the mastery. All may be overcomers."[21]

Among those who stand for Christ, from every nation, kindred, tongue, and people (see Revelation 14:6) will be some who have extensive understanding of Scripture and exceptional keenness of intellect. They may well be the ones who are called before the highest councils on earth to testify of their faith, for "to whom much is given, of him much will be required."[22]

But the Spirit of God is not dependent upon the brilliance of human intellect to accomplish His purposes. "Words will come from the lips of the unlearned with such convincing power and wisdom that conversions will be made to the truth. Thousands will be converted under their testimony."[23] "The poor man is Christ's witness. He cannot appeal to histories or to so-called high science, but he gathers from the Word of God powerful evidence. The truth that he speaks under the inspiration of the Spirit is so pure and remarkable and carries with it a power so indisputable that his testimony cannot be gainsaid."[24] "Strengthened by unquestioning faith in Christ, even the illiterate disciple will be able to withstand the doubts and questions that infidelity can produce, and put to blush the sophistries of scorners."[25]

The assurance derived from these declarations rests not on what the poor, uneducated person can do but on what God can do through anyone who, "by putting self aside, makes room for the working of the Holy Spirit upon his heart."[26] In simple, down-to-earth terms, *any old bush will do*"—*any old bush*—if only *God* is in the bush[27] (see Exodus 3:2, 3)!

The high points

Thus far, we have seen that whatever method we may use in an attempt to arrive at ultimate truth, there is always the possibility of error, misperception, or self-deception, and there is always room for doubt. Consequently, utter certainty about one's own level of perfection is out of reach.

And we have seen that perfection is not a static point in time. Rather, it is dynamic and continues to advance, here and throughout eternity. "The work of transformation from unholiness to holiness is a continuous one."[28] Even "in heaven we are continually to improve."[29] "As knowledge is progressive, so will love, reverence, and happiness increase."[30] "Every faculty will be developed, every capacity increased."[31]

We have also seen that in the great final conflict, the overcomers will likely come from all classes of society. They will not rely on their own achieved level of faultlessness in order to endure. Instead, they will place their full weight of confidence upon the truths of God's Word, on Christ's righteousness, and upon His empowerment to see them through victoriously.

Finally, we recognize that, in the here and now and through the most trying hours of earth's history, doubt will untiringly strive to hinder faith's efforts to bridge the gap between what *can* be confidently demonstrated to be so and what cannot be shown to be indisputable fact; between what *can* be confirmed and what cannot be proved beyond a shadow of a doubt. "Faith is a well-grounded assurance of that for which we hope, a conviction of the reality of things which we do not see" (Hebrews 11:1, Weymouth).

Faith under fire

There are many things that can unsettle faith. Some individuals may be more vulnerable to one type of test of their faith, while other people may find a different set of challenges to be more troubling. What is of no consequence to one person is viewed as an insurmountable obstacle to faith for another. So we turn now to consider some impediments to faith and how these hindrances can be particularly disconcerting to certain individuals.

People who are naturally of an anxious disposition may find their faith under attack by an enemy whose stratagems of worry and guilt are diabolically designed to erode confidence. Chronic worriers have a pervasive sense of impending doom. They may not always be able to clearly identify what awful things are about to happen, but they know that they will be bad for them. Very bad! Even though they know that most of the things they worried about in the past never materialized, they seem unable to shake the ever-present foreboding of imminent trouble.

Professionally speaking, the determination about whether this kind of anxiety is serious enough to warrant professional intervention is informed by the extent to which the worrying interferes with the person's functioning at home, school, and work and within relationships.

In many cases, the worry is subclinical; that is to say, it is not serious enough to require mental health treatment. But if the worries are disquieting to a person's spiritual experience, those apprehensions need to be promptly addressed using spiritual resources and effective remedies. It may also prove helpful for these persons to gauge how often such episodes happen, how long they last, how severe or disabling they are, what triggers them, and what it is about the worries that is so troubling to their faith.

If the person's thoughts turn frequently to aspects of Christian teaching that provoke anxiety, those worries need to be confronted and disarmed. Recurring terrors about dreadful persecution during the time of trouble must be quelled. Deeply unsettling uncertainties about whether it is possible to live a perfect life under the

most adverse of circumstances must be overcome.

It is undeniable that reality-based anxiety is advantageous when it alerts and motivates a person to take appropriate action. If faced with cruel torture and an excruciating death,[32] it would be abnormal to experience zero fear. Total absence of anxiety in anticipation of the very real perils facing God's people would be a cause for serious concern. Healthy levels of anxiety that prompt reasonable action would be appropriate under those circumstances, for "it is often the case that trouble is greater in anticipation than in reality; but this is not true of the crisis before us. The most vivid presentation cannot reach the magnitude of the ordeal."[33]

Unwavering faith

Whether one's fears are healthy or neurotic, they must be prevented from unsettling faith. Sacred history provides the assurance that God is able to miraculously intervene, making people impervious to the flames of persecution, as was the case of Shadrach, Meshach, and Abednego (Daniel 3:27).[34]

He is also able to increase one's capacity to endure suffering, as was evident in the Garden of Gethsemane. "In the supreme crisis, when heart and soul are breaking under the load of sin, Gabriel is sent to strengthen the divine Sufferer, and brace him to tread his blood-stained path."[35] "The angel came not to take the cup from Christ's hand, but to strengthen Him to drink it."[36]

Firm reliance on God's promises of protection and sustaining grace[37] will enable one to dispel troubling thoughts and replace them with abiding peace of mind.[38]

Remorse and regret

While worry looks ahead to fearful presentiments, guilt looks back at freeze-framed wrongdoings that chill the heart with unabating remorse (Psalm 51:3).[39] So preoccupied can one become over past transgressions that present joys become tarnished and drab, and today's rainbows turn to ashen gray.

This pathological guilt refuses to be assuaged by pardon bestowed, restitution made, or punishment endured. To these self-tormented sufferers, no chastisement is ever harsh enough to redress the injury they caused or to undo the damage done.

By contrast, "good" guilt leads to repentance,[40] to forgiveness, and to redemption. "God is faithful and fair. If we confess our sins, he will forgive our sins. He will forgive every wrong thing we have done" (1 John 1:9, NIrV). But there can be no forgiveness for any who believe that they are sin free and who are impervious to the convicting power of the Holy Spirit, because they feel no need to confess.

It is evident that exaggerated worry and guilt impair one's ability to function well and that these twin apprehensions are corrosive to one's faith. Those who are plagued by such guilt and anxiety can benefit from the assistance of faithful Christian counselors who can show them how to restore stability to their disturbed thinking and dispel their unreasonable fears.

Less obvious to many is the fact that the complete absence of worry and guilt is also of grave concern. The worry-free person is at risk of going, without any qualms, into perilous situations where fatal outcomes are prevalent.

And those who never feel the slightest twinge of guilt over sins, large or small, will feel no need to repent or to correct their wrongs. By contrast, the humble saint, whose vision of his unlikeness to Christ becomes progressively clearer the closer he comes to Him,[41] will often bow at the feet of Jesus in contrition and plead for forgiveness and cleansing.[42]

Obviously then, anyone who complacently believes at any time that he is exempt from temptation and immune to transgression is too far distant from Christ to see the beauty of His character and is blind to his own unlikeness to Him. As long as he remains unrepentant, there is no hope for his redemption.[43]

Pathological perfectionism

Many perfectionists keenly feel a third kind of anxiety. They are fiercely driven by their inner disquietude to erect ever more exacting standards of behavior for themselves and often feel driven to go to extreme lengths to conform to highly unrealistic, self-imposed or externally prescribed expectations.

In some instances, their compulsions are rooted in traumatic events from the past and perhaps perpetuated by the irrational belief that if they don't make absolutely sure that everything is under perfect control, very bad things will happen.

For example, a man whose home was destroyed by fire during his childhood due to the carelessness of one of the occupants may have the irresistible urge to check and recheck multiple times that the gas stove is turned off before he can go to bed. He knows that he obsesses excessively about this, that others do not, and that his compulsion to perform his checking behaviors is irrational. Checking once or twice is normal, but thirty times is unreasonable. But that knowledge in no way lessens his overpowering sense of urgency to make absolutely sure that everything is completely safe.

Not surprisingly, this mind-set may also powerfully shape his perception of his standing with God. Instead of seeing the words of Jesus—"You must be perfect, just as your Father in heaven is perfect" (Matthew 5:48, NCV)—as a promise about His transforming power in the life, it is viewed as a formidable, inescapable, unattainable imperative.

So profound is the discrepancy between what he demands of himself and how poorly he is able to comply that he is driven to utter despair and desperate intents. How aptly these words (from a very different context) describe his overwhelming sense of hopelessness: "I looked with desire into the grave. Death appeared to me preferable to the responsibilities I should have to bear."[44]

Beyond receiving professional assistance for his unquiet mind, this despairing perfectionist needs the deep, undisturbable calm that comes from embracing the invitation and promise, "Come to me, all whose work is hard, whose load is heavy; and I will give you relief. Bend your necks to my yoke, and learn of me, for I am gentle and humble-hearted; and your souls will find relief. For my yoke is good to bear, my load is light" (Matthew 11:28–30, NEB).

Twisted self-confidence

Other perfectionists are perfectly pleased with themselves. They exult in the exceptional quality of whatever they do. Along with their penchant for self-congratulation, they have a fondness for favorably comparing themselves with lesser mortals—that is, everyone else. "Oh, God, I thank you that I am not like other people—robbers, crooks, adulterers, or, heaven forbid, like this tax man. I fast twice a week and tithe on all my income" (Luke 18:11, 12, *The Message*). And because they are aware that pride is religiously disapproved, they take delight in putting on display their most highly prized quality—their humility.

Seriously though, there are very talented people with perfectionist tendencies who actually are really, really good people whose lives appear to all observers to be above reproach. Among these individuals are those who truly "do justly, and . . . love mercy, and . . . walk humbly with . . . God" (Micah 6:8, KJV).

Almost indistinguishable from these truly virtuous individuals, however, are some whose overconfidence may imperil their salvation. The amazing human capacity for self-deception[45] can lead people to persuade themselves that all is well when it is not. "Those who accept Christ, and in their first confidence say, I am saved, are in danger of trusting to themselves. . . . Our only safety is in constant distrust of self, and dependence on Christ."[46]

Healthy self-distrust

For high and low, educated and illiterate, rich and poor, distrust of self must be a deepening experience; and an increasing reliance on God to work within them, "both to will and to do of his good pleasure"

(Philippians 2:13, KJV), must prevail. At no time will we be able to make it on our own. At no time will our utter dependence on Him to keep us from sinning be diminished.

This essential self-distrust is not equivalent to low self-esteem. Honesty demands that we shall neither lie to ourselves about how great we are nor about how pitiful we are. Accurate self-knowledge[47] is essential, because it acknowledges both strengths and weaknesses and calls forth praise for gifts bestowed and prayers for overcoming power.

We have noted some of the things that can unsettle one's faith: worry, guilt, anxiety-driven obsessiveness and compulsiveness, self-imposed unrealistic expectations, despair resulting from one's inability to measure up, self-deception, overconfidence in one's own abilities, and low self-esteem. Some individuals may be impervious to some kinds of faith challenges, while they are particularly vulnerable to others. And changing circumstances can make threats to faith appear more or less toxic.

Significant insights

Our initial quest was to discover the means of obtaining unshakable confidence in what we believe. We wanted rock-solid evidence and unanswerable arguments to reinforce our faith. Instead, we discovered that whatever means of knowing we choose, none are fully satisfactory; all have their limitations. So the best we can hope for is to know in part (1 Corinthians 13:12).[48]

Lacking God's omniscience, we aren't able to know with anything like perfect clarity the extent of our inner sinfulness.

We are fully dependent upon Him to reveal to us as much as we can bear (John 16:12)[49] about our bent to evil, about how far short we have fallen, and about our proclivity to relapse.

Next, it became clear that much of what is believed to be so is unprovable. It is true that one can find convincing evidence to support belief, but even the strongest evidence in support of discerned truth is not proof positive; it is not conclusive enough to dispel all doubts.[50] In fact, there would be no need for faith if incontrovertible proof could be provided. By definition, "faith is a well-grounded assurance of that for which we hope, and a conviction of the reality of things which we do not see" (Hebrews 11:1, Weymouth).

Active faith

So how do we acquire this well-grounded assurance? Thankfully, our faith is God given (Romans 12:3)! He will also give us opportunities to exercise our faith, and we can depend on Him to increase our faith (Luke 17:5) in preparation for times of testing and trial. We can strengthen our faith, deepen our assurance, and increase our joy in the Lord by telling and retelling what we believe.

When you have your first opportunity to "speak up and tell anyone who asks why you're living the way you are" (1 Peter 3:15, *The Message*), your witness about how God has affected your life may be very basic and brief. But as you "grow in grace, and in the knowledge of our Lord and Saviour Jesus Christ" (2 Peter 3:18, KJV), your explanation will mature, and your testimony will become more persuasive.

The time may even come when "you will stand trial before governors and kings because you are my [Jesus'] followers.... This will be your opportunity to tell the rulers and other unbelievers about me [Jesus]" (Matthew 10:18, NLT). Under those circumstances, a more closely reasoned and more clearly articulated account of your faith will be necessary. And what you say will need to be wisely adapted to the intellectual prowess of the hearers. Having the well-rehearsed words of God stored in memory will be a great comfort on that day.

But "don't worry about what you'll say or how you'll say it. The right words will be there; the Spirit of your Father will supply the words" (verse 19, *The Message*). "The words you will speak will not be yours; they will come from the Spirit of your Father speaking through you" (verse 20, GNT). "God keeps his promise, and he will not allow you to be tested beyond your power to remain firm; at the time you are put to the test, he will give you the strength to endure it, and so provide you with a way out" (1 Corinthians 10:13, GNT).

Even having mental or physical handicaps does not exclude any of God's children from the high privilege of being witnesses to His goodness. Indeed, the simplest testimony can be profoundly effective. "Men of the highest education and accomplishments have learned the most precious lessons from the precept and example of the humble follower of Christ, who is designated as 'unlearned' by the world."[51]

On the other hand, the Lord may arrange for you to cross paths with someone with a very keen intellect who asks incisive questions about your faith. If you have fortified your mind with carefully reasoned arguments that reinforce your beliefs, you will be well prepared to respond appropriately, dismiss doubts, and refute counterarguments.

In preparation for such an encounter, one would likely have consulted readily available resources beginning, perhaps, with the topical readings in the *Seventh-day Adventist Hymnal*[52] and a comparison of various translations of the Bible.[53] Then one would have advanced to an investigation of the notes in the *Andrews Study Bible*[54] and to an in-depth study of the perspectives presented in the *Seventh-day Adventist Bible Commentary.*[55]

With all these rich resources at our disposal, there still exists a real possibility of reaching erroneous conclusions, even when one most sincerely and diligently searches for truth. "The main thing to keep in mind here is that no prophecy of Scripture is a matter of private opinion" (2 Peter 1:20, *The Message*). In our quest for truth, interdependence with people of faith is indispensable. "Without good direction, people lose their way; the more wise counsel you follow, the better your chances" (Proverbs 11:14, *The Message*). So "let us keep paying attention to one another, in order to spur each other on to love and good deeds" (Hebrews 10:24, CJB).

In conclusion, perfect knowledge of spiritual mysteries is unattainable to us in this life.[56] But more than enough evidence is provided so that one can draw sound conclusions. Yet there remains a gap that separates incomplete knowing from conviction and settled assurance. That chasm must be bridged by faith. Faith the size of a mustard seed[57] (Matthew 17:20) is great enough to bridge any chasm. Fortunately, although "we cannot create our faith,"[58] "God has given to every man his measure of faith,"[59] and we can cherish it and strengthen it by exercising it.

This marvelous gift of faith entails "rendering to God the intellectual powers, [and the] abandonment of the mind and will to God."[60] Now to some this may sound almost as scary as throwing your parachute out of a plane, then jumping out after it in the hope that you will be able to catch up with it and strap it on in time to make a soft landing. That is ultimate presumption. And so is relying on yourself for salvation—that is spiritual suicide.

Blessed assurance

It is infinitely safer to throw yourself into the outstretched arms of God, for "if you trust in the LORD, he will keep you safe" (Proverbs 29:25, NIrV).[61] *He* assures us that on Calvary the cross-crushed Christ did everything necessary to make *us* righteous before the Father. *He* guarantees that "neither death nor life, . . . height nor depth, . . . shall be able to separate us from the love of God which is in Christ Jesus" (Romans 8:38, 39, NKJV)—"not because we hold Him so firmly, but because He holds us so fast."[62] So "if Christ is my Saviour, my sacrifice, my atonement, then I shall never perish."[63] "Let us give thanks to God! He gives us the victory because of what our Lord Jesus Christ has done" (1 Corinthians 15:57, NIrV).

Endnotes

1. Ellen G. White, *Education* (Mountain View, CA: Pacific Press®, 1942), 18. "Every command is a promise; accepted by the will, received into the soul, it brings with it the life of the Infinite One. It transforms the nature and re-creates the soul in the image of God." Ibid., 126. "All His biddings are enablings." Ellen G. White, *Christ's Object Lessons* (Washington, DC: Review and Herald®, 1941), 333.

2. Ellen G. White, *Testimonies for the Church* (Mountain View, CA: Pacific Press®, 1948), 6:331.

3. This question should not be misunderstood to support the fallacious idea that perfection is the result of self-initiated, self-designed, self-implemented personal effort.

4. "First I must see the nail marks in his hands. I must put my finger where the nails were. I must put my hand into his side. Only then will I believe" (John 20:25, NIrV). Cf. "Here is what we announce to everyone about the Word of life. The Word was already here from the beginning. We have heard him. We have seen him with our eyes. We have looked at him. Our hands have touched him" (1 John 1:1, NIrV).

5. The Scriptures. The Spirit of Prophecy also bears the impress of Inspiration. And God sometimes influences the minds of individuals directly. "Your own ears will hear him. Right behind you a voice will say, 'This is the way you should go,' whether to the right or to the left" (Isaiah 30:21, NLT).

6. "The Berean Jews were very glad to receive Paul's message. They studied the Scriptures carefully every day. They wanted to see if what Paul said was true" (Acts 17:11, NIrV).

7. Ellen G. White, *Patriarchs and Prophets* (Mountain View, CA: Pacific Press®, 1958), 432.

8. Ellen G. White, *Testimonies for the Church* (Mountain View, CA: Pacific Press®, 1948), 4:583 (gender neutral).

9. Ellen G. White, *Testimonies for the Church* (Mountain View, CA: Pacific Press®, 1948), 5:705.

10. It is arguably possible that God might reveal information to an individual about his or her standing through a dream, vision, or impression (Joel 2:28). And it is also possible that Satan might appear in the guise of Christ and declare that a person is perfect. While a subjective experience of supernatural revelation should not be summarily dismissed as com-

pletely unreliable, sanctified discernment should be exercised to test the veracity of what is revealed in this atypical way by comparing the manifestation with what is revealed in Scripture. "To the law and to the testimony! If they do not speak according to this word, it is because there is no light in them" (Isaiah 8:20, NKJV).

11. Ellen G. White, "The Whole Duty of Man," *Signs of the Times*, May 16, 1895.

12. "Jesus sits as a refiner and purifier of silver. The furnace in which you may be placed may be very hot, yet you will come forth as gold seven times purified, reflecting the image of Jesus." Ellen G. White, *In Heavenly Places* (Washington, DC: Review and Herald®, 1967), 119.

13. White, *Education*, 105.

14. Ellen G. White, *Maranatha* (Washington, DC: Review and Herald®, 1976), 236.

15. Ellen G. White, *The Acts of the Apostles* (Mountain View, CA: Pacific Press®, 1911), 560, 561.

16. "We are to cry to God daily, 'Create in me a clean heart, O God.' " Ellen G. White, *Manuscript Releases*, vol. 17 (Silver Spring, MD: Ellen G. White Estate, 1990), 115.

17. "All that Christ received from God we too may have." White, *Christ's Object Lessons*, 149.

18. Ellen G. White, "City Work," *Review and Herald*, January 18, 1912.

19. Ellen G. White, *Testimonies for the Church* (Mountain View, CA: Pacific Press®, 1948), 1:203.

20. White, *Christ's Object Lessons*, 65.

21. Ellen G. White, "Faith and Its Effects," *Signs of the Times*, June 10, 1889, 338.

22. Ellen G. White, *Selected Messages*, bk. 2 (Washington, DC: Review and Herald®, 1958), 183.

23. White, *Maranatha*, 252.

24. Ellen G. White, *Last Day Events* (Boise, ID: Pacific Press®, 1992), 206.

25. Ibid., 205.

26. Ellen G. White, *The Desire of Ages* (Mountain View, CA: Pacific Press®, 1940), 250.

27. Ian Thomas, *The Saving Life of Christ* (Grand Rapids, MI: Zondervan, 1961), 70 (emphasis in original).

28. White, *The Acts of the Apostles*, 532.

29. White, *Christ's Object Lessons*, 332.

30. Ellen G. White, *The Great Controversy* (Mountain View, CA: Pacific Press®, 1911), 678.

31. Ibid., 677.

32. "And others had trial of cruel mockings and scourgings, yea, moreover of bonds and imprisonment: They were stoned, they were sawn asunder, were tempted, were slain with the sword: they wandered about in sheepskins and goatskins; being destitute, afflicted, tormented" (Hebrews 11:36, 37, KJV).

33. White, *The Great Controversy*, 622.

34. "And the princes, governors, and captains, and the king's counsellors, being gathered together, saw these men, upon whose bodies the fire had no power, nor was an hair of their head singed, neither were their coats changed, nor the smell of fire had passed on them" (Daniel 3:27, KJV).

35. Ellen G. White, "In Gethsemane," *Signs of the Times*, December 9, 1897, 3 (756).

36. White, *The Desire of Ages*, 693.

37. "We may boldly say, The Lord is my helper, and I will not fear what man shall do unto me" (Hebrews 13:6, KJV). "God Himself has said, 'I will never, never let go your hand: I will never never forsake you' " (Hebrews 13:5, Weymouth). "When you go through deep waters, I will be with you. When you go through rivers of difficulty, you will not drown. When you walk through the fire of oppression, you will not be burned up; the flames will not consume you" (Isaiah 43:2, NLT). "And remember that I am always with you until the end of time" (Matthew 28:20, GW).

38. "You will keep in perfect peace all who trust in you, all whose thoughts are fixed on you!" (Isaiah 26:3, NLT).

39. "For I admit my shameful deed—it haunts me day and night" (Psalm 51:3, TLB).

40. "God sometimes uses sorrow in our lives to help us turn away from sin and seek eternal life. We should never regret his sending it" (2 Corinthians 7:10, TLB).

41. "The closer you come to Jesus, the more faulty you will appear in your own eyes; for your vision will be clearer, and your imperfections will be seen in broad and distinct contrast to His perfect nature." Ellen G. White, *Steps to Christ* (Mountain View, CA: Pacific Press®, 1956), 64.

42. "We shall often have to bow down and weep at the feet of Jesus because of our shortcomings and mistakes, but we are not to be discouraged. Even if we are overcome by the enemy, we are not cast off, not forsaken and rejected of God." Ellen G. White, *Reflecting Christ* (Washington, DC: Review and Herald®, 1985), 123.

43. "There is no salvation without repentance. No impenitent sinner can believe with his heart unto

righteousness. Repentance is described by Paul as a godly sorrow for sin that 'worketh repentance to salvation not to be repented of' (2 Corinthians 7:10). This repentance has in it nothing of the nature of merit, but it prepares the heart for the acceptance of Christ as the only Saviour, the only hope of the lost sinner." Ellen G. White, *Faith and Works* (Nashville: Southern Pub. Assn., 1979), 99.

44. Ellen G. White, *Spiritual Gifts* (Washington, DC: Review and Herald®, 1945), 2:36.

45. "The human mind is the most deceitful of all things. It is incurable. No one can understand how deceitful it is" (Jeremiah 17:9, GW).

46. White, *Christ's Object Lessons*, 155.

47. "If you form too high an opinion of yourself, you will think that your labors are of more real consequence than they are, and you will plead individual independence which borders on arrogance. If you go to the other extreme and form too low an opinion of yourself, you will feel inferior and will leave an impression of inferiority which will greatly limit the influence that you might have for good. You should avoid either extreme. Feeling should not control you; circumstances should not affect you. You may form a correct estimate of yourself, one which will prove a safeguard from both extremes. You may be dignified without vain self-confidence; you may be condescending and yielding without sacrificing self-respect or individual independence, and your life may be of great influence with those in the higher as well as the lower walks of life." Ellen G. White, *Mind, Character, and Personality* (Nashville, TN: Southern Pub. Assn., 1977), 1:274.

48. "All that I know now is partial and incomplete, but then I will know everything completely, just as God now knows me completely" (1 Corinthians 13:12, NLT).

49. "I have much more to say to you, but you are unable at present to bear the burden of it" (John 16:12, Weymouth).

50. "Satan has the ability to suggest doubts and to devise objections to the pointed testimony that God sends, and many think it a virtue, a mark of intelligence in them, to be unbelieving and to question and quibble. Those who desire to doubt will have plenty of room. God does not propose to remove all occasion for unbelief. He gives evidence, which must be carefully investigated with a humble mind and a teachable spirit, and all should decide from the weight of

evidence. God gives sufficient evidence for the candid mind to believe; but he who turns from the weight of evidence because there are a few things which he cannot make plain to his finite understanding will be left in the cold, chilling atmosphere of unbelief and questioning doubts, and will make shipwreck of faith." Ellen G. White, *Counsels for the Church* (Boise, ID: Pacific Press®, 1991), 93.

51. Ellen G. White, *Christian Education* (Battle Creek, MI: International Tract Society, 1893), 199.

52. See readings 698–920 in *Seventh-day Adventist Hymnal* (Hagerstown, MD: Review and Herald®, 1985).

53. A tool to compare translations is on the Bible Study Tools website at https://www.biblestudytools .com/compare-translations/.

54. Jon L. Dybdahl, ed., *Andrews Study Bible* (Berrien Springs, MI: Andrews University Press, 2010).

55. Francis D. Nichol, ed., *The Seventh-day Adventist Bible Commentary*, 7 vols. (Washington, DC: Review and Herald®, 1953–1980).

56. "The secret things belong to the Lord our God. The revealed things belong to us and to our children forever" (Deuteronomy 29:29, CEB).

57. "Truly I tell you, if you have faith as small as a mustard seed, you can say to this mountain, 'Move from here to there,' and it will move. Nothing will be impossible for you" (Matthew 17:20, NIV).

58. "We cannot create our faith, but we can be co-laborers with Christ in promoting the growth and triumph of faith." White, *In Heavenly Places*, 109.

59. "God has given to every man his measure of faith, and each is to walk in faith. He is to show that he has that faith that will rely upon God for help. As God has given to every man his measure of faith, he is to put it into exercise. He is to let his light shine." Ellen G. White, *Sermons and Talks*, vol 2 (Silver Spring, MD: E. G. White Estate, 1994), 133.

60. "Faith is rendering to God the intellectual powers, abandonment of the mind and will to God, and making Christ the only door to enter into the kingdom of heaven." White, *Faith and Works*, 25.

61. Cf. Jeremiah 29:11, NCV: " 'I say this because I know what I am planning for you,' says the Lord. 'I have good plans for you, not plans to hurt you. I will give you hope and a good future.' "

62. Ellen G. White, *That I Might Know Him* (Washington, DC: Review and Herald®, 1964), 80.

63. White, *Selected Messages*, bk. 2, 381.

8

Jesus Christ: Savior and Example

Darius W. Jankiewicz

Introduction

All those who consider themselves Christian, according to the true sense of the word, embrace the biblical truth that Jesus Christ came to this earth to save the lost (John 3:16, 36). The salvation of humanity was singularly accomplished through Christ's death on the cross. This truth has always been at the center of all Christian confessions throughout the ages of Christian history and is traditionally referred to in theological nomenclature as the *passive* obedience of Christ, that is, His voluntary desire to submit Himself to the ignominy of the cross for the sake of lost humanity. Theologians also speak of Christ's *active* obedience when they refer to His righteous and sinless life through perfect fulfillment of God's law. It is Christ's *active* obedience that qualified Him to become the perfect sacrificial Lamb of God who could take "away the sin of the world" (John 1:29).[1] While distinguished, these two aspects of Christ's saving mission—His *passive* and *active* obedience—must never be separated. "The two accompany each other at every point in the Saviour's life."[2] In His passive obedience, Christ paid the price for the sins of humanity; and as a result of His active obedience, Christ's accomplishments are credited to the believer. Believers appropriate both aspects of Christ's work on behalf of humanity through the means of faith.

But Christ did even more than living righteously and dying for the sake of humanity. He also left behind a supreme example of what it means to lead a holy life. While those who choose to follow the God of the Bible are saved solely through the life and death of Christ, the authors of the biblical account do not shy away from the proposition that genuine conviction on the part of the believer will result in a special kind of life. It is the purpose of this chapter to explore the profound richness found in Scripture and the writings of Ellen G. White regarding God's relentless appeal to believers to fulfill His plan for their lives. In the process, I will explore such themes as God's call to holiness during Old Testament times; the identity of Christ and His uniqueness, as well as the extent of His identification with fallen humanity; and finally, the question pertinent to this volume: whether Christ needed to be exactly like us to provide an example of holy living.

The call to holiness during Old Testament times

God is holy! There is little doubt that the holiness of God is one of the most important and prominent themes of the entire Scriptures. In fact, the Hebrew word for "holy," or "to be holy" (*qādaš*), is used to describe one of the most pronounced characteristics of God in the Old Testament.[3]

When God revealed Himself to the Hebrew nation, He did so primarily as a holy Being. "Holy, holy, holy is the LORD Almighty," the seraphim exclaim in Isaiah's vision (Isaiah 6:3). What does it mean that God is holy? The scriptural narrative suggests two basic dimensions of God's holiness. First, God is presented as singularly distinct and separate from all creation (Exodus 15:11; 1 Samuel 2:2; Hosea 11:9).[4] Second, there is an ethical dimension to God's holiness; that is, God is holy in the sense that He is opposed to sin and not in any way defiled by it. Thus, He is morally pure and perfect (Leviticus 19:2–37; Isaiah 5:16).[5]

The Old Testament pronouncements of God's holiness are coupled with His desire for His people to also be holy. The call to "be holy because I, the LORD your God, am holy" (Leviticus 19:2; 20:26), issued at a crucial time in Israel's history and echoed throughout the rest of the Old Testament, appears to be of utmost importance to the existence of the nation. For the Old Testament writers, God Himself was the source of all holiness, and thus it was He who made His people holy if they chose to follow Him (Exodus 31:13; Ezekiel 20:12). The holiness to which God called His people clearly was to be grounded in His own two-dimensional vision of holiness. First, Israel was to be His "treasured possession" and thus a separate or distinct nation from other nations (Exodus 19:6; Leviticus 20:26; Deuteronomy 7:6). This was to ensure Israel's ritual purity and exclusive dedication to the service of God.[6] Second, the Hebrew nation was called by God to reflect His moral and ethical character in its actions. This included following God's commandments as well as

the righteous treatment of other human beings. The Old Testament recounts examples of people who chose to follow this course of action. "Enoch walked faithfully with God; then he was no more, because God took him away" (Genesis 5:24); "Noah was a righteous man, blameless among the people of his time . . . [who] walked faithfully with God" (Genesis 6:9); Job is spoken of by God as "blameless and upright" (Job 1:8); and David is described as a "man after his [God's] own heart" (1 Samuel 13:14). Both aspects of holiness—separateness and ethical behavior—were to be exemplified in the nation of Israel and were essential for the fulfillment of God's mission, which is the salvation of all nations (Isaiah 45:21, 22; 66:18–21).

While in the Old Testament God unrelentingly called His people to adhere to a high ethical and moral standard of holiness, He alone was the absolute standard of holiness. The people of God were continually implored to remember His actions, reflect on His moral character, and replicate His characteristics in their daily lives. It must be emphasized, however, that ultimately they were offered salvation because they had put their faith in God, not because they had become morally pure (Genesis 15:6; Hebrews 11), and it was this total commitment to God that resulted in godly lives. Thus, throughout the Old Testament, it was God Himself who was the great exemplar of holiness for humanity. Echoes of His call, "I am the LORD your God; consecrate yourselves and be holy, because I am holy" (Leviticus 11:44), reverberate throughout the Old Testament.

The theme of God's holiness continues in

the New Testament[7] and, as in the Old Testament, is found to have two basic dimensions: that of separateness from the world (John 17:14; Romans 12:2; Revelation 15:4) and that of ethical or moral holiness (Ephesians 4:1; Philippians 1:27). Thus, according to the New Testament writers, Christian holiness was not represented just in their newfound status in Christ (Hebrews 10:10; 1 Peter 1:9), it was also represented in their characters and thus in their behavior. And once again, God is the great exemplar of both aspects of holiness. Peter thus exhorts the believers: "But just as he who called you is holy, so be holy in all you do; for it is written: 'Be holy, because I am holy' " (1 Peter 1:15, 16). The ethical dimension of God's holiness is also evident in the statements of Jesus, such as, "Be perfect, therefore, as your heavenly Father is perfect" (Matthew 5:48) and the parallel in Luke, "Be merciful, just as your Father is merciful" (Luke 6:36), as well as in Paul's repeated exhortations for believers to live in a manner worthy of "God's holy people" and to resist all forms of temptation and sin (Ephesians 5:3; 1 Thessalonians 4:7). In summary, both the Old and New Testaments urge readers to imitate the holiness of God and thus to be holy.

Jesus as "the holy thing": The uniqueness of Christ in the New Testament

There is one significant difference, however, between the way believers experienced God's holiness in the Old Testament and the New Testament. The Old Testament pronounced God's holiness through theophanies, divine actions, and the words and writings of the prophets. In addition to these, the New Testament revealed God's holiness in and through the person of Jesus Christ, who was "the exact representation of his [God's] being" (Hebrews 1:3). What do we know about Jesus Christ? The New Testament is clear regarding His nature and identity.

Christ's holiness and divinity. Luke's Gospel account begins with a description of Jesus' conception and birth. According to Luke, the angel told Mary that the Holy Spirit "shall come upon thee," and the power of the Most High "shall overshadow thee." As a result of God's action, the one who was to come from Mary's virgin womb was *hagion,* or the "holy thing," and "the Son of God" (Luke 1:35, KJV; the "holy one," NIV). The record of the angel's proclamation leaves one with little doubt as to the special nature of the One who was to be born of Mary. This special Child was not to *become* holy, as was expected of other human beings, but was to *be* holy by nature from the moment of conception. As Derek Tidball notes, "It was [Christ's] nature and character to be separate *from* others, whilst being fully human and sharing human life without reserve."[8] Jesus' extraordinary birth circumstances, the result of a one-of-a-kind divine and human interaction, set Jesus' birth "apart from all other births" and thus confirms His uniqueness.[9] From the time of His birth, Christ was to be *holy* just as His Father in heaven was *holy.*[10] The New Testament writers never discuss how such a birth could be possible or what kind of nature Jesus had.[11] They simply acknowledge that Jesus was "separate" from the rest of humanity by the unique circumstances of His birth.[12]

The concept of Jesus as "the holy one" is

repeated throughout the New Testament, where He is referred to as "the Holy One of God" (Mark 1:24; Luke 4:34) or the Old Testament God, and thus identified as a fully Divine Being. Matthew's Gospel account begins with Jesus being called "Immanuel," or "God with us" (Matthew 1:23). He is spoken of as God (John 1:1; 10:30; 20:28) and referred to as behaving and speaking like God (John 8:58; 14:9). And when Jesus claimed to be "one" with the Father, the Jewish leaders contested His claim, charging Him with blasphemy (John 10:31–33).

Following the example of the Gospel writers, other New Testament authors unabashedly refer to Jesus as God. Paul refers to Christ as "God over all" (Romans 9:5) and "our great God and Savior" (Titus 2:13).[13] Similarly, in Philippians 2:6, Jesus is described as "being in very nature God," and in Hebrews 1:8, Jesus is referred to as God: "Your throne, O God, will last forever." Peter also speaks of Jesus as "our God and Savior" (2 Peter 1:1). Thus, the writers of the New Testament unequivocally equate Jesus Christ with God the Father.[14]

Likewise, Ellen G. White identifies Jesus as "a Son begotten in the express image of the Father's person, and in all the brightness of his majesty and glory, *one equal with God in authority*, dignity, and divine perfection. In him dwelt all the fullness of the Godhead bodily";[15] Christ was "equal with the Father from the beginning."[16] Thus, Ellen G. White identifies the preincarnate Christ as the One who spoke to the people of old: "It was Christ who from the bush on Mount Horeb spoke to Moses saying, 'I AM THAT I AM,' " and thus revealed God to the patriarch.[17] It was Christ who later

led Israel through the pillar of cloud,[18] who instructed Israel and "set up His tabernacle in the midst of our human encampment."[19] It was Christ "who gave to Moses the law engraved upon the tables of stone."[20] This same God later came "in the likeness of men" and "declared Himself the I AM."[21] "In Christ," she boldly asserts, "is life, original, unborrowed, underived. . . . The divinity of Christ is the believer's assurance of eternal life."[22] It is thus indubitable that both the New Testament and Ellen White present Christ as the great I AM of the Old Testament, fully divine, coeternal and coequal in authority with God the Father.[23]

Christ's full divinity carries deep theological significance for humanity. Most important, it identifies Jesus Christ as the only Savior of humanity. The Old Testament writers are clear that no one can usurp or add to God's work of saving humanity. God declares, "I, even I, am the LORD, and apart from me there is no savior" (Isaiah 43:11). Similarly, God exclaims, "You shall acknowledge no God but me, no Savior except me" (Hosea 13:4). As evidenced above, Jesus identifies Himself with the God of the Old Testament. He, the incarnate God of the universe, is thus *the only* Savior of humanity. In other words, no one can contribute anything of substance to God's saving work. Second, because of His full divinity, Christ's death on the cross carries the stamp of all sufficiency. His is the perfect, all-sufficient sacrifice, and nothing can be added that would contribute to the salvation of humanity (1 Peter 1:19; Hebrews 9:14; 10:10).

Christ's humanity. While Christ's full, coequal divinity carries enormous significance, it must also be emphasized that the New Testament affirms His full humanity. At one time in history, the preexistent *logos*, who *was God*, became a human being.[24] During the early Christian centuries, some groups—most notably Docetists and Apollinarians—denied the full humanity of Christ.[25] But this is not what we find in the New Testament. Raoul Dederen argues that Paul's assertion that the preincarnate Christ was *morphē theou*, or "in the form of God" (Philippians 2:6, KJV), indicates that He possessed "the essential characteristics and qualities" of being God. In the same way, Paul's declaration that Jesus took *morphē doulou*, or "the form of a servant [slave]" (verse 7), indicates that He embraced "the essential characteristic and qualities that make a human being what it is."[26] Thus, there can be no doubt that Jesus became fully human and that His humanity was "real and complete."[27] To be sure, the Incarnation did not mean that the Second Person of the Godhead ceased to be God when He became human; rather, while remaining God, the incarnate Son of God took upon Himself human nature, thus becoming God and human at the same time. In Jesus, there was a perfect union of His preexistent, divine nature with human nature, which He voluntarily took upon Himself.

The New Testament clearly teaches the full humanity of Jesus. Notwithstanding the miraculous circumstances of His conception, He came into the world through the natural human process of birth. He matured as every human child. While there was no sin in Him, He looked and lived like all other human beings. He suffered from common physical limitations, such as hunger and tiredness. As with all other human beings, He experienced emotion, and He longed for human companionship and friendship. And ultimately, like every other human being, His life ended in death.[28] "It is apparent," writes Millard Erickson, "that for the disciples and the authors of the New Testament books, there was no question about Jesus's humanity."[29]

Ellen G. White concurs, "[Christ] took human nature. He became flesh even as we are. . . . While in this world, [He] lived a life of complete humanity."[30] Moreover, "Jesus accepted humanity when the race had been weakened by four thousand years of sin. Like every child of Adam He accepted the results of the working of the great law of heredity."[31] "Clad in the vestments of humanity," she further writes, "the Son of God came down to the level of those he wished to save. . . . He took upon him our sinful nature."[32] "Our Saviour," she often affirms, "took humanity, with all its liabilities."[33] Thus, the New Testament writers and Ellen G. White leave little doubt as to the full, or complete, humanity of Christ.

At this point, an important question arises: Why did God choose to become human? The New Testament writers provide a plethora of answers, only a few of which can be mentioned here. First, Christ became human to give evidence of God's initiative in the process of salvation. By becoming human, God showed His commitment to restoring the broken relationship between Himself and humanity (1 Peter 1:20; Revelation 13:8). Through the process of the Incarnation, God bridged the chasm created by sin, thus reuniting humanity to

Himself and providing the possibility of eternal life for humanity.

Second, through the person of Christ, humanity was given the opportunity of truly knowing God. As a result of sin, God's nature had gradually become obfuscated, and humanity had lost a true understanding of who God is. Thus, Christ came to reveal God. "Anyone who has seen me," Jesus said, "has seen the Father" (John 14:9). Jesus, the New Testament authors argued, was the express image of the Father (2 Corinthians 4:4; Hebrews 1:3).

Third, Jesus came to die for humanity. In the person of Christ, God made the ultimate sacrifice on behalf of humanity. The authors of the New Testament clearly understood that, in order for His sacrifice to have full efficacy, God willingly humbled Himself and became human: "Since the children have flesh and blood, he too shared in their humanity so that by his death he might break the power of him who holds the power of death.... For this reason he had to be made like them, fully human in every way, in order that he might become a merciful and faithful high priest in service to God, and that he might make atonement for the sins of the people" (Hebrews 2:14–17). Accordingly, if Jesus had not become human, the efficacy of His sacrifice would be in question.

Fourth, Jesus came to identify with fallen humanity and to provide an example of holy living. To a careful examination of this last point we now turn.

The identification of Christ with the suffering of humanity

While the primary purpose of Christ's incarnation was to reconcile humanity with God through His death,[34] the New Testament also teaches that He came to identify with fallen humanity and to provide comfort for those who struggle with sin. As evidenced previously, Christ embraced humanity thoroughly and completely. Apart from enabling Him to provide atonement for humanity, His identification with humanity allowed the triune God to take up "our infirmities" and carry "our diseases" (Matthew 8:17). As a result, Christ is able to perfectly sympathize with the struggles of "estranged and dysfunctional humanity."[35] Hebrews 4:15 is the locus classicus that expresses this thought: "For we do not have a high priest who is unable to empathize with our weaknesses." Because Jesus came to us as fully human, He knows what it means to live in a world full of sin and fear, wickedness and destruction; to be lonely and homeless, hungry and thirsty; and to be accused and rejected. When He stoops down to us, He does so as the God who has endured human suffering.

Christ's identification with humanity also means that He "has been tempted in every way, just as we are" (verse 15). Ellen G. White suggests that Jesus' experience of all that humanity endures was necessary for two reasons: first, "if we had to bear anything which Jesus did not endure, then upon this point Satan would represent the power of God as insufficient for us";[36] and second, because He suffered in His temptations, He is now "able to help those who are being tempted" (Hebrews 2:18). Thus, while "many say that Jesus was not like us, that He was not as we are in the world, that He was divine, and therefore we cannot overcome as He overcame.... This is not true.... Christ knows the sinner's trials; He knows his temptations. He took upon Himself our nature; He was tempted in all points like as we are. He has wept, He was a man of sorrows, and acquainted with grief."[37] Thus, Christ became a "sharer in all the experiences of humanity, He could feel not only for, but with, every burdened and tempted and struggling one."[38] This knowledge—that Christ suffered temptation like every human being—should be a source of great comfort for all those who struggle with sin.[39]

Furthermore, not only was Jesus "tempted in every way, just as we are" (Hebrews 4:15), Ellen G. White suggests that no other human being has ever been "so fiercely beset by temptation; never another bore so heavy a burden of the world's sin and pain."[40] "Never will man be tried with temptations as powerful as those which assailed Christ."[41] "Christ alone had experience in all the sorrows and temptations that befall human beings."[42] White attributes the greater intensity of Christ's temptations to the fact that His nature was "more exalted, and pure, and holy"[43] than that of other human beings. Thus, "the temptations that Christ withstood were as much stronger than ours as his nobility and majesty are greater than ours."[44] As a result of His suffering, however, "never was there another whose sympathies were so broad or so tender."[45] Moreover, Christ's sympathy for humanity is accompanied by an assurance: due to His identification with and thus understanding of humanity, He can help us overcome temptation. White writes, "He is watching over you,

trembling child of God. Are you tempted? He will deliver. Are you weak? He will strengthen. Are you ignorant? He will enlighten. Are you wounded? He will heal."[46] Because Christ identified with and thus understands the human condition, we can "approach God's throne of grace with confidence, so that we may receive mercy and find grace to help us in our time of need" (Hebrews 4:16). As Louis Berkhof states, "Only such a truly human Mediator, who had experiential knowledge of the woes of mankind and rose superior to all temptations, could enter sympathetically into all the experiences, the trials, and the temptations of man and be a perfect human example for His followers."[47]

Christ as a perfect human example

Identifying with fallen humanity while being without sin (Hebrews 4:15) allowed Jesus Christ to be a perfect example for humans in all areas of life. Beginning with Paul, Christian writers of all persuasions have always affirmed Jesus Christ to be the supreme pattern for moral and ethical behavior. Multitudes of volumes published throughout the centuries exhort Christians to look to Christ alone as the ultimate exemplar of the Christian life.[48]

The theme of "Christ as an example" is extraordinarily vast in the New Testament, as well as in the writings of Ellen G. White.[49] It is, thus, impossible in this short chapter to comprehensively explore the profound depth and richness of this theme as presented in these writings.[50] Thus, this paper will briefly examine just a few areas in which the Scriptures and the writings of Ellen G. White view Christ as the ultimate exemplar for fallen humanity.

First and foremost, Jesus is the quintessential exemplar of the perfect fulfillment of the two great commandments: to love God and one's neighbor (Matthew 22:37–39). The mutual agape love between the Father and the Son serves as an example of the love that Christians should exhibit toward one another.[51] "A new command I give you: Love one another. As I have loved you, so you must love one another" (John 13:34). In Ephesians 5:2, Paul appealed to his readers to "walk in the way of love, just as Christ loved us." Similarly, Ellen G. White frequently affirms that "Christ has given us an example of love . . . , and has enjoined upon his followers to love one another as he has loved us";[52] that "he presented to the world a new phase of greatness in his exhibition of mercy, compassion, and love";[53] and that "Christ is . . . [our] pattern." "[He] has given us an example of pure, disinterested love."[54]

Christ's perfect fulfillment of the two great commandments resulted in genuine obedience in all areas of His life. Jesus is, thus, the ultimate exemplar of obedience to the commandments of God. "The life of Christ is a perfect fulfillment of every precept of this law. . . . His life is our standard of obedience and service."[55] "Christ came to magnify the law and make it honorable. He showed that it is based upon the broad foundation of love to God and love to man, and that obedience to its precepts comprises the whole duty of man. In His own life He gave an example of obedience to the law of God."[56] "And since the law of God is 'holy, and just, and good,' a transcript of the divine perfection, it follows that a

character formed by obedience to that law will be holy. Christ is a perfect example of such a character."[57] It is because of His character that Christ could give us "the example of sinless life."[58]

In addition to this image of Christ as the supreme example of obedience, the New Testament also portrays Christ as an example of self-denial, suffering, and self-sacrifice on behalf of others. "If anyone would come after me, let him deny himself and take up his cross and follow me" (Matthew 16:24, ESV; see also Mark 8:34; Ephesians 5:2; 1 Peter 2:21; Philippians 2:5, 8). Similarly, Ellen G. White writes that Christ taught His disciples "self-sacrifice for the good of others. . . . The true disciple of Christ will follow His example."[59] "Daily we need the fresh revealing of His presence. We need to follow more closely His example of self-renunciation and self-sacrifice."[60] "Christ is the example of every believer. While in the heavenly courts, he chose to lay aside his royal robe and his kingly crown, and come to this earth as one among men, to live a life of poverty and self-denial."[61]

The inspired writers also present Christ as a divine pattern in resistance to temptations. "Because he himself suffered when he was tempted, he is able to help those who are being tempted" (Hebrews 2:18). Similarly, Ellen G. White notes that while Christ's nature was "holy and pure," He was still tempted "in all points as we are." But, as noted above, because "his nobility and majesty are greater than ours," His temptations were also much stronger in magnitude than those experienced by any human being.[62] While the "strength and power" of Christ's temptations will never be experienced by human beings, "it is the privilege of men and women to gain the victory over temptation through the merits of the crucified and risen Saviour, who is familiar with every trial of humanity."[63] Because of His victory over temptations, *"He has left us a bright example,* that we should follow His steps."[64]

Christ is also an exemplar of humility (see, e.g., Matthew 11:29; John 13:13–15). Paul thus implores the believers in Philippi:

Have the same mindset as Christ Jesus:

Who, being in very nature God,
did not consider equality with God
something to be used to his
own advantage,
rather, he made himself nothing,
by taking the very nature of a servant [slave] (Philippians 2:5–7).

Commenting on this passage, Ellen G. White writes, "God permits every human being to exercise his individuality. He desires no one to submerge his mind in the mind of a fellow mortal. Those who desire to be transformed in mind and character are not to look to men, but to the divine Example."[65] Christ's example of humility, so magnificently expressed by Paul in this passage, also forms the foundation for another way in which Christ serves as an example to fallen humanity, namely, as an example of leadership.

Philippians 2:5–7 clearly echoes Jesus' conversation with His disciples when they jostled to secure higher positions in His kingdom. In Mark 10:43–45, Jesus unequivocally pointed to Himself as an example of godly leadership: "Not so with you. Instead, . . . whoever wants to be first must be slave of all. For even the Son of Man did not come to be served, but to serve, and to give his life as a ransom for many." Referring to these passages, Ellen G. White writes,

It is time now for men to humble their hearts before God and to learn to work in His ways. Let those who have sought to rule their fellow workers study to know what manner of spirit they are of. They should seek the Lord by fasting and prayer, and in humility of soul.

Christ in His earthly life gave an example that all can safely follow. He appreciates His flock, and He wants no power set over them that will restrict their freedom in His service. He has never placed man as a ruler over His heritage. True Bible religion will lead to self-control, not to control of one another. As a people we need a larger measure of the Holy Spirit, that we may bear the solemn message that God has given us, without exaltation.[66]

Christ also is the exemplar of "faith and firm trust in God"[67] and of how to relate to others,[68] to exercise mercy,[69] to pray,[70] and to exemplify Him in preaching and teaching as well as in medical and missionary ministry.[71] Christ, thus, serves as the supreme exemplar in a multitude of ways. Both the New Testament writers and Ellen G. White appear to be deeply convicted that, through His example, Jesus provided fallen humanity with all it needs to live godly and fulfilling lives. Ellen G. White concludes, "To save the transgressor of God's law, Christ, the one equal with the Father, came to live heaven before men, that they might learn to know what it is to have heaven in the heart. He illustrated that man must be to be worthy of the precious boon of the life that measures with the life of God."[72]

Thus, it becomes clear that following the example of Christ is not optional for the believer. Only through "fixing our eyes on Jesus" and following His example can Christians experience the abundant life promised by Christ (Hebrews 12:2; John 10:10). It must be noted, however, that while all Christians are beseeched by inspired writers to follow the example of Christ, *following His example is not the means of salvation*. A desire to follow the example of Christ results as a believer understands what Christ accomplished for him or her on the cross. True holiness and obedience always come as a result of hearing, understanding, and accepting by faith the gospel of Jesus Christ. While Christ's life of love, humility, self-sacrifice, and obedience might be attractive to believers and nonbelievers,[73] it is not His example that should primarily attract us to Him but rather the ultimate manifestation of His love on the cross. A true Christian life of humility, obedience, and self-sacrifice is the outcome of accepting Christ as our Substitute. As Ellen G. White affirms, "A work is to be accomplished . . . similar to that which took place at the outpouring of the holy Spirit in the days of the early disciples, when they preached Jesus and him

crucified. Many will be converted in a day; for the message will go with power."[74] And again, "the theme that attracts the heart of the sinner is Christ, and him crucified. On the cross of Calvary, Jesus stands revealed to the world in unparalleled love. Present him thus to the hungering multitudes, and the light of his love will win men from darkness to light, from transgression to obedience and true holiness. Beholding Jesus upon the cross of Calvary arouses the conscience to the heinous character of sin as nothing else can do."[75]

Although no believer in Christ has ever denied that Jesus is the supreme exemplar of ethical and moral behavior, a question has at times been raised regarding the nature of His humanity. Was Jesus' humanity *exactly like ours*? In other words, was His humanity as fallen as ours? And if not, can He be our example?

Was Christ exactly like us?

Throughout Christian history, few thinkers discussed the precise nature of Christ's humanity. The fourth-century theologian Gregory of Nazianzus was one of the first theologians to explore this issue, asserting: "For that which He has not assumed He has not healed."[76] Gregory's assumption was that unless Jesus was exactly like us, the healing of human nature would not have been possible. This position went hand in hand with Gregory's belief that God does not judge newborn infants because there is nothing evil in them at birth.[77] Salvation, thus, consisted primarily in bringing "humans to the same status as the humanity of Jesus Christ";[78] a process labeled by ancient Christians as *theosis*, or "divinization" (also "deification").[79] In later centuries, the view that Christ's human nature was exactly like ours occasionally surfaced within both Catholic and Protestant theology.[80] Nineteenth-century Scottish theologian Edward Irving (1792–1834) became the most vocal proponent of the view that the humanity of Christ was exactly like that of Adam after the Fall.[81] During the latter part of the nineteenth century, a blend of both Gregory's and Irving's positions was adopted by some within the Seventh-day Adventist Church and continues to be held in some Adventist circles today.[82]

So was Jesus exactly like us? Was His human nature like that of every child born after the Fall? It would be highly desirable to obtain clear, unambiguous answers from the inspired writings; however, neither the New Testament nor Ellen G. White provide unequivocal answers to these questions. As evidenced above, both the New Testament and Ellen G. White affirm the full, complete humanity of Christ; however, it must be acknowledged that Ellen G. White also made many statements regarding the "fallen" nature of Christ, the following being but examples: "It was in the order of God that Christ should take upon Himself the form and nature of fallen man";[83] "sinless and exalted by nature, the Son of God consented to take the habiliments of humanity, to become one with the fallen race";[84] "clad in the vestments of humanity, the Son of God came down to the level of those he wished to save. . . . He took upon him our sinful nature."[85] Such statements lead some to conclude that it is seemingly incontrovertible that Jesus' human nature was exactly like that of every child of Adam since the Fall.

On the other hand, it must also be acknowledged that both the New Testament and Ellen G. White indicate that Christ's humanity was *not* the same as ours. Of Christ, it is said that, while yet in the womb, He was a "holy thing" (Luke 1:35, KJV) and that He never sinned (2 Corinthians 5:21). Of us, it is said that we are "shapen in iniquity" (Psalm 51:5, KJV) and that "from birth the wicked go astray; from the womb they are wayward" (Psalm 58:3). While Paul affirmed Christ's full humanity (e.g., 1 Timothy 2:5; 3:16), he nevertheless asserted that Christ had come "in the *likeness* of sinful flesh" (Romans 8:3, KJV; emphasis added) or "in the *likeness* of men" (Philippians 2:7, KJV; emphasis added).[86] Why such ambivalence? Could not Paul have written "in sinful flesh" or "born like all men" and thus avoided ambiguity? According to Thomas Schreiner, Paul's use of this word *likeness* "stresses the identity between Jesus and sinful flesh, yet at the same time it also suggests that he is unique."[87] Raoul Dederen also arrives at a similar conclusion:

Part of Christ's mission was to be truly human. He possessed the essential characteristics of human nature. He was "flesh and blood" (Heb. 2:14), and in all things like His fellow human beings (verse 17). His humanity did not correspond to Adam's humanity before the Fall, nor in every respect to Adam's humanity after the Fall, for the Scriptures portray Christ's humanity as sinless. . . . He came "in the likeness of sinful flesh" (Rom. 8:23). He took human nature in its fallen condition with its infirmities and liabilities and bearing the consequences of sin; but not its sinfulness. He was truly human, one with the human race, except for sin.[88]

The New Testament, thus, testifies to the uniqueness of Christ's humanity. What about Ellen G. White? While it must be acknowledged that many of her statements, in isolation from the totality of her writing, could be understood to mean that Jesus was born "exactly like us," she also makes statements that suggest otherwise: "[Christ is] a brother in our infirmities, but not in possessing like passions."[89]

> It is not correct to say, as many writers have said, that Christ was like all children. . . .
>
> . . . He was God in human flesh. When urged by his companions to do wrong, divinity flashed through humanity, and he refused decidedly.[90]

No other child experienced this because no other child was both divine and human. "He had not taken on Him even the nature of the angels, but humanity, perfectly identical with our own nature, except the taint of sin."[91] Given that all human beings are children of Adam, could one ever argue that all infants are born without "the taint of sin"? "His finite nature was pure and spotless."[92] "His nature was more exalted, and pure, and holy than that of the sinful race for whom he suffered."[93] "His character is superior to ours."[94] "His nobility and majesty are greater than ours."[95] "Jesus was holy and pure."[96]

Except for Christ, has there ever been an infant born on earth who could be described in such words? What would the response be if the parents of a newborn announced to their family and friends that their child's character was purer, holier, and superior to all other newborns? All parents are keenly aware of their children's capacity for sinfulness from a young age. Ellen G. White is aware of this reality when she states that the result of "eating of the tree of knowledge of good and evil is manifest in every man's experience. There is in his nature a bent to evil, a force which, unaided, he cannot resist."[97] Could it be said of Christ that He had "a bent to evil"?[98] Is this what Ellen G. White means when she writes that Christ took upon Himself "the form and nature of fallen man"?[99] While statements like these may lead some to argue that Jesus' human nature was exactly like ours, Ellen G. White herself sheds light on the way she uses the phrase "fallen nature" with reference to Christ: "Christ took our nature, *fallen* but not corrupted."[100] As if this were not enough to settle the matter, in a letter to a Brother Baker she warns him:

> Be careful, exceedingly careful as to how you dwell upon the human nature of Christ. Do not set Him before the people as a man with the propensities of sin. . . .
>
> . . . Never, in any way, leave the slightest impression upon human minds that a taint of, or inclination to corruption rested upon Christ, or that He in any way yielded to corruption.[101]

These and other similar statements are evidence that an insistence that Christ's human nature was exactly the same as ours is unsustainable.

Some theological implications

It is one thing to insist that Jesus' human nature was exactly like ours. It is quite another when the question is reversed: Is our human nature exactly the same as that of Jesus? If we insist that Jesus' human nature was exactly like ours, then logically it seems that we would have to agree that our human nature is exactly the same as His. To unpack the theological implications of such a position, let me pose two further questions: (1) Do newborn infants need a Savior? (2) Did Jesus need a Savior when He was born? An affirmative answer to both of these questions leads to the absurd proposal that, just like every human baby, Jesus needed a Savior when He was born. This was, in fact, the position of Edward Irving, who suggested that one of the reasons that Jesus died on the cross was to redeem His own sinful nature.[102] Such a position cannot be sustained biblically.

The position that Jesus' human nature was identical to ours means that our human nature must be exactly like His. And this position requires a negative response to both of my additional questions. Jesus, being the "holy thing" and having a nature that was "not corrupted" by sin[103] clearly did not need a Savior when He was born. In fact, due to the circumstances of His birth and sinless life, He *never* needed a Savior. But if Jesus' human nature was exactly the same as ours, then the logical conclusion is that human newborns also do not need a Savior, because our natures, like His, would be "fallen but not corrupted."[104] According

to this position, we are not born sinners and begin to need a Savior only when we begin to sin. The ultimate conclusion of this position is that if we are not born sinners and, like Jesus, do not need a Savior when we are born, it is possible to become exactly like Him at some point in life, that is, to become sinlessly perfect. Upon reaching a sinless state, one would need Jesus only as a Sustainer and a Helper rather than as a Savior, relegating Christ's saving activity to the past and therefore denying Christ's ministry in the heavenly sanctuary, for a sinless person no longer needs Christ's high-priestly mediation. Thus, the argument that Jesus' nature was exactly like ours leads to the conclusion that before Jesus returns to earth, it is possible for us to achieve a pre-Fall state of humanity, except for physical infirmities.

Accordingly, it should be evident that the only way to answer our earlier questions—Do newborn infants need a Savior? Did Jesus need a Savior when He was born?—is in the affirmative to the first question and in the negative to the second. Thus, the question of whether Jesus' nature was exactly like ours must be answered both Yes and No. Jesus Christ was unique! "It is not correct to say," Ellen G. White emphatically states "that Christ was like all children."[105] According to Scripture and the writings of Ellen G. White, Christ was fully divine and fully human, and this is where the discussion must end. Parsing Jesus' nature beyond this simple affirmation is counterproductive because it may lead to significant theological aberrations that can negatively affect the spiritual lives of believers.

Did Jesus' human nature really need to be exactly like ours?

Finally, and in conclusion, we need to address the twin questions, Did Jesus' human nature really need to be exactly like ours for Him to function as our example? If not, did He have an advantage over us? The answer to first question is No. Jesus did not need to be exactly like us to function as our example. As evidenced previously, during Old Testament times, God functioned as the supreme exemplar of morals and ethics for Israel. No human being was ever asked to assume such a function. Thus, the people of Israel did not have a human exemplar, and yet God invoked them to follow His example of love, justice, and mercy in their daily lives. They were also to live by faith that one day the divine Messiah would perfectly fulfill the law of God's love (Isaiah 9:6, 7; 61:1, 2). Through the incarnation of Jesus Christ, God in human form, this promise was fulfilled. He did not, however, need to be exactly like us, burdened with inherited inclinations to sin. It was enough for Him to become *fully* human to fulfill the purpose of His coming, that is, to redeem humanity and "to enable men to become sons of God."[106] As Ellen G. White writes, "Christ was treated as we deserve, that we might be treated as He deserves. He was condemned for our sins, in which He had no share, that we might be justified by His righteousness, in which we had no share. He suffered the death which was ours, that we might receive the life which was His."[107] It was Jesus' identification with the human race and His intimate familiarity with the hardships of the human experience that qualified him to be our exemplar. As Ellen

G. White writes, "Since Jesus came to dwell with us, we know that God is acquainted with our trials, and sympathizes with our griefs. Every son and daughter of Adam may understand that our Creator is the friend of sinners. For in every doctrine of grace, every promise of joy, every deed of love, every divine attraction presented in the Saviour's life on earth, we see 'God with us.' "[108]

If Christ's human nature was not exactly like ours, did He have an advantage over us? While purity of nature could certainly be considered as an advantage it must be recognized that because there was not a "taint of sin" in His nature,[109] and because His nature was "more exalted, and pure, and holy than that of the sinful race,"[110] Christ suffered far more than we will ever suffer. The inherent sinfulness of our natures desensitizes us to sin and suffering, and unless it touches us personally, we often react with a degree of indifference to human misery and wretchedness. We take note that two hundred people were killed in an explosion at a market in Baghdad or that five hundred immigrants lost their lives crossing the Mediterranean, but then we move on and read the latest election story. Jesus was not like that. Ellen G. White writes that He was "free from every taint of selfishness,"[111] and therefore, "He was not insensible to ignomiy and disgrace. He felt it all most bitterly. He felt it as much more deeply and acutely than we can feel suffering, as his nature was more exalted, and pure, and holy than that of the sinful race for whom he suffered. He was the majesty of heaven; he was equal with the Father."[112] None of us will ever suffer in the face of sin and temptation as Jesus did.

In *Mere Christianity*, C. S. Lewis addresses the argument that Christ's uniqueness gave Him an advantage over other humans. Some believe, he wrote, that His sufferings and death lose value because "it must have been so easy for him." Lewis responded, "If I am drowning in a rapid river, a man who still has one foot on the bank may give me a hand which saves my life. Ought I to shout back (between my gasps) 'No, it's not fair! You have an advantage! You're keeping one foot on the bank'? That advantage—call it 'unfair' if you like—is the only reason why he can be of any use to me. To what

will you look for help if you will not look to that which is stronger than yourself?"[113] In this view, Christ's advantage affords salvation to humanity.

It is a unique privilege of the Christian to possess the revelation of God through the Holy Scriptures, which give witness to God's effort to save fallen humanity through the life and death of Jesus Christ. It is a further privilege that, through His actions, as revealed in both the Old Testament and the life of Jesus Christ, God showed us His true character and called us to follow His example: "Be holy, because I am holy" (Leviticus 11:44; 1 Peter 1:16).

Endnotes

1. Except where noted otherwise, all Scripture quotations are from the NIV.

2. Louis Berkhof, *Manual of Christian Doctrine* (Arlington Heights, IL: Christian Liberty Press, 2003), 86, 87.

3. Louis Berkhof, *Systematic Theology* (Grand Rapids, MI: Eerdmans, 1994), 73.

4. Ibid., 73.

5. John S. Feinberg, *No One Like Him: The Doctrine of God* (Wheaton, IL: Crossway Books, 2001), 342.

6. Francis D. Nichol, ed., *The Seventh-day Adventist Bible Commentary*, vol. 1 (Washington, DC: Review and Herald®, 1953), 978.

7. In Luke 1:49, Mary refers to God as One whose name is holy; similarly, in 1 Peter 1:15 and Revelation 4:8, we find echoes of the Old Testament proclamation of God's holiness. Feinberg, *No One Like Him*, 341.

8. Derek Tidball, *The Message of Holiness: Restoring God's Masterpiece* (Downers Grove, IL: InterVarsity, 2010), 110 (emphasis in original).

9. Ronald E. Heine, "God Has Spoken in His Son—the Life of Jesus," in *Christian Doctrine: "The Faith . . . Once Delivered,"* ed. William J. Richardson (Eugene, OR: Wipf and Stock, 1983), 154.

10. Several verses later (Luke 1:49), the same designation, *hagion*, is ascribed to God: "holy is his name."

11. In an attempt to explain Jesus' separateness

from the rest of humanity, postapostolic Christianity attempted to answer this question of "how" by developing the teaching that Mary herself was "separate" from the rest of humanity and not touched by sin in any way. Thus, her intrinsic "holiness," which resulted in her "sinless nature," was passed on to Jesus. In 1854, this ultimately resulted in the Roman Catholic dogma of the immaculate conception. There is no support in the New Testament for such a teaching. For a balanced discussion on the theological meaning of the virgin birth, see Millard J. Erickson, *Christian Theology* (Grand Rapids, MI: Baker Academic, 2013), 688–691.

12. Tidball, *Message of Holiness*, 111.

13. These passages may be interpreted as referring either to God the Father and Jesus or to Jesus alone. The majority of commentaries I consulted choose the latter position due to grammatical considerations.

14. For a broader study on the full, coequal, and coeternal divinity of Christ as presented in the New Testament, see Gerhard Pfandl, "The Trinity in Scripture," *Journal of the Adventist Theological Society* 14, no. 2 (Fall 2003): 80–94.

15. Ellen G. White, "Christ Our Complete Salvation," *Signs of the Times*, May 30, 1895, 8 (emphasis added.) Similarly, in "Ask, and It Shall Be Given You," Ellen G. White refers to Christ as "equal with the Father,

Himself all-sufficient, the storehouse of all blessings." *Signs of the Times*, September 5, 1900, 2 (562).

16. Ellen G. White, *Mind, Character, and Personality* (Nashville, TN: Southern Pub. Assn., 1977), 1:352. In many of her statements, Ellen G. White affirms the coequal authority of Jesus with the Father. See, e.g., Ellen G. White, *Counsels on Stewardship* (Washington, DC: Review and Herald®, 1940), 226; *Fundamentals of Christian Education* (Nashville, TN: Southern Pub. Assn., 1923), 179; "Ask, and It Shall Be Given You," 2 (562); *Selected Messages*, bk. 1 (Washington, DC: Review and Herald®, 1958), 371.

17. Ellen G. White, *The Desire of Ages* (Mountain View, CA: Pacific Press®, 1989), 24.

18. Ellen G. White, *Christ's Object Lessons* (Washington, DC: Review and Herald®, 1952), 287.

19. White, *The Desire of Ages*, 23.

20. Ellen G. White, *Patriarchs and Prophets* (Mountain View, CA: Pacific Press®, 1958), 366.

21. White, *The Desire of Ages*, 24. For a collection of Ellen G. White's statements on the preexistence and full divinity of Christ, see also "Statements on Preexistence of Christ: From the Spirit of Prophecy," *Ministry*, May 1945, 14, 18.

22. White, *The Desire of Ages*, 530.

23. Pfandl, "Trinity in Scripture," 88.

24. Raoul Dederen, "Christ: His Person and Work," in *Handbook of Seventh-day Adventist Theology*, ed. Raoul Dederen (Hagerstown, MD: Review and Herald®, 2000), 162.

25. Docetic teachers could not bring themselves to accept that God could become truly man. Instead, they believed that He only *appeared* as a human being. Apollinarians, on the other hand, taught that Jesus' human mind was replaced by the divine mind, which animated His human body. This amounted to the belief that Jesus was not an ordinary human being but rather an odd hybrid of divinity and humanity. Gregg R. Allison, *Historical Theology* (Grand Rapids, MI: Zondervan, 2011), 366, 372, 373.

26. Dederen, "Christ: His Person and Work," 162.

27. Ibid.

28. Erickson, *Christian Theology*, 706–708; Stanley J. Grenz, *Theology for the Community of God* (Nashville, TN: Broadman and Holman, 1994), 358–363.

29. Erickson, *Christian Theology*, 712.

30. Ellen G. White, "The Life and Light of Men," *Signs of the Times*, June 17, 1897, 5 (357).

31. White, *The Desire of Ages*, 49. Ellen G. White wrote many statements on the humanity of Christ. For a comprehensive collection of these statements, see Woodrow W. Whidden, *Ellen White on the Humanity of Christ* (Hagerstown, MD: Review and Herald®, 1997), 105–149.

32. Ellen G. White, "The Word of God," *Advent Review and Sabbath Herald*, August 22, 1907, 8.

33. White, *The Desire of Ages*, 117.

34. Ellen G. White, "Address to the Church," *Advent Review and Sabbath Herald*, April 18, 1893, 241, 242.

35. Donald L. Alexander, *The Humanity of Christ and the Healing of the Dysfunction of the Human Spirit* (Eugene, OR: Wipf and Stock, 2015), 95.

36. White, *The Desire of Ages*, 24.

37. Ellen G. White, " 'Tempted in All Points Like as We Are,' " *Bible Echo*, November 1, 1892, 322.

38. Ellen G. White, *Education* (Mountain View, CA: Pacific Press®, 1903), 78.

39. White, " 'Tempted in All Points,' " 322; cf. Ellen G. White, *Thoughts From the Mount of Blessing* (Mountain View, CA: Pacific Press®, 1955), 13.

40. White, *Education*, 78.

41. Ellen G. White, *Testimonies for the Church* (Mountain View, CA: Pacific Press®, 1948), 4:45; cf. Ellen G. White, *Testimonies for the Church* (Mountain View, CA: Pacific Press®, 1948), 5:426.

42. White, *Education*, 78.

43. Ellen G. White, "The Work of the Minister," *Advent Review and Sabbath Herald*, September 11, 1888, 578.

44. Ellen G. White, " 'In All Points Tempted Like as We Are,' " *Atlantic Union Gleaner*, August 26, 1903, 413 (1).

45. White, *Education*, 78.

46. White, *The Desire of Ages*, 329.

47. Berkhof, *Systematic Theology*, 319.

48. One prominent example includes Thomas à Kempis's *De Imitiatione Christi* (*The Imitation of Christ*). This book was so influential in the thinking of John Wesley that he translated and republished the book under the title *The Christian's Pattern* (New York: Abingdon Press, 1954). *The Imitation of Christ* was also a part of Ellen G. White's personal library. It was referred to positively by E. J. Waggoner in "Humility Wanted," *Signs of the Times*, June 16, 1887, 368, and extracts from the book were published in "Extracts From Thomas a'Kempis," *Advent Review and Sabbath Herald*, December 11, 1855, 83. Quotes from Thomas à Kempis graced the pages of the *Advent Review and*

Sabbath Herald on numerous occasions.

49. Two Protestant movements, seventeenth-century German Pietism and eighteenth-century Methodism, became particularly concerned with the importance of following the example of Christ. The *raison d'être* for these movements' existence was their attempt to revive the spiritually stale state of post-Reformation Protestantism. Roger E. Olson, *The Story of Christian Theology: Twenty Centuries of Tradition and Reform* (Downers Grove, IL: IVP Academic, 1999), 473–475, 489, 490, 510–516. It is not surprising, therefore, that the writings of Ellen G. White, who was familiar with Pietism and intimately connected with Methodism, are permeated with the theme of Christian holiness. True holiness, she is convinced, was something that could be accomplished only by following the example of Christ. Thus, in her writings, one finds literally thousands of references that encourage, exhort, and beseech her readers to fix their eyes on Jesus and to daily walk in His footsteps. In this, she is no different from the New Testament writers, who experienced Jesus' presence in their lives firsthand.

50. A search of Ellen G. White's writings for the words *Christ* and *example* in the same sentence or paragraph revealed more than four thousand entries. The number of references escalates dramatically when one includes words such as *pattern* or *imitation*. Considering the relative ease of access to these writings through electronic means, readers are encouraged to explore this theme in their own time.

51. See, e.g., John 14:31; 15:9; 17:23; Ephesians 5:1, 2; cf. White, *Christ's Object Lessons*, 282.

52. Ellen G. White, "Christ Man's Example," *Advent Review and Sabbath Herald*, July 5, 1887, 417; cf. White, *Testimonies for the Church*, 5:222, 223.

53. Ellen G. White, "No Caste in Christ," *Advent Review and Sabbath Herald*, December 22, 1891, 785.

54. Ellen G. White, *Testimonies for the Church* (Mountain View, CA: Pacific Press®, 1948), 2:169.

55. Ellen G. White, *Testimonies for the Church* (Mountain View, CA: Pacific Press®, 1948), 8:312.

56. Ellen G. White, *The Acts of the Apostles* (Mountain View, CA: Pacific Press®, 1911), 505.

57. Ellen G. White, *The Great Controversy* (Mountain View, CA: Pacific Press®, 1911), 469.

58. White, *The Desire of Ages*, 49.

59. White, *Fundamentals of Christian Education*, 142, 143; cf. 199.

60. Ellen G. White, *The Ministry of Healing* (Mountain View, CA: Pacific Press®, 1942), 457.

61. Ellen G. White, "In Humility of Heart," *North Pacific Union Gleaner*, April 6, 1910, 1; cf. 1 John 3:16.

62. White, " 'In All Points Tempted Like as We Are,' " 1.

63. Ibid.

64. White, *Testimonies for the Church*, 5:426 (emphasis added).

65. Ellen G. White, *Mind, Character, and Personality* (Nashville, TN: Southern Pub. Assn., 1977), 2:428; cf. Ellen G. White, *Testimonies for the Church* (Mountain View, CA: Pacific Press®, 1948), 3:371; White, *Testimonies for the Church*, 5:253.

66. Ellen G. White, *Testimonies for the Church* (Mountain View, CA: Pacific Press®, 1948), 9:275, 276 (emphasis added).

67. Ellen G. White, *Confrontation* (Washington, DC: Review and Herald®, 1970), 49.

68. Ellen G. White, *The Adventist Home* (Nashville, TN: Southern Pub. Assn., 1952), 504.

69. White, "No Caste in Christ," 785.

70. White, *Testimonies for the Church*, 2:203; cf. White, "Ask, and It Shall Be Given You," 2 (562).

71. Ellen G. White, *Child Guidance* (Nashville, TN: Southern Pub. Assn., 1954), 66; Ellen G. White, *Medical Ministry* (Mountain View, CA: Pacific Press®, 1963), 20, 70; White, *Testimonies for the Church*, 5:385; Ellen G. White, *Evangelism* (Washington, DC: Review and Herald®, 1974), 441. Ellen G. White, *Spiritual Gifts* (Washington, DC: Review and Herald®, 1945), 3:123, 124.

72. White, *Fundamentals of Christian Education*, 179.

73. Consider, e.g., Gandhi's famous statement addressed to Christians: "I like your Christ, I do not like your Christians. Your Christians are so unlike your Christ." Gandhi, quoted in Bill Wilson, *Christianity in the Crosshairs* (Shippensburg, PA: Destiny Image Publishers, 2004), 74.

74. Ellen G. White, "The Perils and Privileges of the Last Days (Concluded.)," *Advent Review and Sabbath Herald*, November 29, 1892, 738.

75. Ellen G. White, "The Perils and Privileges of the Last Days," *Advent Review and Sabbath Herald*, November 22, 1892, 723.

76. Gregory Nazianzen, "To Cledonius the Priest Against Apollinarius," in *A Select Library of Nicene and Post-Nicene Fathers of the Christian Church*, ed. Philip Schaff, vol. 7 (Grand Rapids, MI: Eerdmans, 1989).

77. Gregory Nazianzen, "Oration on Holy Baptism,"

in Schaff, *A Select Library of Nicene and Post-Nicene Fathers of the Christian Church*, vol. 7, 40.23, 367; cf. Allison, *Historical Theology*, 345. Gregory was a theological heir of Origen. Olson, *Story of Christian Theology*, 100.

78. Olson, *Story of Christian Theology*, 189. Olson argues that for Gregory, "[Christ's] humanity . . . is the very same humanity that Adam had and that bore the image of God and was destined to share in God's glory in a creaturely way. Christ restored that lost potential, and that is what Scripture means when it describes him as the 'first born among many brothers' and our example." Ibid.

79. By embracing *theosis* as the mode of salvation, Gregory and thinkers like him did not mean to imply that the boundary between the Creator and creature would ever be crossed. They simply meant that believers could become like Christ in His humanity when He was here on earth. For an excellent work on *theosis* in early Christianity, see Vladimir Kharlamov, *Theosis: Deification in Christian Theology* (Cambridge: James Clarke, 2012).

80. Spanish Adoptionists of the eighth and ninth century, e.g., were greatly concerned with the "completeness of our Lord's humanity," ultimately equating His nature with that of humans after the Fall. Alexander Balmain Bruce, *The Humiliation of Christ in Its Physical, Ethical, and Official Aspects* (Grand Rapids, MI: Eerdmans, 1955), 248, 249; cf. Jaroslav Pelikan, *The Growth of Medieval Theology (600–1300)* (Chicago: University of Chicago Press, 1978), 52–54. Seventeenth-century mystic Antoinette Bourignon (1616–1680) also advocated this view of Christ's humanity. Harry Johnson, *The Humanity of the Savior* (Eugene, OR: Wipf and Stock, 1962), 179. The list goes on and includes thinkers such as Pierre Poiret (1646–1719), Johann Conrad Dippel (1673–1734), and Gottfried Menken (1768–1831).

81. For a comprehensive exposition of Irving's views, see Bruce, *The Humiliation of Christ*, 252–256. It must also be noted that prominent twentieth-century theologian Karl Barth also enthusiastically embraces the view of a "post-Fall" or "sinful" nature of Christ. He writes, "There must be no weakening or obscuring of the saving truth that the nature which God assumed in Christ is identical with our own nature. . . . If it were otherwise, how could Christ be really like us? We stand before God characterized by the Fall." *Church Dogmatics*, vol. 1, pt. 2 (London: T & T Clark International, 2004), 153.

82. For a comparison of Irving's views on the human nature of Christ and those of E. J. Waggoner and A. T. Jones, see Remwil R. Tornalejo, "A Comparative Study of the Christology of Edward Irving, Ellet Joseph Waggoner, and Alonzo Trevier Jones" (master's thesis, Adventist International Institute of Advanced Studies, 2009).

83. Ellen G. White, *Spiritual Gifts* (Washington, DC: Review and Herald®, 1945), 4:115.

84. Ellen G. White, "The Plan of Salvation," *Signs of the Times,* February 20, 1893, 247.

85. Ellen G. White, "The Word of God," *Advent Review and Sabbath Herald*, August 22, 1907, 8.

86. Ellen G. White, "The Work of the Minister," 578. In this article, Ellen G. White uses the KJV phrase "in fashion as a man."

87. Thomas R. Schreiner, *Romans* (Grand Rapids, MI: Baker Books, 1998), 403.

88. Dederen, "Christ: His Person and Work," 164, 165.

89. White, *Testimonies for the Church*, 2:202. For further explanation, see endnote 100.

90. Ellen G. White, "And the Grace of God Was Upon Him," *Youth's Instructor*, September 8, 1898, 704, 705.

91. Ellen G. White, *Manuscript* Releases, vol. 16 (Silver Spring, MD: Ellen G. White Estate, 1990), 182.

92. Ibid.

93. White, "The Work of the Minister," 578.

94. White, *The Desire of Ages*, 116.

95. White, " 'In All Points Tempted Like as We Are,' " 1.

96. White, *Testimonies for the Church*, 5:426.

97. White, *Education*, 29.

98. Scripture clearly testifies that there was no hint of sin in Christ. Paul thus wrote "God made him who had no sin to be sin for us" (2 Corinthians 5:21); John emphatically agreed: "And in him is no sin" (1 John 3:5).

99. White, *Spiritual Gifts*, 4:115.

100. White, *Manuscript Releases*, 16:182 (emphasis in original). For an insightful study of Ellen G. White's use of the phrase "sinful nature," see Tim Poirier, "Sources Clarify Ellen White's Christology," *Ministry*, December 1989, 7–9. In his article, Poirier shows that White, in her writings, utilized a useful distinction between "innocent infirmities" and "sinful propensities," which she gleaned from the works of Henry Melvill (one of White's favorite authors) and Octavius Winslow. Accordingly, Adam before the Fall was free from innocent infirmities and sinful propensities. In

contrast, humanity after the Fall is burdened with both. During His incarnation, Christ accepted innocent infirmities but not sinful propensities. He thus possessed "sinful nature" but not exactly the same as ours. Cf. Henry Melvill, *Sermons* (New York: Swords, Stanford, & Co., 1838), 76–97; Octavius Winslow, *The Glory of the Redeemer in His Person and Work* (London: John F. Shaw, 1845), 124–183.

101. Ellen G. White, *Manuscript Releases*, vol. 13 (Silver Spring, MD: Ellen G. White Estate, 1990), 18, 19.

102. Bruce, *The Humiliation of Christ*, 253.

103. White, *Manuscript Releases*, 16:182.

104. Ibid.

105. White, "And the Grace of God Was Upon Him," 704, 705.

106. C. S. Lewis, *The Joyful Christian* (New York: Simon and Schuster, 1977), 50.

107. White, *The Desire of Ages*, 25.

108. Ibid., 24.

109. White, *Selected Messages*, bk. 1, 253.

110. White, "The Work of the Minister," 578.

111. Ellen G. White, "Obedience the Path to Life," *Advent Review and Sabbath Herald*, March 28, 1893, 193.

112. White, "The Work of the Minister," 578.

113. C. S. Lewis, *Mere Christianity* (New York: Collier Books, 1960), 46.

9

What Did Jesus Accomplish on the Cross?

Félix H. Cortez

For the word of the cross is folly to those who are perishing,
but to us who are being saved it is the power of God.

—1 Corinthians 1:18[1]

The folly of the cross

The earliest surviving picture of a crucifixion is a graffito from the second century A.D. found on the Palatine Hill in Rome. It is a caricature of a crucified figure with the head of an ass. To the left, a man stands with his arm raised in worship. Underneath, an inscription says, "Alexamenos worships god."[2]

The idea that a man found guilty and executed on a cross should be worshiped as God was offensive to the ancient mind. In fact, for them, it was the preeminent evidence of the stupidity of the Christian religion, and its enemies always referred to its shame with strong emphasis and malicious pleasure.[3] They called it "madness."[4] Pliny the Younger, who as the Roman governor of Pontus-Bithynia interrogated a number of Christians at the beginning of the second century A.D., referred to Christianity as a form of *amentia* (mental illness) and "a perverse and extravagant superstition."[5] His friend Tacitus, an important Roman historian who probably also interrogated Christians when he was the Roman governor of Asia, knew the shameful fate of its Founder and that the "evil" (*malum*) He instigated spread too quickly in Rome "where all things hideous and shameful . . . become popular."[6]

In the ancient world, the cross was a depraved and distasteful affair. Romans used it, but the sparse reference to it in their literature shows their aversion to it. They considered it a barbarian form of punishment and reserved it for rebels, violent criminals, robbers, and traitors provided "they were also slaves, foreigners, or other nonpersons."[7] Similarly, the Jews detested it.[8] The Law declared that a man impaled on the tree was cursed by God and should not remain there overnight because it would defile the land (Deuteronomy 21:23). There is also evidence that slaves, prostitutes, and others from the lower classes used the word *crux* (cross) as a vulgar taunt.[9] So Cicero argued that "the very word, 'cross,' should be far removed not only from the person of a Roman citizen but from his thoughts, his eyes and his ears."[10] Yet, of all the symbols Christians could have adopted, of all the images they used at the beginning of their history, it was the cross that became the emblem of Christianity. This seems absurd.

The first motifs that we find in the Christian paintings in the catacombs were the peacock (supposedly symbolizing immortality), a dove, the athlete's victory palm, and the fish—the Greek word for fish, *ichthys*, was an acronym for *Iesus*

Christos Theou Huios Soter, meaning "Jesus Christ, Son of God, Savior." Later other themes appeared: Noah's ark, Abraham sacrificing the ram instead of Isaac, Daniel in the lions' den, Jonah being spit out by the fish, a shepherd carrying a lamb, or depictions of miracles such as the healing of the paralytic and the raising of Lazarus.[11] These were symbols of salvation, victory, and caring. The cross, on the other hand, conveyed a sense of defeat and shame and invited derision from both Jews and pagans (Hebrews 12:2; Galatians 5:11). It was a challenge for mission, counterintuitive, and always difficult to explain (1 Corinthians 1:18, 23). Yet it was the cross that became the emblem of Christianity.

The centrality of the cross for the gospel

Scripture asserts that the cross was both necessary and central to God's plans. During His ministry, Jesus taught the disciples, at least three times in plain, explicit language, that "it was necessary" that the Son of man should "suffer many things and . . . be killed" (Mark 8:31, CSB).[12] He also alluded to His death at least eight other times.[13] In addition, the Gospel of John registers seven references made by Jesus in the last week of His ministry to the "hour" of His death.[14] The disciples, however, were unwilling to accept this idea.

The *necessity* of the death of the Son of man was a most astonishing idea.[15] The title "Son of Man" identified Jesus with the glorious, heavenly figure of Daniel 7 who would receive dominion and a kingdom that would never be destroyed:

"I saw in the night visions,

and behold, with the clouds of heaven
   there came one like a son of man,
and he came to the Ancient of Days
   and was presented before him.
And to him was given dominion
   and glory and a kingdom,
that all peoples, nations, and languages
   should serve him;
his dominion is an everlasting dominion,
   which shall not pass away,
and his kingdom one
   that shall not be destroyed"
      (verses 13, 14).

How could this glorious figure, beneficiary of God's dominion over the kingdoms of the earth, be given into the hands of sinners and be executed by the powers from which He was destined to liberate His people? Yet Jesus asserted that the suffering, rejection, and death of the Son of man were *necessary* and that He had come for this specific reason (John 12:27).

The disciples resisted this notion. Peter rebuked Jesus (Mark 8:32, 33; Matthew 16:22, 23), and the rest of the disciples, though distressed (Matthew 17:23; Mark 10:32), failed to understand because the whole matter was simply unthinkable (cf. John 12:34). It was only after the Resurrection, when Jesus explained from the Scriptures that it was *necessary* this should have happened, that they finally understood (Luke 24:26, 44). Therefore, it was because of Jesus' own teaching and emphasis that the cross became central to the apostles' preaching (e.g., Acts 1:16; 17:3). Paul called the gospel simply "the word of the cross" (1 Corinthians 1:18), and the Gospels devote so much attention to the Passion that they could be considered Passion narratives with extended introductions.[16] Thus, Scripture attests that the cross was not simply the result of capricious historical forces or the vileness of Jesus' enemies but the outworking of God's purpose.

The *need* for the cross and the central place it has in the gospel can be understood only in the context of the great controversy between good and evil. This is suggested by the fact that, in addition to the normal Greek noun *stauros* (cross), New Testament authors referred to the cross with the noun *xulon*, which means "tree" (Acts 5:30; 10:39; 13:29; 1 Peter 2:24; cf. Galatians 3:13). The use of the word *tree* for the cross is very significant because it refers back to two important notions of the Old Testament. The first is that by calling the cross a *tree*, New Testament authors clearly meant that Jesus died under the curse of God according to Deuteronomy 21:23. This point is clearly made in Galatians 3:13. The second notion is a little more subtle but no less significant. By calling the cross a *tree*, the apostles alluded to the tree of the knowledge of good and evil in the midst of the Garden of Eden, suggesting that what Adam lost by his disobedience at that tree was recovered by Jesus' obedience at the cross. Paul makes this point explicitly in Romans 5, arguing that while Satan obtained a major victory at the tree of the knowledge of good and evil, God obtained the decisive victory at Calvary.

This connection between Jesus' death on the cross and Adam's fall in Eden is crucial for our understanding of what was achieved at the cross and will provide the foundational perspective from which we will study

what He accomplished there. Jesus and the New Testament authors asserted that the cross was the evidence of God's wisdom and righteousness, the moment of God's victory over—and subjugation of—the forces of evil, and the revelation of God's glory. As we will see, all of these were an irrefutable response to Satan's allegations at the tree.

The tree in the middle of the Garden

When God created Adam and Eve, He put them in the Garden He had planted in Eden. This Garden contained every kind of tree that was "pleasant to the sight and good for food" (Genesis 2:9). In the midst of the Garden was also the tree of life and the tree of the knowledge of good and evil (verse 9). The tree of life symbolized the truth that all life comes from God as a gift. The tree of the knowledge of good and evil, which was denied to Adam and Eve (Genesis 3:3), symbolized the sovereignty of God over the universe. It was a reminder that though God had given humans dominion over everything, they themselves were under the benevolent rule of God.

The significance of the tree of the knowledge of good and evil can be understood only in the context of God's purpose in the creation of humanity. Genesis tells us that God created humanity in His image: "Then God said, 'Let us make man in our image, after our likeness. And let them have dominion over the fish of the sea and over the birds of the heavens and over the livestock and over all the earth and over every creeping thing that creeps on the earth' " (Genesis 1:26).

Scripture suggests that the image of God included moral, physical, relational, and functional aspects of the human nature and role.[17] This passage, however, explicitly relates God's image in humanity to humanity's relationship to creation. Just as God has dominion over the universe, He gave humans dominion over the world. In referring to the creation of humans, Psalm 8 describes them as "crowned . . . with glory and honor," having "dominion over the works of your [God's] hands," and, therefore, made just a little lower than God Himself (verses 5, 6).[18] The earliest readers of the Bible would not have missed the significance of this divine action. Ancient Near Eastern rulers had the practice of erecting an image of themselves in the lands over which they claimed dominion. One such image, dated to the ninth century B.C., was found in Tell Fakhariyeh and had an inscription in Aramaic and Assyrian. The inscription explained that this was the *image* and *likeness* (the same terms used in Genesis 1:26) of King Haddu-yisi.[19] Thus, it was clear that God had created human beings in His image and placed them as rulers on earth to signal His own dominion over creation. The fact that Adam is called a "son of God" (Luke 3:38) has similar implications. Ancient Near Eastern rulers often identified themselves as sons of God, implying that their authority to rule was derived from the gods.[20]

Genesis tells us that humanity's dominion was to be exercised literally by *serving* and *protecting* the earth (Genesis 2:15).[21] Jesus would later affirm this ideal when He taught His disciples: "Whoever would be great among you must be your servant, and whoever would be first among you must be your slave" (Matthew 20:26, 27). Genesis also tells us that God blessed Adam and Eve and commanded them: "Be fruitful and multiply and fill the earth and subdue it" (Genesis 1:28). The plan was that through their *service* and *protection* God's blessing would flow to all creation. God's purpose was that His own benevolent rule (referred to in the New Testament as "the kingdom of God") would be mediated and extended to all creation through the administration of Adam and Eve.

The exalted position of humanity and the significance of the tree of the knowledge of good and evil help us to understand the gravity of humanity's sin. The serpent affirmed that, contrary to God's warning, humans would not die should they eat of the tree; instead, they would become "like God, knowing good and evil" (Genesis 3:1–5). By eating of the tree, Adam and Eve accepted the serpent's claim that God was not as loving as He claimed to be and demonstrated that they believed, instead, that God was selfishly retaining a benefit that was rightfully theirs. They also implied that God was not as righteous as He said He was and that they believed, instead, that God would not destroy them for eating from the tree. Most important, they rebelled against God. Unsatisfied with their exalted position as administrators of the world, they attempted to become God themselves. They did not want to remain in God's image; they wanted to be rulers (gods) in their own right. In short, it was a coup d'état. The irony was, however, that in their attempt to free themselves from their responsibility to God, they fell under the dominion of the serpent, and Satan became the ruler of this world (John

12:31; 14:30; 16:11). These two things—the impeachment of God's character and the dispute over the dominion of the world—are at the core of the great controversy between God and Satan. These issues would be solved only at the cross.

The promise

God did not abandon Adam and Eve to their fate when they rebelled. He promised a Seed to the woman; a *Son* who would destroy the serpent by crushing its head with His heel. He also predicted that, in the same act, the serpent would kill the *Son* through His heel (Genesis 3:15).[22]

God also looked for ways to benefit the world through faithful individuals and their families, as had been His intention through Adam. Noah was the first of such individuals. When God had to destroy humanity because of its wickedness, He found in Noah a righteous person through whom He would provide the ark as a means of salvation from the Flood (Genesis 6). After the Flood, God confirmed to Noah and his family the promises made to Adam. Humanity would continue to have dominion over the animals; God also blessed them and commanded them to "be fruitful and multiply and fill the earth" (Genesis 9:1, 2; cf. Genesis 1:26–28). The purpose of this covenant was to bless and protect creation. That is why God considered this covenant to be not only between Him and Noah but also between Him and creation (Genesis 9:8–17). After the rebellion at the Tower of Babel, God called Abraham in order that through his *seed*—meaning "descendant" or "descendants"—God would bless all the families of the earth. God wanted this to be

a turning point in the history of humanity. The word *curse* has been used five times up to this moment (Genesis 3:14, 17; 4:11; 5:29; 9:25), but God uses the word *bless* five times in His promises to Abraham. His purpose was to bless "all the families of the earth" through Abraham (Genesis 12:1–3). So God promised to make Abraham's descendants a great nation, to multiply them, and to make them exceedingly fruitful in order to bless all the nations of the earth (Genesis 12:1–3; 15:5, 6; 17:4, 6; especially 22:16–18). Like Adam in the beginning, Israel would become God's son (Exodus 4:22; cf. Jeremiah 31:9; Hosea 11:1–4). God wanted to put Israel at the head of the nations and bless it abundantly and through it rule the world (Deuteronomy 28:1–14). Israel at the head of the nations would fulfill a role of service. The Israelites would be a kingdom of priests, a holy nation (Exodus 19:5, 6). Israel would fulfill the priestly functions of mediating the knowledge of God to the nations and blessing them in His name (Deuteronomy 10:8; Numbers 6:22–27). Nevertheless, Israel failed. The Israelites wanted to be like the nations around them and requested a king like those of the other nations; they rejected God's rule over them (1 Samuel 8).

After Israel's request for a king and the failure of Saul, its first king, God found in David a man according to His own heart (1 Samuel 13:14; Acts 13:22). He made a covenant with him and his *seed*. He promised to give David's seed the throne of Israel and adopted that offspring as His own son (2 Samuel 7:13, 14). David immediately understood that this covenant was not only with him, but for all humanity through him (verse 19).[23] The Davidic king would be "the firstborn, the highest of the kings of the earth" and also have a priestly role (Psalms 89:27; 110:4). He would rule over the kings of the earth and defeat and discipline those who opposed Him, but God would bless those who took refuge in Him (Psalm 2:7–12). Sadly, the Davidic kings also failed, and God had to "remove the turban and take off the crown" until One would come through whom He would accomplish His purpose (Ezekiel 21:26, 27).

The tree in the middle of the earth

The turning point in the tragic story of human sin and failure finally came at the cross. God gave His own Son to the human race as the greatest gift of love and grace to raise human beings from the depths of their debased condition. Jesus adopted human nature and was born as the *Seed* of the woman (Luke 3:23–38), the *Seed* of Abraham (Galatians 3:16), and the son of David (Luke 1:32, 33). His mission was to recover what Adam had lost and fulfill the mission Israel and the Davidic kings had failed to accomplish. Scripture's descriptions of the achievements of the cross are multifaceted, because as we have seen, the cross was God's solution to a multifaceted problem. At the cross, Jesus paid the penalty for Adam's rebellion, but He also defeated the devil, recovered the lost dominion over the world, and laid to rest forever the doubts raised regarding God's character of love and righteousness. Thus, the tragedy in the Garden of Eden, with its devastating and wide-ranging consequences, found a unified and astonishing solution at the cross, whose meaning and depth has been

the focus of intense research ever since Jesus died and will continue to be the focus throughout eternity. In the rest of this chapter, I will explore the main aspects of the significance of the cross.

The cross and the wrath of God

The Bible teaches that Jesus died under the wrath of God at the cross. Divine wrath is a relational concept. Scripture relates God's presence to both the *summum bonum* (highest good) of Israel and the ultimate penalty for sin.[24] So God punishes His people by forsaking them,[25] withdrawing His presence,[26] or hiding His face,[27] which results in catastrophes and defeat.[28] Note the following lament: "How long, O Lord? Will you *hide* yourself forever? How long will your *wrath* burn like fire?" (Psalm 89:46; emphasis added).

Jesus' and Paul's descriptions of the penalty for sin included both aspects. Jesus described the punishment for sin both as the breaking of a relationship—the wicked will be rejected and barred from the kingdom and left in outer darkness[29]—as well as retribution[30] and destruction.[31] Similarly, Paul described divine wrath in terms of the breakdown of the relationship between God and sinners and destruction. Romans 1:18–32 affirms that the wrath of God results from humanity's suppression of the truth and that, as a result, God gives people up to the lusts of their hearts, to their degrading passions, and to their debased minds (verses 24, 26, 28). Wrath, then, is a life devoid of God, given over to sin, whose final destiny is complete exclusion from a relationship with God (Romans 9:3; 2 Thessalonians 1:5–10). Paul also described this punishment as the total extinction of sinners at the end of the world. The wicked, he warned, would die (Romans 6:21, 23), perish (Romans 2:12), and be destroyed (Galatians 6:8; 1 Corinthians 3:17; 2 Thessalonians 1:9; Philippians 1:28; 3:19). They would never come back, for their destruction was to be "eternal" (2 Thessalonians 1:9). Thus, the most profound manifestation of God's wrath is the termination of a relationship, which results in destruction.

This relational understanding of the wrath of God helps us to understand how divine punishment is both the normal consequence of committing evil deeds as well as an act of God.[32] While it is true that the final, eternal punishment is God's abandonment of the sinner that results in destruction, this abandonment is the outcome of the sinner's previous abandonment of God.[33] Therefore, by destroying sinners, God honors their freedom to choose to be without Him forever. Death is the penalty for sin (Romans 1:32; 5:12; 6:23) because it separates from God those who have separated themselves from Him, who is the source of life.

Scripture asserts that Jesus died under the wrath of God. Jesus was hanged on a tree (the cross), which according to Deuteronomy 21:23 meant that God had cursed Him. Jesus described His death on the cross as a cup He had to drink (Matthew 26:39).[34] The Old Testament authors often described God's judgment upon the wicked as a cup He gives them to drink:

> For in the hand of the LORD there is a cup
> with foaming wine, well mixed, . . .
> and all the wicked of the earth
> shall drain it down to the dregs

(Psalm 75:8; cf. Job 21:20; Revelation 14:9–11).[35]

The Gospels also say that Jesus was "rejected" (Mark 8:31), delivered over "to the Gentiles" (Mark 10:33; cf. Mark 15:1), mocked at the cross, forsaken by God (Mark 15:34), left in total darkness (Matthew 27:45; Mark 15:33; Luke 22:53; 23:44), and finally destroyed (John 19:34), all of which were signs of the wrath of God in the Old Testament.[36]

But why did Jesus die as a convicted criminal under the judgment of God if He never committed any sin (Hebrews 2:17, 18; 4:15; 7:26–28; 9:14)? He died this death because He suffered God's wrath in our place.[37] For Jesus, the cross was the dreadful moment in which God's wrath on Israel's and humanity's sin would be poured on Him without mercy. According to Paul, Jesus redeemed us from the curse "by becoming a curse for us" (Galatians 3:13, 14; cf. Deuteronomy 21:23). He was referring to the curse upon those who broke the covenant (Deuteronomy 27:26) and the curse upon humanity and creation as a result of Adam's sin (Genesis 3:16–19). He also says that Jesus became sin so that we might "become the righteousness of God" (2 Corinthians 5:21) and be saved from His wrath (Romans 5:9, 10; cf. Romans 3:24–26). As I. Howard Marshall explains, "It is hard to understand this [Christ's becoming sin for us] in any other way than that in dying Christ exhausted the effects of divine wrath against sin."[38] According to Scripture, Jesus bore the ultimate penalty for sin in our stead (Romans 5:6, 8; 2 Corinthians 5:21; Galatians 3:13) and experienced in our place the eternal punishment reserved for the wicked (1 Timothy 2:5, 6; Titus 2:14; 1 John 2:2). Ironically, this action of bearing our sins reveals Jesus' divine identity, because in the Old Testament only God can bear our sins.[39] He is the only one who can forgive, because He bears our sin (Exodus 32:32; Isaiah 43:24, 25; 53:4, 6).

We may wonder why God would not simply forgive Adam and Eve when they sinned against Him as He has asked His children to do.[40] The problem is that Adam's sin was more than a personal affront against God. It was, in fact, as we saw above, a challenge to God's rule and the moral order of the universe. The existence of order in the universe depends, in the end, on the divine reaction to a breach of that order. If no reaction followed a breach of order in the universe, then "there would be no seriousness in the world at all; there would be no meaning in anything, no order, no stability; the world order would fall into ruins; chaos and desolation would be supreme. All order in the world depends upon the inviolability of his [God's] honour, upon the certitude that those who rebel against him will be punished."[41]

The principle of love and service to others is foundational to the well-being of creation, and Adam introduced to this world selfishness and distrust, which are devastating to the order of the universe and our well-being. There is a notion in the Old Testament that "*a wicked action—just like laws of nature which operate so that an action inevitably is followed by a reaction—inevitably results in disastrous consequences.*"[42] This is especially clear in the Old Testament book of Proverbs, which

suggests that evil actions have destructive, built-in consequences.[43] Evil actions have in themselves a weight that weighs down the sinner (Psalms 38:4; 40:12). Thus, sin engenders sadness and tragedy, but the commandments of God are a blessing, a gift, and a wisdom (Deuteronomy 4:5, 6; Isaiah 48:18). God cannot tolerate sin just as a loving father would not allow the presence of a deadly gas in his home. If he loves his children, he will eliminate it. Thus, God's very love for creation requires the destruction of evil. Sin cannot be tolerated; it must be eradicated.[44]

Scripture balances both God's wrath against sin and His love for the sinner by describing Jesus' death on the cross as a sacrifice in which He substituted His life for ours. He died so that we didn't have to die. In the Levitical system, when a person sinned, he could bring an animal to be offered as a sacrifice to make atonement, namely, to bring reconciliation between himself and God: "If he brings a lamb as his offering . . . he shall . . . lay his hand on the head of the sin offering and kill it. . . . [So] the priest shall make atonement for him for the sin which he has committed, and he shall be forgiven" (Leviticus 4:32–35). The sacrifice substituted the life of an innocent animal for the life of the sinner (Leviticus 17:11). Isaiah 53:7 had predicted that the Messiah, God's servant, would be "like a lamb that is led to the slaughter." Thus, John the Baptist called Jesus the "Lamb of God" because as a sacrifice for sin He would carry the sins of the world (John 1:29, 36). Jesus died at the hour of the sacrifice of the paschal lamb.[45] It was the fulfillment of Isaiah's prophecy that God would lay on the Messiah "the iniquity of us all" (Isaiah 53:6); number Him "with the transgressors" (verse 12); and "crush him" (verse 10). This is why Isaiah 53, which explains the death of the Messiah as a sacrificial death in the place of the deaths of many, is the most important Old Testament passage for the New Testament writers.[46] So Jesus died giving His life as a sacrificial death *instead* of many (Ephesians 5:2; Romans 8:3;[47] 1 Corinthians 5:7, 8; Revelation 5:6, 12; 7:14; cf. Mark 10:45; 1 Timothy 2:6; Romans 5:6–8; Galatians 1:4; 1 Corinthians 15:3, 4; 2 Corinthians 5:14, 15).[48]

The cross and the victory of God
Scripture also affirms that Jesus defeated Satan at the cross[49] and delivered us from his power.[50] When Adam and Eve sinned at the tree in the midst of the Garden, they not only committed an offense that required atonement but also became subjugated under the power of an enemy, which required deliverance. Adam's sin was not only a crime but also a defeat. Romans 5:12–21 says that because of the sin of one man death reigned over all human beings, because all sinned. Adam's transgression was similar to being infected with a mortal disease that was then transmitted to all humanity because no one had the resources to fight it. Thus, humanity was subjugated under the power of evil (2 Corinthians 4:4; Ephesians 2:2; Colossians 1:13; 1 John 5:19). A couple of chapters later, Paul shows this to be evident by the fact that even though a person may want to do what the law says, he cannot because there is a law in his flesh that wars against him and makes him captive to the law of sin (Romans 7:14–25).

Death reigns because humanity is powerless before sin. And sin is the sting of death (1 Corinthians 15:56). These are the factors that made possible Satan's oppressive rule over humanity (Hebrews 2:14, 15; cf. John 8:31–44; Romans 6:12–23). Satan rules over us by tempting and deceiving us into sin, and then by accusing us, which results in death. In this sense, he has the power of death (Hebrews 2:14).[51] Thus, George Smeaton argues that "sin was the ground of Satan's dominion, the sphere of his power, and the secret of his strength."[52]

God promised, however, that this subjugation would not be total and would finally be overcome. There would be "enmity" between the serpent and the woman and their descendants, and one of the descendants of the woman would smash the serpent's head (Genesis 3:15). This was accomplished at the cross, where Jesus defeated Satan, the usurping ruler of this world (John 12:31; 14:30; 16:11).

When Jesus began His ministry on earth, it was very clear that He had come to destroy the power of the enemy. He cast out demons (Mark 1:23–25) and healed sicknesses (Matthew 4:23, 24), and nature recognized His lordship (Mark 4:39). His disciples also participated in this assault on the enemy. When they told Jesus how the demons were subjected to them in His name, He told them: "I saw Satan fall like lightning from heaven" (Luke 10:18). He later explained His power over demons as that of a "stronger" man who "overcomes" or triumphs over (*nikao*, "vanquishes") "a strong man" and strips him of his armor and "divides his spoil" (Luke 11:20–22).

The victory over Satan was achieved at

the cross. Three times Jesus said that Satan would be overthrown at the cross (John 12:31; 14:30; 16:11). Ironically, Jesus defeated Satan by dying on the cross. Hebrews says that "through death" Jesus destroyed the one who had "the power of death, that is, the devil" (Hebrews 2:14). Paul explained this in the following way: "[God gave us life] by canceling the record of debt that stood against us with its legal demands. This he set aside, nailing it to the cross. He disarmed the rulers and authorities and put them to open shame, by triumphing over them in him" (Colossians 2:14, 15).

The power of Satan resided in humanity's helplessness to overcome sin and the legal demand of death for those who sinned. But Jesus stripped Satan's weapons from him by living a perfect life and by satisfying the legal demands against us. Thus, Scripture relates Satan's defeat to God's ability to forgive sins because of the cross of Christ (Colossians 2:14, 15).

Adam's original sin was that he rebelled against God at the tree when trying to become like God and take His place. The Son of God, however, became man and was "obedient to the point of death, even death on a cross" (Philippians 2:8). The defeat suffered by Adam at the tree in the middle of the Garden was redeemed by the victory of the Second Adam at the cross. The rebellion at the first tree was solved by total obedience at the second "tree." Satan had been tireless in his attempts to make Jesus sin, but Jesus defeated him (John 14:30; Hebrews 4:15; 7:26-28; 9:14; 10:5-10). He tempted Jesus repeatedly to abstain from the cross but was rebuked (Mark 8:31-33; cf. Matthew 4:8-10; 26:36-44). Finally,

when Jesus hung on the cross, Satan made desperate attempts to get Him to climb down from it (Matthew 27:39-50), but Jesus refused. When Jesus shouted "It is finished" (John 19:30), He stripped Satan of his power and exposed before the universe his weakness.

The victory over sin and death was not achieved at the Resurrection but at the cross. Jesus rose from the dead because He had achieved the victory at the cross. The Resurrection was a demonstration of that victory. And we are invited to participate in Jesus' victory. Paul says that Jesus "was crucified in weakness, but lives by the power of God. For we also are weak in him, but in dealing with you we will live with him by the power of God" (2 Corinthians 13:4; cf. Galatians 2:20; Romans 6:3-11; 8:1-17). As the church preaches the gospel, the victory of Jesus is extended to those who believe in Him (2 Corinthians 10:3-5) and will be consummated in the end when "at the name of Jesus every knee should bow, in heaven and on earth and under the earth" (Philippians 2:10).

Jesus' victory at the cross was total, and we are invited to enjoy its benefits. We can overcome the devil thanks to the cross (Revelation 12:11; cf. 1 John 2:12-14). Our victories do not add anything to Jesus' victory; they serve only as corroborating evidence that Jesus stripped Satan of his weapons and defeated him at the cross. Jesus conquered, and we enjoy the benefits.

The cross and the glory of God

Finally, Scripture also affirms that the cross revealed the glory of God and His Son. When Jesus died, the veil of the temple, which protected the people from the glory of God, was torn in two, revealing the Most Holy Place, which represented the throne room of God (Matthew 27:51). Among other things, this was a powerful symbol that the cross had somehow given us the possibility to look closely at God and into His rule. Jesus expressed this clearly in the Gospel of John. When some Greeks requested to see Him, Jesus said, "The hour has come for the Son of Man to be glorified" (John 12:23) and then explained that this would be accomplished through His death (verses 24–28). Also, when Judas had left the upper room to lead those who would apprehend Him, Jesus said, "Now is the Son of Man glorified, and God is glorified in him" (John 13:31). Finally, in His last prayer, Jesus said, "Father, the hour has come; glorify your Son that the Son may glorify you" (John 17:1). In each case, the reference to the cross was indisputable. Jesus Himself had said at the beginning of His ministry that He would be "lifted up" just as Moses "lifted up the serpent in the wilderness" (John 3:14; cf. 12:32), implying both the manner of His death and its significance. He would die on a cross, but that would be, in fact, an exaltation—a glorification. Similarly, Paul asserted that God gave His Son to die on the cross to demonstrate both His justice and His love, that is, to reveal His character. Jesus' death on the cross "was *to show* God's righteousness, because in his divine forbearance he had passed over former sins. It was to *show* his righteousness at the present time, so that he might be just and the justifier of the one who has faith in Jesus" (Romans 3:25, 26; emphasis added). A couple of chapters later Paul added, "But God *shows* his love for us in

that while we were still sinners, Christ died for us" (Romans 5:8; emphasis added). The cross was, therefore, a revelatory act.

This understanding of the cross actually substantiates John's assertion at the beginning of His Gospel: "The Word became flesh and dwelt among us, and we have seen his glory, glory as of the only Son from the Father, full of grace and truth" (John 1:14). This assertion is very significant. It is an allusion to God's proclamation of His glory to Moses at the mountain (Exodus 34:6). John's expression "full of grace and truth" (Greek: *charis* and *alētheia*) reflects the Hebrew expression in Exodus, "abounding in steadfast love and faithfulness" (*hesed* and *'emet*). These are covenantal terms. "Love" (*hesed*) refers to the firm loyalty that characterizes relationships between relatives, friends, and others with whom one is bound by ties of love and honor. "Faithfulness" (*'emet* = truth) refers to the truth that was spoken when a covenant was made and that is evidenced in acts of loyalty according to the covenant terms.

Our relationship with God has always been based on a covenant relationship of trust and love with Him. Adam broke this covenant (Hosea 6:7), but God maintained it with Noah (Genesis 6:18; 9:9), Abraham (Genesis 15:18), Israel (Genesis 17:19; Exodus 24:7, 8), and David (2 Samuel 7:8–16; 23:5) and finally restored it fully through Jesus (Luke 22:20). God's protection and blessings have always shown that He is a loyal and loving God. His judgments upon the trespassers, however, also show that He spoke "truth" when He made the covenant with them. Thus, Paul says that the gospel reveals God's righteousness

(Romans 1:17), because the cross revealed the depth of God's love as well as His unmovable commitment to truth and justice. It reveals His righteousness, because at the cross He punished fully the transgressions of the wicked. This commitment to truth was so strong that it required the full wrath of God to be poured on His own Son who died in our place (Romans 3:21–26). But the cross also revealed the depth of God's love for us. His commitment to us was so strong that not even the worst of our rebellions and betrayals shook His commitment to our salvation. Christ died for us "while we were still sinners" (Romans 5:8). The cross shows, then, that "it is impossible for God to lie" (Hebrews 6:18). "If we are faithless, he remains faithful—for he cannot deny himself" (2 Timothy 2:13).

Ironically, the cross reveals not only God's love and righteousness but also His greatness and power. According to the Old Testament, God is glorified by His actions. The most important of these are creation and the liberation of Israel from Egypt. "The heavens" (Psalm 19:1), the animals (Psalm 29:9), and "the whole earth" (Isaiah 6:3), that is, all of God's creation, proclaim His glory. Even Solomon, with all his glory, could not match the glory of the lilies of the field and of the grass, the most simple of God's creations (Matthew 6:28, 29). God also revealed His glory when He delivered Israel from Egypt (Numbers 14:22), and the prophets predicted that God's glory would be revealed again when God would bring Israel out of Babylon and restore it to its land. They considered this both a new exodus and a new creation. Jesus revealed His glory by performing powerful miracles

(John 2:11; 11:4, 40), but His greatest act was His victory on the cross (as described earlier), which New Testament authors considered both a new exodus (Luke 9:31)[53] and a new creation (2 Corinthians 5:17; Galatians 6:15; Ephesians 2:15).

Jesus also explained that greatness is attained differently in the kingdom of God than in the world. When James and John, the sons of Zebedee, said to Jesus, "Grant us to sit, one at your right hand and one at your left, in your glory" (Mark 10:37), they were thinking that Jesus, being the Son of man, would be gloriously given "dominion and glory and a kingdom" by the "Ancient of Days" in fulfillment of the prophecy of Daniel 7:13, 14. But Jesus knew that, paradoxically, this glory would be attained at the cross (Mark 10:33, 34). Thus, He asked the brothers whether they could drink the cup that He would drink (verse 38). This cup was the cup of God's wrath that He accepted at Gethsemane as the only way to save us (Mark 14:34–42). Then He explained to them that the greatest in the kingdom of God, the one who exercises dominion and authority, is the servant and slave of all (Mark 10:42–45). This reminds us of Adam, who was given dominion over creation but whose function was to "keep" (serve) creation (Genesis 2:15),[54] and especially of the Messiah, the servant of Yahweh, who would reveal "the arm of the LORD" (Isaiah 53:1) and be highly exalted and who also, paradoxically (at least for us), was burdened like a slave with our sins and grief (Isaiah 52:13–53:12). In the kingdom of God, the greatest is the one who serves. Thus, God Himself, who "sits above the circle of the earth" and to whom

its inhabitants are like grasshoppers;
who stretches out the heavens like a
     curtain
     and spreads them like a tent to dwell in;
who brings princes to nothing,
     and makes the rulers of the earth as
          emptiness (Isaiah 40:22, 23),

who created the universe "by the greatness of his might, and because he is strong in power" (verse 26), is the one who was "burdened" with our sins and "wearied" with our iniquities (Isaiah 43:24). The Hebrew term for "burdened" is *'avad*, which means "to serve" and is the source of the noun *'eved* (servant, slave). The Suffering Servant of Isaiah 53 who bore our griefs and carried our sorrows is Yahweh, the Creator of the universe, who has dominion over all. Thus, the cross also revealed the greatness of God, because it was in this act of deepest service that His role as head over the universe was expressed. Adam forfeited his exalted position by wanting to become God and rule in his own right when he ate of the tree, but the Son of God has exalted His name above every name when He became a man and died as a slave for the benefit of all (Philippians 2:5–11). There is no greater act than this.

This paradox of God's kingdom—exaltation and victory are achieved through sacrifice and abasement—was an integral part of the greatest Messianic prophecies.[55] The Seed of the woman would smash the head of the serpent by having His own heel smashed (Genesis 3:15). A "star" would rise from the "dust of Jacob" (Numbers 24:17; 23:10). A "son" would be born to a "virgin" (Isaiah 7:14). "An anointed one" would be

"cut off" and "have nothing" (Daniel 9:26). A "servant" would be highly "exalted" and "crushed" by God (Isaiah 52:13–53:12).

By revealing both His power and the depth of His love and righteousness through Jesus' death on the cross, God got to the bottom of the problem of sin, to its very root. The serpent had affirmed at the tree of the knowledge of good and evil that, contrary to God's warning, humans would not die should they eat of the tree. Instead, they would become "like God, knowing good and evil" (Genesis 3:1–5). As I said before, by eating of the tree, Adam and Eve accepted the serpent's claim that God was not as loving as He claimed to be; by eating, they showed that they believed that God was selfishly retaining a benefit that was rightfully theirs. They also implied that God was not as righteous or truthful as He said He was and that they believed, instead, that God would not destroy them for eating from the tree. Most important, they rebelled against God. Unsatisfied with their exalted position as administrators of the world, they attempted to become God themselves. They wanted to be rulers in their own right.

At the root of the problem of evil is distrust of God—of His motives and His actions. The serpent had impeached God's character of love and righteousness and misrepresented the nature of His rule. These two things, the impeachment of God's character and the dispute over the dominion of the world, are at the core of the great controversy between God and Satan, between good and evil. But Jesus cleared God's name (John 12:27, 28). At the cross, He demonstrated that God loves us, is loyal to us, and is committed to justice and truth even at the cost of His own life. Jesus also demonstrated the true nature of His government—that His rulership consists of service.

This is why there is power and wisdom in the cross (1 Corinthians 1:18–31). The love and righteousness demonstrated there compel us in ways that nothing else can (2 Corinthians 5:14). The cross reveals that only God can satisfy our deepest desires. It demonstrates that God loves us more than His own life, that we belong and are cherished by Him despite our shortcomings and transgressions, that we are safe because His rule is benevolent and trustworthy, and that the order of the universe is completely secure because His commitment to righteousness is unbending.

There is nothing that we can add to the revelation of God's glory on the cross. Only the Son of God could reveal the glory of God, because He is God Himself. The breadth of that revelation cannot be matched, because there will never be a greater sacrifice than God becoming a slave and carrying the sins of the world. The love and sacrifice of the redeemed is simply a faint reflection of that superior love. We love Him, because He loved us first (1 John 4:19).

Conclusion

What did Jesus accomplish on the cross? The answer to this question depends on your understanding of the problem of sin.[56] The cross was the solution to the problems that arose from the fall of Adam and Eve at the Garden of Eden. What was lost in the tree of knowledge of good and evil was recovered on the cross. On the cross, Jesus endured the full measure of God's wrath against our sins in our place so that we could be restored to a righteous relationship with God. At the cross, Jesus defeated and mastered the enemy, liberating us from the power of sin and death and recovering for us our dominion over the world. At the cross, Jesus revealed the full measure of God's love and righteousness. Because of that supreme revelation, we have learned to trust and love Him.

There has always been a resistance to the cross both inside and outside Christianity. Paul argued that the circumcision party that opposed the gospel and those whose minds were set on earthly things wanted to rid themselves from the offense of the cross (Galatians 6:12; Philippians 3:18, 19; cf. Galatians 5:11). Later on, Docetism, an early Christian heresy, argued that Jesus did not actually die on the cross but only seemed to die.[57] Similarly, Islam also denies that Jesus died on the cross—only that His enemies *thought* He did. For Islam, the cross is inappropriate for a major prophet of God, and the Koran rejects the notion that the cross was necessary, declaring, at least five times, that "no soul shall bear another's burden."[58] Hindus, on the other hand, accept the historicity of the cross but reject its saving significance. Gandhi once wrote, "I could accept Jesus as a martyr, an embodiment of sacrifice, and a divine teacher, but not as the most perfect man ever born. His death on the cross was a great example to the world, but that there was anything like a mysterious or miraculous virtue in it, my heart could not accept."[59] Philosophers have also struggled with the cross. Nietzsche, toward the end of the nineteenth century, rejected Christianity as decadent because of its sympathy toward the weak, and contemptuously dismissed Jesus as "God on the cross."[60]

Yet, during all this time and despite all the attacks, the cross has remained the center of the Christian faith and message. Yes, we glory only in the cross of Christ (Galatians 6:14) because it is the power and wisdom of God (1 Corinthians 1:18–31).

Endnotes

1. Except where noted otherwise, all Scripture quotations are from the ESV.

2. Martin Hengel, *Crucifixion: In the Ancient World and the Folly of the Message of the Cross* (Philadelphia: Fortress Press, 1977), 19; John R. W. Stott, *The Cross of Christ* (Downers Grove, IL: InterVarsity, 1986), 25.

3. Hengel, *Crucifixion*, 19.

4. Justin Martyr, *Apology 1* 13.4.

5. Pliny the Younger, *Epistulae* 10.96.4–8, quoted in Hengel, *Crucifixion*, 2.

6. Cornelius Tacitus, *Annals* 15.44.3, quoted in Hengel, *Crucifixion*, 2.

7. Stott, *Cross of Christ*, 24.

8. Moisés Silva, *New International Dictionary of New Testament Theology and Exegesis*, rev. ed. (Grand Rapids, MI: Zondervan, 2014), 4:357.

9. Hengel, *Crucifixion*, 9.

10. Gerald G. O'Collins, "Crucifixion," in *Anchor Yale Bible Dictionary*, ed. David Noel Freedman (New York: Doubleday, 1992), 1:1208.

11. Stott, *Cross of Christ*, 20, 21.

12. Jesus began to teach explicitly about His death once His disciples had become settled in the belief that He was the Messiah (Mark 8:29; Matthew 16:15–17; Luke 9:20). First prediction: Mark 8:31; Matthew 16:21; Luke 9:22. Second prediction: Mark 9:31; Matthew 17:22, 23; cf. Luke 9:51, 52. The third was in the last trip to Jerusalem: Mark 10:32–34; Matthew 20:17–19; Luke 18:31–34.

13. See Stott, *Cross of Christ*, 28.

14. John 12:23, 27; 13:1; 16:4, 21, 32; 17:1.

15. See Matthew 16:21, 22; Mark 8:31, 32; Luke 9:21; cf. Matthew 26:54; Luke 13:33; 17:25; 22:37; 24:7, 26, 44; John 3:14; 12:34; Acts 1:16; 17:3.

16. Not only do the Gospels devote an important amount of space to the Passion narratives—they occupy between one-third and one-fourth of the three synoptic Gospels and one-half of the Gospel of John—but their plots build momentum toward the cross and depict it as the defining achievement of Jesus Christ. See Stott, *Cross of Christ*, 32.

17. See Richard M. Davidson, "Biblical Anthropology in the Old Testament" (paper presented at the Third International Bible Conference, Jerusalem, Israel, June 16, 2012).

18. According to the Hebrew original text.

19. Paul-Eugène Dion, "Image et ressemblance en araméen ancien (Tell Fakhariyah)," *Science et Esprit* 34 (1982): 151–153.

20. Adolf Deissmann, *Light From the Ancient East: The New Testament Illustrated by Recently Discovered Texts of the Graeco-Roman World*, trans. Lionel R. M. Strachan (London: Hodder & Stoughton, 1927), 346. See also Martin Hengel, *The Son of God: The Origin of Christology and the History of Jewish-Hellenistic Religion*, trans. John Bowden (London: SCM Press, 1976), 25–30.

21. The term *to tend* in the NKJV or *to work* in the ESV translates the Hebrew '*abad*, which means literally "to serve."

22. See Jacques Doukhan, *On the Way to Emmaus: Five Major Messianic Prophecies Explained* (Clarksville, MD: Lederer, 2012), chap. 1.

23. The original text says literally, "This is an instruction for humanity."

24. Stephen Travis, *Christ and the Judgment of God: Divine Retribution in the New Testament* (Basingstoke: Marshall Pickering, 1986), 21–24.

25. Hosea 1:9; Zechariah 7:13, 14; Numbers 32:15.

26. Hosea 5:6; Isaiah 1:15; Zechariah 7:13.

27. Deuteronomy 31:17, 18; 32:20; Micah 3:4; Psalm 89:46.

28. Jeremiah 7:29; 16:10–13; Lamentations 5:20–22 (catastrophes); Jeremiah 12:7–13 (defeat); Psalm 78:56–66 and Psalm 106:40–43 have the same pattern. At other times, it is God's *presence* that brings punishment (Isaiah 2:10–22; 6:5; Hosea 10:8).

29. Matthew 7:13, 14; 22:11–14; 25:10–12, 30; 7:22, 23; 8:11, 12; Luke 13:22–29.

30. Luke 12:46–48; cf. Matthew 11:21, 22; Mark 12:40; Luke 10:12–14.

31. Matthew 3:7–12; 7:19; 13:30; Luke 3:7–9.

32. Stephen B. Chapman, "Reading the Bible as Witness: Divine Retribution in the Old Testament," *Perspectives in Religious Studies* 31, no. 2 (June 2004): 171–190.

33. Notice both aspects in Isaiah's lament: "O Lord, why do you make us wander from your ways and harden our heart, so that we fear you not?" (Isaiah 63:17). "For you have hidden your face from us, and *have made us melt* in the hand of our iniquities" (Isaiah 64:7; emphasis added). See Travis, *Christ and the Judgment of God*, 23, 24. See also Psalm 89:30–46; Isaiah 29:9–16.

34. Cf. Mark 14:36; Luke 22:42; John 18:11.

35. When God confronted Judah because of its unfaithfulness and wickedness, He warned the nation that it would drink the cup of His wrath (Ezekiel 23:32–34). See also Revelation 15:7–16:21.

36. Rejection: Jeremiah 6:30; 7:29; 14:19. To be delivered over to the nations: Leviticus 26:32, 33, 38; cf. Psalm 106:41; Ezra 9:7; Hosea 8:10 (LXX). To be mocked: Psalms 39; 79; 102. Darkness: Exodus 10:21; Amos 8:9, 10; Mark 13:24.

37. See Simon Gathercole, *Defending Substitution: An Essay on Atonement in Paul*, Acadia Studies in Bible and Theology (Grand Rapids, MI: Baker Academic, 2015).

38. I. Howard Marshall, "The Meaning of Reconciliation," in *Unity and Diversity in New Testament Theology: Essays in Honor of George E. Ladd*, ed. Robert A. Guelich (Grand Rapids, MI: Eerdmans, 1978), 123.

39. In the original of Exodus 32:32, "to forgive" literally means that God bears our sins. See also Jacques Doukhan, *On the Way to Emmaus*.

40. Matthew 18:21–35; Mark 11:25; Luke 6:37; 17:3, 4.

41. Emil Brunner, *The Mediator*, trans. Olive Wyon (Philadelphia: Westminster Press, 1947), 444, 445, quoted in Stott, *Cross of Christ*, 122, 123.

42. Klaus Koch, "Is There a Doctrine of Retribution in the Old Testament?," in *Theodicy in the Old Testament*, ed. James L. Crenshaw (Philadelphia: Fortress Press, 1983), 58.

43. Evil actions result in unceasing flight (Proverbs 28:1, 17), falling into the pit (Proverbs 26:27; 28:10), or a snare (Proverbs 29:6). On other occasions, the relationship between an action and its punishment or reward is described by the metaphor of planting and harvesting (Proverbs 11:18, 30) or the path that leads one to bad consequences (Proverbs 11:3, 5). Similarly, the psalmist describes humanity as having only one path, that of good actions (Psalm 25:12, 13, 21). The wicked person, however, deviates from this path, taking a way that leads to sorrows and destruction (Psalms 1:6; 32:10). For more examples, see Koch, "Is There a Doctrine of Retribution?," 62, 63.

44. See Stott, *Cross of Christ*, 122, 123.

45. John 13:1; 18:28; 19:14, 31. See Leslie Hardinge, *With Jesus in His Sanctuary: A Walk Through the Tabernacle Along His Way* (Harrisburg, PA: American Cassette Ministries, 1991), 429–442.

46. Stott, *Cross of Christ*, 145, 146.

47. The expression "for sin" should probably be translated as "a sacrifice for sin." It translates the Greek expression *peri hamartias*, which in the Old Testament denoted the sacrifice of atonement for sin. The same sense is found in 1 Peter 3:18.

48. See Gathercole, *Defending Substitution*; Scott W. Hahn, "Covenant, Cult, and the Curse of Death: Διαθήκη in Heb 9:15–22," in *Hebrews: Contemporary Methods—New Insights*, Biblical Interpretation Series 75 (Leiden: Brill, 2005), 65–88.

49. Colossians 2:15; Hebrews 2:14, 15.

50. First Corinthians 15:57; Romans 8:37; 2 Corinthians 2:14; Revelation 3:21; 5:5; 12:11.

51. Jeremy R. Treat argues that "the reign of Satan therefore is parasitic to the reign of sin (Rom 5:21)." *The Crucified King: Atonement and Kingdom in Biblical and Systematic Theology* (Grand Rapids, MI: Zondervan, 2014), 199–203.

52. George Smeaton, *The Apostles' Doctrine of the Atonement* (Grand Rapids, MI: Zondervan, 1957), 307, 308.

53. The Greek word translated "departure" is *exodus*.

54. The Hebrew term translated "work" is *'avad*, which means "to work for" or "to serve." Its cognate is *'eved*, which means "servant, slave."

55. See Jacques Doukhan, *On the Way to Emmaus*.

56. See Treat, *The Crucified King*, 194, 195.

57. O'Collins, "Crucifixion," 1210.

58. Stott, *Cross of Christ*, 41.

59. Mohandas Gandhi, *Gandhi: An Autobiography* (London: Jonathan Cape, 1966), 113; quoted in Stott, *Cross of Christ*, 42.

60. Stott, *Cross of Christ*, 42, 43.

10

The Significance, Meaning, and Role of Christ's Atonement

Jiří Moskala

Jesus Christ is our atonement (or the atoning sacrifice), for He died for our sins (Romans 3:25; Hebrews 2:17; 1 John 2:2; 4:10).[1] John Wesley declared, "Nothing in the Christian system is of greater consequence than the doctrine of the atonement."[2] Philip E. Hughes and Frank Colquhoun repeat after Leon Morris, "A Christianity which is not cross-centered is not Christianity at all."[3]

This chapter focuses on the meaning of Christ's atonement using as a background the assertion by last generation theology (LGT)[4] proponents that "Jesus is currently [from 1844] making the final atonement"[5] as part of the "cleansing of the [heavenly] sanctuary."[6]

This cleansing in heaven is connected to the cleansing of the faithful believers on earth as interpreted in point 10 of the LGT fourteen-points document: "The sanctuary is cleansed when God has a people who have become so settled into the truth that they will never again be moved to doubt Him or to disobey known duty. The torrent of sin that has needed forgiveness is dried up."[7] This point implies that this last generation of saints will live sinless lives in order to finally and definitively defeat Satan and prove that God is right; thus, they will provide the ground for the vindication of God by their perfection of character and the great controversy can be closed. By their blameless lives, the last generation of saints will prove the validity of God's law and demonstrate that Satan is a liar. The final atonement is then defined in close connection to the entire sanctification and perfection of the final generation of faithful believers, the final defeat of Satan, and the final vindication of God by them.[8]

M. L. Andreasen (1876–1962) developed and made popular LGT with his two publications, namely, *The Book of Hebrews* and *The Sanctuary Service*. According to Andreasen, the atonement has three phases: (1) The first phase was related to Christ's incarnation and earthly sinless life when He "met sin face to face and conquered it."[9] (2) The second phase of atonement included Gethsemane and Christ's death on the cross at Golgotha: "There the sins which He had met and conquered were placed upon Him, that He might bear them up to the cross and annul them."[10] (3) The third and final phase of atonement takes place in the heavenly sanctuary, in the Most Holy Place, after 1844 but also "in the church below. Christ broke the power of sin in His lifework on earth. He destroyed sin and Satan by His death. He is now eliminating and destroying sin in His saints on earth. This is part of the cleansing of the true sanctuary."[11] Andreasen explains that "this phase includes His [Christ's] session at the right hand of God, His high priestly ministry, and the final exhibition of His saints in their last struggle with Satan, and their glorious victory."[12] He states explicitly, "To complete Christ's work and make it efficacious for man, such a demonstration must be made. It must be shown that man can overcome as Christ overcame."[13]

Thus, the final atonement is related to the final defeat of Satan by the saints: "In the last generation God is vindicated and Satan defeated."[14] This means that Andreasen believed that Satan was not completely defeated by Christ's death on the cross: "In His death Christ was victor. But Satan did not give up. He had failed in his conflict with Christ, but he might yet succeed with men.... If he could overcome them he might not be defeated."[15] Andreasen repeats again: "In the last generation God will stand vindicated. In the remnant Satan will meet his defeat.... They will have disproved Satan's accusations against the government of heaven."[16] This is what he calls the "greatest demonstration"[17] of victory over sin.

This is why for Andreasen, "the final demonstration of what the gospel can do in and for humanity is still in the future. Christ showed the way. He took a human body and demonstrated the power of God. Men are to follow His example and prove that what God did in Christ, He can do in every human being who submits to Him. The world is awaiting this demonstration (Rom. 8:19). When it has been accomplished, the end will come. God will have

fulfilled His plan. He will have shown Himself true and Satan a liar. His government will stand vindicated."[18]

This vindication of God and demonstration of the victory over sin will be the most powerful and highly valued because it will be fought in the extremely difficult conditions after the close of probation: "God removes His Spirit from the earth.... God, to make the demonstration complete, does one more thing. He hides Himself. The sanctuary in heaven is closed. The saints cry to God day and night for deliverance, but He appears not to hear.... They must live in the sight of a holy God without an intercessor."[19] Andreasen makes a very serious logical conclusion regarding the result of this scenario: "Through the last generation of saints God stands finally vindicated. Through them He defeats Satan and wins His case. They form a vital part of the plan of God."[20] In the culmination of his explanation, Andreasen boldly claims, "The cleansing of the sanctuary in heaven *is dependent* upon the cleansing of God's people on earth."[21]

This is the description of the final atonement according to LGT. Those who currently defend and follow this LGT make similar assertions about the final defeat of Satan by the faithful last-generation saints:

> Satan still challenges God. "... Where are the people who will keep the law of God perfectly as Jesus did? You are in the sanctuary covering up the mistakes of your people. I have not been defeated yet." God says to Satan, "I will produce these people, through my grace, in the most degenerate age

of earth's history. I will separate them from all sin completely. They will reflect the image of Jesus fully. I will step out of the sanctuary and they will live in the sight of a holy God without an intercessor."

Such a people will be produced that will be the wonder of the whole universe. Through them Satan will be forever defeated. . . .

. . . It is in the 144,000 that Jesus finally wins the great controversy. . . . By the mere fact that they do not fall into sin, but keep the law of God perfectly, Satan is defeated. His case is lost, and he is held fast. . . .

. . . God is going to risk all on the 144,000. . . .

. . . They realize that *everything depends on them.* They realize that they could disgrace God's throne. This is why this company is going to taste more fully than any other people the experience of Jesus.[22]

My response: The foundational biblical truth—Christ's death on the cross defeated Satan

The cross of Jesus lies at the heart of Seventh-day Adventist theology for its unprecedented efficacy. It is the very heart and core of our message. The death of Christ plays the decisive, crucial, central, and dominant position in our Adventist theology and has a tremendous impact for the whole universe in the context of the great controversy. Nothing can replace the centrality and utmost importance of Christ's death (Romans 1:16, 17; 3:22–26; 1 Corinthians 1:30; 2:2; Ephesians 4:21; Philippians 1:21; Colossians

1:27, 28). True Adventism is built around Jesus, and Seventh-day Adventist theology flows from and to the cross of Golgotha. Ellen White powerfully states, "The sacrifice of Christ as an atonement for sin is the great truth around which all other truths cluster. In order to be rightly understood and appreciated, every truth in the word of God, from Genesis to Revelation, must be studied in the light that streams from the cross of Calvary. I present before you the great, grand monument of mercy and regeneration, salvation and redemption,—the Son of God uplifted on the cross. This is to be the foundation of every discourse given by our ministers."[23] And again: "Of all professing Christians, Seventh-day Adventists should be foremost in uplifting Christ before the world."[24] She excellently explains Calvary's significance: "The atonement of Christ is not a mere skillful way to have our sins pardoned; it is a divine remedy for the cure of transgression and the restoration of spiritual health. It is the Heaven-ordained means by which the righteousness of Christ may be not only upon us but in our hearts and characters."[25]

Adventist theology differentiates between the "complete" atonement accomplished by Jesus Christ on the cross and the "completed" atonement in relationship to His intercessory ministry in heaven on humanity's behalf.[26] Atonement is "complete" on the cross but not yet "completed" because it needs to be applied to people's lives. What happened on the cross is an unparalleled, nonduplicable, and unprecedented divine act of salvation (Hebrews 10:12, 14) from which all the benefits flow out, including the intercessory ministry of Christ for us today. Everett Ferguson fittingly underlines that Jesus' "atoning death was a unique and unrepeatable work for human salvation (Heb. 10:12, 14)."[27] Nothing can improve or supplement it, and no one can add anything to Christ's extraordinary sacrifice for humans; salvation is "complete" (Romans 3:21–26; 1 Corinthians 1:18, 23, 24; 2:2; Galatians 2:16, 21; Ephesians 2:4–10).[28] Jesus' mediatory work was made possible only because of this exceptional, unselfish, and once-for-all death for humanity (Hebrews 9:28). Christ's atoning death on Calvary is like a fountain from which all other blessings spring up or like an acorn that contains the whole oak tree. Ellen G. White aptly explains, "When Christ cried out, 'It is finished,' the unfallen worlds were made secure. For them the battle was fought and the victory won. Henceforth Satan had no place in the affections of the universe. The argument he had brought forward, that self-denial was impossible with God, and therefore unjustly required from His created intelligences, was forever answered. Satan's claims were forever set aside. The heavenly universe was secured in eternal allegiance."[29]

But atonement/salvation is not yet completed, because we still live in a sinful world—already saved, but not yet redeemed from this sinful world and transformed. If the atonement had been completed at the cross, then there would no longer be a problem with the evil that surrounds us. The lasting solution to all issues related to evil is an extremely complex task and involves Christ's mediatory work in heaven over a long period of time. Christ's intercessory ministry applies His work of redemption

to individual believers, but it also involves the security of the whole universe (Daniel 7:9, 10, 13, 14; 9:24–27; Ephesians 1:7–10; Revelation 12:7–12).[30] This is what Ellen G. White calls the "final atonement," in contrast to Andreasen's use of that term. For example, consider the following statement: "As the priests in the earthly Sanctuary entered the Most Holy once a year to cleanse the Sanctuary, Jesus entered the Most Holy of the heavenly, at the end of the 2300 days of Dan. viii, in 1844, to make a *final* atonement for all who could be benefited by his mediation, and to cleanse the Sanctuary."[31]

The atonement of Jesus was perfect and complete, as Ellen White puts it: "When the Father beheld the sacrifice of His Son, He bowed before it in recognition of its perfection. 'It is enough,' He said. '*The atonement is complete.*' "[32] "Our great High Priest has made the only sacrifice that is of any value in our salvation. When he offered Himself on the cross, *a perfect atonement was made for the sins of the people.*"[33] Jesus' statement "It is finished" is a powerful confirmation that salvation was secured on the cross for everyone, but actually only those who believe in Christ Jesus will benefit from this greatest sacrifice (John 3:16).[34] Further, the cleansing of the sanctuary is not focused on our work; it is focused on the work of the High Priest in the heavenly sanctuary as it was prefigured by the ceremonies on the Day of Atonement. It is about His ministry (see Leviticus 16);[35] He is our Judge and Intercessor (Genesis 18:25; 1 John 2:1, 2).[36]

The cross was a necessary prerequisite of Christ's salvific, mediatory work for humanity (Romans 3:23–26). His victory over sin (Matthew 4:1–11; Romans 8:3) and His voluntary and substitutionary death for us qualified Him to be our Intercessor. The intercessory ministry of Jesus puts into practice the results of the cross by expanding the efficacy of Calvary. Jesus became sin and a curse for us (Isaiah 53:3–6; 2 Corinthians 5:21; Galatians 3:13), so what was accomplished on the cross almost two thousand years ago now needs to be applied, actualized, and incorporated into our lives in order for us to be restored to His image and have abundant life (John 10:10). He is the God-man, our all-powerful Mediator, because He "gave himself as a ransom for all people" (1 Timothy 2:6; cf. Mark 10:45).[37] He is our Intercessor because He is our Savior. His intercession is a continuation of His saving activity on our behalf—the realization and integration of His work for us on the cross. We need His death and life in order to be spiritually alive (Romans 3:24, 25; 5:10).[38]

Raoul Dederen directly emphasizes the role of Christ's death on the cross: "While His sacrifice for sin was made once for all on the cross (Heb. 7:27; 9:28; 10:11–14), the ascended Christ is making available to all the benefits of His atoning sacrifice."[39] At the moment sin entered the world, Jesus reached down from heaven and stepped in as our Intercessor in anticipation of His victory at the cross. This proleptic reality is best described in the book of Revelation: "The Lamb who was slain from the creation [or better, "foundation"; Greek: katabolé] of the world" (Revelation 13:8).

Thus, the central and cosmic event—namely, Christ's sacrificial and substitutionary atonement—creates the foundation for His two great ministries in which the benefits of this perfect atonement are spelled out, fully expended, and applied: (1) Christ's intercessory ministry in heaven, which He began after His ascension to the heavenly sanctuary and continues until the close of probation; and this ministry was enlarged by (2) Christ's special day of atonement ministry beginning in 1844 in the heavenly sanctuary's Most Holy Place in order to provide the final solution to the cosmic problem of sin. There then follow two tangible executions of the atonement: (1) at the second coming of Christ when eternal life is given to Christ's faithful children (1 Thessalonians 4:13–17; Hebrews 9:28); and (2) at the end of the millennium when all the wicked, the fallen angels, and Satan will be punished and annihilated during the last judgment (Revelation 20:7–15).[40] Thus, the cross of Jesus is the principle point of all phases of atonement, but Calvary is the only place where atonement was actually made. All other phases only apply or execute Christ's victory and merits that flow from the cross.[41]

An excellent illustration of this is the last judgment after the millennium when, according to Ellen G. White's description, the cross of Jesus will be elevated and the drama of sin's entire history will be explained in panoramic view: "Above the throne is revealed the cross; and like a panoramic view appear the scenes of Adam's temptation and fall, and the successive steps in the great plan of redemption."[42] Ellen G. White speaks about the broad understanding of the atonement, which includes the entire plan of salvation: "Human science is too limited to comprehend the atonement. The plan of redemption is so far-reaching that philosophy cannot explain it. It will ever remain a mystery that the most profound reasoning cannot fathom. The science of salvation cannot be explained; but it can be known by experience. Only he who sees his own sinfulness can discern the preciousness of the Saviour."[43]

Critique of the LGT view

Last generation theology of the atonement sounds really good in some respects. Proponents of LGT build a very appealing and striking picture of the last generation of saints, quote biblical texts, stress unique features of Adventism, and use Ellen G. White statements so that it looks like all they propose is well documented and supported by the church. In actuality, the concept of a multiphase atonement is not strange to Adventism, and if rightly understood, it is acceptable Seventh-day Adventist theology. But the way supporters of LGT interpret the phases of the atonement is inadequate and misleading, and their subtle twisting of the intention of texts are unsupportable from a balanced, biblical perspective and from Ellen G. White's writings. In order to explain why this proposition is so problematic, I will focus on crucial issues and the big picture of the atonement that will shed light on many theological details along the way.

The official teaching of the Seventh-day Adventist Church on the atonement is different from what LGT proposes. Last generation theology cannot be accepted on several important grounds:

1. It denies that Christ's sacrificial atonement defeated Satan once for all. The first serious problem is LGT's interpretation of the meaning of Christ's sacrificial atonement on the cross, which significantly diminishes its efficacy, and in so doing, unintentionally diminishes the person and work of Christ. This reduction of the results of the cross can be seen on several crucial levels (especially the first four points in this list). Last generation theology denies that the death of Christ on Calvary definitely, radically, completely, and categorically defeated Satan once and for all. True, LGT accepts that Jesus was victorious at the cross, but this victory was limited to a personal victory between Satan and Jesus and thus partial in its consequences.[44] According to LGT, God *needs* the final generation of the faithful to ultimately defeat Satan and refute his lies.

I am deeply disturbed by such assertions, because they go contrary to the teachings of the Bible and Ellen G. White. Christ's death on the cross was the decisive action of God; it was the efficacious substitutionary atonement for all of our sins (Isaiah 53:3–6; John 1:29; Romans 3:24–26; 5:10; Colossians 2:14, 15; 1 John 2:2; 4:10), and by Christ's atoning death, Satan was decisively and definitely defeated. John certifies this truth:

> "Now have come the salvation and the
>   power
>   and the kingdom of our God,
>   and the authority of his Messiah.
> For the accuser of our brothers and
>   sisters,
>   who accuses them before our God
>   day and night,
>   has been hurled down" (Revelation
>   12:10).

Christ was the victor in His life and on the cross at Golgotha when He took the "sin of the world" upon Himself. Jesus Himself presented this crucial stage of the cross when He stated, "Now is the time for judgment on this world; now the prince of this world will be driven out. And I, when I am lifted up from the earth, will draw all people to myself" (John 12:31, 32). And again, "And about judgment, because the prince of this world now stands condemned" (John 16:11; cf. Romans 8:3). The cross was the fulfillment of the protogospel of Genesis 3:15 about the promised Seed who would crush the head of the serpent, Satan, while the Seed would be "stricken" ("bruised," "bitten") by the serpent (an allusion to the crucifixion of Jesus).[45] Paul testifies that Jesus defeated Satan and death: "Since the children have flesh and blood, he too shared in their humanity so that by his death he might break the power of him who holds the power of death—that is, the devil—and free those who all their lives were held in slavery by their fear of death. . . . For this reason he had to be made like them, fully human in every way, in order that he might become a merciful and faithful high priest in service to God, and that he might make atonement for the sins of the people" (Hebrews 2:14–17). Paul eloquently describes this glorious victory over Satan, evil, and sin as a triumphant procession (see 2 Corinthians 2:14; Ephesians 4:8).[46] Also, the book of Revelation speaks about the pivotal victory of Jesus (Revelation 12:7–12; cf. Luke 10:18). Thus, Satan was judged and categorically defeated, along with everyone who associates with this archenemy of God. Christ's triumphant victory over Satan and his power was the highest demonstration of God's love and justice (Isaiah 53:3–6, 10–12; Romans 1:17; 5:8; 2 Corinthians 2:14; Ephesians 4:8; Colossians 2:15). By this sacrificial atonement, Satan was overpowered; he is a defeated enemy, and now he is waiting for his execution, because his days are numbered (Matthew 25:41; John 16:11; Romans 16:20; Revelation 12:12; 20:10). Ellen G. White powerfully asserts, "In the Saviour's expiring cry, 'It is finished,' the death knell of Satan was rung. *The great controversy which had been so long in progress was then decided, and the final eradication of evil was made certain.*"[47] Do not miss what Ellen G. White conveys here. She is saying that after the cross God is not at risk at all (contrary to Herbert Douglass's assertion in his book's title).[48] Christ's victory is not in jeopardy, threatened, or in peril. Ellen G. White says that Christ's death on the cross "decided" the outcome of the great controversy. This means that once Christ triumphed over Satan at the cross, God's victory was assured, and no one is able to take it from Him (Romans 8:31–39). There is no way that God could thereafter lose the great controversy, despite the claims of LGT.

2. It diminishes the fact that Christ's death vindicated God's character and refuted Satan's claims. Another immense difficulty with LGT is the claim that the last generation of saints will finally provide the ground for vindicating God, without which God's character would not be exonerated. Last generation theology denies that Christ's blameless life and death already provided the full and sufficient grounds for the vindication of God's character and teaches that only the corporate group of faithful believers in the final days of the world's history will be able to do so. But Jesus Christ defeated Satan by His sinless life, for He never sinned (Matthew 4:1–11; John 8:46; 14:30; Romans 8:3; Hebrews 4:15), and thus He refuted Satan's accusation that Adam and his descendants were not able to keep God's law. Christ as the Second Adam (Romans 5:12–21; 1 Corinthians 15:45–49) vindicated God and uprooted Satan's false allegations against the Godhead, and He did it in much worse conditions than the first Adam: "In our humanity, Christ was to redeem Adam's failure. But when Adam was assailed by the tempter, none of the effects of sin were upon him."[49] Ángel Rodríguez rightly proclaims, "In the Bible and the writings of Ellen G. White the cosmic vindication of God is the exclusive result of the sacrificial death of Christ."[50] He supports his statement with the following quotation from Ellen G. White: "By His life and His death, Christ proved that God's justice did not destroy His mercy, but that sin could be forgiven, and that the law is righteous, and can be perfectly obeyed. *Satan's charges were refuted.* God had given man unmistakable evidence of His love."[51] Marvin Moore correctly states that in reality "the *only* Person who vindicated God and brought the plan of salvation to a victorious conclusion was Jesus."[52]

Thus, according to LGT teaching, the last generation is charged with the work that Jesus has already accomplished on the cross: (1) He decisively and once for all defeated Satan; and (2) He revealed who and what the Lord is—His character of love, truth, and justice—and vindicated the triune God before the universe (John 1:14). Ellen G. White explicitly declares that Christ came to the earth and died "to vindicate the character of God before the universe."[53]

This unique, complete, and nontransferable exultant victory of Jesus at Calvary cannot be perfected or supplemented by any group (like the last generation) or added to by anyone else in the entire universe. It is blasphemous to think that we could add to Christ's atoning work by our achievements or do something similar or even better than Christ did. We are totally dependent on God's grace all the time (John 15:4; Philippians 4:13). Ellen G. White fittingly comments on John 15:4, 5 when she states, "You are just as dependent upon Christ, in order to live a holy life, as is the branch upon the parent stock for growth and fruitfulness. Apart from Him you have no life. You have no power to resist temptation or to grow in grace and holiness. Abiding in Him, you may flourish. Drawing your life from Him, you will not wither nor be fruitless."[54] All glory belongs only to God for what Jesus accomplished on the cross in order to defeat our archenemy Satan and his evil forces and for what He does in us (Jeremiah 9:23, 24; Romans 8:31–39; 1 Corinthians 1:31; Revelation 5:9–14). Paul humbly confesses, "But by the grace of God I am what I am" (1 Corinthians 15:10). All victorious people have only followed Christ's steps and participated in His victory, namely, by accepting Him as their Savior and Lord (John 1:12; Romans 6:23; Ephesians 6:10–13; Colossians 1:22; Revelation 12:11). He is the One who gives us victory: "For it is God who works in you to will and to act in order to fulfill his good purpose" (Philippians 2:13; see also John

16:33; Ephesians 2:4–10; 1 Peter 2:8).

Faithful believers of each generation (in both Old and New Testament times) participate in Christ's triumph by receiving victory over the power of sin, giving glory to God, and thus only confirming (not causing) the vindication of our holy and gracious Lord before the universe, because of what Christ's grace and the power of the Holy Spirit accomplished for, in, and through them (Ezekiel 36:26, 27; Romans 6:11–14; 8:4–8; 1 Corinthians 15:10; 2 Corinthians 12:9; Galatians 2:20, 21). The redeemed are victorious because of the Lamb who died for them (Revelation 12:11; 14:4). Job is the primary example of this saving grace in the Old Testament (Job 19:25–27).[55] In each generation, God has had His "perfect" followers (Genesis 6:9; 17:1; 18:3; 2 Samuel 22:24, 26; Job 1:1, 8; 2:3; Ezekiel 14:14, 20). Biblical perfection is never defined as "sinlessness" ("sinlessness" is not even a biblical term) but as "maturity" and "integrity" (Hebrew: *tamim*) and "right directions, goals, and orientation in life" (Greek: *teleios*). This perfection is reflected and demonstrated in a humble walk with God, in a daily surrendering and dedication to Him, in focusing on the things above, and in growing constantly in Him (Micah 6:8; Philippians 3:12–15; Colossians 3:1–4; 2 Peter 3:18).[56] To be perfect means to be as loving, merciful, forgiving, and serving as our heavenly Father is (Matthew 5:48; Luke 6:36; Ephesians 5:1, 2; Colossians 3:14). Only Christ can keep us blameless until His second coming (2 Corinthians 9:8; Ephesians 3:14–21; 5:27; Philippians 3:20, 21; Jude 24, 25).[57]

We can thus be "perfect" only by the continual mediation of Christ on our behalf. Ellen G. White explicitly states, "As the penitent sinner, contrite before God, discerns Christ's atonement in his behalf, and accepts this atonement as his only hope in this life and the future life, his sins are pardoned. This is justification by faith. Every believing soul is to conform his will entirely to God's will, and keep in a state of repentance and contrition, exercising faith in the atoning merits of the Redeemer and advancing from strength to strength, from glory to glory."[58] Till the very end, until the second coming of Christ, all believers are in constant dependence upon the blood of Jesus and His righteousness:

Christ, our Mediator, and the Holy Spirit are *constantly interceding* in man's behalf, but the Spirit pleads not for us as does Christ who presents His blood, shed from the foundation of the world; the Spirit works upon our hearts, drawing out prayers and penitence, praise and thanksgiving. The gratitude which flows from our lips is the result of the Spirit striking the cords of the soul in holy memories, awakening the music of the heart. The religious services, the prayers, the praise, the penitent confession of sin ascend from true believers as incense to the heavenly sanctuary; but passing through the corrupt channels of humanity, they are so defiled that unless purified by blood, they can never be of value with God. They ascend not in spotless purity, and unless the Intercessor who is at God's right hand presents and purifies all by His righteousness, it is not acceptable to God.

All incense from earthly tabernacles must be moist with the cleansing drops of the blood of Christ. He holds before the Father the censer of His own merits, in which there is no taint of earthly corruption. He gathers into this censer the prayers, the praise, and the confessions of His people, and with these He puts His own spotless righteousness. Then, perfumed with the merits of Christ's propitiation, the incense comes up before God wholly and entirely acceptable. Then gracious answers are returned.

O, that all may see that everything in obedience, in penitence, in praise and thanksgiving must be placed upon the glowing fire of the righteousness of Christ. The fragrance of this righteousness ascends like a cloud around the mercy seat.[59]

The whole history of our planet is lived in the light of the cross (Revelation 13:8). "I am troubled by the idea," Marvin Moore states emphatically, "that God is waiting for a final generation to make this demonstration. . . . However, even a casual reading of Hebrews [7:25] makes it clear that *every* Christian in *every* generation is a demonstration that God is able to save to the uttermost those who come to Him through Christ."[60] The atonement of our Lord, namely, accepting the death of Jesus personally, brings victory in our life.[61] Repentant sinners live to God's glory, and God demonstrates through them that His grace is sufficient to save everyone who believes in Christ (John 1:12; 3:16; 5:24; Romans 5:1; 2 Corinthians 12:9; 1 John 5:10–13).

God's amazing grace is a transforming grace (Romans 12:1, 2; 2 Corinthians 3:18; 5:17). There are not two standards of salvation; people have always been saved only by God's grace through faith in our loving God (Genesis 15:6; Psalms 32:1, 2; 51:10–12; Habakkuk 2:4). There are not two ethical criteria for living a life of obedience—a special one for the saints of the last generation who will be alive at the second coming of Jesus in contrast with that of the rest of the generations who have lived on earth (see the biblical examples of the translation of Enoch and Elijah and the resurrection of Old Testament saints, such as Moses, and those who were raised from the dead at the time of Christ's death [Matthew 27:50–53]). There is a whole array of Old and New Testament people who were faithful to God and lived to His glory—Noah, Abraham, Job, Joseph, Ruth, Esther, Daniel, John the Baptist, Peter, Paul—just to name a few. In the spiritual war against sin and evil, we are never able to accomplish more than Jesus accomplished; we are totally dependent[62] on His help, grace, word, and guidance and on the transforming power of the Holy Spirit (Psalm 73:23–28; John 15:4; Philippians 4:13). The apostle Paul proclaims, "Being confident of this very thing, that He who has begun a good work in you will complete it until the day of Jesus Christ" (Philippians 1:6, NKJV).

The triune God vindicates Himself in Christ, and we are invited to recognize, confirm, and proclaim on the basis of His amazing and astounding actions that He is the God of love, truth, justice, and freedom. He provides all the grounds and evidence. God condescends to our level and desires that we discern, understand, and know who He really is: "Taste and see that the LORD is good; blessed is the one who takes refuge in him" (Psalm 34:8). No one in the whole universe has the power to summon God for a trial to judge or evaluate Him, because there is no standard of truth outside of God by which He can be judged. He is the *summum bonum* (James 1:17, 18). But He opens Himself up that we may recognize things correctly and see who He is. God Himself is vindicated by His own actions; He proves that He is what He proclaims Himself to be—the loving, gracious, forgiving, faithful, and just God (Exodus 34:6, 7; Psalm 51:4; Romans 3:4).[63] He even calls on humans to "judge" between Him and them that He is the ultimate caring God: "Now you dwellers in Jerusalem and people of Judah, judge [Hebrew: *shapat*, "to settle (a dispute), decide"] between me and my vineyard" (Isaiah 5:3). Of course, this does not mean that we can bring God into judgment and make a final decision on His actions nor that His "fate" hinges on our judgment. It means that He invites people to recognize the truth of the matter (to make an epistemologically correct personal conclusion), which brings them to a recognition of theodicy. Therefore, God wins the great controversy because He provides all the evidence for who He is and for what He does. At the end, everyone praises God because He is the Holy One who is worthy of all glory and adoration (Ephesians 1:10; Philippians 2:9, 10; Revelation 4:8, 11; 5:9, 10, 12–14; 7:10–12; 15:4).

3. *It ignores the cosmic results of Christ's triumphant victory on the cross.* An additional problem with the LGT teaching is that it does not do justice to the cosmic results of Christ's victorious death on the cross. The cross of Jesus has such an enormous cosmic dimension that human language is unable to describe its magnificent, colossal, and gigantic effects. The enormous benefits of Christ's death include the safety of the whole universe for all eternity (Colossians 1:19, 20; 2:15; Ephesians 1:10; 6:12; Philippians 2:9, 10). Rebellion and sin will never happen again in heaven, because of Jesus Christ's ultimate sacrifice on Golgotha. As mentioned previously, Ellen G. White appropriately explains that the security and well-being of the whole universe, now and throughout all eternity, uniquely depends on the work of Christ accomplished on the cross and not on the performance of the last generation of saints: "The angels ascribe honor and glory to Christ, for even they are not secure except by looking to the sufferings of the Son of God. *It is through the efficacy of the cross that the angels of heaven are guarded from apostasy.* Without the cross they would be no more secure against evil than were the angels before the fall of Satan."[64] She explains that this is why "our little world is the lesson book of the universe. God's wonderful purpose of grace, the mystery of redeeming love, is the theme into which 'angels desire to look,' and it will be their study throughout endless ages. Both the redeemed and the unfallen beings will find in the cross of Christ their science and their song."[65] She admonishes us to learn for ourselves the science of the cross and teach it to our young people: "The revelation of God's love to man centers in the cross. Its full significance tongue cannot utter; pen cannot

portray; the mind of man cannot comprehend. . . . Christ crucified for our sins, Christ risen from the dead, Christ ascended on high, is the science of salvation that we are to learn and to teach."[66] "Let the youth make the word of God the food of mind and soul. Let the cross of Christ be made the science of all education, the center of all teaching and all study."[67]

4. *It disregards the fact that Christ is currently applying the benefits of His substitutionary atonement in the heavenly sanctuary.* The intercessory ministry of Jesus applies to the individual believer the benefits and results of His victorious death on the cross as is clearly explained in Fundamental Belief 24. It is not the case that Jesus is making additional atonement as our Intercessor and our great High Priest in heaven as LGT supporters claim. Our church's official statement is very eloquent that Jesus Christ entered the heavenly sanctuary, where He "ministers on our behalf, making available to believers *the benefits of His atoning sacrifice* offered once for all on the cross [cf. Hebrews 9:26–28]."[68] Ellen G. White relevantly underscores this: "The intercession of Christ in man's behalf in the sanctuary above is as essential to the plan of salvation as was His death upon the cross. By His death He began that work which after His resurrection He ascended to complete in heaven. . . . There *the light from the cross of Calvary is reflected.*"[69] She plainly states that Jesus applies His victory of the cross to believers during His intercessory ministry: "The great Sacrifice had been offered and had been accepted, and the Holy Spirit which descended on the day of Pentecost carried the minds of the disciples from the earthly sanctuary to the heavenly, where Jesus had entered by His own blood, *to shed upon His disciples the benefits of His atonement.*"[70] The same can be said about Christ's heavenly ministry during the antitypical day of atonement when He is actually not making the final atonement but applying to us the results of the cross.[71] We are totally dependent in our daily lives on the high-priestly ministry of Jesus on our behalf in the heavenly sanctuary. Even our best and most noble and spiritual activities need to be covered by His merits, and this will be so until the second coming of Christ.[72]

5. *It blends Christ's two different, but complementary, ministries in heaven.* Last generation theology is not very precise in describing the intercessory ministry of Jesus and His work as High Priest on the antitypical day of atonement. In LGT, it appears that these two different ministries of Jesus Christ are conflated. In contrast to LGT, the Bible depicts these two phases of Christ's ministry in the heavenly sanctuary as complementary but still different in meaning. The first represents the daily ministry in the sanctuary, and the second corresponds to the yearly ministry in the Most Holy Place of the heavenly temple of God. Although the meaning of the cleansing of the heavenly sanctuary affects the cleansing of God's people on earth, according to Seventh-day Adventist Fundamental Belief 24, the emphasis is on God's final solution to the problem of evil.[73] Ellen G. White explains,

Those who are living upon the earth when the intercession of Christ shall cease in the sanctuary above are to stand in the sight of a holy God without a mediator. Their robes must be spotless, their characters must be purified from sin by the blood of sprinkling. Through the grace of God and their own diligent effort they must be conquerors in the battle with evil. While the investigative judgment is going forward in heaven, while the sins of penitent believers are being removed from the sanctuary, there is to be a special work of purification, of putting away of sin, among God's people upon earth. This work is more clearly presented in the messages of Revelation 14.[74]

From 1844 on, the ministry of Jesus Christ in the heavenly sanctuary is expanded. He continues to be our Intercessor, but to His mediatorial work is added the very crucial new high-priestly ministry to cleanse the sanctuary (Daniel 8:14, KJV; Hebrew: *nitsdaq qodesh*).[75] In the last stage of salvation history, Jesus pronounces the final irreversible judgments and presents the concluding solution to the problem of sin in order to close the chapter on humanity's salvation. This simultaneous work of Jesus needs to be properly understood. To confuse the functions of these two important ministries brings complications and obscures Christ's work in heaven. Just as in the earthly sanctuary a priest served daily in this holy precinct by administering forgiveness and reconciliation, so Jesus Christ during His intercessory ministry (daily ministry) applies His righteousness, victory, and merits of the cross to those who accept Him as their personal Savior, forgiving and transforming them by His

grace. Just as once each year on the Day of Atonement the high priest performed a special work of cleansing the sanctuary from all confessed sins, so during the pre-Advent judgment Jesus Christ as the High Priest in the ministry of the antityp- ical day of atonement presents the cases of true believers in Him before the representatives of the entire universe in order for these true believers to be accepted into the heavenly family, thus bringing closure to the long drama of the great controversy (Daniel 7:9, 10, 13, 14). The last generation of believers has no power to determine the time of probation's close by their performance. To finalize the big cosmic issues and close the drama of the great controversy is God's prerogative alone.[76]

6. It falsely claims that the last generation of saints will provide the greatest proof for God's vindication. It is true that believers will live without the intercessory ministry of Jesus after the close of probation, but at that time they will already have been sealed with God's seal,[77] and this seal of the Living God cannot be reversed.[78] LGT maintains that after the close of probation the last generation of saints must provide to the whole universe the final and greatest demonstration and highest proof that they will stay loyal to God and sinless under the worst conditions and circumstances (and thus vindicate God). However, this amounts to the claim that the perseverance of this generation of saints is as great and consequential as Christ's experience. Yet this cannot be so because Christ's temptations, agony, and struggles during His earthly life and on the cross were exceedingly greater than ours, because He took upon Himself the burden of our sin (Isaiah 53:3–6; John 1:29; Romans 5:8; 1 Corinthians 15:3) and experienced God's punishment and wrath upon sin (2 Corinthians 5:21; Galatians 3:13; cf. 1 Thessalonians 5:9). This is something that no human being could ever experience. After the close of probation, the saints will not fall into sin since they are sealed with God's seal and carried during that short period of time by the Holy Spirit.[79] Their victory is not performed by their own strength and power but by Christ's grace and the Holy Spirit, who is their help (John 14:16, 17; 26; 15:26; 16:7–15; Greek: *parakletos*, "one who is called to stand by, to help"; cf. Revelation 12:11) and who gives victory after victory (2 Corinthians 3:18).[80] Thus, the example of the final generation would not prove to the universe something beyond Jesus' accomplishment. Satan would dispute any such claim, because Jesus experienced more difficulties during His incarnation than the final generation could have, either individually or corporately. When Jesus fought against Satan in the full fragility of His humanity, He endured the winepress alone; no one was there to help Him on the cross (see Psalm 22:1–11; Isaiah 63:1–5; Daniel 9:26). Jesus' battle was so real that He could lose His eternal life if He should sin![81] In other words, the greatest demonstration of loyalty to God and the vindication of His name were accomplished by Jesus Christ on the cross when He died for us as the atoning sacrifice (see the preceding points 1 and 2). We are victorious only because we benefit from and participate in Christ's victory, walk humbly with Him, and follow in His footsteps wherever He leads (Micah 6:8; John 15:4, 5; Ephesians 4:1–3; Revelation 12:11; 14:4).

7. *It holds an anthropocentric view.* The activities of the last generation, as presented by the defenders of LGT, seem to be self-centered, focused on the accomplishments and perfect characters of that group. Last generation theology language is very anthropocentric; in the moment of the last generation's ultimate victory, Jesus is actually "hiding." The achievements of the last generation, as portrayed by LGT, seem to put the life and death of Jesus and its merits to the periphery; God's crucial actions seem secondary in importance.

Further crucial biblical and theological observations on Christ's high-priestly ministry with selected Ellen G. White quotations

The work of Christ in the heavenly sanctuary should be understood as the application of the benefits of the atonement already made on the cross, and not as a continuation of the work of atonement that began on the cross or another work of atonement. Christ's heavenly intercessory ministry is currently accompanied by His high-priestly pre-Advent ministry of judgment. On the basis of Daniel 7, 8, the cleansing of the sanctuary and the pre-Advent judgment are references to the same event. Atonement was complete at the cross but needs to be completed by Jesus' intercession, that is, applied, realized, or affirmed in our everyday life in the twenty-first century.[82]

The cross and Jesus' intercessory ministry are the prerequisites for His heavenly sanctuary ministry as High Priest in the Most Holy Place, which began in 1844. He saves completely and then takes the cases of redeemed persons to the pre-Advent judgment, where He affirms before the heavenly beings that these are His people. He demonstrates it, affirms it, and thus reveals that He is their Savior. After the angels and heavenly beings investigate all the records, they affirm Christ's decision because He is the witness who testifies faithfully and truthfully on the basis of their relationship with "the Amen, the faithful and true witness, the ruler of God's creation" (Revelation 3:14). The intercessory ministry of Christ has the power to save and change people. But as in the Old Testament sanctuary service, Christ's high-priestly ministry "only" confirms and reveals the decisions of the redeemed and brings the final solution to the issues related to the great controversy.[83] The investigative judgment does not change their decisions, and no manipulations occur in regard to the facts of their lives. Christ speaks openly and publicly for His saved people, purchased and cleansed by His blood (1 John 1:7, 9; Revelation 5:9; 14:4). This is why we do not need to live in uncertainty; Christ is for us and never against us, so we can have joy and assurance of salvation (Isaiah 33:22; 35:4; John 5:24, 25; Ephesians 2:1–10; 1 John 2:28; 4:17; 5:10–13). Ellen G. White explains the close connection between Jesus' blood poured out for sinners and His intercessory ministry: "As Christ at His ascension appeared in the presence of God to plead His blood in behalf of penitent believers, so the priest in the daily ministration sprinkled the blood of the sacrifice in the holy place in the sinner's behalf."[84]

The primary purpose of the pre-Advent judgment is to secure legally our place in the heavenly family for all eternity with the consent of the universe. Jesus, as the True Witness, will proclaim in front of the heavenly tribunal that we are His, that His grace is sufficient for us, that He made us new persons, and that we are changed by the power of His grace. This pre-Advent judgment is performed in heaven (Daniel 7:9, 10, 13, 14) prior to the second coming of Christ. Seventh-day Adventists explain that this judgment started in 1844 according to the book of Daniel (Daniel 7–9).[85] We are judged by the standard of God's law, the Decalogue, which is the transcript of His character. Jesus Christ is a perfect living example and personification of this law (James 2:12, 13; 1:25; Romans 2:13, 16; 3:21–26; Matthew 16:27; John 8:46; 14:30). He is there for us as our Judge, Advocate (defense attorney), and Intercessor, all at the same time (1 John 2:1). He presents our life in its entirety before the heavenly court as our Faithful and True Witness, so we are not going through investigation alone. We are not standing in front of the court, exposed and abandoned as the court administers its judgment. On the contrary, Jesus is there on our behalf.

This judgment is like the final inspection of a house. Inspection comes after a long period of construction, and at the end comes the process of "sealing," or approving, the work. Part of the affirmative judgment is a review of one's life and a demonstration of the person's orientation and attitudes, and finally results in the confirmation of a judged person. The pre-Advent judgment is thus the last legal procedure before the second coming of Jesus to make clear to the universe who, at the coming of Christ, will be saved and who will be rejected.

The problem of sin will ultimately be resolved only at the end of the millennium when the execution phase of the judgment will occur, which was prefigured in the Day of Atonement with the chasing out and dying of the goat of Azazel (symbolizing Satan) in the wilderness (Leviticus 16:10). The annihilation of the wicked, the evil angels, and Satan will purge the universe from all evil, and the cosmic battle between good and evil, light and darkness, Christ and Satan, will be ended. Thus, the final result of Christ's victory on the cross will be executed, and the whole universe will be put back into total harmony. It will be put at one—"at-one-ment"—which is the true meaning of the atonement. The benefits of the "complete" sacrificial atonement provided on the cross is now "fully completed"; God's victory is secured everywhere and for all eternity (Ephesians 1:10; Philippians 2:9, 10). These benefits will hold the entire universe in perfect harmony, peace, and joy for all eternity. Never again will rebellion against the holy, loving, true, and just God arise. The merits of the cross will guarantee the security of the whole universe throughout eternity! "The third angel closes his message thus: 'Here is the patience of the saints: here are they that keep the commandments of God, and the faith of Jesus.' As he repeated these words, he pointed to the heavenly sanctuary. The minds of all who embrace this message are directed to the most holy place, where Jesus stands before the ark, *making His final intercession for all those for whom mercy still lingers and for those who have ignorantly broken the law of God. This atonement is made for the righteous dead as well as for the righteous living.*"[86]

It is clear that Jesus is not changing or saving the righteous dead (they are already saved in Christ and asleep in the Lord), but He reveals in His final work to the heavenly court His verdict and applies His victory at the cross for them. Thus, He is bringing the final solution to the problem of sin in the pre-Advent judgment. "Then by virtue of the atoning blood of Christ, the sins of all the truly penitent will be blotted from the books of heaven. Thus the sanctuary will be freed, or cleansed, from the record of sin."[87] The final atonement applies the atonement made on the cross and finalizes it, bringing to fruition and conclusion the great controversy. On the Day of Atonement in the earthly sanctuary, everything centered on the work of the high priest, and the people benefited from it, so it is also in Jesus' intercessory work as our High Priest in heaven.

Therefore, the two-phase ministry of Jesus in the heavenly sanctuary is crucial for us. His intercessory ministry brings forgiveness, transformation, and help by building on what He accomplished on Calvary. And Jesus' second ministry in heaven as the all-powerful High Priest guarantees and brings about the final solution to the problem of evil and the complicated issues related to theodicy. Roy Gane aptly summarizes, "When YHWH forgives guilty people, he incurs judicial responsibility . . . by creating an imbalance between justice and kindness that affects his reputation as ruler (cf. 2 Sam 14:9). Restoration of equilibrium is enacted through ritual purification of the sanctuary, which represents vindication of YHWH's administrative justice as he sheds judicial responsibility. As a result, Israelites who show their continuing loyalty to him receive the second benefit of moral cleansing/clearing in the sense that the forgiveness already granted them is confirmed when the Forgiver is vindicated."[88]

Thus, in its results, the two-phase heavenly ministry of Christ "dramatically proclaim[s] that the character of God is just and good."[89] God's caring love and blazing grace will ultimately triumph, and the drama of the great controversy will be finally closed with this astounding, amazing, and marvelous climax. These results will secure God's government for all eternity.

In order not to be under the condemnation of sin, the only solution to our sinful situation is to accept and personally know our great Judge, because in the face of our Judge we can recognize the face of our Savior (Genesis 3:9, 15, 21; Isaiah 63:7–9). This truth is eloquently explained in the following quotation: "Make friendship with Christ today. Put your case in the hands of the great Advocate. He will plead your cause before the Father. Though you have transgressed the law, and must plead guilty before God, Christ will present his precious blood in your behalf; and through faith and obedience, and vital union with Christ, you may stand acquitted before the Judge of all the earth, and he will be your friend when the final trump shall sound, and the scenes of earth shall be no more."[90]

The Lord as Judge is the Redeemer.[91] Walther Zimmerli has it right: "The judgment makes known Yahweh's nature."[92] We are condemned to death, but because

of Jesus' sacrificial substitutionary death, "whoever believes in him shall not perish but have eternal life" (John 3:16; cf. John 1:12; 3:36).[93]

Conclusion

The LGT view on atonement and related events is attractive in many ways. The picture painted regarding last-day events is extremely seductive and appealing to our human fallen nature, in spite of the fact that the last generation of saints will go through an enormously difficult battle with the forces of evil. One might even desire this teaching to be true, because according to this theology the last generation can do something brilliant and extremely significant: (1) it can definitively prove that God is right and vindicate Him in front of the whole universe; (2) it can irrevocably and conclusively defeat Satan; and (3) it can irrefutably decide the verdict of the great controversy by its blameless character and right actions such that the final outcome between good and evil depends on it. Thus, on this last generation depends the final outcome of the cosmic battle between good and evil. How magnificent and solemn a responsibility! No wonder that such a scenario of end-time events motivates its defenders to strive for the final victory over sin and do right things for their great God. Unfortunately, this anthropocentric view cannot be harmonized with the biblical and the Spirit of Prophecy data on several grounds as has been documented in our study. It is a self-centered, human-centered attempt to achieve great things and do it all themselves.

The focus of LGT is on *our* characters and

our actions instead of being God-centered people. In addition, as "beautiful" as the LGT system might appear in some ways, the reality of Christ's fully efficacious and all-sufficient atoning work is far more beautiful; indeed, nothing could be more beautiful. Last generation theology unacceptably downgrades and reduces the meaning of Christ's death on the cross and its efficacy. It is Jesus (and not the last generation saints) who irrevocably, permanently, irreversibly, and irretrievably defeats Satan, vindicates God, and secures eternity for the entire universe, and because of this decisive victory, He will bring the great controversy to its victorious end. There is no justification for marginalizing His radical, perfect, and outstanding victory. Last generation theology's mix of truth with error is highly challenging; its elusive changes in meaning, intention, and theology of the biblical texts and Ellen G. White quotations result in an unacceptable construct and redefinitions of the content of different phases of atonement. Such interpretation is inconsistent and seriously damages the biblical truth on atonement.

The judgment at the cross is the central cosmic event, because the cross of Christ is the central point in human and cosmic history; and at Calvary, in an intense agony of suffering, He fought for our salvation and secured it. In total humility and surrender to His Father, Christ won the decisive victory over Satan, evil forces, and sin. The very safety of the whole universe depends on that key event since the rebellion against the loving Lord started in heaven. Jesus Christ's sacrificial, substitutionary atonement on the cross, built on His perfect earthly life, is the greatest manifestation of God's love and justice. Because of this unprecedented and unique action of God, Satan has no chance, and the future of godly people and the unfallen worlds is guaranteed and protected.

Jesus Christ is our Intercessor in the heavenly sanctuary and is categorically for us and never against us (Romans 8:31–39; Hebrews 7:25). He saves completely. He is also our High Priest who brings the final solution to the problem of evil and presents it to the whole universe during the antitypical day of atonement in order to execute the positive results of His work at His glorious second coming—resurrecting the true believers and transforming those who will be alive at His coming. This brings to His people the tangible and physical results of His work of atonement at the cross for them. Then, at the end of the millennium, He executes and annihilates all the wicked, the evil angels, and Satan in order that sin and evil will be no more. In this way, complete harmony will be restored for all eternity, and everything will be "at-one-ment." Then the atonement of Jesus Christ, the "complete" sacrificial atonement provided on the cross, is fully "completed." The execution and annihilation of evil in all its form brings God's triumph of love and moral power to its peak. Complete harmony, peace, and joy are established, and God's kingdom will be everlasting. Thus, the results of the cross are fully manifested, and the safety of the whole universe is secured and holds together, because of Christ's magnificent act of love and justice. The death of Jesus on the cross will be the highest science studied throughout all eternity. All the redeemed and unfallen angels and worlds will admire the depth, width, length, and height of God's love as expressed at Calvary.

For Christians who are thinking biblically and theologically, to know Christ existentially means eternal life. "Now this is eternal life: that they know you, the only true God, and Jesus Christ, whom you have sent" (John 17:3). This knowledge is focused on the cross of Jesus. As believers in Jesus, we have everything in Him. The apostle Paul makes this clear by constantly repeating a simple phrase: "*en Christo* (in Christ)."[94] We are complete and completed in Him: "In Him you have been made complete, and He is the head over all rule and authority" (Colossians 2:10, NASB). Those who follow the Lamb will triumph with Him, because on the cross He already won the battle with Satan (Revelation 12:10–12; 17:14). The redeemed will humbly acknowledge that it was God who did marvelous things for them: "Lord, you establish peace for us; all that we have accomplished you have done for us" (Isaiah 26:12). "They [God's enemies] will wage war against the Lamb, but the Lamb will triumph over them because he is Lord of lords and King of kings—and with him will be his called, chosen and faithful followers" (Revelation 17:14).

We are called by God to live holy, devoted, dedicated, and sanctified lives for Christ, His church, and the community (John 17:17, 19; Romans 12:1, 2; 15:16; 1 Thessalonians 4:3; 5:23; Hebrews 12:14). All our victories belong to Him (Isaiah 26:12; Romans 5:1; 7:25). Because of His grace, the power of His Word, and the guidance of the Holy Spirit, we can live victorious lives and give glory to God (Ezekiel 36:27; Romans 8:14; Ephesians 5:26). If God's followers are spiritually dead, then God, too, is dead, and Nietzsche's slogan "God is dead" would be right. This is one reason the saved, while rejecting perfectionism, must not diminish the importance of holiness in their lives as a result of Christ's work in them. The church is a spectacle to the world and to the whole universe (1 Corinthians 4:9; Ephesians 3:10). Ellen G. White powerfully explains that this is our role in the closing days of world history:

So the followers of Christ are to shed light into the darkness of the world. Through the Holy Spirit, God's word is a light as it becomes a transforming power in the life of the receiver. By implanting in their hearts the principles of His word, the Holy Spirit develops in men the attributes of God. The light of His glory—His character—is to shine forth in His followers. Thus they are to glorify God. . . .

. . . Men are losing their knowledge of His character. It has been misunderstood and misinterpreted. At this time a message from God is to be proclaimed, a message illuminating in its influence and saving in its power. His character is to be made known. Into the darkness of the world is to be shed the light of His glory, the light of His goodness, mercy, and truth. . . .

. . . *The last rays of merciful light, the last message of mercy to be given to the world, is a revelation of His character of love. The children of God are to mani-*

fest His glory. *In their own life and character they are to reveal what the grace of God has done for them.*

The light of the Sun of Righteousness is to shine forth in good works—in words of truth and deeds of holiness.[95]

Many biblical texts assure us that God is abundant in love and goodness (Exodus 34:6, 7; Psalms 100:5; 117:2; 136; Romans 2:4; 5:5, 8; 1 John 3:1; 4:16). We need to invite people to "taste and see that the LORD is good" (Psalm 34:8) and proclaim the truth about our awesome God of love, grace, and justice in such an attractive way that people will know, love, admire, follow, obey, and worship Him for who He is and for what He did, does, and will do for, in, and through them. In this way they will honor God, live to His glory, and be ready for the second coming of Jesus, as Ellen G. White appropriately confirms: "If you are right with God today, you are ready if Christ should come today."[96]

Endnotes

1. Regarding the meaning of the atonement and the discussion on the different theories of atonement, consult the following publications: David L. Allen, *The Extent of the Atonement: A Historical and Critical Review* (Nashville, TN: B & H Academic, 2016); Sharon L. Baker, *Executing God: Rethinking Everything You've Been Taught About Salvation and the Cross* (Louisville, KY: Westminster John Knox Press, 2013); James Beilby and Paul R. Eddy, eds., *The Nature of the Atonement: Four Views* (Downers Grove, IL: InterVarsity, 2006); Aercio Cairus, *Substitutionary Atonement* (Silver Spring, MD: Biblical Research Institute, 2015); Stephen Finlan, *Problems With Atonement: The Origins of, and Controversy About, the Atonement Doctrine* (Collegeville, MN: Liturgical Press, 2005); Charles E. Hill and Frank A. James III, eds., *The Glory of the Atonement: Biblical, Historical, and Practical Perspectives, Essays in Honor of Roger Nicole* (Downers Grove, IL: InterVarsity, 2004); Donald Macleod, *Christ Crucified: Understanding the Atonement* (Downers Grove, IL: InterVarsity, 2014); A. Graham Maxwell, *Can God Be Trusted?* (Nashville, TN: Southern Pub. Assn., 1977); H. D. McDonald, *Forgiveness and Atonement* (Grand Rapids, MI: Baker Book House, 1984); Leon Morris, *The Atonement: Its Meaning and Significance* (Downers Grove, IL: InterVarsity, 1983); Leon Morris, *The Cross in the New Testament* (Grand Rapids, MI: Eerdmans, 1999); Leon Morris, *Glory in the Cross: A Study in Atonement* (Grand Rapids, MI: Baker Book House, 1979); Richard D. Phillips, ed., *Precious Blood: The Atoning Work of Christ* (Wheaton, IL: Crossway Books, 2009); James I. Packer, *What Did the Cross Achieve? The Logic of Penal Substitution* (Carlisle, PA: Paternoster Press, 1998); Jack Provonsha, *You Can Go Home Again* (Washington, DC: Review and Herald®, 1982); *Seventh-day Adventists Answer Questions on Doctrine*, annotated ed. (Berrien Springs, MI: Andrews University Press, 2003), 271–284; Martyn John Smith, *Divine Violence and the Christus Victor Atonement Model* (Eugene, OR: Pickwick Publications, 2016); John Stott, *The Cross of Christ* (Leicester: InterVarsity, 1986); Derek Tidball, David Hilborn, and Justin Thacker, eds., *The Atonement Debate: Papers From the London Symposium on the Theology of Atonement* (Grand Rapids, MI: Zondervan, 2008); J. Denny Weaver, *The Nonviolent God* (Grand Rapids, MI: Eerdmans, 2013).

2. John Wesley, *A Compend of Wesley's Theology*, ed. R. Burtner and R. Chiles (Nashville, TN: Abingdon, 1954), 79. Atonement theories attempt to explain why Jesus came to earth and why He had to suffer and die. These theories are numerous: substitutionary, satisfaction, *Christus Victor*, government, moral influence, ransom, recapitulation, and many others. Each theory is usually right in what it affirms but wrong in what it denies. No one theory can adequately put together all the richness and complexity of the mystery of the cross. The meaning of the death of Christ is bigger, greater, and broader than the human mind can comprehend, explain, or imagine. Throughout all eternity, we will study the science of the cross and learn more. The more we understand, the more we will be amazed and in awe of our gracious and holy Lord.

3. Morris, introduction to *Glory in the Cross*, 6. The original quotation is on page 91 of that work.

4. Also sometimes called "final generation theology." In this article, "last generation theology" has been abbreviated as LGT.

5. Last generation theology's point 9 of fourteen points; see "Last Generation Theology in 14 Points," LastGenerationTheology.org, http://web.archive.org/web/20140303230550/http://lastgenerationtheology.org/lgt/ori/ori-lgt14.php.

6. Ibid., point 10. The ninth point of "Last Generation Theology in 14 Points" is entitled "Jesus Is Currently Making the Final Atonement" and reads as follows: "Jesus' atonement was promised in Eden. With His incarnation and then death as our Substitute on the cross, His atoning work was begun. He rose from the dead and went to heaven in A.D. 31 to represent us before the Father, who received His sacrifice for us. Through that sacrifice we can be right with God as soon as we accept His gift of forgiveness and heart cleansing. In A.D. 1844 He entered the second apartment of the heavenly sanctuary, commencing the closing phase of His atonement. Today, Jesus is making the final atonement."

7. The full text of LGT's point 10 reads, "Neither Luther nor the Millerite Adventists living in 1844 finished the Reformation or understood the angel messages of Revelation 14 and 18. The cleansing of the heavenly sanctuary is connected to the cleansing and purifying of lives on earth. The sanctuary is cleansed when God has a people who have become so settled into the truth that they will never again be moved to doubt Him or to disobey known duty. The torrent of sin that has needed forgiveness is dried up. Christ's presence remains with those who have chosen Him. The Holy Spirit empowers obedience even after the ministry of forgiveness is closed." "Last Generation Theology in 14 Points." For details see, Larry Kirkpatrick, *Cleanse and Close: Last Generation Theology in 14 Points* (Highland, CA: GCO Press, 2005).

8. Kirkpatrick claims, "The work done in us by the Holy Spirit is part of the atonement." *Cleanse and Close,* 85. But the work of the Holy Spirit in us is called *sanctification,* not atonement.

9. M. L. Andreasen, *The Book of Hebrews* (Washington, DC: Review and Herald®, 1948), 59.

10. Ibid., 59.

11. Ibid., 60.

12. Ibid., 59.

13. Ibid., 58.

14. M. L. Andreasen, *The Sanctuary Service* (Washington, DC: Review and Herald®, 1947), 303, 304.

15. Ibid., 310.

16. Ibid., 315.

17. Ibid., 312.

18. Ibid., 299.

19. Ibid., 317, 318. But the last sentence of LGT's point 10 presupposes help from the Spirit of God: "The Holy Spirit empowers obedience even after the ministry of forgiveness is closed."

20. Andreasen, *The Sanctuary Service,* 319.

21. Ibid., 321 (emphasis added).

22. Dennis Priebe, "Will the Great Controversy End Soon?" Dennis Priebe Seminars, http://www.dennispriebe.com/new/node/45 (emphasis added). For more on firsthand material from the proponents of LGT, see Kirkpatrick, *Cleanse and Close.* These fourteen points are the manifesto of LGT. See also lesson 16 of Dennis Priebe's Bible study on righteousness by faith: "Thus the perfect character developed by God's people is crucially important in the final resolution of the great controversy between Christ and Satan. This is the real reason for stressing the concept of perfection in God's end-time people. God claims that total obedience is possible. Satan claims that a sinful nature and character make obedience impossible. Who is telling the truth? Only God's final generation can prove that Satan is a liar." "Why Is It so Important?" Dennis Priebe Seminars, http://www.dennispriebe.com/new/node/44. See also M. L. Andreasen, *The Last Generation* (Malo, WA: Light Bearers Present Truth Ministries, 1989), and Herbert E. Douglass, *God at Risk: The Cost of Freedom in the Great Controversy Between God and Satan* (Roseville, CA: Amazing Facts, 2004) 27, 107, 110–117, 226, 382–385, 391, 392, 396–404, 439–446.

23. Ellen G. White, *Gospel Workers* (Washington, DC: Review and Herald®, 1915), 315.

24. Ibid., 156. See also Ellen G. White Comments, in *The Seventh-day Adventist Bible Commentary,* ed. Francis D. Nichol, vol. 5 (Washington, DC: Review and Herald®, 1956), 1137, 1138; Ellen G. White, *The Acts of the Apostles* (Mountain View, CA: Pacific Press®, 1911), 560.

25. Ellen G. White, Letter 406, 1906, quoted in Ellen G. White Comments, in *The Seventh-day Adventist Bible Commentary,* ed. Francis D. Nichol, vol. 6 (Washington, DC: Review and Herald®, 1957), 1074.

26. See, e.g., the statement by Dr. W. G. C. Murdock, the former dean of the Seventh-day Adventist Theological Seminary, at the 1980 General Conference Session in Dallas, Texas: "Seventh-day Adventists have

always believed in a complete atonement that is not completed." Quoted in Morris L. Venden, *Never Without an Intercessor: The Good News About the Judgment* (Boise, ID: Pacific Press®, 1996), 140. The full "at-one-ment," i.e., the complete harmony between God and His creation, will be reached when sin is eradicated and evil is no longer present (1 Corinthians 15:24–28; Ephesians 1:10). This full harmony will be restored at the end of the millennium (Revelation 21; 22).

27. Everett Ferguson, *The Church of Christ: A Biblical Ecclesiology for Today* (Grand Rapids, MI: Eerdmans, 1996), 282.

28. Ferguson rightly claims that "Jesus' sacrificial death, therefore, was a ministry that the church cannot continue.... Jesus' redemptive sufferings were complete and cannot be added to. The church, nonetheless, shares in Jesus' redemptive work; she, too, exists to seek and save the lost. God's goal is the salvation of all (1 Tim. 2:4), and the church participates in that. God works through her to bring the benefits of Jesus' atoning death to bear on lost human lives. This is accomplished through the church's proclaiming the message of the atonement, demonstrating redemption in its life, and working for the redemption of all people." Ibid., 282.

Ellen G. White explains, "The intercession of Christ in man's behalf in the sanctuary above is as essential to the plan of salvation as was His death upon the cross. By His death He began that work which after His resurrection He ascended to complete in heaven.... There the light from the cross of Calvary is reflected." *The Great Controversy* (Mountain View, CA: Pacific Press®, 1950), 489.

The intercessory ministry of Jesus Christ for sinners will cease at the close of probation (Revelation 15:8; 16:1; cf. Revelation 22:11).

29. Ellen G. White, "Lessons From the Christ-Life," *Advent Review and Sabbath Herald*, March 12, 1901, 161.

30. "Christ is mediating in behalf of man, and the order of unseen worlds is preserved by His mediatorial work." Ellen G. White, *Messages to Young People* (Nashville, TN: Southern Pub. Assn., 1930), 254. "Not only men, but angels, will ascribe honor and glory to the Redeemer, for even they are secure only through the sufferings of the Son of God. It is through the efficacy of the cross that the inhabitants of unfallen worlds have been guarded from apostasy. Not only those who are washed by the blood of Christ, but also the holy angels, are drawn to him by his crowning act of giving his life for the sins of the world." Ellen G.

White, unpublished testimony, quoted in J. O. Corliss, "Our Special Privilege for This Time," *Home Missionary*, May 1, 1897.

31. Ellen G. White, *Spiritual Gifts* (Washington, DC: Review and Herald®, 1945), 1:161 (emphasis added).

32. Ellen G. White, "Without Excuse," *Advent Review and Sabbath Herald*, September 24, 1901, 615 (emphasis added).

33. Ellen G. White, "The Only True Mediator," *Signs of the Times*, June 28, 1899, 1 (emphasis added).

34. For an outstanding discussion on the unlimited atonement, see Allen, *The Extent of the Atonement*.

35. The goat for the Lord was offered on the altar, and its blood (representing Christ's death) was applied and administered in the Most Holy Place.

36. For a variety of different meanings of the divine judgment, see Jiří Moskala, "The Gospel According to God's Judgment: Judgment as Salvation," *Journal of the Adventist Theological Society* 22, no. 1 (2011): 28–49.

37. Unless noted otherwise, all Scripture quotations in this chapter are from the NIV.

38. Ellen G. White underlines the importance of studying and understanding the atonement and Christ's mediation:

Satan invents unnumbered schemes to occupy our minds, that they may not dwell upon the very work with which we ought to be best acquainted. The archdeceiver hates the great truths that bring to view an *atoning sacrifice* and an *all-powerful mediator*. He knows that with him everything depends on his diverting minds from Jesus and His truth. Those who would share the benefits of the Saviour's mediation should permit nothing to interfere with their duty to perfect holiness in the fear of God. The precious hours, instead of being given to pleasure, to display, or to gain seeking, should be devoted to an earnest, prayerful study of the word of truth. The subject of the sanctuary and the investigative judgment should be clearly understood by the people of God. All need a knowledge for themselves of the position and work of their *great High Priest*. Otherwise it will be impossible for them to exercise the faith which is essential at this time or to occupy the position which God designs them to fill. Every individual has a soul to save or to lose. Each has a case pending at the bar of God. Each must meet the great Judge face to face. How important, then, that every mind contemplate often the solemn scene when the judgment shall sit and the books shall be opened, when, with Daniel, every individual must stand in his lot, at the end of the days. All who have received the light upon these subjects are to bear testimony of the *great truths* which God has committed to them. The sanctuary in heaven is the very center of Christ's work in behalf of men. It concerns every soul living upon the earth. It opens to view the plan of redemption, bringing us down to the very close of time and revealing the triumphant issue of the contest between righteousness and sin. It is of the utmost importance that all should thoroughly investigate these subjects and be able to give an answer to everyone that asketh them a reason of the hope that is in them (*The Great Controversy*, 488, 489; emphasis added).

39. Raoul Dederen, "Christ: His Person and Work," in *Handbook of Seventh-day Adventist Theology* (Hagerstown, MD: Review and Herald®, 2000), 187.

40. For Ellen G. White's three different understandings of the notion of atonement as (1) complete atonement accomplished on the cross; (2) the High-Priestly ministry of Jesus in the heavenly sanctuary; and (3) the plan of salvation in a broad way, see the insightful article by Denis Fortin, "The Cross of Christ: Theological Differences Between Joseph H. Waggoner and Ellen G. White," *Journal of the Adventist Theological Society* 14, no. 2 (Fall 2003): 131–140, especially 138, 139.

41. When sacrificial atonement is implemented in these two additional phases, one can say that the atonement was "made." For an understanding of the panorama of the seven phases of God's plan of salvation in the form of His judgments seen from the perspective of the cross of Jesus, see Jiří Moskala, "Toward a Biblical Theology of God's Judgment: A Celebration of the Cross in Seven Phases of Divine Universal Judgment (An Overview of a Theocentric-Christocentric Approach)," *Journal of the Adventist Theological Society* 15, no. 1 (Spring 2004): 138–165.

42. White, *The Great Controversy*, 666.

43. Ellen G. White, *The Desire of Ages* (Mountain View, CA: Pacific Press®, 1940), 494, 495. See also ibid., 565, 566; *The Great Controversy*, 503. Ellen G. White makes the point that atonement is the all-encompassing plan of salvation:

In the typical service the high priest, having made the *atonement* for Israel, came forth and blessed the congregation. So Christ, at the close of his work as a mediator, will appear, "without sin unto salvation" (Hebrews 9:28), to bless his waiting people with eternal life. As the priest, in *removing* the sins from the sanctuary, confessed them upon the head of the scapegoat, so Christ will place all these sins upon Satan, the originator and instigator of sin. The scapegoat, bearing the sins of Israel, was sent away "unto a land not inhabited" (Leviticus 16:22); so Satan, bearing the guilt of all the sins which he has caused God's people to commit, will be for a thousand years confined to the earth, which will then be desolate, without inhabitant, and he will at last suffer the full penalty of sin in the fires that shall destroy all the wicked. Thus the great plan of redemption will reach its accomplishment in *the final eradication of sin*, and the deliverance of all who have been willing to renounce evil. (*The Great Controversy*, 485, 486: emphasis added).

44. Kirkpatrick speaks about Christ's victory over sin, not Satan (see *Cleanse and Close*, 88), and then he explains explicitly: "When we are so settled into the truth, both doctrinally and experientially, that we cannot move, we will no longer sin. We will stop sending sins into the heavenly sanctuary to be forgiven. . . . All this Satan has denied and misrepresented, but today he is being proven wrong. . . . There is no longer any need to forgive sin in His people, even ignorant sin, because no more sin will be there." Ibid., 96, 97. But the Bible and the Spirit of Prophecy declare that we need to be constantly covered by Christ's grace and His merits. See Jiří Moskala, "The Meaning of the Intercessory Ministry of Jesus Christ on Our Behalf in the Heavenly Sanctuary," *Journal of the Adventist Theological Society* 28, no. 1 (2017): 3–25.

45. Walter C. Kaiser Jr., *The Messiah in the Old Testament*, Studies in Old Testament Biblical Theology (Grand Rapids, MI: Zondervan, 1995), 36–42; see also Afolarin O. Ojewole, *The Seed in Genesis 3:15: An Exegetical and Intertextual Study* (Berrien Springs, MI: Adventist Theological Society Publications, 2002).

46. Gustaf Aulén, *Christus Victor: An Historical Study of the Three Main Types of the Idea of the Atonement* (New York: Macmillan, 1969).

47. White, *The Great Controversy*, 503 (emphasis added).

48. See Douglass, *God at Risk*.

49. White, *The Desire of Ages*, 117. Jesus lived a victorious life, and it was sufficient to prove that Adam could obey God. Jesus, as the Second Adam, in much more challenging circumstances and with a weakened body that was already affected by several millennia of sin, was victorious and never sinned. He lived a perfect, blameless life of submission and obedience to God's law.

50. Ángel Manuel Rodríguez, "Theology of the Last Generation," *Adventist Review*, October 20, 2013, 42, http://www.adventistreview.org/2013-1528-p42.

51. White, *The Desire of Ages*, 762 (emphasis added).

52. Marvin Moore, *The Close of Probation* (Nampa, ID: Pacific Press®, 2014), 214 (emphasis in original).

53. The full quotation is as follows:

But the plan of redemption had a yet broader and deeper purpose than the salvation of man. It was not for this alone that Christ came to the earth; it was not merely that the inhabitants of this little world might regard the law of God as it should be regarded; but it was to vindicate the character of God before the universe. To this result of His great sacrifice—its influence upon the intelligences of other worlds, as well as upon man—the Saviour looked forward when just before His crucifixion He said: "Now is the judgment of this world: now shall the prince of this world be cast out. And I, if I be lifted up from the earth, will draw all unto Me." (John 12:31, 32). The act of Christ in dying for the salvation of man would not only make heaven accessible to men, but before all the universe it would justify God and His Son in their dealing with the rebellion of Satan. It would establish the perpetuity of the law of God and would reveal the nature and the results of sin (Ellen G. White, *Patriarchs and Prophets* [Mountain View, CA: Pacific Press®, 1958], 68, 69).

54. Ellen G. White, *Steps to Christ* (Mountain View, CA: Pacific Press®, 1956), 69.

55. See Jiří Moskala, "The God of Job and Our Adversary," *Journal of the Adventist Theological Society* 15, no. 2 (Spring 2004): 104–117, https://digitalcommons.andrews.edu/jats/vol15/iss2/7/.

56. See especially White, *Steps to Christ*, 62, 63.

57. See Jiří Moskala, "Genesis 3 as a Model for Understanding the Nature of Sin and Salvation," *Journal of the Adventist Theological Society* 27, nos. 1–2 (2016): 117–152; and Jiří Moskala, "Sin," in *The Ellen G. White Encyclopedia*, ed. Denis Fortin and Jerry Moon (Hagerstown, MD: Review and Herald®, 2013), 1164–1167.

58. Ellen G. White Comments, in Nichol, *Seventh-day Adventist Bible Commentary*, 6:1070.

59. Ellen G. White, MS 50, 1900, quoted in Ellen G. White Comments, in Nichol, *Seventh-day Adventist Bible Commentary*, 6:1077, 1078 (emphasis added). See also White, *Patriarchs and Prophets*, 352, 353; Ellen G. White, *Selected Messages*, bk. 1 (Hagerstown, MD: Review and Herald®, 1958), 344.

60. Moore, The *Close of Probation*, 213 (emphasis in original). This is in direct contradiction to Kirkpatrick's assertion that only the last generation proves that God is right: "As followers of Christ, our lives offer evidence as to whether God or Satan has been right in the great controversy." Kirkpatrick, *Cleanse and Close*, 100; see also his statement on page 96: "All this Satan has denied and misrepresented, but today he is being proven wrong." The Bible, on the other hand, proclaims that God vindicates His name through His people who are faithful to Him and through His church (His followers participate in Christ's victory). As the apostle Paul states, "His intent was that now, through the church, the manifold wisdom of God should be made known to the rulers and authorities in the heavenly realms, according to his eternal purpose that he accomplished in Christ Jesus our Lord" (Ephesians 3:10, 11). See also Ezekiel 36:20–28; on the topic of vindication in the book of Ezekiel, see Jiří Moskala, "Notes on the Literary Structure of the Book of Ezekiel," in *Meeting With God on the Mountains: Essays in Honor of Richard M. Davidson*, ed. Jiří Moskala (Berrien Springs, MI: Old Testament Department, Seventh-day Adventist Theological Seminary, Andrews University, 2016), 102–110.

61. Ellen G. White Comments, in Nichol, *Seventh-day Adventist Bible Commentary*, 6:1070.

62. Ellen G. White writes,

The religion of Christ uplifts the receiver to a higher plane of thought and action, while at the same time it presents the whole human race as alike the objects of the love of God, being purchased by the sacrifice of His Son. At the feet of Jesus, the rich and the poor, the learned and the ignorant, meet together, with no thought of caste or worldly pre-eminence. All earthly distinctions are forgotten as we look upon Him whom our sins have pierced. The self-denial, the condescension, the infinite compassion of Him who was highly exalted in heaven, puts to shame human pride, self-esteem, and social caste. Pure, undefiled religion manifests its heaven-born principles in bringing into oneness all who are sanctified through the truth. All meet as blood-bought souls, alike dependent upon Him who has redeemed them to God (White, *Gospel Workers*, 330).

63. See the excellent insights by Edward Zinke in E. Edward Zinke and Roland R. Hegstad, *The Certainty of the Second Coming* (Hagerstown, MD: Review and Herald®, 2000), 81–89. There is no statement in Scripture that would say that God "is judged," because no one in the entire universe has the authority to judge God. Even Satan, with all his accusations, is powerless to summon God to judgment. He can only complicate the situation. So in view of these lies, the Lord reacts, and as the highest Judge, He prevails in all His judgments (Psalm 51:4), because He is the absolute truth—good, just, and holy. The verb *titsdaq* in this verse is in the Qal, not in the Niphal, meaning "to be in the right," "to be just," and not "to be justified/vindicated." (The NIV translates correctly: "So you are right in your verdict and justified when you judge.") Romans 3:4 cites this text, and even though many modern versions translate in the passive that God "may be justified" and "is judged," the verb *dikaiothes* is in the subjunctive aorist passive, second person singular, and the infinitive *krivesthai* is in the present middle or passive. It is obvious that these Greek terms parallel the thoughts of Psalm 51:4, thus referring to God judging, not that He is being judged. The NIV rightly translates this: "Let God be true, and every human being a liar. As it is written: 'So that you may be proved right when you speak and prevail when you judge' " (Romans 3:4). God Himself vindicates His character in front of the whole universe, but the Bible states that He does it also through the true believers (Ezekiel 36:23) and even through the destruction of Gog (Ezekiel 38:16, ESV). Ellen G. White confirms that the faithful followers of God vindicate Him and His law (see, e.g., *Testimonies to Ministers* [Mountain View, CA: Pacific Press®, 1923], 58; *Faith and Works* [Nashville, TN: Southern Pub. Assn., 1979], 42; *Testimonies for the Church*, vol. 5

[Mountain View, CA: Pacific Press®, 1948], 317, 746; *Selected Messages*, bk. 3 [Hagerstown, MD: Review and Herald®, 1980], 395), but it is never stated that vindication is performed only by the last generation. How do God's people vindicate Him? By trusting God, honoring Him, being faithful, defending God's law, serving others unselfishly, and witnessing to the victory of Jesus on the cross (Revelation 12:11); thus, they are living evidences of the efficacy and transforming power of the death of Christ and confirm that Jesus defeated the evil forces (Ephesians 3:10, 11; Colossians 2:15). In His mercy, God vindicates Himself by involving His people from all generations in this process of affirmation of Christ's triumphant victory (Ephesians 1:10; Colossians 2:10; Revelation 13:8). This vindication is done by God, by the power of the Holy Spirit, by His grace, and by His Word, which is then reflected in human lives (Romans 12:1, 2; 2 Corinthians 3:18), and never by the achievement or performance of God's people.

64. Ellen G. White, "What Was Secured by the Death of Christ," *Signs of the Times*, December 30, 1889, 786 (emphasis added).

65. White, *The Desire of Ages*, 19, 20. See also White, *The Great Controversy*, 651.

66. Ellen G. White, *God's Amazing Grace* (Washington, DC: Review and Herald®, 1973), 178.

67. Ellen G. White, *The Ministry of Healing* (Mountain View, CA: Pacific Press®, 1942), 460.

68. Emphasis added. For the full text of Fundamental Belief 24, see endnote 73.

69. White, *The Great Controversy*, 489 (emphasis added).

70. Ellen G. White, *Early Writings* (Washington, DC: Review and Herald®, 1973), 260 (emphasis added).

71. The Bible in the description of the Day of Atonement uses the language of "making" atonement (see Leviticus 16:10, 16; cf. Leviticus 4:20, 26), and Ellen G. White employs this biblical language too (see, e.g., *The Great Controversy*, 418–422). But we need to ask the question about the meaning of the term *making*, because its interpretation is determined only by the biblical-theological context: Jesus "made" the atonement on the cross, and then during His intercessory ministry as our High Priest or during the pre-Advent judgment, Christ's victory is applied to believers through the immense riches of His benefits springing from the cross and bringing the problem of sin and the drama of the great controversy to its conclusion and

final solution. This special work of atonement during the Day of Atonement is performed in close connection with His work on the cross. We may say that the atonement of the cross was applied, and thus "made" or "accomplished." The Hebrew term *yom hakippurim* literally means "the Day of Atonements"; note the plural of extension and intensity. See E. Kautzsch, ed., *Gesenius' Hebrew Grammar*, trans. A. E. Cowley, 2nd ed. (New York: Oxford University Press, 1910), 396, 397, which may allude to this direction.

72. For the details, see Moskala, "Meaning of the Intercessory Ministry."

73. Fundamental Belief 24, "Christ's Ministry in the Heavenly Sanctuary," reads as follows:

There is a sanctuary in heaven, the true tabernacle that the Lord set up and not humans. In it Christ ministers on our behalf, *making available to believers the benefits of His atoning sacrifice offered once for all on the cross.* At His ascension, He was inaugurated as our great High Priest and, began His intercessory ministry, which was typified by the work of the high priest in the holy place of the earthly sanctuary. In 1844, at the end of the prophetic period of 2300 days, He entered the second and *last phase of His atoning ministry,* which was typified by the work of the high priest in the most holy place of the earthly sanctuary. It is a work of investigative judgment which is part of the ultimate disposition of all sin, typified by the cleansing of the ancient Hebrew sanctuary on the Day of Atonement. In that typical service the sanctuary was cleansed with the blood of animal sacrifices, but *the heavenly things are purified with the perfect sacrifice of the blood of Jesus.* The investigative judgment reveals to heavenly intelligences who among the dead are asleep in Christ and therefore, in Him, are deemed worthy to have part in the first resurrection. It also makes manifest who among the living are abiding in Christ, keeping the commandments of God and the faith of Jesus, and in Him, therefore, are ready for translation into His everlasting kingdom. This judgment vindicates the justice of God in saving those who believe in Jesus. It declares that those who have remained loyal to God shall receive the kingdom. The completion of this ministry of Christ will mark the

close of human probation before the Second Advent. (Lev. 16; Num. 14:34; Ezek. 4:6; Dan. 7:9-27; 8:13, 14; 9:24-27; Heb. 1:3; 2:16, 17; 4:14-16; 8:1-5; 9:11-28; 10:19-22; Rev. 8:3-5; 11:19; 14:6, 7; 20:12; 14:12; 22:11, 12.) (*28 Fundamental Beliefs* [Silver Spring, MD: General Conference of Seventh-day Adventists, 2015], 10, https://www.adventist.org/fileadmin/adventist.org/files/articles/official-statements/28Beliefs-Web.pdf; emphasis added).

74. White, *The Great Controversy*, 425. On the interpretation of what it means and does not mean to stand in the sight of a holy God without a mediator, see chapter 12 in this book, "Misinterpreted End-Time Issues: Five Myths in Adventism."

75. To interpret Daniel 8:14 properly, one needs four words in English to translate the Hebrew word *nitsdaq* (Niphal perfect, third person singular masculine, from the root *tsadaq*), which is a hapax legomenon and encapsulates a very rich meaning: "cleanse," "justify," "restore," and "vindicate." See Richard M. Davidson, "The Meaning of *Niṣdaq* in Daniel 8:14," *Journal of the Adventist Theological Society* 7, no. 1 (Spring 1996): 107–119.

76. One biblical text and a key quotation of Ellen G. White are used to prove that we have the power to decide the time of Christ's second coming:

Biblical text. The text about speeding, or hastening the Second Coming (2 Peter 3:12) needs to be understood in its context. Jesus delays His coming as God desires to save everyone. If I accept Jesus as my personal Savior and also help others to find Jesus and repent, then I am hastening Christ's coming, because He does not need to wait any longer for me or for the people to whom I witnessed. The more people who make decisions for God, the sooner God could close the time of probation. The context thus emphasizes *evangelism.* But this does not mean that we have a final say—that is God's prerogative—but we have the privilege to hasten His second coming by cooperating with His mission. There is a healthy tension in the text between our hastening Jesus' coming and the reality that our actions have no power to "push" forward His coming. He desires people to be ready for His coming even though the day of the Lord will come like a thief (2 Peter 3:10). Christ strongly desires to have in His triumphant procession, after His second coming, as many redeemed as possible, because He "wants all people to be saved and to come to a knowledge of the truth" (1 Timothy 2:4; cf. John 3:16) and He takes "no pleasure in the death of anyone" (Ezekiel 18:32). This is why He waits in His mercy for people to respond positively to His offers of salvation (2 Peter 3:9). Ellen G. White clearly declares, "By giving the gospel to the world it is in our power to hasten our Lord's return. We are not only to look for but to hasten the coming of the day of God. 2 Peter 3:12, margin. Had the church of Christ done her appointed work as the Lord ordained [to evangelize the world], the whole world would before this have been warned, and the Lord Jesus would have come to our earth in power and great glory." *The Desire of Ages*, 633, 634. See also Ellen G. White, *Education* (Oakland, CA: Pacific Press®, 1903), 264; *Christ's Object Lessons* (Battle Creek, MI: Review and Herald®, 1900), 340; *Selected Messages*, bk. 1, 68, 69; *The Great Controversy*, 618–620.

Ellen G. White quotation. The popular Ellen G. White quotation is from page 69 of *Christ's Object Lessons*: "Christ is waiting with longing desire for the manifestation of Himself in His church. When the character of Christ shall be perfectly reproduced in His people, then He will come to claim them as His own." Again it must be seen in its context. Ellen G. White speaks about the fruit of the Holy Spirit, and she encourages God's followers to let God transform their lives in order for them to reflect His unselfish character of love, grow in Him, and help others to know Him and be saved. It is a call to live a holy life and be faithful to God's disposition in order to evangelize the world by our lives, words, and actions because He will come soon. It is important to note that nowhere in the Bible or in Ellen G. White's writings is there a statement that the last generation of the faithful will defeat Satan and that by living perfect lives they will finally vindicate God and cause the finishing of the cleansing of the heavenly sanctuary and the closing of the great controversy. This silence is eloquent enough for believers to abandon such thinking and not to speculate on this matter. See Revelation 12:10–12 and also Ellen G. White, *Early Writings*, 71; *Last Day Events* (Boise, ID: Pacific Press®, 1992), 221; *Testimonies for the Church*, 5:216; *Education*, 156.

77. See Revelation 7:2–4; 9:4; 14:1; 22:4. Ellen G. White explains that the sealing occurs first and then follows the ceasing of Jesus' intercessory ministry:

When the third angel's message closes, mercy no longer pleads for the guilty inhabitants

of the earth. The people of God have accomplished their work. They have received "the latter rain," "the refreshing from the presence of the Lord," and they are prepared for the trying hour before them. Angels are hastening to and fro in heaven. An angel returning from the earth announces that his work is done; the final test has been brought upon the world, and all who have proved themselves loyal to the divine precepts have received "the seal of the living God." Then Jesus ceases His intercession in the sanctuary above. He lifts His hands and with a loud voice says, "It is done;" and all the angelic host lay off their crowns as He makes the solemn announcement: "He that is unjust, let him be unjust still: and he which is filthy, let him be filthy still: and he that is righteous, let him be righteous still: and he that is holy, let him be holy still." Revelation 22:11. Every case has been decided for life or death. Christ has made the atonement for His people and blotted out their sins (*The Great Controversy*, 613, 614).

78. Ellen G. White declares,

In 1844 our great High Priest entered the most holy place of the heavenly sanctuary, to begin the work of the investigative judgment. The cases of the righteous dead have been passing in review before God. When that work shall be completed, judgment is to be pronounced upon the living. How precious, how important are these solemn moments! Each of us has a case pending in the court of heaven. We are individually to be judged according to the deeds done in the body. In the typical service, when the work of atonement was performed by the high priest in the most holy place of the earthly sanctuary, the people were required to afflict their souls before God, and confess their sins, that they might be atoned for and blotted out. Will any less be required of us in this antitypical day of atonement, when Christ in the sanctuary above is pleading in behalf of His people, *and the final, irrevocable decision* is to be pronounced upon every case? (*Selected Messages*, bk. 1, 125; emphasis added).

79. For the details regarding what it means to be

carried by the Holy Spirit after the close of probation, see chapter 12 in this book, "Misinterpreted End-Time Issues: Five Myths in Adventism."

80. On this specific point I am in agreement with Herbert E. Douglass, even though otherwise I disagree with his LGT views. See pages 159, 354, 385, in his book *God at Risk*, where he explains what it means to live without an intercessor after the close of probation.

81. See White, *The Desire of Ages*, 49: "Yet into the world where Satan claimed dominion God permitted His Son to come, a helpless babe, subject to the weakness of humanity. He permitted Him to meet life's peril in common with every human soul, to fight the battle as every child of humanity must fight it, *at the risk of failure and eternal loss*" (emphasis added). See also ibid., 131: "Never can the cost of our redemption be realized until the redeemed shall stand with the Redeemer before the throne of God. Then as the glories of the eternal home burst upon our enraptured senses we shall remember that Jesus left all this for us, that He not only became an exile from the heavenly courts, but for us took *the risk of failure and eternal loss*" (emphasis added).

82. The sanctuary language and its typology help us to understand it. The sacrifice (representing Jesus Christ) was offered on the altar as the atoning sacrifice in the courtyard (pointing to Christ's atoning death), and then its blood was cashed in, applied to the Holy Place (representing His intercessory ministry), and later to the Most Holy Place on the Day of Atonement (representing Christ's high priestly ministry).

83. Different terms can be used to explain various aspects of the pre-Advent judgment: (1) affirmative judgment: I want to coin this new name for this particular judgment from the perspective of the redeemed, because God in front of the universe affirms or confirms the relationship established between Himself and the believers during their lifetimes; (2) revelatory judgment (from God's perspective): because Christ reveals to the entire universe who are His true followers as well as the ethical dynamics of the relationship between Himself and His faithful children, and He unmasks the antichrist who plays being God and His agent of salvation; (3) demonstrative judgment: God presents facts to heavenly beings and shows them our attitudes to Him, His law, people, nature, and sin as well as explaining who He is, what He is doing, and that when dealing with sin He is the God of love, truth, and justice; and (4) investiga-

tive judgment: angels and heavenly beings need this judgment in order to have more insight into the great controversy, including why God saves some while He does not accept others into heaven.

84. Ellen G. White, *Counsels for the Church* (Boise, ID: Pacific Press®, 1991), 347, 348.

85. For detailed exegetical and theological insights of the pre-Advent judgment, see Moskala, "Toward a Biblical Theology of God's Judgment," 152–155; Gerhard F. Hasel, "Divine Judgment," in Dederen, *Handbook of Seventh-day Adventist Theology*, 833–846; William H. Shea, *Daniel 7–12: Prophecies of the End Time*, The Abundant Life Bible Amplifier (Nampa, ID: Pacific Press®, 1996), 85–166; Richard M. Davidson, "Meaning of *Niṣdaq*," 107–119; Edward Heppenstall, *Our High Priest: Jesus Christ in the Heavenly Sanctuary* (Washington, DC: Review and Herald®, 1972), 107–129; Norman Gulley, *Christ Is Coming! A Christ-Centered Approach to Last-Day Events* (Hagerstown, MD: Review and Herald®, 1998), 410–437. It is important to differentiate between an eschatological time in general, inaugurated by the first coming of Jesus, and a specific prophetic time of the end, starting in 1798 and 1844 according to the historicist school of prophetic interpretation (Daniel 7–9). For the explanation of this prophetic eschatological time and the chronological aspect of the judgment, see especially the following studies: William H. Shea, *Selected Studies on Prophetic Interpretation*, Daniel and Revelation Committee Series, vol. 1 (Washington, DC: Review and Herald®, 1982), 67–171; Jacques Doukhan, *Secrets of Daniel: Wisdom and Dreams of a Jewish Prince in Exile* (Hagerstown, MD: Review and Herald®, 2000), 100–156; Jacques Doukhan, *Daniel: The Vision of the End* (Berrien Springs, MI: Andrews University Press, 1987), 11–44, 153; Richard M. Davidson, "In Confirmation of the Sanctuary Message," *Journal of the Adventist Theological Society* 2, no. 1 (1991): 93–114. See also a pertinent dissertation written by Gerhard Pfandl, *The Time of the End in the Book of Daniel*, Adventist Theological Society Dissertation series, vol. 1 (Berrien Springs, MI: Adventist Theological Society, 1992), 272, 314, 317.

86. White, *Early Writings*, 254 (emphasis added).

87. White, *Counsels for the Church*, 348.

88. Roy E. Gane, *Cult and Character: Purification Offerings, Day of Atonement, and Theodicy* (Winona Lake, IN: Eisenbrauns, 2005), 379, 380.

89. Ibid., 380.

90. Ellen G. White, "A Vital Connection With

Christ," *Signs of the Times*, July 27, 1888, 450.

91. For further study, see Zachman's outstanding article in which he argues about the unity of justice and love and explains that "the judgment of God is an expression of the love of God." Randall C. Zachman, "The Unity of Judgment and Love," *Ex Auditu* 20 (2004): 152.

92. Walther Zimmerli, *The Fiery Throne: The Prophets and Old Testament Theology*, ed. K. C. Hanson (Minneapolis: Fortress Press, 2003), 106.

93. About the meaning of the death of Jesus Christ as an atoning sacrifice and substitution, see especially Raoul Dederen, "Christ's Atoning Ministry on the Cross," insert, *Ministry*, January 1976, 3C–30C; Morris, *Glory in the Cross*; Leon Morris, *The Apostolic Preaching of the Cross*, 3rd ed. (Grand Rapids, MI: Eerdmans, 1965); Morris, *The Atonement*; Stott, *The Cross of Christ*; Alister E. McGrath, *The Mystery of the Cross* (Grand Rapids, MI: Zondervan, 1988); H. D. McDonald, *The Atonement of the Death of Christ* (Grand Rapids, MI: Baker, 1985).

94. Paul employs this tiny but all-encompassing "phrase, *en Christo*, or its close equivalent at least 163 times in his writings." Alan J. Torrance, "Reclaiming the Continuing Priesthood of Christ: Implications and Challenges," in *Christology, Ancient and Modern: Explorations in Constructive Dogmatics*, ed. Oliver D. Crisp and Fred Sanders (Grand Rapids, MI: Zondervan, 2013), 190.

95. White, *Christ's Object Lessons*, 414–416 (emphasis added). Consider also the following extremely relevant quotations: "Love is the basis of godliness. Whatever the profession, no man has pure love to God unless he has unselfish love for his brother. But we can never come into possession of this spirit by trying to love others. What is needed is the love of Christ in the heart. When self is merged in Christ, love springs forth spontaneously. The completeness of Christian character is attained when the impulse to help and bless others springs constantly from within—when the sunshine of heaven fills the heart and is revealed in the countenance." Ibid., 384.

"A true, lovable Christian is the most powerful argument that can be advanced in favor of Bible truth. Such a man is Christ's representative. His life is the most convincing evidence that can be borne to the power of divine grace. When God's people bring the righteousness of Christ into the daily life, sinners will be converted, and victories over the enemy will be gained." Ellen G. White, "A Call to Greater Consecration," *Advent Review and Sabbath Herald*, January 14, 1904.

96. Ellen G. White, *In Heavenly Places* (Washington, DC: Review and Herald®, 1967), 227.

11

What Is the State of the Last Generation?

Ranko Stefanovic

This chapter deals with the question of the state of the last generation of God's people before the Second Coming. It addresses three assertions that are used in support of last generation theology (LGT): (1) Revelation 7 refers to the last generation as a select group in contrast to the rest of believers; (2) Revelation 14:1–5 shows that the last generation will reach a level of particular holiness and moral perfection that has not been reached by any previous generation; and (3) Ellen G. White, in her writings, states that the last generation will reach an absolutely sinless condition in order to be able to go through the time of trouble.

In addressing these three assertions, we will first provide an exegetical analysis of Revelation 7 and Revelation 14:4, 5. Then we will examine the statements of Ellen G. White that, according to LGT advocates, point to the absolutely sinless state of the last generation of the redeemed.

The last generation as the 144,000

Revelation 7 describes the last generation of the saved in terms of the sealed 144,000 (verses 1–8). The chapter further mentions an incalculable great multitude standing before God's throne in white robes and praising God for their salvation (verses 9–17). While Seventh-day Adventists generally agree that the 144,000 are the saints who will be alive at the second coming of Christ, there is disagreement regarding their relationship to the great multitude. The traditional view has been that in contrast to the sealed 144,000, who represent the last generation, the great multitude comprises the redeemed of all ages.[1] But the prevailing understanding among Adventists today is that the 144,000 and the great multitude are one and the same group of God's saved people, pictured from two different perspectives. The latter is the position taken in this chapter.

Purpose of Revelation 7

Important to an understanding of the 144,000 and the great multitude is an understanding of the place of Revelation 7 in the organizational structure of the vision of the seven seals. This chapter is part of the vision of the sixth seal and is inserted parenthetically between the sixth and seventh seals. The scene of the sixth seal describes the heavenly signs of the Second Coming (Revelation 6:12–14) followed by Christ's coming (verses 15, 16). At this point, John observes people of all walks of life and every social strata running in terror to hide themselves from God's presence. The scene concludes with the question "Who is able to stand?" on the day of wrath (verse 17). Chapter 7 provides the answer: those who will be able to stand in the great day of God's wrath are the sealed 144,000 (see verses 1–8). This shows that Revelation 7 concerns exclusively the end-time saints who will be alive at the time of the Second Coming. God's people in general are referred to in Revelation 20:4–6.

Sealing of the end-time saints (Revelation 7:1–3)

Revelation 7 opens with a scene of four angels standing at "the four corners of the earth" (verse 1) who are restraining four destroying winds from harming the earth, the sea, and the trees. The expression "the four corners of the earth" (i.e., the four points of the compass) denotes the global significance of the scene.

In the Old Testament, winds represent destructive forces by which God executes judgments upon the wicked (Isaiah 66:15, 16; Jeremiah 23:19, 20; Hosea 13:15). The blowing of the winds correlates with God's wrath in Revelation 6:17. It is another way of referring to the seven last plagues to be poured upon the wicked right before the Second Coming (Revelation 15; 16), which are referred to as the pouring out of God's wrath (Revelation 15:1; cf. Revelation 14:10).

These destructive forces are being restrained while the sealing of God's people takes place (Revelation 7:3). In the Bible, the primary meaning of *sealing* is "ownership." Paul explains that the meaning of the divine sealing is that "the Lord knows those who are His" (2 Timothy 2:19).[2] God recognizes those who are His and seals them with the Holy Spirit (2 Corinthians 1:21, 22; Ephesians 1:13, 14). By grieving the Holy Spirit, one may lose his or her sealing (Ephesians 4:30). At the time of the end, the

seal of God on the forehead distinguishes God's people from the worshipers of the beast who are identified by the mark of the beast on their foreheads or right hands (cf. Revelation 13:16, 17, with Revelation 14:1).[3]

At the time of the end, the sealing also functions as a sign of protection. The seal of God upon the forehead protects God's people from the harm of the seven last plagues.[4] The backdrop of this whole idea is Ezekiel's vision concerning the destruction of Jerusalem before the Exile in which the mark on the forehead distinguished those who were faithful to God from the unfaithful and idolatrous and, as such, provided them with protection from the impending judgment (Ezekiel 9:1–11). As in Ezekiel's vision, so in Revelation 7, the seal identifies God's people and protects them from the eschatological blowing of the winds of the seven last plagues. With this, the question that was posed in Revelation 6:17 regarding who will be able to stand on the day of the great wrath receives the ultimate answer.

The sealed 144,000 (Revelation 7:4–8)

Eventually, the sealing of the saints is complete, and John hears the number of those who are sealed as 144,000 from "every tribe of the sons of Israel" (Revelation 7:4). The evidence shows that this number of the sealed saints is symbolic rather than literal.

First of all, the beginning of the whole passage is symbolic (verses 1–3): the four corners of the earth, the four winds and their blowing, the earth, the sea, and the trees, the seal of God, and the sealing. In Revelation 14:1–5, the description of the 144,000 is also symbolic: they have not defiled themselves with women, for they are virgins, and they follow the Lamb wherever He goes. The terms *women*, *virgins*, and the *Lamb* are all symbols. Since all of these are symbolic, so also is the number 144,000.

Second, the number 144,000 is made up of 12,000 multiplied by the twelve tribes of Israel. If the number 144,000 is literal, so must be the tribes. The fact is, however, that the twelve tribes of Israel are not in existence today.[5] In addition, the list of the twelve tribes in Revelation 7 is not a regular list of the tribes of Israel—Judah is listed as the first tribe instead of Reuben. Also, the tribes of Dan and Ephraim are excluded from the list, and Joseph and Levi are included instead. The most likely reason for the exclusion of Dan and Ephraim is because these two tribes apostatized and were associated with idolatry in the Old Testament.[6] The 144,000 constitute the true and loyal people of God (Revelation 14:4, 5); they follow the Lamb wherever He goes (verse 4). There is no place among them for the unfaithfulness that characterized the tribes of Dan and Ephraim.

This shows that the list of the tribes in Revelation 7 is theological rather than historical. The twelve tribes in Revelation 7 clearly stand for the whole people of God (James 1:1). The number 144,000 signifies the totality of God's end-time people who are sealed and ready to enter the great tribulation at the end of history.

The great multitude (Revelation 7:9–17)

After having heard the number of those who have been sealed, John sees "a great multitude which no one could count, from every nation and all tribes and peoples and tongues, standing before the throne and before the Lamb, clothed in white robes" (Revelation 7:9). At this point, some questions arise: What is the relationship between the 144,000 and this group? Are they two different groups of God's people—the former being the last generation of the saints and the latter the redeemed of all ages? The evidence suggests that the 144,000 and the great multitude are the same group under different names and perspectives.

First, the relationship between the 144,000 and the great multitude is defined by the literary features "I heard" and "I saw," which occur often in the book. When in vision, John often hears something. When he actually sees what he has heard about, it appears to him in a different symbol. For instance, in Revelation 5:5, he hears that the Lion from the tribe of Judah has overcome; when he eventually takes a look, he sees the Lamb instead of a Lion (verse 6). Both the Lion and the Lamb represent Christ; the Lion shows what Jesus did, and the Lamb shows how He did it. Likewise, in Revelation 17:1, John hears that the great prostitute Babylon sits on many waters. But when he sees the prostitute, she sits upon the scarlet beast (verse 3). The same kind of hearing-seeing occurrences may be observed in other places in Revelation.[7]

This is also the situation in Revelation 7. In verse 4, John only hears that the number of the sealed saints is 144,000. But he does not see them as such because they are spread throughout every nation, tribe, people, and tongue. They are now ready to enter the great tribulation. When in Revelation 7:9 he actually sees them, they appear to him as an incalculable great multitude coming out of the great tribulation.[8] Thus, the 144,000 and the great multitude appear to be the same group of end-time saints described from different perspectives.

Next, the 144,000 are called "the bond-servants of our God" (verse 3); and the great multitude are described as the ones who "serve" God in His temple (verse 15; see also Revelation 22:3).[9] Furthermore, Revelation 7 shows that both the 144,000 and the great multitude must go through the great tribulation of the last days. The 144,000 are sealed before the winds are unleashed to blow. As the sealing is completed, they have to go through the tribulation of the seven last plagues. The great multitude consists of the ones who have come out of the great tribulation (see Revelation 7:14). The following chart confirms this:

Revelation 7:9	Revelation 7:13–15
After these things I looked, and behold, a great multitude which no one could count, from every nation and all tribes and peoples and tongues, standing *before the throne* and before the Lamb, *clothed in white robes*, and palm branches were in their hands (emphasis added).	Then one of the elders answered, saying to me, "These who are *clothed in the white robes*, who are they, and where have they come from?" . . . And he said to me, "These are the ones *who come out of the great tribulation*. . . . For this reason, they are *before the throne* of God" (emphasis added).

Finally, in dealing with the question of the relationship between the 144,000 and the great multitude, we must remember,

as it was shown before, that the purpose of Revelation 7 is to provide the answer to the question raised in Revelation 6:17: "Who is able to stand?" While the 144,000 provides the immediate answer to that question,[10] a further answer is given in the portrayal of the great multitude who are seen as "standing" before God's throne as they have come out of the great tribulation (verses 9, 14). One may notice that the word *stand* is used in both Revelation 6:17 and Revelation 7:9.[11]

All of this shows that the great multitude is not set in contrast to the 144,000, but it is a further description of the 144,000.[12] The 144,000 and the great multitude are the same group of end-time saints defined under different names. Both groups refer to the last generation of saints who will have to go through the great tribulation of the seven last plagues and who will be alive at the Second Coming.

The militant and triumphant church

Another question arises: Why is the end-time church described under these two different symbols and names? The answer is that the 144,000 and the great multitude describe the end-time church from different historical perspectives.

In Revelation 7, the 144,000 are the end-time people *on earth*. They are sealed and ready to enter the great tribulation of the seven last plagues. The number 144,000 consists of 12 × 12 × 1,000. The number twelve is a symbol of the church.[13] The 144,000 signify the totality of God's end-time people. In the Old Testament, the number 1,000 (Hebrew: *'eleph*) is a basic military unit of the ancient Israelite army.

It appears the description of the end-time saints is modeled after ancient Israel going to war.[14] Thus, the 144,000 represent the church militant symbolically organized into 144 military units of a thousand.[15] They are on earth ready to engage in the final battle with the satanic army—the number of which is 200 million (Revelation 9:16).[16] In Revelation 17:14, they are referred to as the "called and chosen and faithful" who have joined Christ the Lamb in the final war of this earth's history.

But John did not see them as such in chapter 7; he has only heard that their number was 144,000. At the announcement of the number of those who were sealed, the destructive forces of the winds are unleashed, and the seven last plagues are poured out upon rebellious humanity. At that point, the sealed 144,000 were to enter into the great tribulation of the seven last plagues. But the great tribulation of the seven last plagues is not portrayed in Revelation 7 but later, in chapter 16. This is the reason why in chapter 7 there is no further description of the 144,000 as they are entering the great tribulation.

When John actually sees them in vision, they appear to him as a great multitude *in heaven* that have come out of the tribulation of the seven last plagues (Revelation 7:14). The war is over, and they are now the church triumphant, no longer organized into military divisions. They appear as a great incalculable multitude, not because of their uncountable number but because they stand in contrast to the countable 144,000.[17] As such, they stand before the throne of God, celebrating the great victory, and are about to receive their reward.

Preliminary (first) conclusion

Revelation 7 does not point to two distinct groups of the redeemed—the 144,000 who will be alive at the Second Coming and the great multitude that comprises the redeemed of all ages. In the context of the overall purpose of Revelation 7 in the organizational structure of the vision of the seven seals, the focus of chapter 7 is not on God's people of all ages but is exclusively on the last generation who will go through the great tribulation of the seven last plagues. This points to the 144,000 and the great multitude as the same group of saints referred to under different names.

Thus, Revelation 7 does not show that the 144,000 constitute an end-time select group separated from the larger body that will be granted special privileges that are not available to the rest of the faithful. All of God's people living before the Second Coming who choose to be faithful will be sealed, not just a small select number. In God's kingdom there are no clans or ranks; before God's throne, the redeemed are all dressed in the white robes granted by Christ (see Revelation 19:8). The robes of the last generation are made white in "the blood of the Lamb" (Revelation 7:14). Their salvation is a result of Christ's great victory achieved on the cross; it is not based on their own holiness and works (verse 10). This victory is the privilege of all the saved people of God, not just the last generation.[18] It is the blood of Christ that makes all the redeemed without distinction and equal before God.

The characteristics of the 144,000

As we have seen, Revelation 7:1–8 describes

the 144,000 as the church militant on earth, ready to go through the great tribulation of the seven last plagues, while verses 9–17 describe the 144,000 as the church triumphant in heaven after they have come out of the great tribulation. Revelation 14:1–5 gives a more detailed description of this group and portrays them as the church triumphant, standing with the Lamb on Mount Zion with the name of God inscribed on their foreheads. Isaiah envisioned the ransomed of the Lord returning to Mount Zion with joyful singing (Isaiah 35:10; 51:11). This is a further indication that the 144,000 are the great multitude of the saints standing before the throne of God in Revelation 7:9–17.

The new song they are heard singing is related to the shout of the great multitude: "Salvation to our God who sits on the throne, and to the Lamb" (Revelation 7:10). This also points to the saved saints standing on the sea of glass; they have won the victory over the beast and its image and are now singing the song of Moses and the Lamb (Revelation 15:1–4). No doubt the shout of the great multitude (Revelation 7), the new song of the victorious 144,000 (Revelation 14), and the song of Moses and the Lamb of the victorious saints (Revelation 15) are three facets of the same song offered to God for providing salvation to His people during the final crisis, just as the Israelites celebrated God's acts of salvation from the Egyptians at the Exodus (Exodus 15). The 144,000 have gone through a special time in this world's history. Their faithfulness has been tested in a special way. Yet they have remained unswervingly loyal to God. There is nothing in their song to

show that either their salvation or their victory over the beast results from their achievements and merit. God provided the victory for them. Thus, the new song is a song of their experience of what God has done for them.

Revelation 14:4, 5 provides a threefold description of their characteristics, telling us about who and what they truly are: (1) they have not defiled themselves with women; (2) they have been purchased from among men as firstfruits to God; and (3) no lie has been found in them, for they are blameless. We will now have a closer look into each of these characteristics.

They have not defiled themselves with women. The 144,000 are first described as "the ones who have not been defiled with women, for they have kept themselves chaste" (Revelation 14:4).[19] This defilement with women must be taken in a symbolic sense due to the symbolic language of Revelation. Otherwise, it would seem that the 144,000 has to comprise only individuals who have never had sexual relations. The symbol of a "woman" in the Bible is used regularly for the church, whether faithful or apostate.[20] Paul wrote to the Corinthians: "I betrothed you to one husband, so that to Christ I might present you as a pure virgin" (2 Corinthians 11:2). Revelation talks about the harlot Babylon and her daughters—apostate churches— seducing the governing world powers into illicit relationships with them (Revelation 17:1–5; 18:3, 9).

The Greek word *molunō* (defile, soil) occurs only three times in the New Testament in a figurative sense with reference to moral defilement. In 1 Corinthians 8:7,

Paul talks of a defiled conscience. Revelation 3:4 mentions a small number of believers in Sardis who have not soiled their garments with the pollution of the pagan environment. This is undoubtedly the meaning that the word *defiled* has in connection with the 144,000.

The imagery of the 144,000 as the ones who have not defiled themselves with women in the final crisis mirrors the Old Testament practice of Israelite soldiers who, before going into battle, were required to keep themselves ritually pure by not having sexual relations with women (Deuteronomy 23:9–11; 1 Samuel 21:4, 5).[21]

This ancient ceremonial practice is undoubtedly a backdrop for the portrayal of the 144,000 as the church militant that joins Christ in the final battle against the satanic army (cf. Revelation 17:14; 19:14). As such, they have not spiritually defiled themselves with Babylon and her daughters with whom it is said that all the nations of the earth have committed fornication (Revelation 14:8; 17:2; 18:3). "These are the ones who follow the Lamb wherever He goes" (Revelation 14:4). It is in this sense that their characterization as "virgins" must be understood. In Revelation 17:14, they are described as the "chosen and faithful." They have kept themselves spiritually pure and chaste and have remained unwaveringly faithful to Christ as they are engaged in the final battle.[22]

Purchased from among men as firstfruits to God. A further characteristic of the 144,000 is that they are the ones who "have been purchased from among men as first fruits to God and to the Lamb" (Revelation 14:4). In the New Testament, the Greek word

agorazō (purchase) is used metaphorically to describe what Christ did (1 Corinthians 6:20; 7:23; Revelation 5:9). In ancient Israel, the firstfruits were the best of the harvest, set aside for God, while the people were permitted to use the rest of the harvest for themselves (Exodus 34:26).

In the Bible, the term *firstfruits* is also used metaphorically for God's people in their totality, in distinction from the rest of the people in the world. Jeremiah refers to all Israel as redeemed from Egypt and "holy to the Lord, the first of His harvest" (Jeremiah 2:3). Likewise, James refers to all redeemed Christians as "the first fruits among His creatures" (James 1:18). One may notice that the term refers to God's people as a whole, never to a small group separated from the larger body.

The 144,000 are the firstfruits, *aparchē*, not as separated from other believers but in the sense that they have been purchased by the blood of Christ and so are separate from the rest of the people in the world ("they have been purchased from among men" [Revelation 14:4]). While the people in the world who have sided with the beast and received the mark of the beast are set for judgment (cf. verses 17–20), the sealed saints are, as the firstfruits, separated for God and sealed with the name of God. In Revelation 14:14–16, they are distinct from humanity in general as the grain harvest. And this does not apply to a separate group; it applies to all the sealed believers at the time of the end.

They are blameless. The final characteristic of the 144,000 is that "no lie was found in their mouth; they are blameless" (verse 5). This echoes Zephaniah's prophecy:

"The remnant of Israel will do no wrong
And tell no lies,
Nor will a deceitful tongue
Be found in their mouths" (Zephaniah
3:13).

The "lie," *pseudos*, mentioned here is more than common untruthfulness. It stands in contrast to the truth, *alētheia*. It is the lying of the antichrist power—falsehood with the purpose of deceiving people in the world (Revelation 13:14; 16:13, 14; 19:20). Thus, the NKJV translates it appropriately as "deceit." Such a deceitful lie, or falsehood, is not found in the 144,000 (cf. Revelation 21:27; 22:15), for they refuse to participate in the end-time deception.

In the Septuagint (LXX), the Greek term translated as "blameless," or "without blemish" (Greek: *amōmos*), basically translates the Hebrew word *tāmîm*, which in the Old Testament is a standard cultic word denoting the unblemished condition of sacrificial animals (cf. Numbers 6:14, LXX). Thus, in the New Testament, the word *blameless* (*amōmos*) appropriately applies to Christ while He was on earth (Hebrews 9:14; 1 Peter 1:19).

Throughout the Bible, the words *unblemished* and *blamelessness* are the standard terms that describe the people who are faithful and dedicated to God. In the Greek Old Testament (LXX), *amōmos* is used for Abraham (Genesis 17:1) and Job (Job 1:1). In the New Testament, the word also applies to the lives of Christians who are to be holy and without blemish before God. Believers were chosen "before the foundation of the world" to be "holy and blameless before Him" (Ephesians 1:4). The word describes, in particular, the condition of the church

at the Second Coming (Ephesians 5:27; Philippians 2:15; Colossians 1:22; Jude 24). Paul wished for the Thessalonians to be preserved blameless (1 Thessalonians 5:23). "Therefore, beloved," Peter wrote, "since you look for these things, be diligent to be found by Him in peace, spotless and blameless" (2 Peter 3:14). All these texts show that blamelessness is not an exclusive characteristic of the last generation of saints because all these admonitions applied equally to the original recipients of these letters two thousand years ago, not just to those who will live at the time before the Second Coming.

Thus, the blamelessness of the 144,000 does not refer to an absolute, sinless perfection, but rather it refers to their fidelity and total commitment to Christ. To be blameless means to walk with God just as Abraham and Job did; these people were blameless but not absolutely sinless.[23] In the closing days of this world's history, when the majority of people renounce their loyalty to God and side with the satanic trinity, the 144,000 reflect the true character of Christ as acceptable to God. Thus, they stand in contrast to those who have hardened their hearts in sin and unbelief and have willingly and knowingly chosen falsehood and have accepted the mark of the beast. In those days, the 144,000 will reflect the true character of Christ. They have washed their robes and made them white in the blood of the Lamb, and as such, they are found "spotless and blameless" before God (2 Peter 3:14).

Second conclusion

In describing the 144,000 sealed saints, Revelation 14:1–5 affirms what seems to be clear in Revelation 7. In God's kingdom, there will not be two distinct groups of the saved—the last generation who will be sinless and, as such, enjoy special privileges in God's kingdom in contrast with the rest of the saved who will not reach such a sinless state. Like the rest of the Bible, Revelation does not show that God has set for the last generation a higher standard of righteousness and obedience than the one He has set for the faithful before them. He requires from the last generation the same as He has required from every previous generation: to live a holy life of preparation for Christ's return.[24] And His conditions for salvation have never changed.

The last generation is not a group of "super saints" who will reach a level of holiness that was not attainable by other people of God.[25] It is true that their loyalty and obedience will be tested in a unique way; however, their victory will be achieved on the same grounds as that of the redeemed of all ages. Salvation is a result of the saving grace of God rather than one's own holiness and works. "For by grace you have been saved through faith; and that not of yourselves, it is the gift of God; not as a result of works, so that no one may boast" (Ephesians 2:8, 9). The only hope of God's people, particularly of the last generation, is in Christ's grace. It is through Christ's grace that God's people win the full victory over sin and find themselves in their eternal home.

Ellen G. White on the state of the last generation

Last generation theology proponents claim that Ellen G. White states in her writings that the last generation will reach sinless

perfection in order to be able to go through the time of trouble during the last crisis. They point in particular to two statements in *The Great Controversy* in which she states that during the time of the trouble, God's people will have to stand without a mediator or intercessor. For the advocates of sinless perfection, the statement that God's people will have to stand without a mediator or intercessor during the final trouble is "one of the strongholds of their position."[26]

Therefore, we will look into and examine these two statements in their literary contexts and in conjunction with Ellen G. White's other statements on the state of the last generation in order to find out whether she speaks of a state of sinlessness in the last generation right before the Second Coming.

Going through the time of trouble without a mediator. The first of the two aforementioned statements is found in chapter 24 of *The Great Controversy*, which is titled, "In the Holy of Holies." Here, Ellen G. White describes the investigative judgment in the heavenly sanctuary prior to the Second Coming. The whole subject is dealt with in the context of the Great Disappointment of the Millerites in 1844. Although the Millerites were expecting Christ to come, they were obviously "not yet ready to meet the Lord. There was still a work of preparation to be accomplished for them."[27] Then she gives this warning: "Those who are living upon the earth when the intercession of Christ shall cease in the sanctuary above are to stand in the sight of a holy God without a mediator. Their robes must be spotless, their characters must be purified from sin by the blood of sprinkling. Through the grace of God and their own diligent effort they must be conquerors in the battle with evil."[28]

During the cleansing of the sanctuary, forgiveness is still available. "While the investigative judgment is going forward in heaven, while the sins of penitent believers are being removed from the sanctuary, there is to be a special work of purification, of putting away of sin, among God's people upon earth."[29] Then, when this work of preparation is done, God's people will be ready for Christ's coming. The close of probation marks the end of the investigative judgment, and the destiny of all has been decided.

In the rest of the chapter, Ellen G. White goes on to explain Christ's high-priestly ministry in the Holy of Holies in the heavenly sanctuary and how this subject came to be gradually understood by the early Adventists. "Though this was not at first understood by Adventists, it was afterward made plain as the Scriptures . . . began to open before them."[30]

The whole purpose of the chapter is to explain what the Millerites missed in their understanding of what truly happened on October 22, 1844. There is nothing in this whole chapter showing that Ellen G. White taught that, before the close of probation, God's people will reach the state of sinless perfection. What she endeavored to show was that the final generation needs intercession until the close of probation.[31] But the time after the close of probation is without a mediator because all cases have been decided, so the sinner "will no longer be able to switch sides."[32]

The second "without a mediator or intercessor" statement is found in chapter 39, which is titled, "The Time of Trouble." This statement is set in the context of her comments on Daniel 12:1, talking about Michael arising at the time of the final distress. With the closing of the preaching of the gospel, "Jesus ceases His intercession in the sanctuary above" and "mercy no longer pleads for the guilty inhabitants of the earth."[33] Every "case has been decided for life or death. Christ has made the atonement for His people and blotted out their sins. The number of His subjects is made up."[34] It is in this context that she makes the following statement:

> When He leaves the sanctuary, darkness covers the inhabitants of the earth. In that fearful time the righteous must live in the sight of a holy God without an intercessor. The restraint which has been upon the wicked is removed, and Satan has entire control of the finally impenitent. . . . Unsheltered by divine grace, they [the righteous] have no protection from the wicked one. Satan will then plunge the inhabitants of the earth into one great, final trouble. As the angels of God cease to hold in check the fierce winds of human passion, all the elements of strife will be let loose.[35]

Then she turns to describe the experience of God's people after the close of probation: "The people of God will then be plunged into those scenes of affliction and distress described by the prophet as the time of Jacob's trouble."[36]

There is nothing in this whole description

that points to a state of absolute sinlessness for God's people after the close of probation. The statement "the righteous must live in the sight of a holy God without an intercessor" is given in the context of the time of trouble characterized by intensive demonic activities as Satan and his angels stir up the world against God's faithful people.[37] During that perilous time, God's people will have to "live in the sight of a holy God without an intercessor," which means that they will have to trust God and that His presence is with them. But one may note that nowhere does Ellen G. White indicate that they will have to go through that time without their Savior.

The state of the last generation. Does Ellen G. White teach in her writings that the last generation of the saints is to be in a state of sinless perfection before the close of probation? For one thing, in her writings, she repeatedly urges Adventists to prepare for the Second Coming. They have to win the victory over every cherished and willful sin. She taught that God expects from His people nothing less than the perfection of their character. She regularly defines this character perfection in terms of reflecting fully the character of Christ in His human nature. In some of her earliest writings, she states, "Those who receive the seal of the living God and are protected in the time of trouble must reflect the image of Jesus fully."[38] In 1911, she makes a similar declaration: "Now, while our great High Priest is making the atonement for us, we should seek to become perfect in Christ. Not even by a thought could our Saviour be brought to yield to the power of temptation. . . . This is the condition in which

those must be found who shall stand in the time of trouble."[39]

She also writes, "The Lord requires perfection from His redeemed family. He expects from us the perfection which Christ revealed in His humanity."[40] In another place, she writes, "By the power of the Holy Spirit the moral image of God is to be perfected in the character. We are to be wholly transformed into the likeness of Christ."[41] And again: "The ideal of Christian character is Christlikeness. As the Son of man was perfect in His life, so His followers are to be perfect in their life. . . . His character is to be ours."[42]

God will accept only those who are determined to aim high. He places every human agent under obligation to do his or her best. Moral perfection is required of all. Never should we lower the standard of righteousness in order to accommodate inherited or cultivated tendencies to wrongdoing. We need to understand that imperfection of character is sin.

The question must be asked: In urging God's people to perfection of character, did Ellen G. White have in mind a state of absolute sinlessness? An important principle in reading her writings is to interpret her unclear statements in light of the clear ones. Thus, in an effort to find the answer to that question, we will consider Ellen G. White's two descriptions of the condition of the last generation after the close of probation.

The time of Jacob's trouble. In the rest of the aforementioned chapter "The Time of Trouble" in *The Great Controversy*, Ellen G. White describes the experience of God's people during the time after the close of probation, which she refers to as "the time of Jacob's trouble"—the expression taken from Jeremiah 30:7.[43] She likens their experience to the experience of Jacob the night before meeting his brother Esau. As Satan turned Esau against Jacob, so in the final crisis he will stir up the wicked against God's people to destroy them.[44] As he accused Jacob before God on account of his sins, so he will direct his accusations against them. Satan "has an accurate knowledge of the sins which he has tempted them to commit, and he presents these before God. . . . He declares that the Lord cannot in justice forgive their sins and yet destroy him and his angels."[45]

As Satan accuses God's people, their confidence in God is greatly tested. "They are fully conscious of their weaknesses and unworthiness. Satan endeavors to terrify them with the thought that their cases are hopeless, that the stain of their defilement will never be washed away."[46] While surrounded by enemies who are trying to destroy them, their "fear that every sin has not been repented of" is overwhelming.[47]

Now comes Ellen G. White's significant statement that rebuffs the idea that she taught that the last generation will be in a sinless state during the time of trouble. She describes the time of Jacob's trouble as the refining "furnace of fire" where God's people will be purified as gold is tried in fire. What are God's people to be purified of? Ellen G. White explains, "God's love for His children during the period of their severest trial is as strong and tender as in the days of their sunniest prosperity; but *it is needful for them to be placed in the furnace of fire; their earthliness must be consumed, that the image of Christ may be perfectly reflected.*"[48] Here, Ellen G. White states clearly that God's people

will not, during the time of trouble, reflect the image of Christ absolutely perfectly. The reason that God will place the saved into this furnace of fire is because "their earthliness must be consumed, that the image of Christ may be perfectly reflected." This shows that even after the close of probation, there will still be in God's people some lingering earthliness that they have to be purged of. It is only after this earthliness is consumed that Christ's image will be perfectly reflected in them.

Zechariah's vision of Joshua and the Angel. That Ellen G. White did not hold the idea of the sinless perfection of the last generation during the final crisis is also evident in the chapter "Joshua and the Angel" in volume 5 of *Testimonies for the Church.* After reflecting on Zechariah's vision of Joshua in Zechariah 3, she states, "Zechariah's vision of Joshua and the Angel applies with peculiar force to the experience of God's people in the closing up of the great day of atonement."[49] Furthermore, she describes the condition of God's people as they are going through the trial of the final crisis after the close of probation:

As Joshua was pleading before the Angel, so the remnant church, with brokenness of heart and earnest faith, will plead for pardon and deliverance through Jesus their Advocate. *They are fully conscious of the sinfulness of their lives, they see their weakness and unworthiness, and as they look upon themselves they are ready to despair.* The tempter stands by to accuse them, as he stood by to resist Joshua. *He points to their filthy garments, their defective charac-*

ters. *He presents their weakness and folly, their sins of ingratitude, their unlikeness to Christ, which has dishonored their Redeemer.* He endeavors to affright the soul with the thought that their case is hopeless, *that the stain of their defilement will never be washed away.* He hopes to so destroy their faith that they will yield to his temptations, turn from their allegiance to God, and receive the mark of the beast.[50]

It may be seen here that, as Ellen G. White explains, even after the close of probation, the final generation is humble, and they are fully cognizant of their sinfulness and their need of Christ's merits. Then she makes an identical declaration to the one she made in the discussion on the time of Jacob's trouble: "Their earthliness must be removed that the image of Christ may be perfectly reflected; unbelief must be overcome; faith, hope, and patience are to be developed."[51] But the earthliness of God's people has been atoned for. They are sealed, and their salvation has been secured.

As the people of God afflict their souls before Him, *pleading for purity of heart, the command is given, "Take away the filthy garments" from them,* and the encouraging words are spoken, "Behold, I have caused thine iniquity to pass from thee, and I will clothe thee with change of raiment." The spotless robe of Christ's righteousness is placed upon the tried, tempted, yet faithful children of God. The despised remnant are clothed in glorious apparel, nevermore to be defiled by the cor-

ruptions of the world. . . . Their sins are transferred to the originator of sin. And *the remnant are not only pardoned and accepted,* but honored. . . . These are they that stand upon Mount Zion with the Lamb, having the Father's name written in their foreheads. They sing the new song before the throne, that song which no man can learn save the hundred and forty and four thousand, which were redeemed from the earth.[52]

If the final generation has achieved a state of absolute sinlessness before the close of probation, why are they, according the above statement, "pleading for purity of heart"? Ellen G. White makes it clear that after the close of probation, there is still a lingering "earthliness"—deficiencies and shortcomings—that must be removed in order that the image of Christ may be perfectly reflected in them. Her statement that the saints' "faith, hope, and patience are to be developed" shows that these virtues are still in the process of development after the close of probation. The same situation is found with her statement that in answer to the prayers of the saved, their "filthy garments" are removed and the "spotless robe of Christ's righteousness is placed" upon them so that they are "nevermore to be defiled by the corruptions of the world." As such, they are fully "pardoned and accepted" by God. This all takes place after the close of probation.

Final conclusion

A closer look into Ellen G. White's statements on the state of the last generation shows that while she teaches that God's people will have to stand perfect before God at the Second Coming, nowhere does she teach that God's people will reach a particular state of absolute sinlessness before the close of probation and that, after the close of probation, they will no longer have sin in any shape or form and, thus, they will not have the need of Christ's atoning grace. On the contrary, she constantly insists that sinlessness is unattainable in this life. God's people will never reach a sinless state as long as they are in this flesh: "As long as Satan reigns we shall have self to subdue, besetments to overcome, and there is no stopping place, there is no point to which we can come and say we have fully attained."[53] In the year 1888, she stated, "We cannot say, 'I am sinless,' till this vile body is changed and fashioned like unto His glorious body. But if we constantly seek to follow Jesus, the blessed hope is ours of standing before the throne of God without spot or wrinkle, or any such thing; complete in Christ, robed in His righteousness and perfection."[54]

Seven years later, she penned a similar statement: "When the conflict of life is ended, when the armor is laid off at the feet of Jesus, when the saints of God are glorified, then and then only will it be safe to claim that we are saved and sinless."[55]

While in her writings Ellen G. White constantly urges God's people to perfection of character, in her two extensive descriptions of the condition of the faithful after the close of probation, she explains clearly that the faithful will have to go through "the fiery furnace" of the time of trouble to be purified as gold is tried in fire, that their lingering "earthliness must

be removed that the image of Christ may be perfectly reflected." As with the situation of Jacob the night before he was to meet his brother Esau, so Satan endeavors to terrify God's people during the time of trouble, saying that "the stain of their defilement will never be washed away." In likening their situation to that of the high priest Joshua in Zechariah 3, she states they are "fully conscious of the sinfulness of their lives, they see their weakness and unworthiness, and as they look upon themselves they are ready to despair." Satan is there beside them, pointing to "their filthy garments, their defective characters ... their weakness and folly, their sins of ingratitude, their unlikeness to Christ." He terrifies them that "their case is hopeless, that the stain of their defilement will never be washed away." Then their "filthy garments" are replaced with "the spotless robe of Christ's righteousness." It is then that God's people will be "not only pardoned and accepted, but honored." These descriptions of the state of God's people during the time of trouble show that God's people after the close of probation will still have their sinful nature and will not be in a state of absolute, sinless perfection.

Woodrow Whidden suggests that, in light of Ellen G. White's wider soteriology, her statements regarding the perfect state of the last generation that will not need the intercession of Jesus must be understood as meaning that

> God's sealed and faithful people are regarded as perfect in the sense that they are no longer cherishing sin or committing overt sins—sins that are

deliberately or willfully performed. However, they will be imperfect in the sense that they still have sinful natures, so that all they do is less than the best. They still have unavoidable deficiencies, but they do not indulge in or commit premeditated acts of sin. Jesus is still making up for their "unavoidable deficiencies," "defects," "shortcomings," "mistakes," and "errors," but He is no longer mediating for the unsealed—the rebellious, willful, high-handed, sin-excusing sinners.[56]

Thus, Ellen G. White is in line with the rest of the Bible. Nowhere in the Bible is perfection equated with absolute sinlessness.[57] Biblical perfection refers to a total commitment and loyalty to God that reflects His character but that allows for the possibility of incidental and accidental weaknesses and mistakes.[58] The indwelling Holy Spirit is the divine power that enables God's character to be exhibited in the life of the genuine believer and that gives the victory over sin.[59] But as long as God's people are in this flesh, they will have to grow in grace until they stand before their Savior in an uncorrupted body (i.e., after glorification; see 1 Corinthians 15:51–55). Only then will the final eradication of the sinful nature be experienced.

At this point, we will conclude with Ellen G. White's appeal: "Live the life of faith day by day. Do not become anxious and distressed about the time of trouble, and thus have a time of trouble beforehand. Do not keep thinking: 'I am afraid I shall not stand in the great testing day.' You are to live for the present, for this day only. To-morrow is not yours. To-day you are to maintain the victory over self."[60]

Endnotes

1. This view goes back to Uriah Smith, who held that Revelation 7:1–8 referred to the 144,000, while verses 9–12 referenced the great multitude, and verses 13–17 were a description of the 144,000. In Smith's view, the 144,000 were the last generation and the great multitude were the redeemed of all ages, so the ones coming out of the great tribulation could only be the 144,000. See Uriah Smith, *Daniel and Revelation* (Battle Creek, MI: Review and Herald®, 1897), 466, 467.

2. Unless noted otherwise, all Scripture quotations in this chapter are from the NASB.

3. The above Pauline statements show that sealing is not limited only to the last generation, for it was experienced by the faithful in Paul's time. Revelation shows that the test of faithfulness in the final crisis will focus on the keeping of God's commandments (see Revelation 12:17; 14:12). In particular, the fourth commandment will become the test of obedience to God (Revelation 14:7). As the Sabbath has been the sign of God's people in Old Testament times (Exodus 31:12–17; Ezekiel 20:12, 20), so it will be the sign of loyalty to God at the time of the end. The eschatological sealing and the fourth commandment of the Decalogue are closely related in the book of Revelation.

4. Although God's people will be protected from the harmful effects of the seven last plagues, Revelation 7:16 clearly shows that they will, in a certain measure, suffer hunger, thirst, and the scorching heat of the sun during the trial of the plagues. Before the plagues are poured out, God's people are assured that He will be close to them during those difficult times. He will care for them just as much as He cared for Elijah during the time of severe famine in Palestine (1 Kings 17:5–16).

5. During the Assyrian conquest, the ten tribes of the northern kingdom of Israel were taken into captivity (2 Kings 17:6–23), where they soon merged with other nations and, thus, disappeared from history. The two remaining tribes, Judah and Benjamin, were those who were known in the New Testament era as

"Jews." They were scattered throughout the Roman Empire after the destruction of Jerusalem in A.D. 70. The Judaism of today does not consist of the original twelve tribes. See William Hendriksen, *More Than Conquerors: An Interpretation of the Book of Revelation* (1940; repr., Grand Rapids, MI: Baker, 1997), 111.

6. Dan was the first of the tribes to turn to idolatry (Judges 18:27–31) and later became a center of idolatrous worship competing with the temple worship in Jerusalem (1 Kings 12:28–30). The Jews of John's day believed that the antichrist would come out of the tribe of Dan (cf. Dan 5:4-7 in *The Testaments of the Twelve Patriarchs*). Likewise, the tribe of Ephraim in the Old Testament became the symbol of idolatry (2 Chronicles 30:1, 10; Hosea 4:17; 8:11). The psalmist describes the tribe of Ephraim as those who "did not keep the covenant of God and refused to walk in His law" (Psalm 78:10). Cf. Douglas Ezell, *Revelations on Revelation: New Sounds From Old Symbols* (Waco, TX: Word Books, 1977), 61.

7. See Revelation 1:10–12; 9:16, 17; 21:9, 10.

8. Beatrice S. Neall, "Sealed Saints and the Tribulation," in *Symposium on Revelation—Book I*, ed. Frank B. Holbrook, Daniel and Revelation Committee Series, vol. 6 (Silver Spring, MD: Biblical Research Institute, 1992), 263.

9. Ekkehardt Mueller, "Who Are the 144,000 and the Great Multitude?," in *Interpreting Scripture: Bible Questions and Answers*, ed. Gerhard Pfandl, Biblical Research Institute Studies, vol. 2 (Silver Spring, MD: Biblical Research Institute, 2010), 434.

10. Ibid.

11. Ibid.

12. Neall, "Sealed Saints," 269.

13. In the Old Testament, twelve is the number of the tribes of Israel as the people of God; in the New Testament, it is also the number of the church, which is built upon the foundation of the twelve apostles (Ephesians 2:20). In the vision of the New Jerusalem, the names of the twelve tribes of Israel are inscribed on the twelve gates of the city and the names of the twelve apostles on its twelve foundation stones (Revelation 21:12–14).

14. E.g., Exodus 18:21; 25; Numbers 1:16; 10:4; 31:3–6; 1 Samuel 8:12; 18:13; 22:7.

15. *The War Scroll* envisions the eschatological war in the following way: "To organize the arm[ies] of your chosen ones in its thousands and its myriads, together with your holy ones and your angels, to di-

rect the hand in battle, [and destroy] the rebels of the earth by your great judgments." 1QM XII, 4, 5; see also 1QM IV, 1, 2; V, 3; Florentino García Martínez, ed., *The Dead Sea Scrolls Translated: The Qumran Texts in English*, trans. Wilfred G. E. Watson (New York: Brill, 1994), 97, 98.

16. Revelation 19:18 shows that Satan's end-time army is also organized into military units of 1,000 (Greek: *chiliarchos*; denoting a commander of a thousand troops). They are mentioned also in the scene of the sixth seal, trying to hide themselves from Christ's coming (Revelation 6:15).

17. Richard P. Lehmann suggests that the "innumerable" multitude echoes the promise made to Abraham that his offspring would be innumerable like the sand on the seashore. "The Remnant in the Book of Revelation," in *Toward a Theology of the Remnant: An Adventist Ecclesiological Perspective*, ed. Ángel Manuel Rodríguez (Silver Spring, MD: Biblical Research Institute, 2009), 92.

18. E.g., the "overcomers" in Sardis were promised that they would walk before Christ clothed in white clothes (Revelation 3:4, 5). The praise of the great multitude acknowledging God and the Lamb for their salvation (Revelation 7:10) echoes the praise of the twenty-four elders to the Lamb in Revelation 5:9, 10 for redeeming with His blood people "from every tribe and tongue and people and nation."

19. Literally, "for they are virgins [*parthenoi gar eisin*]." *Parthenos* means "virgin," but it may also mean "young woman." In the New Testament, the word is used metaphorically with reference to fidelity to Christ. In 2 Corinthians 11:2, Paul says to the Corinthians believers that he has betrothed them to one Husband, Christ, so he is eager to present them as "a pure virgin" to Him; in other words, he wants to keep them pure and chaste for Christ.

20. In the Bible, a woman is often used as a symbol for God's people, both in the Old Testament (Isaiah 54:5, 6; Jeremiah 3:20; Ezekiel 16:8–14; Hosea 1–3; Amos 5:2) and in the New (2 Corinthians 11:2; Ephesians 5:25–32). The same is true in Revelation. The symbol of a pure and faithful woman consistently stands for the church faithful to God (Revelation 12:1–6, 13–17; 19:7, 8; 22:17), while a prostitute symbolizes the apostate and unfaithful (Revelation 17:1–6; 19:2).

21. The Dead Sea Scrolls show that this concept was still known among the first-century Jews. See 1QM VII, 3–6, in Martínez, *Dead Sea Scrolls*, 105, 106.

22. Craig S. Keener, *Revelation*, The NIV Application Commentary (Grand Rapids, MI: Zondervan, 2000), 371.

23. See Jean R. Zurcher, *Christian Perfection* (Washington, DC: Review and Herald®, 1967), 26–35.

24. Roy Adams, *The Nature of Christ: Help for a Church Divided Over Perfection* (Hagerstown, MD: Review and Herald®, 1994), 130.

25. Hendriksen, *More Than Conquerors*, 152.

26. Woodrow W. Whidden II, *Ellen White on Salvation: A Chronological Study* (Hagerstown, MD: Review and Herald®, 1995), 131.

27. Ellen G. White, *The Great Controversy* (Nampa, ID: Pacific Press®, 2005), 424.

28. Ibid., 425.

29. Ibid.

30. Ibid., 431.

31. Whidden asks in this regard,

What, then, did she [Ellen G. White] mean when she spoke of a perfection that does not need the mediation of Jesus? Does she mean that they will not need Christ's grace or that Christ will no longer be sustaining them in their severe trial? Will they have built up such a reservoir of grace within that they will no longer have to look without to Christ? If the answer is yes to these questions, then the entire thrust of Ellen White's understanding of salvation would be severely distorted—even stood on its head. It would have been strange for one who had so consistently urged believers to look away from self and constantly to behold and trust in Jesus as their advocate and mediator now to urge them to begin to look within for some internal, subjective stockpile of strength (*Ellen White on Salvation*, 135).

32. Ibid., 134.

33. White, *The Great Controversy*, 613.

34. Ibid., 613, 614.

35. Ibid., 614; see also 649.

36. Ibid., 616.

37. Ibid., 614; see also Ellen G. White, *Early Writings* (Hagerstown, MD: Review and Herald®, 1999), 279–285.

38. White, *Early Writings*, 71.

39. White, *The Great Controversy*, 623.

40. Ellen G. White, *Child Guidance* (Hagerstown, MD: Review and Herald®, 1999), 477.

41. Ellen G. White, *Testimonies to Ministers and Gospel Workers* (Mountain View, CA: Pacific Press®, 1962), 506.

42. Ellen G. White, *The Desire of Ages* (Nampa, ID: Pacific Press®, 2005), 311.

43. White, *The Great Controversy*, 616–621.

44. Ibid., 618.

45. Ibid.

46. Ibid., 619.

47. Ibid.

48. Ibid., 621 (emphasis added).

49. Ellen G. White, *Testimonies for the Church* (Mountain View, CA: Pacific Press®, 1948), 5:472.

50. Ibid., 473 (emphasis added).

51. Ibid., 474.

52. Ibid., 475, 476 (emphasis added).

53. Ellen G. White, *Testimonies for the Church* (Mountain View, CA: Pacific Press®, 1948), 1:340.

54. Ellen G. White, " 'Abide in Me,' " *Signs of the Times*, March 23, 1888, 178; also in Ellen G. White, *Selected Messages*, bk. 3 (Washington, DC: Review and Herald®, 1980), 355.

55. Ellen G. White, "The Whole Duty of Man," *Signs of the Times*, May 16, 1895; also in White, *Selected Messages*, bk. 3, 355, 356.

56. Whidden, *Ellen White on Salvation*, 136.

57. See Hans K. LaRondelle, *Perfection and Perfectionism: A Dogmatic-Ethical Study of Biblical Perfection and Phenomenal Perfectionism*, 2nd ed., Andrews University Monographs, Studies in Religion, vol. 3 (Berrien Springs, MI: Andrews University Press, 1975), 159–245; see also Zurcher, *Christian Perfection*, 102–107.

58. See Zurcher, *Christian Perfection*, 33, 34.

59. Ibid., 33, 34.

60. Ellen G. White, "The Light of the World (Concluded.)," *Signs of the Times*, October 20, 1887, 625.

12

Misinterpreted End-Time Issues: Five Myths in Adventism

Jiří Moskala

When I accepted the Lord Jesus Christ as my personal Savior in my early teens, I genuinely rejoiced in the gift of salvation. But almost simultaneously, I was deeply disturbed and perplexed by a message preached by some pastors regarding last-day events. They claimed that no one could be sure of salvation because we do not know when our names will be called during the pre-Advent judgment. Thus, as it was explained to me, only at the very end of time, after the shaking period, would believers know whether they had passed the investigation and could be sure of their redemption. I was profoundly frustrated. I wanted to be saved, have assurance of the forgiveness of my sins, experience the joy of salvation, and receive the seal of God, but this complete uncertainty led me to an unhealthy self-examination.

This teaching seemed to be in direct contradiction to the explicit instruction of the Holy Scriptures (see texts such as John 1:12; 3:16, 17, 36; 5:24; 6:47; 1 John 1:7–9; 2:1, 28; 4:17; 5:12, 13). I did not know what to do with all these claims and the insecurity I felt; tension tortured my conscience. Salvation is a future reality, these pastors insisted. I was deeply confused and discouraged because, on the one hand, I believed that I was saved in Jesus Christ (in spite of all my fragility, He is my Savior!), but on the other hand, I had to wait for God's seal in order to be approved at the end of the probation period. I was not able to make sense of all these contradictory thoughts.

My spiritual life was unbalanced, and I lived in fear of the future. Even though I believed in God, I was torn within myself because if I had to wait until the end time to know for sure what would happen to me, everything might be different at that time from what I hoped. And, of course, the time of probation was painted with dreadful colors; it was a nightmare to think about the time of judgment and Christ's second coming. Feelings that I was lost brought a keen sense of desperation—"I would never belong in the kingdom of heaven; I wouldn't make it." My faith was shaken, and thoughts about my weak faith led to the conclusion that probably everything I did was in vain and that maybe I had deceived myself with the notion of being saved in Christ.[1] The thought that even stronger attacks against my faith would come at the end of the world's history only added to my anxiety. How could I survive during that time when mercy would no longer be granted?

Worse than that, I was told that at the very end of human history, when the time of probation and God's door of mercy would close and Satan's attacks would intensify, I would have to live without any help from God. I was also told that I would have to make it through the last-day events on my own because the Holy Spirit would be taken from the earth and Jesus would cease to be my Intercessor! Believers would be left alone and on their own. If I struggled now, I reasoned, how could I make it through when Satan's anger and activities would culminate without any restrictions?

This mistaken and distorted thinking (as I understand it today) robbed me of the assurance and joy of salvation. I was scared of God, afraid of His judgment, and fearful of the time of the end. I was concentrating on myself, my performance, and my achievements and lived in spiritual schizophrenia. It was a very unfortunate situation because my attitude toward God was not built on gratitude or motivated by love for what He had done and was graciously doing for me. Needless to say, my youthful years were a very sober struggle of faith and full of fear and anxiety.

When I analyze that spiritual uncertainty today, I realize my unpleasant Christian experience was built on five misunderstandings that assumed that the Bible and/or the Spirit of Prophecy (1) teach that believers will receive the seal of God only at the end of time; (2) caution against the assurance of salvation; (3) affirm that living believers can be called to appear in the pre-Advent judgment and be examined at any time; (4) proclaim that after the close of probation the Holy Spirit will be removed from the earth, meaning that believers will be without any supernatural

help; and (5) declare that believers in Jesus Christ will be on their own when the door of mercy is closed because Christ will cease to be their Intercessor. Thus, their characters must be especially strong in order to be victorious against the forces of evil in this final short period of time. I now understand that I cannot make it to heaven on my own because salvation, from beginning to end, is an undeserved gift from God to repentant sinners who surrender to Him and accept Him as their personal Savior through faith. It is only this amazing grace of God that makes us fit for God's kingdom.

Even though it is impossible in one chapter to deal in depth with all five of these important issues, nevertheless, in what follows I will summarize the crucial objections to each of these misunderstandings. Let me stress that, although believed by some Adventists, all five are myths—misleading propositions built on false presuppositions—and need to be corrected because only truth can set us free (John 8:31, 32). All are erroneous in their core teaching. The reasoning behind them is a human construct that mixes truth with error; the Bible and Ellen G. White's writings present a very different picture. Let me explain why this kind of theology is fatally flawed and how these mistakes distort biblical teaching as well as how the true biblical teaching, supported by the Spirit of Prophecy, makes us free, trusting, trustworthy, joyful, and full of abundant life.

1. God's two seals: The seal of the gospel and the apocalyptic seal

The Bible teaches about two seals of God, not only one. This was an astounding and unexpected biblical discovery for me, personally. It was profoundly encouraging to me when I read in two places in Paul's epistle to the Ephesians about the very comforting truth concerning the first seal of God—the seal of the gospel. I always heard about the end-time sealing only in the book of Revelation. Understanding about the seal of the gospel helped deepen my Adventist identity and brought to my Christian walk with the Lord a new dimension, fresh insights, renewed commitment, and deep joy.

The two seals are different; they are given at different times but are complementary. Only those who receive the first seal will receive the second one—just as with the gift of the Holy Spirit, only those who receive the early rain will be recipients of the latter rain. The first seal is received at the beginning of our spiritual journey with our gracious and awesome Lord, and the second one comes at the very end of time, just prior to the close of probation. Where do we find the biblical data for these two seals?

The first seal. The first relevant biblical passage is the following: "And you also were included in Christ when you heard the message of truth, the gospel of your salvation. When you believed, you were marked in him with a seal [Greek: *esphragisthēte*[2]], the promised Holy Spirit, who is a deposit guaranteeing our inheritance until the redemption of those who are God's possession—to the praise of his glory" (Ephesians 1:13, 14).[3] Paul plainly states that at the moment one gives his or her life to Jesus and believes in Him, the Holy Spirit seals that believer in Christ for the day of redemption. What a wonderful, liberating, and reassuring truth! The Spirit of God marks Christ's followers with the seal of salvation right when they first believe. I propose to call this seal "the seal of the gospel."

This clear biblical teaching brought great relief to my troubled heart when I searched for the assurance and joy of salvation. For the first time in my life, I clearly understood that I did not need to wait until the time of the end to be sealed by God because at the moment I began to trust in Him and gave my life to Jesus I was sealed, marked, by the Holy Spirit. This was incredible news to me. I have found that Ellen G. White links this sealing with conversion: "Oh, that the youth and children would give their hearts to Christ! What an army might then be raised up to win others to righteousness! . . . Do not many of them [parents] think that the minister should take the burden and see to it that their children are converted and that the seal of God is placed upon them?"[4]

The sequence of thoughts in this passage in Ephesians is clear: (1) we hear the word of truth—the gospel of salvation; (2) we believe in Jesus Christ; (3) we are sealed by the Holy Spirit; and (4) the Holy Spirit is given to us as a deposit (Greek: *arrabōn*; Ephesians 1:14; 2 Corinthians 1:22) or as a firstfruit (Greek: *aparchē*; Romans 8:23, 24). This means that He is a pledge and guarantor of our salvation and redemption. Thus, the Holy Spirit is guaranteeing our inheritance, that is, salvation. He is guaranteeing our redemption for when we will be God's possession in our entirety at the end of time. Then we will have a perfect relationship with God face-to-face.[5]

The gift of the Spirit is like a down

payment of the inheritance we have in God. This first "deposit" guarantees complete future payment. The Spirit is the initial installment in our salvation as well as the promise and assurance that our full future inheritance and salvation will be delivered. Salvation does not depend on our achievements, performance, or actions; it is thoroughly and uniquely God's work. The Greek word *arrabōn* (noun, nominative masculine singular common) means "pledge," "guarantee" (of what is to come). This term is used also in 2 Corinthians 1:22, where the ideas of "sealing" and "guaranteeing" are put together, and also in 2 Corinthians 5:5, where the Holy Spirit is given to us as a deposit or guarantor.

This is why Paul encourages believers not to "grieve the Holy Spirit of God, with whom you were sealed [Greek: *esphragisthēte*] for the day of redemption" (Ephesians 4:30).[6] This is the second text referring to the seal of the gospel. It is significant that the Greek word *esphragisthēte* occurs only twice in the New Testament, namely, in our two texts—Ephesians 1:13 and Ephesians 4:30—and always in relation to believing in Christ. Pay close attention to Paul's affirmation in both texts that the sealing by the Holy Spirit is a past event for those to whom he was writing: "You *were* sealed." Believers in Christ are sealed by the Holy Spirit for the future event of total redemption.

Paul exhorts Christians to maintain proper ethical behavior because obedience flows from a living faith (see Christian ethics in a nutshell in Ephesians 4:31–5:6). This sealing is God's gift, His response to our response to His love, to our openness and surrender to Him. Note that the Ephesian believers already have the Holy Spirit, and for that reason they should not disappoint and sadden Him by wrong actions and the behavior described in this passage: "Get rid of all bitterness, rage and anger, brawling and slander, along with every form of malice." "But among you there must not be even a hint of sexual immorality, or of any kind of impurity, or of greed, because these are improper for God's holy people" (Ephesians 4:31; 5:3). Christians should be imitators of God, following His example as dearly loved children, and walk in love (Ephesians 5:1, 2).

Paul's phrase "do not grieve the Holy Spirit of God" (Ephesians 4:30) is an exhortation to not act like God's people in the past (see the identical terminology in Isaiah 63:10), because when we experience the Spirit, we need to let Him change our hearts in order to fulfill the will of God. Why live contrary to Him, whose ownership seal we wear, when we in fact are living in violation of our eternal destiny?

Sealing in the time of the Old Testament had several functions. Three principle purposes were (1) as a sign, or proof, of authenticity; (2) as a sign of ownership; and (3) as a sign of approval, like a signature functions for us today. By sealing us, God proclaims that we belong to Him, that we are His own, that He approves and accepts our little faith in order that we may grow in Him, and that He will help us to live authentic lives of love, faith, and hope (1 Corinthians 13:13; 2 Peter 3:18). All these nuances are present in God's sealing of those who believe in Him. In Paul's time, sealing was also a sign of ownership, of belonging to, as well as an approval of a product. It was like an autograph and gave a sense of validity and genuineness: "Now it is God who makes both us and you stand firm in Christ. He anointed us, set his seal of ownership on us, and put his Spirit in our hearts as a deposit, guaranteeing what is to come" (2 Corinthians 1:21, 22). "Now the one who has fashioned us for this very purpose is God, who has given us the Spirit as a deposit, guaranteeing what is to come" (2 Corinthians 5:5). The possession implied by the seal is God's possession of His people, not their possession of salvation (Ephesians 1:14; see also Malachi 3:17).

The "you" in Ephesians 1:13 and 2:11 refers to the Gentile believers in Christ in Ephesus. Through their union with Christ, they belonged to Him, and the Holy Spirit put His stamp on them in order to seal that relationship. Thus, here there is no uncertainty of salvation because the Holy Spirit is the guarantor of that redemption (cf. John 5:24; Ephesians 2:4–10). Having believed, they are sealed by the Spirit for the day of redemption. It is significant that sealing by the Spirit is mentioned in both parts of this epistle. In the first part (Ephesians 1–3), which is more theological or doctrinal, Paul presents the indicative of the gospel, or root of our salvation, and reminds Christians of their calling and the riches of God's grace. Then in the second part (chapters 4–6), which demonstrates the consequences of salvation, namely, the imperative of the gospel and ethical behavior, he exhorts Christ's followers to live in a manner appropriate to their calling—to show by obedience the fruits of their faith—and explains how to praise the Lord by walking faithfully with Christ.

No one can put a seal on himself or herself. The sealing is God's action for us in which there is no "but" or "perhaps." We not only need to "marry" Jesus but need to stay happily married to Him. By staying in Christ, we have this assurance of salvation as we wait for the second coming of Jesus Christ and the final judgment (1 John 2:28; 4:17).

The second seal. The other seal of God is described in the book of Revelation. This seal is not in contradiction to the first one but is a complementary, matching one, like the early rain is supplemented by the latter rain. This seal is like a final stamp on a completed document. Its purpose is not focused on salvation or redemption but has to do with protection.

This eschatological or apocalyptic seal (Greek: *sphragis*) is plainly mentioned in Revelation, which describes God's faithful followers receiving it at the end of time in order to be able to go through the final events and be protected from the last seven plagues (Revelation 7:2, 3; 9:4). This seal of God is in contrast to the mark (Greek: *charagma*) of the beast, which people are solemnly warned not to receive (Revelation 13:16, 17; 14:9, 11; 16:2; 19:20; 20:4) because the recipients of this mark are those who are *not* ready for the second coming of Christ and who will perish.

Ezekiel 9 is the background of this imagery in Revelation and clearly demonstrates that only those who are sealed are protected from impending destruction. What happened before the fall of Jerusalem in 587–586 B.C. is a type for marking God's faithful followers with the seal of God at the time of the end (see especially Ezekiel

9:3–6). In the book of Revelation, those who have the seal of God are protected from the outpouring of God's wrath, and they will be able to stand on that great day (Revelation 6:17; 7:3). The commands in both Ezekiel and Revelation are similar: "Do not touch anyone who has the mark" (Ezekiel 9:6), and John records the order to the four angels: "Do not harm" (Revelation 7:3). The seal of God shields His people in the time of the outpouring of the divine judgment of condemnation. The seal is put on the foreheads of true believers as a sign of protection.

This apocalyptic seal affirms who are God's faithful children at the time of the end. It is not by chance that in the climax of the three angels' messages, the Spirit of God says of them: "They will rest from their labor, for their deeds will follow them" (Revelation 14:13). These faithful ones are God's inheritance, resting in the Lord until the day of redemption. Salvation is never an anthropocentric endeavor but a theocentric one. We cannot take it into our hands. We do not possess salvation; it comes to us as God's prepared gift that we can only accept or reject. God possesses us; we belong to Him. One needs to stay "in Christ," and this is "a central motif in Paul."[7] Christ is the guarantor of our sealing, because He received a seal of approval on His work of salvation on our behalf when He lived on earth: "Do not work for food that spoils, but for food that endures to eternal life, which the Son of Man will give you. For on him God the Father has placed his seal of approval" (John 6:27). Ranko Stefanovic fittingly comments: "All classes of human society are commanded to receive the mark of the beast. To receive the mark of the beast means to belong to the beast and worship it. The mark of the beast is, thus, an antithesis of God's seal ([Revelation] 14:1). Just as the seal identifies those who belong to God, so the mark of the beast identifies those who belong to and worship the beast. While the sealing signifies the Holy Spirit's working presence in human hearts (Eph. 1:13–14; 4:30), the mark of the beast counterfeits the work of the Holy Spirit."[8]

When comparing the two seals of God, one may say the following: the first seal may be called the "seal of the gospel" and the second one, "the apocalyptic seal." The first is a seal of salvation, and the second is the seal of protection. Each is irreplaceable, and they cannot be interchanged. The sealing is done by the Holy Spirit. One seal is a seal of acceptance, and the other is a seal of final ratification. The first seal is declarative, and the second one is affirmative. This second seal confirms one's faithfulness in following the Lamb and God's leadership in one's life, doing His will, keeping His commandments, and living according to His revealed Word (Revelation 7:14–17; 12:17; 13:10; 14:4, 5, 12; 17:14; 19:10). These were sealed by the Spirit at the time of their acceptance of Jesus Christ as their Savior; but, according to the book of Revelation, they will have continued walking with God in order to receive the final eschatological seal of God at the close of time and be able to go through the final showdown and stand before the Son of Man (Luke 21:36). Although the seal of the gospel can be broken by rebellion and a lack of repentance, the apocalyptic seal is permanent.

2. The assurance and joy of salvation

The assurance of salvation is plainly taught in Scripture. God declares that when we are in Christ, we can have full confidence and bold assurance in regard to the divine judgment and His second coming.[9] Consider carefully the following texts:

> Say to those with fearful hearts,
>   "Be strong, do not fear;
> your God will come,
>   he will come with vengeance;
> with divine retribution
>   he will come to *save* you" (Isaiah 35:4; emphasis added).

"Very truly I tell you, whoever hears my word and believes him who sent me has eternal life and will not be judged but has crossed over from death to life" (John 5:24). "Dear children, continue in him, so that when he appears we may be *confident and unashamed* before him at his coming" (1 John 2:28; emphasis added). "This is how love is made complete among us so that we will have *confidence* on the day of judgment" (1 John 4:17; emphasis added). Both of the texts from 1 John underline that faithful, dedicated Christians should have bold confidence (Greek: *parrēsia*) and assurance for the day of judgment and Jesus' coming.

The apostle Paul underlines that when we are in Christ, we are His and no one can stand against or separate us from the love of God: "Therefore, there is now *no condemnation* for those who are in Christ Jesus" (Romans 8:1; emphasis added; see also verses 31–39; Ephesians 2:4–7). In a crystal-clear way, the apostle John proclaims, "Whoever has the Son *has* life; whoever does not have the Son of God does not have life. I write these things to you who believe in the name of the Son of God so that you may *know* that you *have* eternal life" (1 John 5:12, 13; emphasis added; see also John 1:12; 3:16, 17, 36; 6:47; 10:28, 29; Romans 5:1–5; Ephesians 2:1–14; 1 John 1:7–9; 2:1; 3:1). Surprisingly often, the Bible speaks about eternal life in the present tense. We have salvation here and now; of course, by faith—only at the second coming of Jesus will it be a physical reality.

There are two extreme attitudes toward God's marvelous gift of salvation. One group of Christians has *too little or no assurance* of salvation and experiences internal struggles with doubts, frustrations, and fears. The other group has *too much assurance* and is asleep on the pillow of self-assurance and self-deception.[10] Where does the balance lie? Only the Word of God can provide it—living in harmony with the revealed will of God by His grace and the power of the Holy Spirit. Long ago, Socrates famously asserted that "the unexamined life is not worth living."[11] The apostle Paul also encourages healthy introspection: "Examine yourselves to see whether you are in the faith; test yourselves. Do you not realize that Christ Jesus is in you—unless, of course, you fail the test?" (2 Corinthians 13:5; cf. 1 Corinthians 11:28).

Ellen G. White very vividly paints the assurance of salvation for Christ's followers: "If you give yourself to Him, and accept Him as your Saviour, then, sinful as your life may have been, for His sake you are accounted righteous. Christ's character stands in place of your character, and you are accepted before God just as if you had not sinned."[12] Her statement that "there is danger in taking the position that many do take in saying, 'I am saved' "[13] is often taken out of context, and her intention is distorted. She wants to stress that one should not live in a false assurance by claiming to be saved and then disobeying the explicit commandments of God: "God's holy law is the only thing by which we can determine whether we are keeping his way or not. If we are disobedient, our characters are out of harmony with God's moral rule of government, and it is stating a falsehood to say, 'I am saved.' No one is saved who is a transgressor of the law of God, which is the foundation of his government in heaven and in earth."[14]

She further warns against self reliance and cheap grace:[15] "All those who say, 'I am saved! I am saved!' but do not obey God's commandments, are resting their salvation on a false hope, a false foundation. No one who has an intelligent knowledge of the requirements of God, can be saved in disobedience."[16] She powerfully explains, "The gospel does not weaken the claims of the law; it exalts the law and makes it honorable. Under the New Testament, no less is required than was required under the Old Testament. Let no one take up with the delusion so pleasant to the natural heart, that God will accept of sincerity.... God requires of His child perfect obedience."[17]

In this sense, Ellen G. White clearly warns against the idea of "once saved, always saved" and explains the issue in the context of staying vigilant in faith:

We are never to rest in a satisfied condition, and cease to make advance-

ment, saying, "I am saved." When this idea is entertained, the motives for watchfulness, for prayer, for earnest endeavor to press onward to higher attainments, cease to exist. No sanctified tongue will be found uttering these words till Christ shall come, and we enter in through the gates into the city of God. Then, with the utmost propriety, we may give glory to God and to the Lamb for eternal deliverance. As long as man is full of weakness,—for of himself he cannot save his soul,—he should never dare to say, "I am saved." ... It is he that endureth unto the end that shall be saved.[18]

She further explains that in the matter of salvation we cannot rely on our feelings; we are saved because God said so, not because we feel we have salvation: "There are many who conclude that they are saved, simply because they have good impressions; but this is not enough. The entire affection must be renovated. Every individual must learn by experimental knowledge where lies his true strength. No one can leave his first love without a forfeiture of the Christian character."[19]

On the other hand, Ellen G. White also states that Christ's followers must have an assurance of salvation: "It is essential to have faith in Jesus, and to believe you are saved through Him."[20] She describes the joy of salvation that the Gentiles who responded to the preaching of the gospel in the early church had: "The Spirit of God accompanied the words that were spoken, and hearts were touched.... And the speaker's words of assurance that the 'glad tidings' of salvation were for Jew and Gentile alike, brought hope and joy to those who had not been numbered among the children of Abraham according to the flesh."[21] Study carefully Ellen G. White's warning against self confidence as well as her words on the assurance of salvation we have *only* in Christ:

> Those who accept the Saviour, however sincere their conversion, should never be taught to say or to feel that they are saved. This is misleading. Every one should be taught to cherish hope and faith; but even when we give ourselves to Christ and *know that He accepts us*, we are not beyond the reach of temptation. . . .
>
> Those who accept Christ, and in their first confidence say, I am saved, are in danger of trusting to themselves. They lose sight of their own weakness and their constant need of divine strength. They are unprepared for Satan's devices, and under temptation many, like Peter, fall into the very depths of sin. We are admonished, "Let him that thinketh he standeth, take heed lest he fall." 1 Corinthians 10:12. *Our only safety is in constant distrust of self, and dependence on Christ.*[22]

As followers of Christ, we need to learn how to live in the healthy tension every sincere believer experiences—full confidence in Christ and complete mistrust in self. It is not easy to balance this paradox of our faith and avoid the extreme positions that lie on both ends. We need to be constantly focused on Him: "We are to be found day by day abiding in the Vine, and bringing forth fruit, with patience, at our home, in our business; and in every relation in life manifesting the Spirit of Christ."[23] In this process, we need to look persistently to Jesus (John 15:5; Philippians 4:13; Hebrews 12:2) and not concentrate on ourselves and the fruit-bearing, which is the natural result of cultivating a close fellowship with Him: "Connected with Jesus Christ, they will be wise unto salvation. They will be fruit-bearing trees."[24]

Unfortunately, many are not sure whether they are saved in Christ and are constantly baffled by fear and plagued with doubts regarding whether they will be able to go through the last-day events victoriously. Instead, we must know how to consciously live in a steady pressure of "already" but "not yet." We have eternal life but not yet; we are saved but not yet; we are perfect in Christ but not yet; we sit with Christ by the right side of the heavenly Father but not yet. Thus, we can experience the true joy of salvation. We need to wait for the second coming of Christ when we will see Him face-to-face because then our present hope of redemption will become tangibly factual.

3. God's apocalyptic sealing—at any time?

It is significant to realize that God's closing the cases of the saints of the Most High who will live through the final end-time crisis and presenting them to the innumerable representatives of heavenly beings during the pre-Advent judgment (see Daniel 7; 8) is one and the same event as their receiving the apocalyptic seal (Revelation 7:1–4), even though these are described from two different perspectives. The final affirmation in heaven of those who will be alive to greet Jesus at His second coming is the time of receiving the apocalyptic seal.

Questions then arise: When, precisely, will the believer who will be alive at the second coming of Christ receive the apocalyptic seal of the Living God? Does the Bible teach that the cases of the living can be brought before God at any time during the pre-Advent judgment before the close of probation? These are troubling questions for many. If our names can be presented to the heavenly court at any time, it looks as though it would be unfair: "God appears hard, unjust, and arbitrary. Why should He finalize on a person's destiny prior to the close of probation, since life has not ended and that person still possesses the power of choice?"[25]

God certainly judges according to an individual's decision. At the time of the end, there will be such pressing circumstances that people will have to decide on which side they stand—with God or with the forces of evil, presented in the book of Revelation as the dragon, the beast out of the sea, the beast out of the earth, the image of the beast, and the false prophet (see Revelation 13–18). The book of Revelation mentions God's activity of the sealing of His people in the time of the end (Revelation 7:1–4) and warns against receiving the mark of the beast (Revelation 14:9–11).

On the basis of biblical teaching, which is expanded in Ellen G. White's writings, one may conclude that the apocalyptic seal is given to God's faithful followers only after the final global crisis, immediately before the close of probation. At that time, the image of the beast is formed and the forceful demands of that power are presented. Ellen G. White explains,

> The image of the beast will be formed before probation closes; for it is to be the great test for the people of God, by which their eternal destiny will be decided. . . .
>
> This is the test that the people of God must have *before they are sealed.* All who prove their loyalty to God by observing His law, and refusing to accept a spurious sabbath, will rank under the banner of the Lord God Jehovah, and will *receive the seal of the living God.* Those who yield the truth of heavenly origin and accept the Sunday sabbath, will receive the mark of the beast.[26]

Ellen G. White also teaches more specifically when the mark of the beast will be received:

> No one has yet received the mark of the beast. The testing time has not yet come. There are true Christians in every church, not excepting the Roman Catholic communion. None are condemned until they have had the light and have seen the obligation of the fourth commandment. But when the decree shall go forth enforcing the counterfeit sabbath, and the loud cry of the third angel shall warn men against the worship of the beast and his image, the line will be clearly drawn between the false and the true. Then those who still continue in transgression will re-

ceive the mark of the beast.

With rapid steps we are approaching this period. When Protestant churches shall unite with the secular power to sustain a false religion, for opposing which their ancestors endured the fiercest persecution, then will the papal sabbath be enforced by the combined authority of church and state. There will be a national apostasy, which will end only in national ruin.[27]

Ellen G. White also explicitly proclaims, "Sundaykeeping is not yet the mark of the beast, and will not be until the decree goes forth causing men to worship this idol sabbath. The time will come when this day will be the test, but that time has not come yet."[28]

The assertion that the name of a believer might be taken into judgment at any time before the close of probation and sealed for eternity is thus not correct on several grounds: (1) the eschatological sealing comes only after apostate Protestantism unites with Catholicism and enforces the keeping of Sunday; (2) the Sunday law will be a catalyst to cause people to choose between God's law or human demands, to make their final decision for or against God, His law, and His people; and (3) only then will the seal of God or the mark of the beast be given to people corporately. Douglas Bennett explains this crucial point very well when he states, "It seems appropriate to suggest that the close of probation will occur for all the living [nearly] simultaneously and that this can only be after all the living have met a supreme test that exposes the true condition

of each heart before the universe."[29]

Today there is still time to prepare oneself and others for the final crisis by preaching the gospel, educating, teaching, and serving others so that they will be ready to stand before the Son of man at His second coming. God's apocalyptic sealing of the living will not occur at just any time but only after the final test. Those who have chosen God's side will be approved, affirmed at the heavenly court (Daniel 7:9, 10, 13, 14).

4. Living without the Holy Spirit after the close of probation

Another myth in Adventism is built on a serious misinterpretation of biblical teaching as well as of the Spirit of Prophecy; namely, that the Holy Spirit is gradually withdrawing from our world until He will be completely absent and humans will be left without Him. Some assume that everyone, including believers after the close of probation, will be without His help. This erroneous belief is based on a misunderstanding of a statement by Ellen G. White that, if studied in context, shows that she was talking about the Holy Spirit gradually leaving the *wicked* world. She writes, "All fornicators will be outside the City of God. Already God's angels are at work in judgment, and *the Spirit of God is gradually leaving the world*. The triumph of the church is very near, the reward to be bestowed is almost within our reach, and yet iniquity is found among those who claim to have the full blaze of heaven's light."[30] Also carefully study the following quotations:

The days in which we live are solemn and important. *The Spirit of God is grad-*

ually but surely being withdrawn from the earth. Plagues and judgments are already falling upon the *despisers* of the grace of God. . . .

The agencies of evil are combining their forces, and consolidating. . . . Great changes are soon to take place in our world, and the final movements will be rapid ones.[31]

"The restraining Spirit of God is even now being withdrawn from the world. Hurricanes, storms, tempests, fire and flood, disasters by sea and land, follow each other in quick succession."[32] "The time is at hand when there will be sorrow in the world that no human balm can heal. The Spirit of God is being withdrawn."[33]

"*The wicked* have passed the boundary of their probation; the Spirit of God, persistently resisted, has been at last withdrawn. Unsheltered by divine grace, they have no protection from the wicked one. Satan will then plunge the inhabitants of the earth into one great, final trouble."[34]

"So when the irrevocable decision of the sanctuary has been pronounced and *the destiny of the world* has been forever fixed, the inhabitants of the earth will know it not. *The forms of religion will be continued by a people from whom the Spirit of God has been finally withdrawn.*"[35]

Thus, it is very evident that Ellen G. White underlines that the Holy Spirit is withdrawn from the *wicked* world. But He will stay with God's faithful followers in even more abundant measure to transform them into God's image and enable them to accomplish God's given mission. Already in *Early Writings*, Ellen G. White explains

that the outpouring of the Holy Spirit at the very end will have two functions: (1) to finish the preaching of the gospel before the second coming of Christ; and (2) to help the saints go through the perilous period of the seven plagues.[36] Believers will never live without the Holy Spirit. The latter rain of the Holy Spirit will be given in abundance to them (Joel 2:23, 28, 29).

Jesus Christ explains this truth explicitly in the parable of the ten virgins (Matthew 25:1–13). Only the five wise virgins had oil in abundance, sustaining the flame of their lamps (i.e., their living relationship with Christ); because of this oil, they were ready to welcome the Bridegroom and enter into the joy of His wedding. The oil represents the transforming power of the Holy Spirit of God, who enables people to be true lights and to obey God (Ezekiel 36:25–27).[37] Those believers who allow God to change their characters are sealed by the Spirit for the final victory. It will be the Holy Spirit who will carry them victoriously through the final short period of crisis: "The time of trouble, trouble such as was not since there was a nation [Daniel 12:1], is right upon us, and we are like the sleeping virgins. We are to awake and ask the Lord Jesus to place underneath us His everlasting arms, and *carry us through* the time of trial before us."[38] Paul states that "those who are led by the Spirit of God are the children of God" (Romans 8:14). We do not need to fear that we will fail because we are completely in God's hands.

5. Living without an Intercessor

How often I have heard in different congregations of our church the thought that believers will be on their own when they have to live without an Intercessor after probation ends. This half-truth is related to the erroneous thinking that the end-time apocalyptic sealing and the closure of our cases in the heavenly judgment before the second coming of Christ are two different events. In reality, however, they are distinct, though closely related.

When our names are called during the pre-Advent judgment, Jesus as the True Witness of our lives presents our principal choices, deep convictions, and life orientation before the universe's representatives (Daniel 7:9, 10, 13, 14). If we are found hidden "in Christ," then our destiny is sealed with the seal of the Living God, and we will be protected from the seven last plagues and be ready for the second coming of Christ. After probation, when the door of mercy has closed, Jesus Christ will no longer be our Mediator because He has already saved us "completely" (Hebrews 7:25). The fact that Jesus will no longer serve as our Mediator, however, is often interpreted to mean that at this time believers will have to live without God's help, so they must develop a strong character and a firm will in order to go victoriously through the final crisis while the evil forces will no longer be restrained by God's mercy (Revelation 7:1–3; 14:9–11; 15:6–8). Such an interpretation of the end-time scenario is false.

It is true that Jesus Christ will no longer perform His mediatorial ministry for His people when probation closes, but this does not mean that they will live independently of Him nor that He will forsake them. Jesus never abandons His followers (see John 10:27, 28; 15:5; etc.), and even though they will live at this time without His special intercessory work (they are already saved by His grace), they will never for one moment live without Christ's presence and power. By then, every sincere believer will have decided to live in total dependence upon God and will have chosen to trust and love Him, and this close relationship will continue and grow throughout all eternity.

During Jacob's night struggle with the preincarnate Jesus, Christ's presence with him was closer than before, and as a result, he received His blessing and "saw God face to face" (see Genesis 32:24–30; cf. Jeremiah 30:7). Jacob's victorious wrestling with God is a type of the faith experience of Christ's followers at the time of the end. The real struggles of faith bring Christ's faithful even closer to Him. This fellowship of love, faith, and hope with our Lord Jesus Christ will never be broken or interrupted. Even in the time of trouble, our faith will continue to grow, and Jesus will cover our sinful nature with His merits until we are glorified at the Second Coming (1 Corinthians 15:50–57; Philippians 1:6; 3:12–15, 20, 21; 1 John 3:2–5; Jude 24, 25).[39]

To live without a Mediator, then, does not mean to live without the sustaining and empowering grace of Christ through the help of the Holy Spirit (Daniel 12:1; Hebrews 4:16), because without His help we are powerless (John 15:5; Philippians 4:13). Believers will continually need divine assistance in order to stand against the forces of evil (Revelation 12:17; 17:14). In other words, believers will never be on their own, because they are not able to resist evil by their own strength. Jesus is their only power and security (Romans 1:16, 17; 8:1–5;

1 Corinthians 1:18, 22–24, 30; 2:2), and He has promised to be with His people until the very end of the world (Matthew 28:20).

Amazingly, not only will Jesus be with His followers but so also will the Holy Spirit and even the Father as well (Isaiah 57:15; 66:2). The presence of the Father will be marked by the help of His angels (Psalm 34:7; Hebrews 1:14). Paul aptly declares, "Being confident of this, that he who began a good work in you will carry it on to completion until the day of Christ Jesus" (Philippians 1:6).[40]

Summary

I have argued in this chapter that the five interpretations of the Bible and the Spirit of Prophecy that were presented are in error for the following reasons:

1. There are two seals of God. The seal of God is not given only once, as many assume. The seal of the gospel, salvation, is given at the beginning of our spiritual journey with Christ, and the apocalyptic protective seal is later given to those who will thereafter live through the final crisis. This latter seal affirms that those who receive it unselfishly serve others, earnestly seek to save people for eternity, and love God, His law, and His values. Each seal has a unique but complementary role. Only those who received the first seal can receive the second one. Thus, only those who are sealed by the gospel seal can be marked at the end of time by the eschatological seal that will protect them in the time of trouble when probation is closed. It is a seal of life in the midst of destruction and ruin; it is a seal of final redemption.

2. The Bible presents the assurance of

salvation. God is for us and never against us. He saves us completely. We may know that we have eternal life and have passed from death to life. We can even now rejoice in the gift of salvation. We can have a bold assurance, because this assurance comes from God, based on what He accomplished for us, not on our achievements. We need only to stay in Christ and dwell every day in Him (see John 5:24; 1 John 2:28; 3:1–5). Assurance of salvation is always in view of Jesus' work and His merits and in maintaining a living, trustful relationship with God. Salvation is never dependent upon us, our performance and works, because they are the fruits of our redemption in Christ Jesus. Good deeds are important for the salvation of others but not for our salvation.

3. The apocalyptic sealing will not occur at just any time, but only after the Sunday law is issued and people make their decision for or against God. The final Sabbath-Sunday controversy will result in an outward expression of either loyalty and love for God or obedience to the ungodly powers aimed against Him, His law, and His people (Revelation 17:15).

4. The Holy Spirit will never be taken away from believers. On the contrary, the Spirit will be given to them in an even greater portion, and it will be the Holy Spirit who will carry them through the final time of crisis. The Holy Spirit will leave the wicked, stubborn world, but we will be safe in God's hands.

5. Genuine believers will never live without Christ—only without His special intercessory ministry after the close of probation. He secured our salvation on the cross, and we do not need to worry about being abandoned without His sustaining grace. During Jacob's fight when the patriarch was wrestling with God, the Lord was closer to him than ever. This will be the experience of God's people after probation is closed. They will be empowered by Jesus' constant presence as Jacob was sustained and blessed by Him.

Conclusion

These five myths, although believed by some in Adventism, are not biblically substantiated or sustainable. We can face tomorrow with full confidence because we are in God's hands and He is in ultimate control of our lives and world events. We can trust Him, and our destiny depends on this relationship between us and our gracious and holy Lord. We can rely on the firm prophetic Word of God and look forward with hope. The hope of the second coming of Jesus is called the "blessed" hope (Titus 2:13), so we can rejoice in this life, having full confidence in Him (1 John 2:28; 4:17), having our eyes fixed on Jesus (Hebrews 12:2). This is why we do not need to listen to different conspiracy theories regarding last-day scenarios, but rather we need to cultivate God's presence in our lives and serve others with joy (Revelation 14:6, 7). God is in charge and in ultimate control, and we can fully trust Him. We do not need to be, and should not be, *fear-centered* Seventh-day Adventist Christians

but a *hope-centered* people. The return of Jesus is the ultimate good news for humanity; He is the only way to the bright future.

God does not want to keep people from heaven. He is not a goalie trying to protect His kingdom, allowing only a few to enter. He wants all to be saved (1 Timothy 2:3, 4) because He has no delight in the death of the wicked (Ezekiel 18:23, 32). Punishment is a strange act for Him (Isaiah 28:21) because He is the God of life (Deuteronomy 30:20). Isaiah expressed the Lord's desire exceptionally well:

> Yet the Lord longs to be gracious to you;
>   therefore he will rise up to show you
>   compassion.
> For the Lord is a God of justice.
>   Blessed are all who wait for him!
>   (Isaiah 30:18).

Thus, correct theology always culminates in doxology. Paul relevantly declares, "Praise be to the God and Father of our Lord Jesus Christ, who has blessed us in the heavenly realms with every spiritual blessing in Christ" (Ephesians 1:3), and again, "Now to him who is able to do immeasurably more than all we ask or imagine, according to his power that is at work within us, to him be glory in the church and in Christ Jesus throughout all generations, for ever and ever! Amen" (Ephesians 3:20).

Endnotes

1. An excellent book on self-deception was published by Gregg A. Ten Elshof, *I Told Me So: Self-Deception and the Christian Life* (Grand Rapids, MI: Eerdmans, 2009).

2. *Esphragisthēte* is a verb (indicative aorist passive second person plural) that means "you were sealed" or "marked" (from the Greek verb *sphragizō*, "to seal, secure with a seal, mark with a seal, set apart by a seal, affix to be true, acknowledged, proved") and is speaking about a community of faith—believers in Christ Jesus.

3. Biblical quotations in this chapter are from the NIV, unless otherwise noted.

4. Ellen G. White, *The Adventist Home* (Washington, DC: Review and Herald®, 1980), 188.

5. The presence of the Holy Spirit in the lives of believers is not only evidence of one's present salvation in Christ but also a pledge and guarantee of one's future inheritance and a down payment on that inheritance. Paul speaks also about having the firstfruits of the Spirit: "Not only so, but we ourselves, who have the firstfruits of the Spirit, groan inwardly as we wait eagerly for our adoption to sonship, the redemption of our bodies. For in this hope we were saved. But hope that is seen is no hope at all. Who hopes for what they already have?" (Romans 8:23, 24).

6. Ephesians 4:30 is mentioned among the list of exhortations. The reference to "the day of redemption" in this verse is Paul's unique emphasis in the epistle to the Ephesians and in its context points to the second coming of Christ (see Ephesians 1:14).

7. " 'In Christ' with its 164 occurrences, 36 of which are in Ephesians, is much more likely the central motif, or at least *a* central motif in Paul." Klyne Snodgrass, *Ephesians*, The NIV Application Commentary (Grand Rapids, MI: Zondervan, 1996), 57 (emphasis in original).

8. Ranko Stefanovic, *Plain Revelation: A Reader's Introduction to the Apocalypse* (Berrien Springs, MI: Andrews University Press, 2013), 163.

9. For details, see Jiří Moskala, "The Gospel According to God's Judgment: Judgment as Salvation," *Journal of the Adventist Theological Society* 22, no. 1 (2011): 28–49.

10. Ten Elshof, *I Told Me So*.

11. Thomas C. Brickhouse and Nicholas D. Smith, *Plato's Socrates* (Oxford: Oxford University Press, 1994), 201, 202.

12. Ellen G. White, *Steps to Christ* (Mountain View, CA: Pacific Press®, 1956), 62.

13. Ellen G. White, *Selected Messages*, bk. 1 (Washington, DC: Review and Herald®, 1958), 373.

14. Ibid., 315. Also Ellen G. White, "The Truth as It Is in Jesus," *Advent Review and Sabbath Herald*, June 17, 1890, 369.

15. God's grace is never cheap because Christ gave Himself for it, but some treat grace cheaply. See Dietrich Bonhoeffer, *The Cost of Discipleship* (New York: Macmillan, 1959), 43–49.

16. Ellen G. White, " 'If My Words Abide in You,' "

Signs of the Times, December 28, 1891.

17. White, *Selected Messages*, bk. 1, 373, 374.

18. White, "The Truth as It Is in Jesus," 369.

19. Ellen G. White, "Christ Gives Repentance (Concluded.)," *Signs of the Times*, August 18, 1890.

20. White, *Selected Messages*, bk. 1, 373.

21. Ellen G. White, *The Acts of the Apostles* (Mountain View, CA: Pacific Press®, 1911), 172, 173.

22. Ellen G. White, *Christ's Object Lessons* (Battle Creek, MI: Review and Herald®, 1900), 155 (emphasis added). Not only our safety, but that of the whole universe lies in beholding and understanding the meaning of Jesus' sacrifice. It is the effectiveness of what He accomplished on the cross that secures the universe against sin and not our achievements or sinlessness or even that of angels: "The angels ascribe honor and glory to Christ, for even they are not secure except by looking to the sufferings of the Son of God. It is through the efficacy of the cross that the angels of heaven are guarded from apostasy. Without the cross they would be no more secure against evil than were the angels before the fall of Satan." Ellen G. White, "What Was Secured by the Death of Christ," *Signs of the Times*, December 30, 1889, 786. See Ephesians 1:3, 10; Philippians 2:9–11; Colossians 1:19, 20.

23. Ellen G. White, "The Conditions of Fruit Bearing," *Signs of the Times*, April 18, 1892.

24. Ellen G. White, *Daughters of God* (Hagerstown, MD: Review and Herald®, 2005), 16. See also Ellen G. White, *The Desire of Ages* (Mountain View, CA: Pacific Press®, 1940), 674–680.

25. Douglas Bennett, "The Good News About the Judgment of the Living," *Adventist Review*, June 16, 1983, 14.

26. Ellen G. White, Letter 11, 1890, quoted in Ellen G. White Comments, in *The Seventh-day Adventist Bible Commentary*, ed. Francis D. Nichol, vol. 7 (Washington, DC: Review and Herald®, 1957), 976 (emphasis added).

27. Ellen G. White, *Evangelism* (Washington, DC: Review and Herald®, 1946), 234, 235.

28. Ellen G. White, Manuscript 118, 1899, quoted in Ellen G. White Comments, in Nichol, *Seventh-day Adventist Bible Commentary*, 7:977. God has His people in Babylon, which is why He calls them out of this fallen religious system: "Come out of her, *my people*" (Revelation 18:4; emphasis added). We need to love Babylonians while at the same time proclaiming Babylon's fall and denouncing her sins. This is analogous to the well-known statement "Love the sinner, but hate the

sin." We need to relate to other Christians charitably and present God's last message in a very attractive way. Ellen G. White declares, "There needs to be a waking up among God's people, that His work may be carried forward with power. . . . We need to understand that God will add to the ranks of His people men of ability and influence, who are to act their part in warning the world. All in the world are not lawless and sinful. God has many thousands who have not bowed the knee to Baal. There are God-fearing men in the fallen churches. If this were not so, we should not be given the message to bear, 'Babylon the great is fallen, is fallen. . . . Come out of her, My people.' " Ellen G. White, Letter 51, 1902, quoted in *Evangelism*, 558, 559. "Furthermore, in the eighteenth chapter of the Revelation the people of God are called upon to come out of Babylon. According to this scripture, many of God's people must still be in Babylon." Ellen G. White, *The Great Controversy* (Mountain View, CA: Pacific Press®, 1911), 383.

29. Bennett, "Good News," 15.

30. Ellen G. White, *Testimonies to Ministers and Gospel Workers* (Mountain View, CA: Pacific Press®, 1962), 431 (emphasis added).

31. Ellen G. White, *Testimonies for the Church* (Mountain View, CA: Pacific Press®, 1948), 9:11 (emphasis added). Also in White, *Evangelism*, 31, 32.

32. Ellen G. White, *Testimonies for the Church* (Mountain View, CA: Pacific Press®, 1948), 6:408.

33. Ellen G. White, *Prophets and Kings* (Mountain View, CA: Pacific Press®, 1943), 277.

34. White, *The Great Controversy*, 614 (emphasis added).

35. Ibid., 615 (emphasis added).

36. "At that time the 'latter rain,' or refreshing from the presence of the Lord, will come, to give power to the loud voice of the third angel, and prepare the saints to stand in the period when the seven last plagues shall be poured out." Ellen G. White, *Early Writings* (Washington, DC: Review and Herald®, 1945), 86.

37. For details, see White, *Christ's Object Lessons*, 414.

38. Ellen G. White, Letter 54, 1906, quoted in Ellen G. White, *Manuscript Releases*, vol. 3 (Silver Spring, MD: Ellen G. White Estate, 1990), 305 (emphasis added.)

39. The good news is that Jesus Christ regenerates and changes our hearts (John 3:3–5), forgives all our sins (Isaiah 1:16–19; 1 John 1:8, 9), liberates us from the bondage of sin (John 12:31, 32), and transforms our lives (Romans 12:1, 2; 2 Corinthians 5:17; 1 John 3:1–3). If the Son gives freedom, we are indeed free. Sin began with pride but is defeated by humility. There is hope for us, because sin was overcome by the humble person Jesus Christ, who is the guarantor of freedom, peace, and joy. Our sinful nature does not disappear through conversion or repentance; however, our sinful nature, tendencies, or inclinations (inherited or cultivated) can be controlled by the power of the Holy Spirit, His Word, and God's grace (Romans 7:25; 8:1–11). Until the Second Coming, we will have our sinful nature, and only then will believers be completely transformed and receive an incorruptible body (1 Corinthians 15:50–57; Philippians 3:20, 21). We are not able on our own to do good deeds. Good deeds are a result of the transforming power of God's grace and the work of the Holy Spirit (John 1:12; 15:1–5; Romans 1:16, 17; 8:1–4; 1 Corinthians 1:18–25, 30, 31; 2:12–15; Galatians 5:22, 23; Ephesians 2:10; Philippians 4:13; 1 Peter 2:9, 10).

40. For additional insight into how God works with His people from the beginning till the end and sanctifies and helps them, see Philippians 3:12–15; 4:13; Jude 24, 25; 1 Thessalonians 5:23, 24; 2 Thessalonians 3:3; 2 Corinthians 3:5; Revelation 3:10; Hebrews 12:1. See also White, *The Great Controversy*, 615, 623.

13

The Second Coming of Christ: Is There a "Delay"?

Jo Ann Davidson

Modern media news regularly describes a worldwide restlessness and instability. Seventh-day Adventists watching this are reminded of biblical prophecies as they observe turmoil in nature, warring postures in more and more countries, and prevalent skepticism. Even Jesus warned, "When the Son of Man comes, will He really find faith on the earth?" (Luke 18:8).[1]

The last century has witnessed an ever-deepening loss of belief in God, the authority of Scripture, and the church. There has also been a loss of confidence in modern secular ideologies, such as belief in progress, government, politics, and the Enlightenment's ideas of "salvation" (humanity solving any and all problems given enough time). There is little conviction of any life beyond the here and now, with heaven and eternal life dismissed as childish illusions.

Biblical writers, however, present a very different perspective: God is in the shadows, moving human history toward His promise to end the evil dragon's reign and make "all things new" (Revelation 21:5). Scripture opens in Genesis, chapters 1–11, by presenting a historical beginning of this world along with a worldwide flood. On that basis, later biblical writers trace a literal end of this present sinful world with God's righteous kingdom restored.

Biblical prophecies point to major future cosmic events, including judgment and the second coming of Christ—aspects of God's final, definitive acts toward this world. There will be no uninvolved spectators at that time, for the entire world will be affected. The seriousness of the end time is not avoided in Scripture because the final, decisive remedy is certain. Biblical writers also nail down prophecy with their often-repeated, spine-tingling "Thus says the LORD." For God Himself insists,

As the rain and the snow come down
    from heaven,
And do not return there without water-
    ing the earth
And making it bear and sprout,
And furnishing seed to the sower and
    bread to the eater;
So will *My word be which goes forth from
    My mouth;*
It will not return to Me empty,
Without accomplishing what I desire,
And without succeeding in the matter
    for which I sent it (Isaiah 55:10, 11,
    NASB; emphasis added).

Because "last things" center on the second coming of Jesus, attention to them has always been a paramount Seventh-day Adventist concern; it's why we call ourselves "Adventists." This belief is not based on futuristic human constructions, for various biblical writers point to the second advent of Jesus. For example, "According to His promise we are looking for new heavens and a new earth, in which righteousness dwells" (2 Peter 3:13, NASB). Even though human promises and hopes are often disappointing, the prophets insist that both the content and certainty of biblical prophecies can be trusted.

Bible writers do warn against trying to peer into the future. But their concern is always about the source: "Give no regard to mediums and familiar spirits; do not seek after them, to be defiled by them; I am the LORD your God" (Leviticus 19:31). And God explains why:

> Thus says the LORD, your Redeemer,
> And He who formed you from the womb:
> "I am the LORD, who makes all things,
> Who stretches out the heavens all alone,
> Who spreads abroad the earth by Myself;
> Who frustrates the signs of the babblers,
> And drives diviners mad;
> Who turns wise men backward,
> And makes their knowledge foolishness;
> Who confirms the word of His servant,
> And performs the counsel of His mes-
>   sengers" (Isaiah 44:24–26).

Any study of the future must be grounded in God's Word. He is the only One who can guarantee that "none of his words fall to the ground" (1 Samuel 3:19; cf. Isaiah 44:26; Joshua 21:45). Furthermore, in spite of the claims of modern "open theism," God insists that foretelling the future is proof of His divinity:

> "Present your case," the LORD says.
> "Bring forward your strong arguments,"

> The King of Jacob says.
> Let them bring forth and declare to us
>   what is going to take place;
> As for the former events, declare what
>   they were,
> That we may consider them and know
>   their outcome.
> Or announce to us what is coming;
> Declare the things that are going to
>   come afterward,
> That we may know that you are gods
>   (Isaiah 41:21–23, NASB).

> "Remember the former things long past,
> *For I am God, and there is no other;*
> *I am God, and there is no one like Me,*
> *Declaring the end from the beginning,*
> *And from ancient times things which have*
>   *not been done,*
> *Saying, 'My purpose will be established,*
> *And I will accomplish all My good plea-*
>   *sure';...*
> *Truly I have spoken; truly I will bring it to*
>   *pass.*
> *I have planned it, surely I will do it"* (Isaiah
>   46:9–11, NASB; emphasis added).

Divine prediction of the future is not the counterpart of secular fortune-telling. It never deals with whom one should marry or what job one should take or who the next president will be. In the Bible, peering into the future is *never* to satisfy idle curiosity. Divine prediction always deals with the very core of human existence—confrontation with Jesus Christ, who came once as Savior and who will "appear a second time" as "King of kings" (Hebrews 9:28; Revelation 17:14).[2] This second appearance will be the climax of human history and distinguishes the event from secular futurism. Christian expectation is not directed to various unrelated or mystical events in the future—it is directed to Jesus Himself.

In the end, everything will be open before the throne of God and of the Lamb. Life will be revealed *as it really is*, exposing all human deceptions. There will be no more justification of persecution and torture in God's name—as Jesus foretold would happen.[3] All excuses and all motives will be known. Life as it actually happened will be disclosed. In the meantime, we are urged to be "alert and sober," with keen spiritual insight and our minds girded up.[4] Perhaps recalling Christ's parable of the sleeping bridal party, Paul urges, "So then let us not sleep as others do, but let us be alert and sober" (1 Thessalonians 5:6, NASB; cf. 1 Peter 5:8).

But we are still here! And our Christian expectation is sometimes taunted, because Jesus hasn't come yet. After all, He did say some two thousand years ago, "Behold, I am coming quickly" (Revelation 22:7).

Contemporary thinking about eschatology

Because of all the time that has lapsed since Jesus promised to come "quickly," some Christians since the nineteenth century have offered alternative explanations:

- Some have argued that God's kingdom has already appeared, being achieved through human genius as life's problems are resolved. It is assumed, with evolutionary optimism, that all disease will eventually be conquered and political cooperation will halt all wars, and the human condition will continue to improve.[5]

- Others decided that the New Testament teaches that there would be only a short time between Christ's resurrection and His second coming and that any eschatology must be consistent with what has actually transpired. Thus, many centuries later, the New Testament must be outdated and completely wrong.

- Yet others suggested that perhaps the Second Coming already occurred at Christ's resurrection when the earth shook, rocks split, tombs opened, and the bodies of saints were raised (Matthew 27:51–53). Since the cosmic Second Coming has not occurred, the gripping supernatural events of the Resurrection are suggested as marking the "end."[6]

- Some have argued for a "timeless end time," seeing the Second Coming as a symbol of the unending seriousness of every moment of life. There will be no dramatic climax of history, no literal cosmic event. Instead, a decisive moment will come individually for each person with a crucial crisis marking the gravity of God's presence.[7]

Presently, many Christians have determined that Christ's promise to come again has failed, calling for various reinterpretations of His words—anything but a literal, global event.

But this is a dangerous way to think, for connecting the Second Coming to literal salvation acts that have already occurred rejects what the Bible writers have written so explicitly and authoritatively. God is the

Lord of history, and He sovereignly promises an actual glorious cosmic event. Modern reinterpretations of biblical prophecies deprive Christ of His glory!

Perhaps the faith of earlier believers wasn't threatened when Jesus didn't return immediately because they recalled God's former acts in history. All through Scripture, fulfillment of divine promises involves waiting.

Delay in the Old Testament

1. Eve thought the promise of Genesis 3 was to be fulfilled in her firstborn son. "The Saviour's coming was foretold in Eden. When Adam and Eve first heard the promise, they looked for its speedy fulfillment. They joyfully welcomed their first-born son, hoping that he might be the Deliverer. But the fulfillment of the promise tarried."[8]

2. Enoch prophesied divine judgment and the coming of Christ, which didn't happen in his lifetime.[9]

3. The patriarch Job, in the midst of extreme suffering, looked to the future with hope:

> "For I know that my Redeemer lives,
> And He shall stand at last on the earth;
> And after my skin is destroyed, this I
>   know,
> That in my flesh I shall see God,
> Whom I shall see for myself,
> And my eyes shall behold, and not another.
> How my heart yearns within me!" (Job
>   19:25–27).

4. Noah, having never seen rain, warned about a coming flood for 120 years. He was called a fanatic and ridiculed by the scientists of the day.[10] Moreover, after entering the ark, he waited another seven days for the rain to begin, further testing his faith.[11]

5. Abraham and Sarah waited until he was a hundred years old and she was ninety for the first of his promised heirs that were to be "as numerous as the stars in the sky." Yet Abraham died believing the promise (Hebrews 11:12, 13, NIV).

6. Abraham was also told that his progeny would have to endure slavery and wait to be delivered until the iniquity of the Amorites was full.[12] The Exodus was delayed until probation granted to the Amorites ended.[13]

7. The children of Israel, forced into slavery in Egypt, yearned for deliverance for hundreds of years, and "because of the bondage . . . they cried out" and waited for emancipation (Exodus 2:23).

8. Many of the hymns Israel sang in worship begged God for help: "I will say unto God my rock, Why hast thou forgotten me? why go I mourning because of the oppression of the enemy?" (Psalm 42:9, KJV). "How long will the enemy mock you, God? Will the foe revile your name forever? Why do you hold back your hand, your right hand?" (Psalm 74:10, 11, NIV). Their "how long" pleas point to a passing of time that is troubling:

> How long, LORD?
> Will You hide Yourself forever?
> Will Your wrath burn like fire?
> Remember how short my time is;
> For what futility have You created all
>   the children of men?

What man can live and not see death?
Can he deliver his life from the power of
    the grave?

Lord, where are Your former loving-
    kindnesses,
Which You swore to David in Your
    truth? (Psalm 89:46–49).

9. In the book of Isaiah, the question is asked, " 'Watchman, what of the night?' The watchman said: 'The morning comes, and also the night' " (Isaiah 21:11).[14] The answer implies that having to live with delay must not be interpreted as God failing to keep His promise.

10. God also addressed Israel's yearning for deliverance from their Babylonian captivity through His words to Ezekiel:

And the word of the Lord came to me, saying, "Son of man, what is this proverb that you people have about the land of Israel, which says, 'The days are prolonged, and every vision fails'? Tell them therefore, 'Thus says the Lord God: "I will lay this proverb to rest, and they shall no more use it as a proverb in Israel." But say to them, "The days are at hand, and the fulfillment of every vision. For no more shall there be any false vision or flattering divination within the house of Israel. *For I am the Lord. I speak, and the word which I speak will come to pass*; it will no more be postponed; for in your days, O rebellious house, I will say the word and perform it," says the Lord God' " (Ezekiel 12:21–25; emphasis added).

Decades in captivity had passed without deliverance, which led to doubting, to which the Lord responded that none of His words would be delayed any longer (verse 28). Critics may contend that delay implies failure of the divine promises, but God insists differently.

11. After his dramatic visions of the future, Daniel was told he must wait: "You, go your way till the end; for you shall rest and will arise . . . at the end of the days" (Daniel 12:13).

12. Habakkuk despairs of never-ending violence:

O Lord, how long shall I cry,
    And You will not hear?
Even cry out to You, "Violence!"
    And You will not save (Habakkuk 1:2),

to which Yahweh answers:

"Write the vision,
And make it plain on tablets,
That he may run who reads it.
For the vision is yet for an appointed
    time;
But at the end it will speak, and it will
    not lie.
Though it tarries, wait for it;
Because it will surely come,
It will not tarry" (Habakkuk 2:1–3; emphasis added).

13. God explains to His petulant prophet Jonah the reason for His deferred judgment on the violent Ninevites: "Should I not pity Nineveh, that great city, in which are more than one hundred and twenty thousand persons who cannot discern between

their right hand and their left—and much livestock?" (Jonah 4:11). He desires to extend grace to both the morally ignorant Ninevites and their innocent animals.

New Testament "waiting"

1. Martha and Mary told Jesus after their brother Lazarus died, "If You had been here, my brother would not have died" (John 11:21, 32). Jesus did not come at once at their urgent request. He waited and then performed a greater miracle.[15]

2. The parable of the wedding party that sleeps because of the delay of the bridegroom (Matthew 25) hints at an unforeseen passing of time before the wedding. Notably, Jesus gives this "parable of delay" immediately after discussing the future destruction of Jerusalem and the end of the world (Matthew 24).[16]

3. All during Christ's earthly ministry, the disciples kept thinking Jesus would shortly establish His kingdom. Their overpowering disappointment at His crucifixion changed only after Christ's resurrection.

4. After Pentecost and the gift of the Holy Spirit, Peter preached in terms of what is "afar off" when the church began its work between Christ's two advents (Acts 2:39). The pouring out of the Holy Spirit did not mean rejecting belief in the Second Coming. Instead, the persecuted first-century followers of Jesus were included in God's promises to the patriarchs in Hebrews 11: "Therefore we also, since we are surrounded by so great a cloud of witnesses, let us lay aside every weight, and the sin which so easily ensnares us, and let us run *with endurance* the race that is set before us" (Hebrews 12:1; emphasis added). All believers

will share the same glorious destiny, for "none of them [in the Old Testament] received what had been promised, since God had planned something better for us so that only together with us would they be made perfect" (Hebrews 11:39, 40, NIV).

Nowhere in the New Testament is there any suggestion that belief in the Second Coming should be jettisoned. There are indicators that His coming had been expected soon, which caused Paul to counsel the Thessalonians that certain things must happen first (2 Thessalonians 2:1–12). But faith in God's promises was never lost, nor was expectation muffled. The literal death and resurrection of Christ buoyed up the believers' optimism and assured glorious prospects for the future.

5. There were those who scoffed at the second coming of Jesus: "Where is the promise of His coming? For since the fathers fell asleep, all things continue as they were from the beginning of creation" (2 Peter 3:3, 4). Jude also describes "mockers" in the last time (Jude 18) who display haughty certainty in their supposedly irrefutable arguments.

But believers were counseled to beware of such attitudes (2 Peter 3:1, 8, 14, 17). Scoffing reflects a false philosophy of history. Bible writers confront such skeptical understandings and reject the scoffers' illegitimate interpretations. The continuous duration of time is not any kind of divine failure; instead, it is evidence of God's patience. He has promised that evil will never rise again. And He can do this because He will have permitted sin and all its deadly results to be fully displayed, which will leave no sympathy for it anymore.[17]

Biblical promises concerning the future are emphatic and based on God's great mercy: "But do not ignore this one fact, beloved, that with the Lord one day is like a thousand years, and a thousand years are like one day. *The Lord is not slow about his promise as some count slowness, but is patient with you, not wanting any to perish, but all to come to repentance*" (2 Peter 3:8, NRSV; emphasis added). The continuity of time is never evidence of false prophecy.[18] Believers can anticipate Christ's return with all earnestness and diligence (verses 10, 12, 14, 18), for divine promises are certain.

Human existence is a mere "day that has just gone by" (Psalm 90:4–6) compared to God's eternity. We cannot possibly evaluate time from His infinite perspective. God hints at this through the numerous ways of measuring time found in His creation: a fly or a mosquito lives to the ripe old age of three weeks (if not swatted sooner); twelve to fifteen years is considered a full age for domesticated cats and dogs; Jewish tradition points to the divine design of the retina, which receives an upside-down picture of what is seen, to remind us that what is being seen is not the full and correct picture.

6. The apostle Paul instructed the Thessalonians that a series of events must take place prior to Jesus' return (2 Thessalonians 2:1–12).

7. The book of Revelation intimates passing of time. For example, the vision of the "souls under the altar":

And when he had opened the fifth seal, I saw under the altar the souls of them that were slain for the word

of God, and for the testimony which they held: And they cried with a loud voice, saying, How long, O Lord, holy and true, dost thou not judge and avenge our blood on them that dwell on the earth? And white robes were given unto every one of them; and it was said unto them, that they should *rest yet for a little season*, until their fellowservants also and their brethren, that should be killed as they were, should be fulfilled (Revelation 6:9–11, KJV; emphasis added).

Notably, from Genesis to Revelation, there is no call to calculate the exact date for the second coming of Christ. Rather, there is an urgent attentive watching for it, as Jesus invites, "Let your waist be girded and your lamps burning; and you yourselves be like men who wait for their master, when he will return from the wedding, that when he comes and knocks they may open to him immediately" (Luke 12:35, 36). This attitude is contrasted with that of the unfaithful servant who says to himself, "My master is delaying his coming," and so does not bother to get ready (verses 45–47). Although he knew what to do, he was unprepared for his master's arrival.

Ever since the closing of the 2,300-day prophecy of Daniel 8, date setting is not possible, yet Christ's coming should not be unexpected, which gets to the heart of the issue. Jesus declares, "If you will not watch, I will come upon you as a thief, and you will not know what hour I will come upon you" (Revelation 3:3; cf. 1 Thessalonians 5:1, 2). Suddenness will not be a problem for those who have earnestly anticipated the

Lord's return, as Paul wrote to the Thessalonians: "But you, beloved, are not in darkness, for that day to surprise you like a thief" (1 Thessalonians 5:4, NRSV). It does demand constant vigilance and preparation. The danger lies in being careless or forgetful. Jesus referred to this, speaking of those destroyed by the Flood that they were without watchfulness "and knew not until the flood came, and took them all away" (Matthew 24:39, KJV; cf. Luke 17:26–30). In fact, the word regularly translated "quickly" would be more fairly translated "suddenly."

As we wait for the Second Coming, we can become pessimists, doubting the Word of God and suggesting false interpretations of His promises. Or we can settle into denial with the scoffers who think heaven is an illusion. But the sentiment of Scripture is very different:

> The voice of one crying in the wilderness:
> "Prepare the way of the LORD;
> Make straight in the desert
> A highway for our God.
> Every valley shall be exalted
> And every mountain and hill brought low;
> The crooked places shall be made straight
> And the rough places smooth;
> The glory of the LORD shall be revealed,
> And all flesh shall see it together;
> For the mouth of the LORD has spoken"
> (Isaiah 40:3–5).

This is a royal announcement heralding the arriving King. The composer Handel was challenged to write music to these glorious words.[19] Other hymn writers also wanted to exalt the Second Coming: "Lift up the trumpet, and loud let it ring! Jesus is coming again!"[20] "Lo, He comes, with clouds descending!"[21] "Wake, awake, for night is flying,"[22] and "Watch, ye saints, with eyelids waking!"[23]

On the other side of the coin

While we wait, we must not fall into another mistaken notion: thinking that the timing of the Second Coming is dependent on us reaching some standard of perfection:

- There are those who argue that Jesus has not yet returned because of His less-than-perfect followers—that if only there had been more concentrated efforts on reaching perfection, Jesus would have come by now. This position is often linked to a quote from Ellen G. White: "When the character of Christ shall be perfectly reproduced in His people, then He will come to claim them as His own."[24]
- Others suggest that Christ could have come earlier if believers had been more diligent to carry out the divine commission of witnessing—that because we haven't, the "delay" continues.

But these perspectives do not manifest an adequate understanding of Scripture or of Ellen G. White. Will there ever be a time when we will be good enough for Jesus to come? This is a critical issue.

A fundamental principle for interpreting Scripture (and for interpreting Ellen G.

White, who constantly turns us to Scripture) needs to be reviewed. The Old and New Testaments are a complete system of truth. Thus, the entire canon must be carefully studied to correctly understand what it actually teaches. In this case, understanding what it means to be ready when Jesus returns must be informed by more than one text and/or quotation.

For example, the Old Testament highlights Moses as a lawgiver, the spokesperson for God. He received, wrote down, taught, applied, and expounded God's law, often repeating God's call for commitment to His law. And Moses was fully aware of the dangers of legalism and hypocrisy. His great desire was that Israel might come to know the grace and love of God by the circumcision of the *heart* (Deuteronomy 30:6) and that by responding to His grace they would keep His commands (verse 10). By means of the law, they could get a correct sense of what sin is and, by asking for forgiveness, become a people privileged to enjoy God's holy presence. The law was a gift of God (Romans 9:4) and a positive means of instructing His children how to abide in His presence (Leviticus 26:11-13; cf. 2 Timothy 3:16, 17). But believers always need to be covered by Christ's righteousness. No one can ever be good enough to be saved, as the opening words of the Decalogue underscore:

And God spoke all these words, saying:

"I am the LORD your God, who brought you out of the land of Egypt, out of the house of bondage. You shall have no other gods before Me" (Exodus 20:1-3).

Obedience to the law has never been the way to earn salvation. God states at the outset of the Decalogue that He is first a Savior and Deliverer from slavery![25] First, He saved Israel from Egypt, and then He spoke His law to them. This sequence is significant.

There on Mount Sinai God covenanted Himself to a certain group of people—people who had not distinguished themselves by being good and faithful. But Yahweh chose them, which had nothing to do with any of their spiritual attainments. The opposite is true. They were selected in spite of themselves; for if there is one thing noticeable about the children of Israel, it is that they did not deserve their election, even falling into deep apostasy just after their covenant with God had been established at Mount Sinai.[26]

The great apostle Paul also insisted that the only reason anyone can be saved is because God, in His bountiful grace, declares that the person is righteous through Christ Jesus.[27] Paul's endless thankfulness for God's grace is a lesson many Christians need to learn, enabling believers to come a long way toward truly appreciating the gospel.

When Paul insists, "There is no distinction" (Romans 10:12), he means that before God there is no distinction between Jew and Gentile, godly and ungodly, believer and pagan, "good guys" and "bad guys." All are in bondage to the power of sin. Being "religious" does not do any good, nor does being "spiritual." Paul is clear: there is nothing we can do about our sinful nature; we cannot free ourselves from its imprisoning grip. Romans 7 carefully spells this out; as that great evangelist Paul concludes, "Who will deliver me from this body of death?" (verse 24). Repentance is a sign of the Holy Spirit at work in us, convicting us of sin[28] so that we can repent and find and accept God's amazing grace.

Every one of us is a condemned sinner until Jesus comes. Because sin is very blinding, this crucial insight does not come easily. We need to look unblinkingly at sin and its power even in the lives of "good" Christians, for even our very best is tainted by sin.[29] All of us, even the most fervent believers, will ever need the justifying grace that God offers to sinners:

> But we are all like an unclean thing,
> And all our righteousnesses are like filthy
>   rags;
> We all fade as a leaf,
> And our iniquities, like the wind,
> Have taken us away (Isaiah 64:6; emphasis added).

Martin Luther understood this, stating that we need to repent even for our good deeds. Thomas Cranmer knew this, confessing: "We have erred, and strayed from [God's] ways like lost sheep. We have followed too much the devices and desires of my own heart."[30] This is not easy to admit. All of us, even "good" Christians, participate to one degree or another in some form of denial, keeping consciousness of our sinfulness at bay. The true blunder is to fail to recognize this. The truly tragic person is not the one who commits a crime or causes harm to others. The truly tragic person is the "good" person who finds it hard to acknowledge that even our good deeds need forgiveness because of what Ellen G. White

terms our "corrupt channels of humanity":

The religious services, the prayers, the praise, the penitent confession of sin ascend from true believers as incense to the heavenly sanctuary, but passing through the corrupt channels of humanity, they are so defiled that unless purified by blood, they can never be of value with God. They ascend not in spotless purity, and unless the Intercessor, who is at God's right hand, presents and purifies all by His righteousness, it is not acceptable to God. All incense from earthly tabernacles must be moist with the cleansing drops of the blood of Christ. He holds before the Father the censer of His own merits, in which there is no taint of earthly corruption. He gathers into this censer the prayers, the praise, and the confessions of His people, and with these He puts His own spotless righteousness. Then, perfumed with the merits of Christ's propitiation, the incense comes up before God wholly and entirely acceptable. Then gracious answers are returned.

Oh, that all may see that everything in obedience, in penitence, in praise and thanksgiving, must be placed upon the glowing fire of the righteousness of Christ. The fragrance of this righteousness ascends like a cloud around the mercy seat.[31]

Paul uses the word *justification* more often than the word *forgiveness*, meaning that we sinners will not only be forgiven, we will also be justified—declared righteous by God! Because of the sacrifice of Jesus, who took the sentence of our condemnation upon Himself, grace is bestowed on us. This is the grand news of the Christian faith. Connected with the grace we receive will come the discovery that we are among those who have not only been forgiven but also reckoned righteous by God through faith in Jesus. There is not one of us who can claim any sort of special merit for who we are or what we do. Rather, we are part of the worldwide human family of sinners who daily need to rediscover our utter dependence on the faithfulness and mercy of God. One hymn writer caught this biblical teaching: "Just as I am, without one plea, but that Thy blood was shed for me, and that Thou bid'st me come to Thee . . ."[32]

This means that we need to understand that we are not just those who commit a little error here and a minor mistake there. No; all of us are fully embedded in a world of ungodliness. We are not innocent bystanders to the sinfulness of the human race. If we aren't aware of the degree to which sin undermines even the most noble of our efforts, we will find ourselves in a type of self-righteousness and will not even notice that we continue to fail God and people and need to repent. We will never be able to hold up our characters and our good deeds as something to be proud of. None of us will ever be able to claim to be heirs of His promises as a reward for our righteousness.

The biblical narratives of those who followed God clearly illustrate this. Notice the statement about Abraham: "He believed the LORD; and the LORD reckoned it to him as righteousness" (Genesis 15:6, NRSV), or "Abram put his faith in the LORD, who

reckoned it to him as righteousness" (REB). At that time, Abraham was eighty-five years old (Genesis 16:3, 16). Fourteen years before his circumcision (Genesis 17:24), Abraham was "reckoned" righteous by God! After that, he deliberately deceived Abimelech. This helps us to understand the maturing process of sanctification. Even Abraham, who is noticeably highlighted in the "Faith Hall of Fame" of Hebrews 11, could never claim perfection. He was constantly growing in his relationship with God.

And God expects from those who walk with Him nothing less than He expected from Enoch, Noah, and Abraham—namely, perfection. God's standard of righteousness is not lowered as sanctification continues. The meaning of *tamim*, "perfect" (e.g., Genesis 17:1), signifies "integrity" and "maturity," as further defined in Psalms 15:2; 24:4; and Micah 6:8. This is what Jesus wants from His followers—the *pursuit* of holiness, justice, righteousness, love, and peace.

We need to understand the divine definitions of *good* and *bad* and how good we need to be to qualify as "good." For "bad" is something more than "missing the mark" (as *hamartia* is usually defined) or transgressing the law. Biblical narratives reveal that sin is much more serious than this; being "good" is much more than a matter of merely "not sinning."

Sin is not defined by comparing ourselves to others, like the Pharisee Jesus described: "God, I thank You that I am not like other men—extortioners, unjust, adulterers, or even as this tax collector" (Luke 18:11). The Pharisee did not understand that sin cannot be defined by any human standard but only by grasping how deeply every person is embedded and entangled in the deadly condition of sin. We are not merely victims of sin but actual inhabitants. In the final judgment, we won't be able to fall back on such excuses as, "Nobody's perfect," or "We all make mistakes." Sin is the universal human condition, and because it is so blinding, it never will become fully obvious to us unless we constantly align ourselves with God. "Fallen man is not simply an imperfect creature who needs improvement; he is a rebel who must lay down his arms."[33] Only as we cling to Jesus in repentance will this ever become clear.

Perhaps modern casual familiarity with the divine has brought about this corresponding effect of a dampened conviction of our sinful nature. Exposure to God's naked, unveiled, overwhelming glory would quickly correct this superficial thinking. Recall that whenever Jesus' divinity flashed through humanity, people were thrown to the ground,[34] for there is a humanly unbridgeable, fatally serious abyss between a holy God of righteousness and sinful humanity.

This is illustrated in the Sermon on the Mount. When confident believers hold up their "good deeds," Jesus responds that He does not know them (Matthew 7:21–23). Those who think they are "good enough" are going to learn that they built on the wrong foundation. Those who have been merely "religious" are going to discover that God was looking for something else. And those who counted on their "goodness" will learn that some people whom they thought were not "good enough" will be given salvation.

Throughout history, Christians seem to have become accustomed to an accommodating standard of righteousness far below the holiness of God. But Ellen G. White instructs that true growth in sanctification is a painful process:

> The closer you come to Jesus, the more faulty you will appear in your own eyes; for your vision will be clearer, and your imperfections will be seen in broad and distinct contrast to His perfect nature. This is evidence that Satan's delusions have lost their power; that the vivifying influence of the Spirit of God is arousing you.
>
> No deep-seated love for Jesus can dwell in the heart that does not realize its own sinfulness. The soul that is transformed by the grace of Christ will admire His divine character; but if we do not see our own moral deformity, it is unmistakable evidence that we have not had a view of the beauty and excellence of Christ.[35]

Growth in sanctification by a true follower of Jesus will always be experienced as an ever increasing consciousness of one's sinfulness. The biblical narratives disclose that those who truly grew in grace were precisely those who most intensely sensed their human sinfulness. There was no self-applause of personal goodness. The great apostle Paul understood this: "This is a faithful saying and worthy of all acceptance, that Christ Jesus came into the world to save sinners, of whom I am chief" (1 Timothy 1:15). Even the prophet Daniel, of whom nothing sinful is recorded in Scripture, prayed to be forgiven. And Ellen G. White urges Daniel's example as something we need to learn from: "As we have clearer views of Christ's spotless and infinite purity we shall feel as did Daniel when he beheld the glory of the Lord and said: 'My comeliness was turned in me into corruption' (Daniel 10:8). We cannot say, 'I am sinless' till this vile body is changed and fashioned like unto His glorious body. But if we constantly seek to follow Jesus, the blessed hope is ours of standing before the throne of God without spot, or wrinkle, or any such thing, *complete in Christ, robed in His righteousness and perfection.*"[36]

One pastor recalls his experience of growing in sanctification:

> The first church I served in called me back to preach twenty-five years after I left. On my way to the church . . . I remembered how foolish and brash I was when they had me as an assistant pastor. That saying, "Seldom right, never in doubt" fit me pretty well then. I thanked God for his and their patience with me. I thanked him that he somehow managed to use me. I said to the Lord, "I was really in over my head then, wasn't I?" I distinctly heard the Lord answer, "So what makes you think you're in your depth now?"[37]

The truly saved will ever be acknowledging and thanking God for His grace. In the Christian hymn "Glorious Things of Thee Are Spoken," the hymn writer got it right: "Savior, if of Zion's city, I through grace a member am . . ."[38]

Ellen G. White speaks of a striving after righteousness because of love for the Savior, but that growth in grace will never be adequate for our salvation. She makes this clear many times, including her discussion of one of Zechariah's visions:

> As Satan accused Joshua and his people, so in all ages he accuses those who are seeking the mercy and favor of God. In the Revelation he is declared to be the "accuser of our brethren," "which accused them before our God day and night." Revelation 12:10. The controversy is repeated over every soul that is rescued from the power of evil and whose name is registered in the Lamb's book of life. . . .
>
> *Man cannot meet these charges himself. In his sin-stained garments, confessing his guilt, he stands before God. But Jesus our Advocate presents an effectual plea in behalf of all who by repentance and faith have committed the keeping of their souls to Him. He pleads their cause and vanquishes their accuser by the mighty arguments of Calvary.* His perfect obedience to God's law, even unto the death of the cross, has given Him all power in heaven and in earth, and He claims of His Father mercy and reconciliation for guilty man. To the accuser of His people He declares: " 'The Lord rebuke thee, O Satan.' These are the purchase of My blood, brands plucked from the burning." *Those who rely upon Him in faith receive the comforting assurance:* "Behold, I have caused thine iniquity to pass from thee, and I will clothe thee with change of raiment."

White continues by insisting that

All that have put on the robe of Christ's righteousness will stand before Him as chosen and faithful and true. Satan has no power to pluck them out of the hand of Christ. Not one soul that in penitence and faith has claimed His protection will Christ permit to pass under the enemy's power. . . .

The fact that the acknowledged people of God are represented as standing before the Lord in filthy garments should lead to humility and deep searching of heart on the part of all who profess His name.[39]

And significantly, her visionary description of the climactic day of Christ's return mentions no confident cheering by the redeemed:

As the living cloud comes still nearer, every eye beholds the Prince of life. . . . A diadem of glory rests on his holy brow. His countenance outshines the dazzling brightness of the noonday sun. "And he hath on his vesture and on his thigh a name written, King of kings, and Lord of lords."

Before his presence, "all faces are turned into paleness." . . . And "the faces of them all gather blackness." *The righteous cry with trembling, "Who shall be able to stand?"* The angels' song is hushed, and there is a period of awful silence. Then the voice of Jesus is heard, saying, "My grace is sufficient for you." The faces of the righteous are lighted up, and joy fills every

heart. And the angels strike a note higher, and sing again, as they draw still nearer to the earth.[40]

God has never revealed the exact date when Jesus will come. He only promises that it will come "suddenly." This does not mean that history has no direction or goal. God remains sovereign in the timing of human history. Looking for the Second Coming is a way of discerning this while acknowledging that what is promised is true. Nor is the great Second Coming dependent upon our perfection or we would never be saved, because there is no such thing as human righteousness.

But God promises through His prophet: "He shall reign over the house of Jacob for ever; and of his kingdom there shall be no end" (Luke 1:33, KJV). We don't need to think "delay" or underestimate the certainty of the divine promise. The second coming of Christ is the promised climax of the Christian gospel, grounded in God's glorious righteousness and grace demonstrated all through salvation history, as the psalmist chants: "The Lord has made known His salvation; His righteousness He has revealed in the sight of the nations" (Psalm 98:2). God's faithful believers have ever failed their Lord, but He has never forsaken His people.

Yes, much time has passed since Jesus promised to come. Perhaps most Christians, at one time or another, will wonder why evil still seems to triumph and ponder how it can get any worse. But the powerful promise of God is greater than any of our doubts or fears. And secular scoffing need not crush our faith. Whatever doubts or negative emotions, whatever spiritual emptiness may threaten, it is no match for the promise and power of God!

> The nations will see your righteousness,
> And all kings your glory;
> And you will be called by a new name
> Which the mouth of the Lord will designate.
> You will also be a crown of beauty in the hand of the Lord,
> And a royal diadem in the hand of your God. . . .
> And as the bridegroom rejoices over the bride,
> So your God will rejoice over you (Isaiah 62:2, 3, 5, NASB).

"Behold," says Isaiah, "the darkness shall cover the earth, and gross darkness the people; but *the Lord shall arise upon thee*, and *his glory shall be seen upon thee*" (Isaiah 60:2, KJV; emphasis added).

Both the Old and New Testaments present glorious descriptions of God's kingdom restored. There will be the re-union of the first and Second Adam, along with feasting at the marriage supper of the Lamb, with Jesus serving. We will be able to study the glories of creation with the Creator as Instructor: " 'Now we see through a glass, darkly.' We behold the image of God reflected, as in a mirror, in the works of nature and in His dealings with men; but then we shall see Him face to face, without a dimming veil between. We shall stand in His presence and behold the glory of His countenance."[41]

Only by God's grace will anyone, even "good sinners," be saved. And those who eagerly await His glorious appearing will be highly motivated to share this amazing grace, longing for the praise of the Lamb to reach "every tribe and tongue and people and nation" (Revelation 5:9). As believers come ever closer to Jesus, waiting for His glorious appearing will not diminish their eagerness, for they know it will be worth the wait!

"Even so, come, Lord Jesus"—quickly come! (Revelation 22:20).

Endnotes

1. Unless otherwise noted, all Scripture quotations are from the NKJV.

2. "So Christ was offered once to bear the sins of many. To those who eagerly wait for Him He will appear a second time, apart from sin, for salvation" (Hebrews 9:28).

3. "They will put you out of the synagogues; yes, the time is coming that whoever kills you will think that he offers God service" (John 16:2).

4. "Therefore gird up the loins of your mind, be sober, and rest your hope fully upon the grace that is to be brought to you at the revelation of Jesus Christ" (1 Peter 1:13).

5. E.g., Albrecht Ritschl, *The Christian Doctrine of Justification and Reconciliation: The Positive Development*

of the Doctrine (Edinburgh: T & T Clark, 1900).

6. See Albert Schweitzer, *The Quest of the Historical Jesus: A Critical Study of Its Progress From Reimarus to Wrede*, trans. W. Montgomery (London: Adam and Charles Black, 1954).

7. E.g., Karl Barth, *The Epistle to the Romans* (London: Oxford University Press, 1933).

8. Ellen G. White, *The Desire of Ages* (Oakland, CA: Pacific Press®, 1898), 31. The Hebrew grammar of Genesis 4:1 suggests this.

9. "Now Enoch, the seventh from Adam, prophesied about these men also, saying, 'Behold, the Lord comes with ten thousands of His saints, to execute judgment on all, to convict all who are ungodly among them of all their ungodly deeds which they

have committed in an ungodly way, and of all the harsh things which ungodly sinners have spoken against Him' " (Jude 14, 15).

10. "Noah stood like a rock amid the tempest. Surrounded by popular contempt and ridicule, he distinguished himself by his holy integrity and unwavering faithfulness. . . . His solemn voice fell upon the ears of that generation in regard to events, which, so far as human wisdom could judge, were impossible." Ellen G. White, *Patriarchs and Prophets* (Battle Creek, MI: Review and Herald®, 1890), 96.

11. "For seven days after Noah and his family entered the ark, there appeared no sign of the coming storm. During this period their faith was tested. It was a time of triumph to the world without. The apparent delay confirmed them in the belief that Noah's message was a delusion, and that the Flood would never come. Notwithstanding the solemn scenes which they had witnessed—the beasts and birds entering the ark, and the angel of God closing the door—they still continued their sport and revelry, even making a jest of these signal manifestations of God's power. They gathered in crowds about the ark, deriding its inmates with a daring violence which they had never ventured upon before." Ibid., 98, 99.

12. "Then He said to Abram: 'Know certainly that your descendants will be strangers in a land that is not theirs, and will serve them, and they will afflict them four hundred years' " (Genesis 15:13).

13. "Through the symbols of the great darkness and the smoking furnace, God had revealed to Abraham the bondage of Israel in Egypt, and had declared that the time of their sojourning should be four hundred years. 'Afterward,' He said, 'shall they come out with great substance.' Genesis 15:14. Against that word, all the power of Pharaoh's proud empire battled in vain. On 'the self-same day' appointed in the divine promise, 'it came to pass, that all the hosts of the Lord went out from the land of Egypt.' " Exodus 12:41." White, *The Desire of Ages*, 32.

14. "For thus the Lord has said to me: 'Within a year, according to the year of a hired man, all the glory of Kedar will fail; and the remainder of the number of archers, the mighty men of the people of Kedar, will be diminished; for the Lord God of Israel has spoken it' " (Isaiah 21:16, 17).

15. Ellen G. White comments,

Christ beheld the whole scene, and after the

death of Lazarus the bereaved sisters were upheld by His grace. Jesus witnessed the sorrow of their rent hearts, as their brother wrestled with his strong foe, death. He felt every pang of anguish, as He said to His disciples, "Lazarus is dead." But Christ had not only the loved ones at Bethany to think of; He had the training of His disciples to consider. They were to be His representatives to the world, that the Father's blessing might embrace all. For their sake He permitted Lazarus to die. Had He restored him from illness to health, the miracle that is the most positive evidence of His divine character would not have been performed. . . .

In delaying to come to Lazarus, Christ had a purpose of mercy toward those who had not received Him. He tarried, that by raising Lazarus from the dead He might give to His stubborn, unbelieving people another evidence that He was indeed "the resurrection, and the life." He was loath to give up all hope of the people, the poor, wandering sheep of the house of Israel. His heart was breaking because of their impenitence. In His mercy He purposed to give them one more evidence that He was the Restorer, the One who alone could bring life and immortality to light (*The Desire of Ages*, 528).

16. "As Christ sat looking upon the party that waited for the bridegroom, He told His disciples the story of the ten virgins, by their experience illustrating the experience of the church that shall live just before His second coming." Ellen G. White, *Christ's Object Lessons* (Battle Creek, MI: Review and Herald®, 1900), 406.

17. Ellen G. White speaks eloquently of this:

Through Christ's redeeming work the government of God stands justified. The Omnipotent One is made known as the God of love. Satan's charges are refuted, and his character unveiled. Rebellion can never again arise. Sin can never again enter the universe. Through eternal ages all are secure from apostasy. By love's self-sacrifice, the inhabitants of earth and heaven are bound to their Creator in bonds of indissoluble union.

The work of redemption will be complete.

In the place where sin abounded, God's grace much more abounds. The earth itself, the very field that Satan claims as his, is to be not only ransomed but exalted (*The Desire of Ages*, 26).

18. Ellen G. White addresses this principle when she describes the first advent of Christ:

The Saviour's coming was foretold in Eden. When Adam and Eve first heard the promise, they looked for its speedy fulfillment. They joyfully welcomed their first-born son, hoping that he might be the Deliverer. But the fulfillment of the promise tarried. Those who first received it died without the sight. From the days of Enoch the promise was repeated through patriarchs and prophets, keeping alive the hope of His appearing, and yet He came not. The prophecy of Daniel revealed the time of His advent, but not all rightly interpreted the message. Century after century passed away; the voices of the prophets ceased. The hand of the oppressor was heavy upon Israel, and many were ready to exclaim, "The days are prolonged, and every vision faileth." Ezekiel 12:22.

But *like the stars in the vast circuit of their appointed path, God's purposes know no haste and no delay* (*The Desire of Ages*, 31; emphasis added).

19. In his sacred oratorio *Messiah*.

20. Jesse E. Strout, "Jesus Is Coming Again," 1872.

21. Charles Wesley, "Lo! He Comes," 1758.

22. Philip Nicolai, "Wake, Awake, for Night Is Flying," 1599.

23. Phoebe Palmer, "Watch, Ye Saints," 1844.

24. White, *Christ's Object Lessons*, 69.

25. Seeing this connection, Jewish engravings of the ten precepts of the Decalogue include the "prologue" with the first commandment.

26. God Himself describes this through Ezekiel (chap. 16).

27. "For all have sinned and fall short of the glory of God, *being justified freely by His grace* through the redemption that is in Christ Jesus" (Romans 3:23, 24; emphasis added).

28. As Jesus promises, "It is to your advantage that I go away; for if I do not go away, the Helper will not come to you; but if I depart, I will send Him to you.

And when He has come, He will convict the world of sin, and of righteousness, and of judgment" (John 16:7, 8).

29. The book of Proverbs manifests this important biblical principle: "All the ways of a man are pure in his own eyes, but the LORD weighs the spirits" (Proverbs 16:2). "Pride goes before destruction, and a haughty spirit before a fall" (verse 18). "There is a generation that is pure in its own eyes, yet is not washed from its filthiness" (Proverbs 30:12). Thus, the really crucial question is, Are we deceived about ourselves? How *do* we stand before *God*?

30. Thomas Cranmer, "General Confession."

31. Ellen G. White, *Selected Messages*, bk. 1 (Washington, DC: Review and Herald®, 1958), 344 (emphasis added). Note that even our *prayers* must be covered with Christ's righteousness.

32. Charlotte Elliott, "Just as I Am," 1834.

33. C. S. Lewis, *Mere Christianity* (New York: The Macmillan Co., 1965), 59.

34. One example is when Jesus cleansed the temple:

The piercing look of Jesus swept over the desecrated court of the temple. All eyes were turned toward Him. Priest and ruler, Pharisee and Gentile, looked with astonishment and awe upon Him who stood before them with the majesty of heaven's King. Divinity flashed through humanity, investing Christ with a dignity and glory He had never manifested before. Those standing nearest Him drew as far away as the crowd would permit. Except for a few of His disciples, the Saviour stood alone. Every sound was hushed. The deep silence seemed unbearable. Christ spoke with a power that swayed the people like a mighty tempest: "It is written, My house shall be called the house of prayer; but ye have made it a den of thieves." His voice sounded like a trumpet through the temple. The displeasure of His countenance seemed like consuming fire. With authority He commanded, "Take these things hence." John 2:16. . . .

. . . They were now more terrified than before, and in greater haste to obey His command. There were none who dared question His authority. Priests and traders fled from His presence (White, *The Desire of Ages*, 590).

35. Ellen G. White, *Steps to Christ* (Mountain View, CA: Pacific Press®, 1956), 64.

36. Ellen G. White, *That I May Know Him* (Washington, DC: Review and Herald®, 1964), 361 (emphasis added). Ellen G. White is very clear that salvation comes only by being fully clothed with Christ's robe of righteousness:

> Those who are indeed purifying their souls by obeying the truth will have a most humble opinion of themselves. The more closely they view the spotless character of Christ, the stronger will be their desire to be conformed to his image, and the less will they see of purity or holiness in themselves. But while we should realize our sinful condition, *we are to rely upon Christ as our righteousness, our sanctification, and our redemption. We cannot answer the charges of Satan against us. Christ alone can make an effectual plea in our behalf. He is able to silence the accuser with arguments founded not upon our merits, but on his own* ("The Return of the Exiles—No. 9: Joshua and the Angel," *Advent Review and Sabbath Herald*, January 2, 1908, 9; emphasis added).

> The law requires righteousness,—a righteous life, a perfect character; and this man has not to give. *He cannot meet the claims of God's holy law. But Christ, coming to the earth as man, lived a holy life, and developed a perfect character. These He offers as a free gift to all who will receive them. His life stands for the life of men. Thus they have remission of sins that are past, through the forbearance of God. More than this, Christ imbues men with the attributes of God. He builds up the human character after the similitude of the divine character, a goodly fabric of spiritual strength and beauty. Thus the very righteousness of the law is fulfilled in the believer in Christ.* God can "be just, and the justifier of him which believeth in Jesus." Romans 3:26 (White, *The Desire of Ages*, 762; emphasis added).

37. Ben Patterson, *God's Prayer Book: The Power and Pleasure of Praying the Psalms* (Carol Stream, IL: Tyndale House, 2008), 271.

38. John Newton, 1779.

39. Ellen G. White, *Counsels for the Church* (Nampa, ID: Pacific Press®, 1991), 352 (emphasis added).

40. Ellen G. White, *The Great Controversy* (Oakland, CA: Pacific Press®, 1888), 641 (emphasis added).

41. Ellen G. White, *Maranatha* (Washington, DC: Review and Herald®, 1976), 356.

14

The Triumph of God's Love

John C. Peckham

In the great controversy, God's character of love has been called into question by the false accusations of the devil that God is not entirely loving and just. By slandering God's name, the enemy has attempted to displace confidence in God and usurp God's place for himself (cf. Ezekiel 28:12–18; Isaiah 14:12–14).[1] As has been seen in this book, just how God's character is vindicated over and against the allegations and charges of the accuser is a matter of great significance to Adventist theology, with far-reaching implications for faith and life. In light of the materials in the preceding chapters, we are now in a position to very briefly revisit the primary issues and questions that have been addressed in this book relative to God's character and the last generation:[2]

- What is sin? How can humans overcome sin, and what does that mean?
- What is *justification*, and how does it function? How can humans be justified in the sight of God?
- What is *sanctification*, and how does it function in the process of salvation? Can humans be "perfect"? Why and in what way is sanctification the work of a lifetime?
- What does it mean to be holy? How should we live in light of the soon coming of Jesus?

- How should we understand our "struggle" with sin, and how might if affect our mental health?
- How can Jesus be both our Savior and our example? Was Jesus just like us? Would He need to be in order to be our perfect and sufficient example?
- Just what did Jesus accomplish on the cross? Was it effective and sufficient?
- What is the meaning and significance of the atonement? Was Satan defeated at the cross?
- What is the state of the last generation?
- Who vindicates God's character, and what does that mean?
- Why hasn't Jesus returned yet to take His people home? Why does the great controversy continue?

Revisiting the issues and questions pertinent to last generation theology

Each of the questions above is bound up with the significant disagreement about just how the controversy over God's character is settled and the part that humans are to play in this cosmic drama. Specifically, each of these questions relates, in some significant way, to the disagreement over whether God provides for Himself the means and grounds of victory in the great controversy (particularly by definitively defeating Satan at the cross) or whether a demonstration by a last generation of absolutely "perfect" humans is needed in addition to Christ's life, death, and resurrection.

On the nature of sin. The last generation theology (LGT) view that some group of humans must become absolutely sinless and "perfect" prior to Christ's second coming fosters a view of the human condition that downplays the infection of sin and sinful inclinations inherited by all humans due to the Fall. Instead, LGT tends to reduce sin to merely actions that transgress God's law, while correspondingly denying or downplaying the bent disposition of the human condition, with its unchosen, inborn, propensities toward evil. This allows LGT to at least give the impression that humans may *perfectly* overcome sin in all respects by force of the human will. This seems to overlook the fact that the human will is itself infected and severely constrained by sin. As Jeremiah 17:9 puts it, "The heart is more deceitful than all else and is desperately sick; who can understand it?"[3] (cf. Genesis 8:21; Psalms 51:5; 58:3; Ephesians 2:3). It is no coincidence that "all have sinned and fall short of the glory of God" (Romans 3:23) and that "there is none righteous, not even one" (Romans 3:10; cf. Psalm 14:1–3; 1 Kings 8:46; Ecclesiastes 7:20). Thus, in God's "sight no man living is righteous" (Psalm 143:2).

On the other hand, as has been seen in the previous chapters of this book, if sin is more than mere actions, including an infection of our very being and character, the free will of humans is severely constrained by this enslaving, alien force of sin (cf. Romans 6:6, 12, 13, 16–18; 7:14, 17–20). If this is so, given that we humans

are as powerless to change our nature as the leopard is to change its spots (Jeremiah 13:23), the solution to sin must come from outside of us.[4] Left to our own devices, we humans would be hopelessly lost. "Sin has marred and well-nigh obliterated the image of God in man."[5] It is only the primary and prior (prevenient) work of God that enables us to receive the free gift of salvation by faith (cf. Jeremiah 31:3; 1 John 4:19). This, among other reasons, is why we need a Savior—particularly (as will be discussed later) a Savior who is not infected with sin as we are.

On the nature of justification. Before moving to the implications of the LGT view for the nature and work of Christ, however, we turn to the issue of how the conception of sin relates to how we should understand salvation. Last generation theology has tended to criticize and sometimes reject the forensic nature of justification as a legal declaration of righteousness (imputed righteousness) and has tended to confuse, and sometimes even conflate, justification and sanctification. Further, some have contended that justification refers only to forgiveness of past sins so that once one has been justified, one can be acceptable in God's sight only by an infused righteousness of Christ that makes one righteous.

But we have seen in the previous chapters that justification in Scripture is a judicial declaration of acquittal by God based on the righteousness of Christ and not the righteousness of the one who is justified. As such, justification is the imputation of the merits of Christ's righteousness (cf. Romans 5:15–19), not the imparted righteousness of Christ (which refers to sanctification).[6] While justification and sanctification cannot be separated, they can and must be distinguished.

On the nature of sanctification. Further, we have seen that sanctification is no less by faith than is justification. Yet whereas justification is the work of a moment, consisting of Christ's righteousness being imputed to the believer, "sanctification is the work of a lifetime," consisting of Christ imparting His righteousness to the believer.[7]

Further, as the "work" of a lifetime (specifically, Christ's ongoing work in us who believe), sanctification is never completed prior to glorification and Christ's second coming.[8] In this regard, as Ellen G. White puts it, "So long as Satan reigns, we shall have self to subdue, besetting sins to overcome; so long as life shall last, there will be no stopping place, no point which we can reach and say, I have fully attained. Sanctification is the result of lifelong obedience."[9]

On the nature of "perfection." The fact that sanctification is the result of lifelong obedience entails that perfectionism is in significant error, not only because it tends to lead people to emphasize human works but also because it maintains that one can reach a "stopping place" before Christ comes (cf. Philippians 3:12)—namely, a state of absolute, sinless "perfection." But as we have seen previously, this expectation of absolute perfection turns (at least, in part) on adopting the absolutist Greek philosophical conception of perfection as "something totally and absolutely free of errors, mistakes, or anything short of an idealist and faultless view of perfect behavior and attitudes."[10] This absolutist conception of perfection has become a

common way of understanding the English term *perfect*, in contrast to the biblical conception and terminology for *perfect*, which refers to completeness and maturity.[11]

This has massive ramifications for, among other things, understanding Christ's command: "Therefore you are to be perfect, as your heavenly Father is perfect" (Matthew 5:48). Perfectionists often cite this command as evidence that humans can and must be perfect in the sense of absolute sinlessness. But the biblical conception of "perfect" (*teleios*) points in a rather different direction, and this is evinced by the context of both Matthew 5 and its parallel in Luke 6. Just previous to this command in Matthew 5, Jesus points out that humans tend to love only those who love them, but God, in contrast, loves everyone. If you love only those who love you (even the "tax collectors" do this much), your "love" is woefully incomplete—that is, imperfect. Conversely, God loves everyone; that is, He loves completely, or perfectly. As such, when Jesus says, "Therefore you are to be perfect, as your heavenly Father is perfect" (Matthew 5:48), the context suggests that this should be understood as conveying the idea that you are to show love to everyone even as the Father loves everyone.

This not only fits with the biblical understanding of sanctification as closely associated with growing in love but also corresponds to the parallel in Luke 6. There, just after Jesus conveys that we are not only to love those who love us but to love even our enemies as God does (Luke 6:34, 35, paralleling Matthew 5:44–47), Luke goes on to quote Jesus as saying, "Be merciful, just as your Father is merciful" (Luke

6:36)—instead of, "Therefore you are to be perfect, as your heavenly Father is perfect" (Matthew 5:48). *Merciful* is one of the major New Testament terms for *love*, evincing that the "perfection" to which Christ calls His followers is a complete love for others, which the Scriptures elsewhere emphasize as the identifying marker of those who follow Christ (John 13:35; cf. 1 John 4:20).[12]

So Christians can and must grow in love, but sanctification cannot be fully achieved at any moment during one's life prior to glorification. Sanctification is a lifelong process that culminates in glorification (cf. 1 Corinthians 15:52–55). Thus, contrary to the claims of perfectionists, Ellen G. White states, "We cannot say 'I am sinless,' till this vile body is changed and fashioned like unto His glorious body" (cf. 1 John 1:8–10).[13]

Although we cannot become absolutely, sinlessly perfect until glorification, we can and should attain character perfection— that is, a mature disposition of unselfish love for God and others that manifests itself in the way we relate to God and others.[14] This can be brought about only by the prevenient love of God: "We love, because He first loved us" (1 John 4:19). As Ellen G. White puts it, "While we cannot claim perfection of the flesh, we may have Christian perfection of the soul. Through the sacrifice made in our behalf, sins may be perfectly forgiven. . . . Through faith in His blood, all may be made perfect in Christ Jesus."[15] As such, although "if we say that we have no sin, we are deceiving ourselves and the truth is not in us" (1 John 1:8), Christ has made a way for us to be cleansed as described in the very next verse: "If we

confess our sins, He is faithful and righteous to forgive us our sins and to cleanse us from all unrighteousness" (verse 9).

On the call to, and nature of, holiness. In this regard, the rejection of perfection*ism* in this book in no way supports licentiousness or the shirking of one's duty to holy living. Above all people, Christians should be holy and live lives of love. As Peter puts it, "What sort of people ought you to be in holy conduct and godliness" (2 Peter 3:11; cf. Ephesians 1:4; 5:27; 1 Peter 1:15, 16). But the holy living prescribed for the followers of Christ in the last days, as we have seen in chapter 6, entails far more than merely refraining from external sins. External obedience and abstinence from the commission of particular sins is not enough. The believer motivated by love will not only be concerned with abstaining from sins but also will be concerned to make a positive impact by actively loving and serving others, thus not focusing only on sins of *commission* but also sins of *omission* (cf. the parable of the good Samaritan in Luke 10:25–37 and Christ's teaching regarding the sheep and the goats in Matthew 25:34–46). Further, despite the vital importance of obedience and abstaining from intentionally committing sin (cf. the biblical distinction between intentional and unintentional sins), genuine obedience and the overcoming of sinful *actions* can be accomplished only by a work of God in us that we embrace by faith.

This is because *genuine* obedience itself flows from a disposition of love. Yet we humans are incapable of generating a genuine disposition of love in and of ourselves due to our fallen nature that is infected by sin. "We love, because He first loved us" (1 John 4:19). In other words, "only by love is love awakened."[16] In this regard, "love" should never be set in opposition to God's law or law-keeping: "Love is the fulfillment of the law" (Romans 13:10). Indeed, Christ, drawing from the Old Testament, identified the greatest commandments as love for God and love for one's neighbor (Matthew 22:37–40; Mark 12:29–31; cf. Leviticus 19:34; Deuteronomy 6:5). At the same time, attempts at law-keeping without love are worse than clanging cymbals (cf. 1 Corinthians 13:1). One cannot genuinely *keep* the law without love, because the law is a transcript of God's character of love and the internal motivation of love that impels the external actions is necessary for any action to truly be in correspondence to God's law of love.[17]

Christ Himself emphasized this deeper significance in the antitheses (Matthew 5:17–48), repeatedly pointing to the deeper nature of sin within our very desires and inclinations and calling for a deeper kind of transformation that can be brought about only by the work of God from outside of us. We can take hold of this transforming work by faith, but only because God has first laid hold of us (cf. Philippians 3:12).[18] In this regard, while our sinful nature will remain until glorification, if we surrender to God, He can and will instill and grow in us a disposition of love that reflects the love that He has graciously bestowed on us (cf. Philippians 1:6).

On the practical, spiritual ramifications of perfectionism. Conversely, misunderstanding God's commands, laws, and expectations might have a massive negative impact on one's own spiritual and mental well-being. As mentioned in chapter 1, I have ministered to many Adventists who have desperately tried to be absolutely perfect—and failed. Their failure to achieve absolute perfection had devastating consequences on their faith and well-being (and often on the well-being of their families as well) because they had no assurance of salvation in the last days. Many of them simply gave up, while others became depressed and very critical of others.

For me, then, this is far more than an academic question. What we believe about our sinful condition and how God saves us from it has massive ramifications on our practical life and well-being and the well-being of our church. I firmly believe that we must help our people, especially our young people, understand both the genuine Christian call to holiness that is motivated by love and that is itself a response to God's love as well as to the grace and mercy of Christ who "always lives to make intercession for" us (Hebrews 7:25) and, as Ellen G. White puts it, makes up for our "unavoidable deficiencies."[19] Thus, our assurance is not in ourselves or in the power of our wills; we have assurance in Christ "who gave Himself for us" (Titus 2:14) and who will finish the good work He began in us if we only surrender to Him (Philippians 1:6). His victory assures our salvation, if only we believe (i.e., trust) in Him. As Paul puts it, "I have been crucified with Christ; and it is no longer I who live, but Christ lives in me; and the life which I now live in the flesh I live by faith in the Son of God, who loved me and gave Himself up for me" (Galatians 2:20).

On the nature of Christ as Savior and example. Many have been taught that they *can* and *must* be just like Jesus in order to be "worthy" of salvation. Last generation theology contends that we can be absolutely sinless *just as* Christ was absolutely sinless. In this regard, the claim goes, Christ must have inherited the same sinful condition and inclinations toward sinning that plague us. If Jesus did not, LGT claims, then He was not fully human like us. But if Jesus was *just* like us and still was absolutely sinless, then it follows that we may also become absolutely sinless by following His example.

Ellen G. White is explicit that, while Christ is our example, we cannot be *just* like Him: "Christ is our pattern, the perfect and holy example that has been given us to follow. We can never equal the pattern; but we may imitate and resemble it according to our ability."[20] This definitively affirms that Christ can be "our example" while denying that we can be *just* like Him. In order to recognize that Jesus was not just like us, you need only entertain this question: Have you ever been tempted to turn stones into bread as Jesus was in the temptation narrative (cf. Matthew 4)?[21] Of course not, because you lack the ability to do so.

Whereas we are only human, Christ became fully human while remaining fully divine.[22] Christ took upon Himself "humanity, perfectly identical with our own nature, except without the taint of sin."[23] Further, "in Him there is no sin" whatsoever (1 John 3:5; cf. John 14:30). In this regard,

> we must not think that the liability of
> Christ to yield to Satan's temptations

degraded His humanity and He possessed the same sinful, corrupt propensities as man.

> . . . Christ took our nature, *fallen* but not corrupted.[24]

As such, Christ is a "brother in our infirmities, but not in possessing like passions."[25]

But what about the claims of LGT that if Jesus was not just like us, (1) He was not fully human, or (2) He had some advantage that nullifies His vindication of God's law by His perfect life? To see the problem with the first claim, we need only ask whether Adam and Eve were "fully human" prior to the Fall.[26] Of course, they were. Thus, full humanity does not require the possession of a fallen, sin-infected nature. If anything, it is we who are less than fully human. With regard to the second claim that unless Jesus was infected with the sinful condition in the precise way that we are He could not act as our example, the charge raised by the enemy in the great controversy was not whether someone already *infected* by sin could perfectly keep God's law. Satan's charge was that God's law was not fair and just in the context of perfectly sinless beings. Christ's perfect life and voluntary sacrificial death for us proved this claim to be utterly false.[27]

On the "thorn" in our "flesh." Some LGT advocates claim that any denial that humans can become absolutely sinless and perfect prior to glorification amounts to a denial of the power of God. But the issue here is not one of power. If the conflict was a matter of power, there could be no conflict. Similarly, if the total overcoming of sin by humans was merely a matter of the exercise of divine power, there would be no sin. There must be some other reason why our sinful nature is not eradicated immediately. There must be some other explanation why, even if one prays with full sincerity that God will remove one's inclinations to sin, God does not do so (cf. the "thorn" in Paul's flesh, 2 Corinthians 12:7).[28] Recall, in this regard, the words of Ellen G. White: "*So long as Satan reigns*, we shall have self to subdue, besetting sins to overcome; so long as life shall last, there will be no stopping place."[29] Here White indicates that the struggle with sin will not end until the conclusion of Satan's reign—that is, the removal of the enemy's usurping rule at the Second Coming.

Therefore, the infection of our natures by sin and our inherited propensity to sin will not be removed prior to the second coming of the true King. This is not because God lacks the power to transform our natures here and now. God is all powerful (omnipotent), which entails that He possesses the sheer power to transform us. Indeed, He will transform our nature at glorification (cf. 1 Corinthians 15:52–55). Apparently, something about the way the great controversy is set up grants the enemy some jurisdiction ("so long as Satan reigns") to antagonize fallen humans prior to Christ's second coming. The issue, then, is not one of power at all but of timing and God's larger purposes at work (cf. Revelation 12:12).

Further, as noted above, given that humans inherit a nature that is infected with sin so that we cannot save ourselves and, without God's intervention, would be hopelessly lost, we *must* have a Savior who

Himself is not *infected* with sin as we are and thus does not Himself need a Savior. This is one reason why, despite LGT's claims to the contrary, in order to be our Savior, Jesus could not have been *just* like us. If He were just like you and me, He would Himself need a Savior. Christ was affected by sin, but He was not infected by sin, and this is why He could save us from sin.[30]

On Christ's work of atonement. Christ's perfect life and death definitively defeated Satan, and this is a common theme of the New Testament (e.g., Revelation 12:10; cf. Colossians 2:15). As Ellen G. White puts it, at the cross, "Satan knew that he had been defeated in his purpose to overthrow the plan of salvation."[31] Among the largest problems with LGT is that it denies that the work of Christ was and is sufficient, apart from the work of mere humans, to demonstrate that God's law is perfect and just. As we have seen, Christ provided a complete and once-for-all atonement for us at the cross. As Jiří Moskala explained in chapter 10, the atonement was "complete" but not "completed" at the cross. Thus, there is no need or place for an additional phase of the atonement via human action in order for God to win the great controversy.

God provides for Himself the fully sufficient means and grounds of victory in the great controversy (cf. Genesis 22:8, 13, 14). Christ has definitively defeated Satan at the cross, effectively refuting the devil's charges and thus providing effective grounds for the full vindication of God's character before the onlooking universe. Whereas LGT contends that another demonstration relative to God's character is needed, a demonstration to be provided by the "perfect" last generation of humans, Ellen G. White affirms that only Christ could accomplish this work. As she puts it, "His character must be manifested in contrast to the character of Satan. This work only one Being in all the universe could do. Only He who knew the height and depth of the love of God could make it known."[32] This work, which could be done by "only one Being in all the universe," Christ has done, once and for all.

The role of humans in this cosmic drama is not to add anything to God's victory but is a missional role of proclamation and witnessing to the truth of God's unimpeachable character and law of love, spreading the good news, and reflecting God's character as imitators of Christ's love, as a means to help people recognize God's goodness, love, and justice.[33] Whereas this missional role has significant ramifications, the activity of humans does not provide any grounds for the vindication of God's character or His victory in the great controversy. The essential point here, as noted earlier, is that God Himself wins the victory in the great controversy, and this victory is not contingent upon something added by mere creatures. Christ effectively refuted Satan's false charges against God's character, law, and moral government at the cross and has thus defeated the enemy.

On the "crisis" of the delay. Why has Christ not returned? What is taking so long? Some call this the crisis of the delay. While we are not privy to the timing of the Second Coming or all of God's reasons for tarrying, it is worth remembering that God's modus operandi throughout Scripture is to have a "delay" before the execution of judgment.

At least in part, this delay is motivated by His desire to save as many as possible (cf. 2 Peter 3:9). Before Christ returns, the gospel is to be spread to the entire world. Although God has defeated Satan at the cross, not everyone has recognized this or had the opportunity to recognize it. We are told that this mission to the world will be complete before Christ comes, and *then* the end will come (Matthew 24:14). Given Adventist eschatology, of which we can only scratch the surface here, every living person will have an opportunity to make their final decision for or against Christ before He comes. Only then will probation close.

While other factors are surely at work,[34] the emphasis in Scripture is on the mission to make disciples of all nations (see the Great Commission in Matthew 28:19, 20). In this regard, while we should not mistake the mission of the last generation as an additional phase of atonement or in any way as providing grounds for God to win the great controversy that He would otherwise lose, we must not overlook the missional importance of the witness of God's people throughout the ages and in the last generation.

On the mission of love. In one of my favorite statements by Ellen G. White, she writes,

> The last rays of merciful light, the last message of mercy to be given to the world, is a revelation of His character of love. The children of God are to manifest His glory. In their own life and character they are to reveal what the grace of God has done for them.
>
> The light of the Sun of Righteousness is to shine forth in good works—

in words of truth and deeds of holiness.[35]

As Christ's followers, then, we are called to a higher standard for the sake of the mission. If we claim the name of Christ by proclamation but deny Christ by the way we live, not only will we fail to attract people to Christ and His love, but we might inoculate them against the gospel. I believe this missional proclamation and reflection of God's love is precisely what is at issue in another of Ellen G. White's statements: "Christ is waiting with longing desire for the manifestation of Himself in His church. When the character of Christ shall be perfectly reproduced in His people, then He will come to claim them as His own."[36]

At times, this statement has been taken to mean that Christ has not yet returned because He is waiting for a group to be perfectly sinless and thus provide sufficient grounds to vindicate God's character and close the great controversy. But the character of Christ is love, and I take this statement to be in reference to the way Christians should manifest love to God and to others. As such, this statement is eminently missional.

That this is so is evident from what Ellen G. White writes directly following the quotation above: "It is the privilege of every Christian not only to look for but to hasten the coming of our Lord Jesus Christ, (2 Peter 3:12, margin). Were all who profess His name bearing fruit to His glory, how quickly the whole world would be sown with the seed of the gospel. Quickly the last great harvest would be ripened, and Christ would come to gather the precious grain."[37]

Notice that, in context, Ellen G. White is talking about the completion of the Great Commission. If we were to inculcate and display Christ's character of love, we would not be able to help but proclaim the good news, and our witness would be exceedingly attractive. As 2 Peter 3 puts it, the way we live might hasten the Second Coming in a missional way: "What sort of people ought you to be in holy conduct and godliness, looking for and hastening the coming of the day of God" (verses 11, 12).

If my reading is correct, this dovetails with Christ's command to be "perfect" in Matthew 5, which we have already seen is a command to love completely rather than partially. The mission of the last generation is indeed to proclaim and reflect to everyone God's character, which is love (1 John 4:16, 17).[38] This cannot be done merely by abstaining from evildoing, as important as that is; it must also be manifested in a positive demonstration of love. "By this all men will know that you are My disciples, if you have love for one another" (John 13:35; cf. 1 John 4:20; 1 Peter 4:8). In this regard, "Only by love is love awakened."[39]

Although not absolutely sinless or "perfect" (in the absolutist Greek philosophical sense), the last generation will be a people devoted to Christ and reflecting His love; a people who "follow the Lamb wherever He goes" (Revelation 14:4). Yet this devotion to Christ will not provide the grounds either for God's vindication or for the vindication of the saints themselves. All our righteousness is filthy rags, and apart from Christ's intercession, nothing we bring could be acceptable in God's sight (Isaiah 64:6; 1 Peter 2:5). Yet Christ "always lives to make intercession" for us (Hebrews 7:25). As Ellen G. White puts it,

> The religious services, the prayers, the praise, the penitent confession of sin ascend from true believers as incense to the heavenly sanctuary, *but passing through the corrupt channels of humanity, they are so defiled that unless purified by blood, they can never be of value with God.* They ascend not in spotless purity, and unless the Intercessor, who is at God's right hand, presents and purifies all by His righteousness, it is not acceptable to God. All incense from earthly tabernacles must be moist with the cleansing drops of the blood of Christ. He holds before the Father the censer of His own merits, in which there is no taint of earthly corruption. He gathers into this censer the prayers, the praise, and the confessions of His people, and with these He puts His own spotless righteousness. Then, perfumed with the merits of Christ's propitiation, the incense comes up before God wholly and entirely acceptable. Then gracious answers are returned.[40]

Apart from God's mercy, then, no one could stand before God. Yet we can boldly approach the throne of grace because of Christ's work (Hebrews 4:16, KJV). We can have confidence in the judgment only because God will vindicate all who have faith in Him. In this regard, one should understand that while the last generation will "live in the sight of a holy God without an intercessor," this generation will

have already been sealed.[41] Part of Christ's ministry will have ceased, but the sustaining presence of the Holy Spirit will not be absent. The last generation will live by faith in Christ and dependence on the Holy Spirit and will never be left nor forsaken (cf. Hebrews 13:5; Matthew 28:20).

On the glory that belongs to God alone. This missional work of believers cannot, and does not, provide the grounds for God to be vindicated. It merely attests and proclaims the character of God, not only in word but also in reflecting God's love in action. In this regard, perhaps the greatest problem with LGT is that it makes God's victory in the great controversy dependent upon the fidelity of mere creatures, entailing that divine revelation and action are insufficient to win the great controversy and must be supplemented by human action. This appears to be at direct odds with Paul's statement, "Let God be found true, though every man be found a liar" (Romans 3:4). It does not follow that if humans reject God, God is not just. The evil decisions of humans have no bearing on God's justice. Even if every human being rejected God, that would not change the fact that God is just.[42] God's love and righteousness have been ultimately, definitively, and indisputably demonstrated by His self-giving work of redemption, which was supremely manifested at the cross (Romans 3:25; 5:8).

Whereas the "accuser of our brethren" (Revelation 12:10) claims that God cannot justly redeem sinners, God in Christ demonstrates His justice in making atonement while yet providing forgiveness, cleansing, and full reconciliation for all who believe in Christ. In this, God shows Himself to be both "just and the justifier" of all who believe (Romans 3:26). Accordingly, no one is in a position to "bring a charge against God's elect" (Romans 8:33), and no one can take believers out of God's hand (verses 38, 39). God vindicates and redeems sinners who accept Christ as Savior and Lord, and He vindicates Himself in a way that will finally be recognized by everyone in the universe. In the end, every knee shall bow and every tongue shall confess (Romans 14:11; cf. Philippians 2:10; Revelation 5:13).

It is worth noting that the confessions and doxologies in Revelation do not point to the accomplishments of the redeemed. Humans, along with the heavenly host, praise *God* in humility. The redeemed praise the only One who was found worthy to open the seals; the One to whom all glory and honor belongs (Revelation 5:9). Christ shares the fruits of His victory, but the glory and honor of victory belong to God the Father, Son, and Spirit alone (cf. Isaiah 42:8).

In the end, then, God's love triumphs over all. God Himself provides the full and sufficient means and grounds to vindicate His character. No additional work is necessary. God is the victor and will be so with or without our loyalty and service. The victory and the glory thus belong to God and God alone, and He will finally eradicate sin and evil and suffering forevermore. "And He will wipe away every tear from their eyes; and there will no longer be any death; there will no longer be any mourning, or crying, or pain; the first things have passed away" (Revelation 21:4).

In His graciousness, God extends the spoils of victory to all who are in Christ. We,

by faith in Christ's fully effective and sufficient work, may be adopted as God's children and thus as heirs to the inheritance that Christ has won for us (cf. Romans 8:15; Galatians 4:5; Ephesians 1:5). Thus, we can partake of God's victory; there is a place for us at the wedding feast of the Lamb. Yet we must never forget that this place was not won by our works or our contribution but was won *for us* by the Lamb who was slain. Worthy, then, is the Lamb to receive all glory and power and honor forever and ever!

Conclusion

God is love. Those are the first and the last three words of Ellen G. White's epic Conflict of the Ages series, beginning with *Patriarchs and Prophets* and ending with *The Great Controversy*, and everything in between testifies that God's character is love. It is not what we do as humans that provides the grounds to vindicate God's character. It is God's work in the plan of salvation that manifests His righteousness and love, finally eradicating every doubt in the universe that God is indeed love and that His moral government is entirely just and above reproach. Although we have a missional role in this controversy to proclaim and reflect God's love to others, the story is about God's own manifestation of His character as the One who gives everything, even His own life, to reconcile the world unto Himself. Ellen G. White thus fittingly concludes the last book of the series, *The Great Controversy*, with this beautiful paragraph, with which I will also conclude this book: "The great controversy is ended. Sin and sinners are no more. The entire universe is clean. One pulse of harmony and gladness beats through the vast creation. From Him who created all, flow life and light and gladness, throughout the realms of illimitable space. From the minutest atom to the greatest world, all things, animate and inanimate, in their unshadowed beauty and perfect joy, declare that God is love."[43]

Endnotes

1. See Richard M. Davidson, "Ezekiel 28:11–19 and the Rise of the Cosmic Conflict," in *The Great Controversy and the End of Evil*, ed. Gerhard Pfandl (Silver Spring, MD: Review and Herald®, 2015), 57–69. See also Richard M. Davidson, "And There Was Gossip in Heaven," *Adventist Review*, January 24, 2013.

2. In what follows I will make frequent reference to the writings of Ellen G. White because so much of LGT is based on what I consider to be faulty interpretations of her writings. While I am confident that the view set forth in this book can be demonstrated from Scripture alone, the writings of Ellen G. White shed significant light on the issues.

3. Unless otherwise noted, all Scripture quotations are from the NASB.

4. "It is impossible for us, of ourselves, to escape from the pit of sin in which we are sunken. Our hearts are evil, and we cannot change them. . . . Education, culture, the exercise of the will, human effort, all have their proper sphere, but here they are powerless. They may produce an outward correctness of behavior, but they cannot change the heart; they cannot purify the springs of life. There must be a power working from within, a new life from above, before men can be changed from sin to holiness. That power is Christ. His grace alone can quicken the lifeless faculties of the soul, and attract it to God, to holiness." Ellen G. White, *Steps to Christ* (Mountain View, CA: Pacific Press®, 1956), 18.

5. Ellen G. White, *Christian Education* (Battle Creek, MI: International Tract Society, 1894), 63.

6. "The righteousness by which we are justified is imputed; the righteousness by which we are sanctified is imparted. The first is our title to heaven, the second is our fitness for heaven." Ellen G. White, "Qualifications for the Worker," *Advent Review and Sabbath Herald*, June 4, 1895, 353. Both of these are received by surrender to Christ: "Both our title to heaven and our fitness for it are found in the righteousness of Christ. The Lord can do nothing toward the recovery of man until, convinced of his own weakness, and stripped of

all self-sufficiency, he yields himself to the control of God." Ellen G. White, *The Desire of Ages* (Oakland, CA: Pacific Press®, 1898), 300.

7. Ellen G. White, *Christ's Object Lessons* (Battle Creek, MI: Review and Herald®, 1900), 65.

8. It is particularly telling that Paul, who had the grounds to boast like few others, explicitly denied having achieved perfection and exhorted believers to focus on continuing to run the race. He writes, "Not that I have already obtained it or have already become perfect, but I press on so that I may lay hold of that for which also I was laid hold of by Christ Jesus. Brethren, I do not regard myself as having laid hold of it yet; but one thing I do: forgetting what lies behind and reaching forward to what lies ahead, I press on toward the goal for the prize of the upward call of God in Christ Jesus" (Philippians 3:12–14).

9. Ellen G. White, *The Acts of the Apostles* (Mountain View, CA: Pacific Press®, 1911), 560, 561.

10. Denis Fortin, in chapter 5 of this book.

11. See the discussion in chapter 5. Further, see especially Hans K. LaRondelle, *Perfection and Perfectionism: A Dogmatic-Ethical Study of Biblical Perfection and Phenomenal Perfectionism* (Berrien Springs, MI: Andrews University Press, 1975). See also George R. Knight, *I Used to Be Perfect: A Study of Sin and Salvation* (Berrien Springs, MI: Andrews University Press, 2001); Edward Heppenstall, "How Perfect Is 'Perfect' or Is Christian Perfection Possible?," Biblical Research Institute, July 23, 1998, https://www.adventistbiblicalresearch .org/materials/theology-salvation/how-perfect -perfect-or-christian-perfection-possible.

12. This should not be taken to imply any denial of the distinction in Scripture between love for other Christians and love for others in general. Both are commanded, but they are not the same. See John C. Peckham, *The Love of God: A Canonical Model* (Downers Grove, IL: IVP Academic, 2015).

13. Ellen G. White, " 'Abide in Me,' " *Signs of the Times*, March 23, 1888, 178. The full quote is as follows: "As we have clearer views of Christ's spotless

and infinite purity, we shall feel as did Daniel, when he beheld the glory of the Lord, and said, 'My comeliness was turned in me into corruption.' We cannot say 'I am sinless,' till this vile body is changed and fashioned like unto His glorious body. But if we constantly seek to follow Jesus, the blessed hope is ours of standing before the throne of God without spot or wrinkle, or any such thing, complete in Christ, robed in His righteousness and perfection."

14. Ellen G. White helpfully speaks of being perfect in terms of development like the stages of growth in a plant. She writes, "As in nature, so in grace; there can be no life without growth. The plant must either grow or die. As its growth is silent and imperceptible, but continuous, so is the development of the Christian life. At every stage of development our life may be perfect; yet if God's purpose for us is fulfilled, there will be continual advancement. Sanctification is the work of a lifetime." White, *Christ's Object Lessons*, 65. See the further discussion by Fortin in chapter 5.

15. The wider context of this quotation is as follows:

And while we cannot claim perfection of the flesh, we may have Christian perfection of the soul. Through the sacrifice made in our behalf, sins may be perfectly forgiven. Our dependence is not in what man can do; it is in what God can do for man through Christ. When we surrender ourselves wholly to God, and fully believe, the blood of Christ cleanses from all sin. The conscience can be freed from condemnation. Through faith in His blood, all may be made perfect in Christ Jesus. Thank God that we are not dealing with impossibilities. We may claim sanctification. We may enjoy the favor of God. We are not to be anxious about what Christ and God think of us, but about what God thinks of Christ, our Substitute. Ye are accepted in the Beloved. The Lord shows, to the repenting, believing one, that Christ accepts the surrender of the soul, to be molded and fashioned after His own likeness (Ellen G. White, *Selected Messages*, bk. 2 [Washington, DC: Review and Herald®, 1958], 32, 33).

16. White, *The Desire of Ages*, 22.

17. Paul exhorts, "Faith, hope, love, abide these three; but the greatest of these is love" (1 Corinthians 13:13). As a sinner, I can be saved only by faith in Christ (justification), and through His work in my life, grow in love toward God and fellow humans (sanctification), also by faith, while I expectantly hope and wait for the day when I will be like Him (glorification). I am indebted to my colleague Martin Hanna for highlighting this framework in personal discussions.

18. It is no coincidence that the antitheses of Matthew 5 build up to the command of Matthew 5:48, "Therefore you are to be perfect." The context should remind us that Christ is pointing to the deeper matter of the heart, which we cannot change.

19. Ellen G. White, *Selected Messages*, bk. 3 (Washington, DC: Review and Herald®, 1980), 196. The wider quotation is as follows:

Jesus loves His children, even if they err. They belong to Jesus and we are to treat them as the purchase of the blood of Jesus Christ. Any unreasonable course pursued toward them is written in the books as against Jesus Christ. He keeps His eye upon them, and when they do their best, calling upon God for His help, be assured the service will be accepted, although imperfect.

Jesus is perfect. Christ's righteousness is imputed unto them, and He will say, "Take away the filthy garments from him and clothe him with change of raiment." Jesus makes up for our unavoidable deficiencies. Where Christians are faithful to each other, true and loyal to the Captain of the Lord's host, never betraying trusts into the enemy's hands, they will be transformed into Christ's character. Jesus will abide in their hearts by faith (Ibid., 195, 196).

Elsewhere, she writes,

When it is in the heart to obey God, when efforts are put forth to this end, Jesus accepts this disposition and effort as man's best service, and He makes up for the deficiency with His own divine merit. But He will not accept those who claim to have faith in Him, and yet are disloyal to His Father's commandment. We hear a great deal about faith, but we need to hear a great deal more about works. Many are deceiving their own souls by living an easygoing, accommodating, crossless religion. But

Jesus says, "If any man will come after me, let him deny himself, and take up his cross, and follow me" ("To Perfect the Christian's Character," *Signs of the Times*, June 16, 1890, 7, quoted in *Selected Messages*, bk. 1 [Washington, DC: Review and Herald®, 1958], 382).

20. Ellen G. White, "Conquer Through the Conqueror," *Advent Review and Sabbath Herald*, February 5, 1895, 81. She continues,

When we fall, all helpless, suffering in consequence of our realization of the sinfulness of sin; when we humble ourselves before God, afflicting our souls by true repentance and contrition; when we offer our fervent prayers to God in the name of Christ, we shall as surely be received by the Father, as we sincerely make a complete surrender of our all to God. We should realize in our inmost soul that all our efforts in and of ourselves will be utterly worthless; for it is only in the name and strength of the Conqueror that we shall be overcomers.

21. Notice, here, as Darius Jankiewicz explains in chapter 8, although Christ was tempted in all things like as are we (Hebrews 4:15), His temptations were actually greater than ours.

22. Some people mistakenly think Christ laid aside His divinity, but Ellen G. White is clear in this regard that "Christ had not exchanged his divinity for humanity; but he had clothed his divinity in humanity." Ellen G. White, "Satan's Malignity Against Christ and His People," *Advent Review and Sabbath Herald*, October 29, 1895, 689. Elsewhere, she stated, "He veiled his divinity with the garb of humanity, but he did not part with his divinity." "Lessons From the Second Chapter of Philippians: Talk by Mrs. E. G. White, May 13, 1905," *Advent Review and Sabbath Herald*, June 15, 1905, 8. Further, "Our Lord was tempted as man is tempted. He was capable of yielding to temptations, as are human beings. His finite nature was pure and spotless, but the divine nature that led Him to say to Philip, 'He that hath seen Me hath seen the Father' also, was not humanized; neither was humanity deified by the blending or union of the two natures; each retained its essential character and properties." Ellen G. White, *Manuscript Releases*, vol. 16 (Silver Spring, MD:

Ellen G. White Estate, 1990), 182.

23. White, *Manuscript Releases*, 16:181. "In Christ dwelt the fullness of the Godhead bodily. This is why, although tempted in all points like as we are, He stood before the world, from His first entrance into it, untainted by corruption, though surrounded by it." Ellen G. White, *Manuscript Releases*, vol. 17 (Silver Spring, MD: Ellen G. White Estate, 1990), 337.

He had not taken on Him even the nature of the angels, but humanity, perfectly identical with our own nature, except without the taint of sin. A human body, a human mind, with all the peculiar properties, He was bone, brain, and muscle. A man of our flesh, He was compassed with the weakness of humanity. The circumstances of His life were of that character that He was exposed to all the inconveniences that belong to men, not in wealth, not in ease, but in poverty and want and humiliation. He breathed the very air man must breathe. He trod our earth as man. He had reason, conscience, memory, will, and affections of the human soul which was united with His divine nature (White, *Manuscript Releases*, 16:181).

24. White, *Manuscript Releases*, 16:182 (emphasis in original). A lot of confusion is caused by misunderstanding the way Ellen G. White sometimes talks about the "fallen" or "sinful nature" that Christ took upon Himself. She tends to use the terms quite differently than we do today. She used "fallen" and "sinful nature" to refer to Christ taking on innocent infirmities but expressly denied that He took upon Himself sinful human passions or propensities to sin. See, in this regard, the helpful article by Tim Poirier, "Sources Clarify Ellen White's Christology" *Ministry*, December 1989, 7–9.

25. Ellen G. White, *Testimonies for the Church*, vol. 2 (Washington, DC: Review and Herald®, 1948), 202. Further, she writes:

Be careful, exceedingly careful as to how you dwell upon the human nature of Christ. *Do not set Him before the people as a man with the propensities of sin.* He is the second Adam. The first Adam was created a pure, sinless being, without a taint of sin upon him; he was in the image of God. He could fall, and he did fall through transgressing. Because of sin, his posterity was born with inherent propensities of disobedience. But Jesus Christ was the only begotten Son of God. He took upon Himself human nature, and was tempted in all points as human nature is tempted. He could have sinned; He could have fallen, but not for one moment was there in Him an evil propensity. He was assailed with temptations in the wilderness, as Adam was assailed with temptations in Eden. . . .

These words ["that holy thing" (Luke 1:35, KJV)] are not addressed to any human being, except to the Son of the Infinite God. *Never, in any way, leave the slightest impression upon human minds that a taint of, or inclination to corruption rested upon Christ, or that He in any way yielded to corruption.* He was tempted in all points like as man is tempted, yet He is called that holy thing. It is a mystery that is left unexplained to mortals that Christ could be tempted in all points like as we are, and yet be without sin. The incarnation of Christ has ever been, and will ever remain a mystery. That which is revealed, is for us and for our children, but let every human being be warned from the ground of making Christ altogether human, such an one as ourselves: for it cannot be. The exact time when humanity blended with divinity, it is not necessary for us to know. We are to keep our feet on the rock, Christ Jesus, as God revealed in humanity (Ellen G. White, *Manuscript Releases*, vol. 13 [Silver Spring, MD: Ellen G. White Estate, 1990], 18, 19; emphasis added).

Elsewhere, she writes,

It is not correct to say, as many writers have said, that Christ was like all children. He was not like all children. . . . His *inclination to right* was a constant gratification to his parents. . . .

No one, looking upon the childlike countenance, shining with animation, *could say that Christ was just like other children.* He was God in human flesh. When urged by his companions to do wrong, *divinity flashed through humanity,* and he refused decidedly. In a moment he

distinguished between right and wrong, and placed sin in the light of God's commands, holding up the law as a mirror which reflected light upon wrong (" 'And the Grace of God Was Upon Him,'" *Youth's Instructor*, September 8, 1898; emphasis added).

26. This is not to suggest that Christ was just like Adam and Eve before the Fall either. He was both like and unlike us; He took upon Himself the innocent infirmities that plagued humankind but not the sinful propensities or passions. See the discussion of this by Jankiewicz in chapter 8.

27. Whereas LGT claims that, in addition to Christ's work, there must be a group of humans who become perfectly sinless and thus provide the grounds for God's character to be vindicated by demonstrating that God's law can be perfectly kept by humans, Christ has already demonstrated that Christ's law can be kept by a human and has fully vindicated God's law and character.

28. I am not suggesting that the thorn in Paul's side was a sinful nature but simply noting the parallel that he prayed that God would remove a chronic trial from him—and it was not removed. Paul does not indicate or suggest that God lacked the power to remove it, but God did not remove it for some reason or reasons, to which Paul was not entirely privy.

29. White, *The Acts of the Apostles*, 560, 561 (emphasis added).

30. See the discussion in chapter 8.

31. Ellen G. White, "The Unchangeable Character of the Law," *Signs of the Times*, September 23, 1889, 577. Further, "When Christ cried out, 'It is finished,' the unfallen worlds were made secure. For them the battle was fought and the victory won. Henceforth Satan had no place in the affections of the universe. The argument he had brought forward, that self-denial was impossible with God, and therefore unjustly required from His created intelligences, was forever answered. Satan's claims were forever set aside. The heavenly universe was secured in eternal allegiance." Ellen G. White, "Lessons From the Christ-Life," *Advent Review and Sabbath Herald*, March 12, 1901, 161.

32. White, *The Desire of Ages*, 22.

33. In this regard, there is a limited sense in which humans might "vindicate" God—that is, in the sense of being a witness and thereby *showing* to the world what is already the case about God's character and

law. Nothing that humans do *makes it the case* that God is just or *makes it the case* that He is vindicated when He otherwise would not have been. The full and effective grounds of God's vindication are provided by God Himself. Further, the investigative judgment will "vindicate" God (again, in the sense of *showing* that God's judgments are just, not *making it the case* that they are just) by showing that He is just in saving those whom He has saved. In this regard, as Whidden puts it: "What Christ did in His incarnation has *meritoriously* settled the issue of defeating Satan, especially with regard to his charges against God that obedience is impossible and the faith response of His people will *evidentially* vindicate God in saving them. Thus their manifestation of the fruit of the Spirit in their lives provides *evidence(s)* that their faith was genuine and that God was just in giving them eternal life." Woodrow Whidden, "Ellen White and LGT: A Review and Evaluation of Her Key Statements" (unpublished paper). In this way, Ellen G. White sometimes speaks of the believers' involvement in the vindication of God, but this is not restricted to the last generation; it is part of the missional witnessing work of God's people throughout the ages. See, again, Whidden, "Ellen White and LGT." Here, however, it would be a mistake to think that the failure of any individual human, or humans collectively, in this regard would remove or reduce God's justice or make it the case that He is not vindicated, because any human who fails to surrender to God's work will not be judged righteous by Him in any case. It simply is the case that all God's judgments are only and always just, and the records of this world's history will definitively bear this out.

34. For this and the rest of the events of the last days to come to fruition, a number of factors must be in place, not all of which are within God's purview to bring about (given His commitment to the freedom required for love)—similar to Israel walking around in the wilderness. God could have taken Israel to the Promised Land via a direct route, but they were not willing (cf. Matthew 23:37).

35. White, *Christ's Object Lessons*, 415, 416.

36. Ibid., 69.

37. Ibid.

38. Notice, further, that 1 John 4:17 speaks of how we might have "confidence in the day of judgment"

in relationship to love being "perfected with us" (cf. the earlier discussion of Matthew 5:48 and Luke 6:36).

39. White, *The Desire of Ages*, 22.

40. White, *Selected Messages*, bk. 1, 344 (emphasis added). Just previous to this, she writes, "Christ, our Mediator, and the Holy Spirit are constantly interceding in man's behalf, but the Spirit pleads not for us as does Christ, who presents His blood, shed from the foundation of the world; the Spirit works upon our hearts, drawing out prayers and penitence, praise and thanksgiving. The gratitude which flows from our lips is the result of the Spirit's striking the cords of the soul in holy memories, awakening the music of the heart." Ibid.

Elsewhere, she adds,

> We are saved through the merit of the blood of Christ, but Christ's righteousness does not cover the sin of transgressing God's law, without repentance. We must do all in our power to keep the commandments of God, *and then He will impute unto us his righteousness,* because we believe in Christ and seek to obey the divine law. This is the reason that Christ came to this world, that he might bring his righteousness to man, that man might lay hold of his strength, and make peace with God. *God accepts the efforts of man to keep the law, because Christ imputes his righteousness to him.* We could not keep the law in our own strength ("The Unchangeable Character of the Law," 578; emphasis added).

41. Ellen G. White, *The Great Controversy* (Mountain View, CA: Pacific Press®, 1911), 614. See the discussion of this by Moskala in chapter 10.

42. The only way that I can see that God's justice might be contingent upon what a human does is relative to the possible discrepancy between God's favorable judgment of a human and their sustained wickedness in contrast to that judgment. But this does not occur because God finally judges favorably only those who are willing to be saved, and God brings His good work to completion in all who are willing (see Philippians 1:6).

43. White, *The Great Controversy*, 678.